RIMBAUD

RIMBAUD

PIERRE PETITFILS   *Translated by Alan Sheridan*

UNIVERSITY PRESS OF VIRGINIA   *Charlottesville*

Translation copyright 1987
by the Rector and Visitors of the University of Virginia
First published 1987

Originally published in 1982 as
Rimbaud by Pierre Petitfils
© Editions Julliard, 1982

Library of Congress Cataloging-in-Publication Data

Petitfils, Pierre.
   Rimbaud.

   Translation of: Rimbaud.
   Bibliography:
   Includes index.
   1. Rimbaud, Arthur, 1854–1891—Biography.
2. Poets, French—19th century—Biography.
I. Sheridan, Alan.   II. Title.
PQ2387.R5Z754513   1987   841'.8   [B]   87-6109
ISBN 0-8139-1142-7

Printed in the United States of America

CONTENTS

La place ducale and its fountain, Charleville, in Rimbaud's time.

rthur, seated, and Frédéric Rimbaud at
eir first communion.

imbaud, front row, third from left, age ten, at the Institution Rossat, Charleville.
Courtesy Musée Rimbaud de Charleville-Mézières)

Rimbaud as a high school student.

Rimbaud at the prow of his "drunken boat," drawing attributed to André Gill published in Album zutique.

The Old Mill and the branch of the Meuse at Charleville, where The Drunken Boat *was written.*

Ernest Delahaye, childhood friend of Rimbaud.

Georges Izambard, *teacher of rhetoric at* *the Collège, Charleville.*

Germain Nouveau.

Charleville during the German occupation in 1871, a view familiar to Rimbaud.

Paul Verlaine at the time Rimbaud knew him.

Paul Auguste (Charles) Bretagne, caricature by Paul Verlaine.

*The house where the Rimbauds lived from 1869 to 1875, Quai de la Madeleine
(today Quai Arthur-Rimbaud).*

Rimbaud, photograph by Carjat, September 1871.

Rimbaud, sketch by Forain. The legend—"Stings on Contact"—alludes to the dinner during which Rimbaud stabbed the photographer-poet Carjat.

Rimbaud, gouache by Fantin-Latour.

*The house in London at 34 Howland St.,
where Rimbaud and Verlaine lived in
1872.*

Young London coachman, sketch by Rimbaud, 1872.

Rimbaud, sketch by Paul Verlaine.

Voyelles.

A noir, E blanc, I rouge, U vert, O b[leu]
Je dirai quelque jour vos naissances lat[entes]
A, noir corset velu des mouches éclat[antes]
Qui bombinent autour des puanteurs cr[uelles]

Golfes d'ombre; E, candeurs des vapeurs e[t]
Lances des glaciers fiers, rois blancs, fris[sons]
I, pourpres, sang craché, rire des lèvres
Dans la colère ou les ivresses pénitente[s]

U, cycles, vibrements divins des mers v[irides]
Paix des pâtis semés d'animaux, paix des [rides]
Que l'alchimie imprime aux grands fronts s[tudieux]

O suprême Clairon plein des strideurs ét[ranges]
Silences traversés des Mondes et des Ang[es]
— Ô l'Oméga, rayon violet de Ses Yeu[x]

Autograph copy of Rimbaud's sonnet Vowels, *given by the poet to Emilie Blémont*

A. RIMBAUD

UNE

SAISON EN ENFER

PRIX : UN FRANC

BRUXELLES

ALLIANCE TYPOGRAPHIQUE (M.-J. POOT ET COMPAGNIE)

37, rue aux Choux, 37

1873

The only book published by Rimbaud.

PARIS. - Rue Campagne-Première - C. F.

*ue Campagne-Première, Paris. In 1872 Rimbaud lodged in the attic of the hotel
en on the left.*

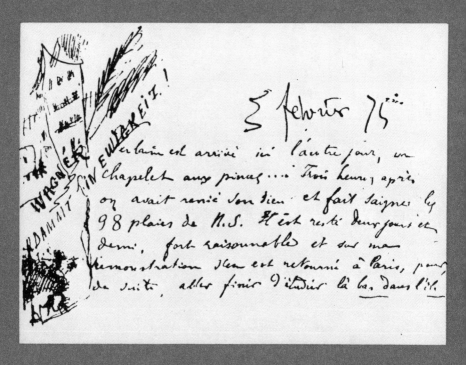

Letter from Rimbaud, Stuttgart, February 1875, to Delahaye.

Rimbaud encountering his friend Delahaye on a street in Charleville in October 1875, drawing by Delahaye.

Rimbaud returning on foot from Vienna, in the Ardennes, drawing by Delahaye.

Rimbaud helping with the harvest at his mother's farm in 1879, drawing by his sister Isabelle on the cover of an account book.

Mme Rimbaud's farm at Roche.

La Maison Bardey, Aden, where Rimbaud lived and worked for a number of years.

Aden-Camp. Rimbaud lodged at the grand Hôtel de l'Univers, which can be seen on the left.

Rimbaud at Harar.

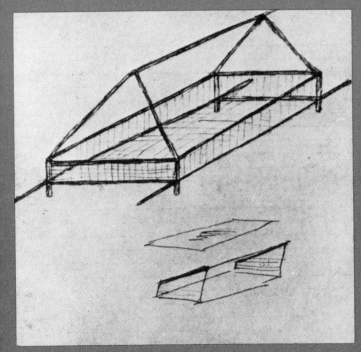

...gn for a stretcher, sketched by Rim-...d for his last trip from Harar to ...a.

...mbaud several days before his death, ...awn by his sister Isabelle.

Rimbaud's notes made for his last trip, made on a stretcher, from Harar to the coast.

Tomb of Arthur and the Rimbaud family at Charleville-Mézières.

INTRODUCTION

Adding yet another book to the pyramid of works that have appeared on Rimbaud—over three hundred to date throughout the world—may seem an insignificant undertaking. After so many subjective appreciations, so many scholarly but disappointing studies of an author who wrote so little, does one not run the risk of swelling still further the incommensurate plethora of commentary and of deepening still further the obscurity that surrounds the poet? However, to recount the events of his life certainly runs counter to present academic fashion, which dictates that the work is sufficient unto itself, any knowledge of the author being superfluous, if not actually harmful: the circumstances and incidents of his life are mere anecdote; all that matters is the message that he left. Although some defense of this thesis may be made in certain cases—one thinks of Mallarmé, for instance, whose self-effacing life bears no relation to his glittering poetry—it is radically false in the case of poets like Verlaine or Rimbaud, who burned out their lives at the fire of poetry. This immolation is their message. Everything that Verlaine wrote has an autobiographical resonance, while in the case of Rimbaud it would be utterly gratuitous to ignore the stages of his "way of the cross": his stifling youth at the hands of a tyrannical mother, his rebellion (Sartre may well be right when he wrote in Saint Genêt: "Genius is not a gift, it is the way out one invents in desperate cases"), his furious desire to bring every- thing down, to raze everything and to set up in its place some splendid, if utopian world, his cruel disappointment when he realized his failure, the fury with which he trampled on his loves and dreams, and, last, his decision to throw himself into adventure and action—in fact to throw himself at the mercy of a destiny determined to track him down and punish him for trying to free himself from the human condition.

Because Rimbaud's life was short (thirty-seven years), it must be seen as a whole. Many commentators, for no other reason than their own personal taste, are interested only in bits of it, the revolutionary phase, for example, or that of adolescent rebellion; others deliberately ignore the last ten years of his life in Africa, when he "went back to prison," as André Breton put it, because in their eyes those years marked his break with poetry. One actually invites misunderstanding if one makes hasty judgments on isolated episodes, on the grounds that his life was too disjointed to be taken as a whole. Nothing could be further from the truth: on the contrary, his life has the logic of a Greek tragedy.

Disconcerted by the contradictory aspects of the char- acter (there has even been a Rimbaud who had no other aim in life than to make money), some critics have taken it into their heads that in order to explain it one has only to select the right key from the bunch, that of the childhood or the hashish smoking, that of paranoia or mental derangement, that of homosexuality or Hinduism, that of the occult sciences or magic—not to mention the personal keys of those who, identifying themselves with Rimbaud, speak of themselves when they think they are speaking about him. When no single key works perfectly, they give up, declaring that our poet-seer is an impenetrable mystery, myth or void. This is not new: already, in 1892, one year after his death, Adolphe Retté, signing his painting, Fra Diavolo, *wrote in the Hermitage: "Arthur Rimbaud the adventurer never existed, Arthur Rimbaud is a myth." We know how successfully the key of myth was exploited in the 1950s.*

These are some of the false trails that have misled those who, their heads filled with an ideology, have lost sight of the man of flesh and blood that Rimbaud was. In this respect it is striking to observe how little of the mass of writings concerning him is biographical. On this crucially important subject, the number of serious biographical works—setting aside fictional lives and compilations—amounts to no more than about half a dozen. There is Jean-Marie Carré's La Vie aventureuse de Jean Arthur Rimbaud *(Plon, 1926, new editions in 1943 and 1949), a good, if rather literary work, but one terribly incomplete in relation to present knowledge; the works of Enid Starkie, Colonel Godchot, Vernon Underwood, François Ruchon, Daniel de Graaf, and, last,* La vie d'Arthur Rimbaud, *which I wrote long ago with Henri Matarasso (Hachette, 1962, with a preface by Jean Cocteau), which is really no more than a handbook, and is now out of print.*

Now that Rimbaud is "within reach" (Alain Borer), the time has come for a biography of him whose sole ambition will be truthfulness and clarity, an account based on contemporary eyewitnesses and documents, with no preconceived doctrine; in short, a work that will strive to show rather than to demonstrate.

If Rimbaud is so little known, in spite of the mass of commentary on him, it is because people have persisted in trying to explain him in rational terms, a Cartesian shortcoming that drives us at all costs to "understand" him—as if a poem or a poet could be "understood." The truth is that the poet eludes us because he belongs to another world—and this is particularly true of Rimbaud, who, when he was practic-

ing "second sight," returned to his true country, far, far away from our choked planet, where, as he himself says in a splendid line: "Notre pâle raison nous cache l'infini."

Note to the Virginia edition: *The translations of Rimbaud's verse are by Wallace Fowlie, from his bilingual edition,* Rimbaud: Complete Works, Selected Letters *(Chicago: University of Chicago Press, 1966). These are literal translations, intended to aid understanding of the originals, rather than to stand as poems in their own right. All other translations in this book are by Alan Sheridan.*

RIMBAUD

Nul n'ignore plus que la Poésie est une solitude effrayante,
une malédiction de naissance, une maladie de l'ame.

JEAN COCTEAU

J'ai même toujours vu qu'il est impossible
de vivre plus péniblement que moi.

ARTHUR RIMBAUD

1

Family Ties

On the edges of the massifs of Ardenne and Argonne, the Attigny region is fairly flat country consisting of plowed fields and meadows bordered with woodlands and watered by innumerable streams. The dwellings, grouped in hamlets, give an impression of poverty and drabness. "In that region of the Ardennes," writes Paul Claudel, "poor harvests, a tiny group of slate roofs, and, always on the horizon, the legendary line of the forests. A country of springs, where the limpid water, captive in its depths, slowly turns upon itself; the blue-green Aisne, congested with water lilies, and three long yellow reeds emerging from the jade."[1]

The land forms men's characters, it is said. One imagines that here, in the past, the peasants must have clung tenaciously to this meager soil, at which they worked hard and long. These peasants must also have needed resources of courage and patience to resist foreign invasions; first the Normans, then the English, then the Germans, on several occasions—in the seventeenth century, in 1815, in 1870, in 1914, in 1940.

And yet Attigny had been an important town where church councils and plenary courts had been held. For a time the history of France had been made there. Clovis II built his palace there. Pepin the Short was baptized there in the presence of Charlemagne, whose son, Louis the Pious, made his public penitance there. Of that former glory only a few vestiges remain, notably the foundations of the Dôme, a sixteenth-century palace, in the town center.

At that time, at Sainte-Vaubourg, not far away, was a vast estate with castle, chapel, park, gardens, fish ponds, hot springs, and summer houses, belonging to the seigneur of Roche. Nearby, at Wallart, was another seigneury, evidence of which is to be found in parchment documents of the fourteenth century. The countryside around was cultivated by villeins, many of whom, from time immemorial, were called Cuif.

As their descendant Arthur Rimbaud remarked, it needed the Declaration of the Rights of Man and of the Citizen for these churls to emerge out of the shadow of the manor houses.

Indeed, one of these Cuifs, Jean-Baptiste, born in 1714, acquired in 1789 part of the former estate of Roche, from Louis Le Seur, canon of the collegiate church of Mézières. In 1791 he rebuilt the farmhouse, putting his initials on the facade, and, having gotten a taste for such things, built or restored other houses in the hamlet of Roche, as well as several farmhouses in the surrounding district, in particular that of Fontenille, between Roche and Voncq, whose lands were leased to his father, Nicolas. It was at Fontenille that our Jean-Baptiste Cuif usually resided. We do not know at what date he decided to settle at Roche and cultivate his lands, which extended to Méry and Chuffilly. The poor fellow was unaware that the place had a curse on it.

This story was to take in the family drama that was to be played out there, then the spiritual drama that his great-grandson Arthur Rimbaud was to experience there, up to the ultimate drama, the destruction by the Germans, on October 12, 1918, of the farmhouse and all its outbuildings except for a barn, rebuilt in 1933, which was destroyed in turn in May 1940, together with a number of houses in the neighborhood that had belonged to Mme Rimbaud.

It does not seem that his son Jean (1759–1828) inherited his enterprising character; all that we know of him is that he married a young lady called Marguerite Jacquemart.

So we come to the poet's grandfather, Jean Nicolas Cuif (1789–1858), a farmer at Roche, who married Marie-Louise Félicité Fay, like him from a farming family. His daughter Vitalie, the future Mme Rimbaud, always spoke of him in affectionate terms ("My good father"), and, on the occasion of his exhumation in 1900, remarked that he was "very tall and very strong."[2]

Everything has its roots in the past. It is probable that Arthur Rimbaud would have been different if his mother had been another woman. For her destiny was set by a serious event that took place on June 9, 1830, the death of her mother, née Fay, at the age of twenty-six, leaving three young children: Charles-Auguste (two months old), herself, Marie Catherine Vitalie (five years old), and Jean Charles Félix (six years old).

So the family found itself motherless. The father did what he could, and did not remarry. The grandmother, née Jacquemart, did her share in the upbringing of the children, but young Vitalie soon turned out to be an efficient young mistress of the household. One can imagine her at sixteen, working on the farm from morning till night, serious, thrifty, energetic, and uncommunicative. There were few leisure activities, other than the occasional walk to Vouziers or to the Aisne canal, which she saw being built. For the most part, her life was a matter of duties and responsibilities. She realized early on that she could never depend on her brothers.

At seventeen, the elder brother, following an incident that nearly brought him before the magistrates (a brawl? a theft?), signed up in the African army (1841). The younger brother, Charles-Auguste, a lazy fellow, who drank heavily, was little better. Vitalie suffered a great deal from their misdemeanors, for she placed the reputation of her family name above everything. One has to admit that her lot was not a very happy one: joyless, with little free time, and no recognition of what she did from anyone, her life consisted entirely of work, which got more and more burdensome with every day as her father and grandmother grew older. Anyone who has had to experience such a youth will have a view of life quite different from that of someone who has enjoyed a pampered childhood, whose parents have tried to hide the harsh realities of life from their children. Is it surprising, then, if she soon grew stiff inside her armor of duty, and had such a horror of laziness, waste, and profligacy?

Since she held the pursestrings, she refused to give any money to her good-for-nothing brother Charles-Auguste, knowing only too well what he would do with it. One can imagine the angry scenes that took place in the farmhouse at Roche. One day he had had enough and married a young woman, Marguerite Adélaïde Misset (February 10, 1852). He was twenty-two.

Since she was no longer in sole command of the household, Vitalie decided to leave at the end of the same year. Her father accompanied her to Charleville, where, in the center of the town, 12 Rue Napoléon, he rented the rooms on the second floor of a simple house, the first floor of which was, and still is, occupied by a bookshop.

Vitalie's father must have had to go back to Roche quite often, for marriage had done nothing to improve his son. Vitalie, for her part, bore her idleness and loneliness with haughty courage. What fate awaited this poor, uprooted girl? She could well end up as a bigoted old maid, useless and ignored. On the other hand, she could marry. But she saw no one, except perhaps a few women neighbors. Yet Charleville was a pleasant, lively town:

it was very congested on market days and local trade was thriving. It was a rather extraordinary town: perfectly straight streets laid out by Charles of Gonzaga, duke of Mantua, in the early seventeenth century; a marvelous ducal square covering an area of one hectare, with a beautiful fountain at its center; and, between wooded slopes, the Meuse meandered gracefully around the town. The local bourgeoisie consisted of the rich merchants, notables, and industrialists of the Meuse valley, that somber valley echoing to the din of forges and foundries, which extended into Belgium—but the Cuifs had no access to that enclosed social world. Vitalie hardly went out except to do her errands at the market or to perform her devotions in church.

Then, at the end of 1852, quite by chance, when she was twenty-seven years old, she made the acquaintance of a handsome, thirty-eight-year-old army officer, Captain Frédéric Rimbaud, who, like her, had come to the Place de la Musique to hear the band of the 47th infantry regiment, then billeted at Mézières.[3] This was something of a miracle, for the reserved, almost rough-mannered Vitalie did not make friends easily. She was not pretty, but it is quite possible that an army officer, after a harsh life under the African sun, and anxious to start a family, would have been attracted by her serious manner and proud bearing. Things began to move very quickly: no useless sentimentality. On January 3, 1853, the couple had a draft marriage contract drawn up by Maître Descharmes, a notary at Charleville.[4] The settlement chosen was one whereby only acquests, or noninherited property, came into joint ownership; the future wife's personal property consisted of dues and credits to be recovered from her mother's estate. Furthermore, old M. Cuif undertook to favor none of his other children more than his daughter.

On January 15 Captain Rimbaud applied to the commanding officer of the 4th military division for permission to marry Mlle Vitalie Cuif, on whom her father had settled a dowry of 30,000 francs, and who could expect a handsome inheritance estimated at 46,000 francs. As soon as permission was granted, the marriage took place on February 8, 1853. The bridegroom's witnesses were his colonel, Baron Lemaire, and one of his fellow officers, Captain Gabillot; the bride's witnesses were her uncles through marriage, Charles Moraine de Rilly-aux-Oies and Pierre Augustin Pierlot d'Allan'huy.

And where did he come from, this handsome Captain Rimbaud? If we trace his ancestry back, we come to a more agreeable region than Roche, in fact to Nantilly (Saône-et-Loire), "a tiny village stuck in the midst of greenery," Jacques Foucart tells us, "with a church spire pointing up among the trees, a few kilometers from Gray."[5] Foucart fails to mention the pleasant hillside planted with vines. In fact, Captain Rimbaud's ancestors were vine-growers.

The family tradition, mentioned by Paterne Berrichon,[6] according to which the Rimbauds were descendants of the comtes d'Orange, is therefore incorrect, as was any connection with the Provençal troubadour Rimbaut de Vauqueyras (1180–1270).[7] The name Rimbaud comes from *ribaud*, a word of Teutonic origin meaning prostitute (*ribbe*). In the Middle Ages, the *ribauds* were mercenaries who went to war only to loot—and Arthur, our poet, knew this when he wrote in *Une saison en enfer:* "Ma race ne se souleva jamais que pour piller" (My race never rose up except to loot). The word *ribaud* entered the Occitan language in the Low Latin forms of *ribaldus* or *rimbaldus*. In his *Dictionnaire Provençal*, Mistral cites the term *Casso Ribaud* (*ribauds*-chasers) to denote a curfew (Marcel Coulon).

At Nantilly, then, lived two vinegrowers, the brothers Rimbaud, Guil-laume (1669–1739) and Gabriel (1680–1735), each with a large family. Jean-François, one of Gabriel's sons, born in 1730, set up in Nantilly as a cobbler. He was an unstable man, moving from parish to parish. At the age of forty-seven, now a widower, he remarried. His bride was a young woman of twenty-five, Marguerite Brodt (or Brotte), the daughter of a master tailor. She led him such an impossible life that one Sunday morning in the year 1792, when his son was only six years old, he fled without either stockings or coat, and nothing was heard of him again.[8] Marguerite Brodt, for her part, remar-ried, first to a Danish deserter called Francen, then to a peddler, and ended her days in utter destitution.

The only child of the Rimbaud-Brodt marriage, Didier, the poet's grand-father, born on April 19, 1786, set up business as a tailor at Parcey. On June 27, 1810, he married Catherine Taillandier, a farmer's daughter. At twenty-eight, we find him a master tailor at Dôle in the Jura. He died on May 18, 1852.

It was at this time that the spelling of the surname became fixed: up till then it had been variously spelled as Rimbaut, Rimbaux, Rimbault, Rim-beaud.

The Rimbaud-Taillandier marriage produced four children, two of whom, it is said, met their deaths in the riots of 1830, but this has not been confirmed. On the other hand, we can trace perfectly the only surviving child, Frédéric, who managed to raise himself above the monotony of these dreary lives: he became a soldier.[9]

Born on October 7, 1814, at Dôle, he joined that 46th infantry regiment at the age of eighteen, on the advice of a cousin, a retired army officer. He had to wait seven years before being promoted to the rank of sergeant-major on May 6, 1839. Later, after being commissioned a sublieutenant, on April 13, 1841, he embarked for Algeria with a battalion of light infantry.

These *chasseurs à pied*, who later came to be known as the "*chasseurs d'Orléans*," were constantly in action around Tlemcen against the bands of Abd el-Kader. An officer in the same battalion, Captain Bazaine, spoke well of him.

In 1845, now a full lieutenant, Frédéric Rimbaud was ordered to rejoin the depot at Tlemcen, and this fact no doubt saved his life, for his battalion was decimated in a skirmish at Sidi Brahim. He then exchanged the sword for the pen: in July 1845, he was transferred to the Department for Arab Affairs; then, in June 1847, he was made head of the Arab Bureau at Sebdou. Sebdou was a small outpost of 280 men, 80 kilometers from the Moroccan frontier. There his duties were purely administrative, to research and write up bimonthly reports on the enemy's activities, the attitude of the tribes, the situation of the markets, local affairs (justice, police, taxation, etc.). He carried out his duties more than competently. Some of his reports, now in the Archives de la France d'outre-mer, have been published.[10] There is a study on grasshoppers, dating from June–July 1849, written in an excellent style, which reveals that his handwriting is strangely similar to what was to be that of his son, Arthur. His writings are marked by their clarity, conciseness, and precision. He had a knack of marshaling his material, without either heaviness or inappropriate literary flourishes: his work is that of a methodical, clear-headed clerk. He also left several works in manuscript, notably a *Military Correspondence*, a *Treatise on Military Eloquence*, and a *Book of War*. As his son's first biographers, Jean Bourguignon and Charles Houin, wrote, "These are enormous works. The first consists of 700 very large pages, covered by small handwriting; it is accompanied by commentaries and analyses. The second is a treatise comparing ancient orators with modern ones, whose speeches had been published by an officers' club under the same title about 1818. The third is remarkable for its many plans and for its accounts of episodes that took place during expeditions in Algeria, the Crimea, and Italy."[11]

This information comes from Isabelle Rimbaud, Arthur's sister, for, when these researchers came to see her, their mother refused to open her mouth or to show them these manuscripts. We understand from Jean Bourguignon that Mme Rimbaud used the large pages to wrap up things she bought at Charleville market. To complete the list of Frédéric Rimbaud's works, we should add an annotated French grammar (which has been found), and various Arabic papers, in particular an exercise book entitled "Jokes, puns, etc." (which has been lost); mention has also been made of an annotated Koran.

Lieutenant Rimbaud remained at Sebdou until 1850, well after the surrender of Abd el-Kader (1847). He returned to France on June 26 and must have vegetated in some depot before being transferred with the rank of captain to the 2d battalion of the 47th regiment of the line, stationed in the Ardennes. The headquarters and the 2d battalion were billeted at Mézières, the 1st battalion at Givet, and the depot at Rocroi.

The captain must have been dreadfully bored in his small garrison town, with its quiet, narrow streets. How he must have hankered after the sun, the sand, the surprise attacks, the responsibilities, the permanent danger!

Then, on the Place de la Musique, at Charleville . . .

Vitalie must have felt some affection for her handsome officer. She dreamed of starting a family, held together by the good principles of morality and religion, of having many children, whom she would bring up strictly in order to prepare them for the hurts and disappointments of life. For his part, the captain could appreciate the solid virtues of this farmer's daughter: inexhaustible energy, an elevated sense of duty, an innate thrift, and strict views on dress.

The young couple set up house in M. Cuif's apartments, 12 Rue Napoléon.

Before moving on, perhaps we should make a rapid sketch of the couple, of whom we have no photograph or drawing.

This is what Pierre Dufour (his literary pseudonym was Paterne Berrichon) has to say about his mother-in-law, Vitalie Rimbaud: "She was a woman of above average height, with dark brown hair, a slightly swarthy complexion, a broad forehead, a straight nose, and a thin mouth. She was slim, with large, knotty hands. She seemed proud and energetic."[12]

He recognizes that beneath this rigid exterior were hidden "qualities of unusual depth and delicacy," and adds that she was of a very nervous disposition, and that during her childhood she had been given to sleepwalking. Last, one has to admit that she could write well. Her letters, published by Mme Briet, have a nobility and simplicity of style reminiscent of the Grand Siècle.[13]

Jean Bourguignon depicts her as a peasant woman of average height with a rather red, deeply wrinkled face, and very light blue eyes. "I never once saw her laugh or smile," adds Louis Pierquin, one of Arthur's friends.

The qualities that Captain Rimbaud had discerned in her were certainly, at a distance, virtues, but, unfortunately, they turned out on closer acquaintance to be unbearable defects. Her very deep religious faith was often indistinguishable from the most bigoted intolerance: she combined the narrowness of mind of the Jansenists with the mental rigor of the Huguenots. There was a good deal of Phariseeism in her, too, for the opinion of others counted for much in her eyes. She judged people by their fortune, rather than their merits, and despised the poor and the disinherited, assuming that they were themselves responsible for their lot.

Her decisiveness concealed an utter absolutism: she could tolerate no slight to her authority, no advice, no criticism. It was hardly surprising if she quarreled with all her neighbors, and indeed with everybody. A dutiful wife? Yes, the captain certainly had that! But where duty is concerned, what one does is perhaps less important than how one does it. Many people find joy and satisfaction in doing their duty. For her, it was rather a matter of surly self-satisfaction and pride. This does not mean that she was incapable of love: however, the object of her love was expected to comply docilely with her will. "God has given me a strong heart, full of courage and energy," she wrote to Paul Verlaine. The more people resisted her, the more she tightened her grip. If, later, she complained of having been unhappy, of having suffered, of having wept a great deal, it was because her discipline had turned most people away. As we shall see, her husband left her, her eldest son, just to spite her, became a newspaper seller, then signed up for five years in the army; as for her younger son, Arthur, he had only one idea in his head: to place the greatest possible distance between himself and her. It did not take much for her to break with her daughter, the gentle Isabelle, who committed the crime of marrying an undistinguished scribbler in Paris instead of a good local farmer.

Marcel Coulon describes her wittily as a mixture of Brutus the Elder and Mme Lepic, the mother of Poil de Carotte. No less wittily, Verlaine called her "the mother of the Gracchi."[14]

We know very little about Captain Rimbaud and this gap in our knowledge impedes our understanding of his son. Paterne Berrichon never saw him, but he had no doubt caught a glimpse of some portrait of him, since he describes him as "a man of average height, fair-haired, with a high forehead, blue eyes, a short, slightly turned up nose, a full mouth, sporting, as was then the fashion, moustache and imperial."[15] He adds that he was of a "changeable, indolent, and violent" character. He was later to prove incapable of adapting himself to any situation that did not please him. Indeed his handwriting reveals a mixture of impulsiveness and pride. However, the deductions of certain biographers are quite gratuitous: the fact that he had been transferred to Arab departments does not prove that he had been an alcoholic; nor did the fact that he belonged to particularly mobile regiments, constantly moving from one garrison to another, mean that he was a vagabond. Lastly there is no proof of his anticlericalism; the fact that he was buried "with the prayers and ceremonies of the Church" would tend to prove the contrary. But it may well be (and one can sympathize) that he was irritated by his wife's bigotry. "Twenty times a day," writes Mme Briet, "she would kneel down when she passed a small statue of the Virgin placed in the outer wall at Roches,[16] on the garden side. Every evening, before retiring to her room, she would bless the house, and, from her bed, the young maid Marie."[17]

There, then, are the husband and wife—for better or for worse.

It was soon to be for the worse.

2

First Steps

When old M. Cuif gave his son Charles-Auguste a fairly large sum of money to put the farm at Roche on its feet (by buying equipment, seed, etc.), by way of compensation for what he had done for Vitalie, he thought that at last he had earned the right to some peace and quiet. Unfortunately, the good-for-nothing went back to drinking and to mistreating his wife so much that she was forced to return to her parents. Left alone, he became a permanent cause of scandal. It is said that he would force his visitors at gunpoint to drink with him until they were drunk. Was his father aware of what was going on? We cannot be sure, for he was not a man to tolerate shame: he would rather have given up living with his daughter and resume the running of the farm. Soon his presence at Charleville became necessary, for the young couple's honeymoon was of short duration. On May 1, 1853, less than three months after the wedding, Captain Rimbaud had to leave his already pregnant wife to rejoin his regiment in the Lyonnais region.

Nine months after the wedding, on November 2, 1853, a son, Jean Nicolas Frédéric, was born. The child was put out to nurse near Mézières, while his father roamed around Romans, Annonay, and Valence.

At the beginning of the year 1854 the captain returned to Charleville on leave, and, though he was delighted to kiss his son, he realized soon enough that he hated children—which did not stop him making his wife pregnant again.

That same year, 1854, in the course of which he was decorated with the Legion of Honor (August 9), was marked by fresh trouble at Roche. While he was dissipating the last of his father's money, Charles-Auguste received a surprise visit from his brother, Jean Charles, tanned by the Algerian sun, who was at once nicknamed "the African." Sickened at the sight of his younger brother spending the day sobering up after the previous night's dissipation, Jean Charles "bought" the farm and began to run it. Unfortunately, he did not have time to prove himself, for he died on December 3, 1854. The cause of his death is unknown.

By that time, Mme Rimbaud was the mother of a second son, Jean Nicolas Arthur, the future poet, who was born on October 20, at six o'clock in the morning. The captain was not present at the birth; a few days before, he had had to return to Lyon.

The birth was registered by the grandfather, Jean Nicolas Cuif, and witnessed by Jean-Baptiste Hémery,[1] a town-hall clerk, and Prosper Letellier, the bookseller on the first floor, who owned the building in which they lived. The baptism was celebrated on November 20 in the chapel of the then Grand Prieuré (the church of Notre-Dame was not built until 1860), by a curate, the Abbé Constant Grison. The godfather was grandfather Cuif, and the godmother Rosalie Cuif, no doubt a cousin.

The "Rimbaud myth," the golden legend of his life, began at once. Paterne Berrichon omits no detail learned from Isabelle, his wife, Arthur's sister, that might show that an exceptional human being had just appeared on the surface of the earth. For instance, he was born with his eyes open (a sign of his future curiosity), and, when only a few months old, he appears to have left the cushion on which he had been placed, and crawled off to the door of the apartment—his first attempt at running away!

He was soon put out to nurse at Gespunsart, near the Belgian frontier, with a good nailsmith and his wife. One day his mother went to see him and was surprised to find him half naked in a salt chest, while his foster brother was wearing the baby clothes that had been made for Arthur.

But let us leave the gospel account of the childhood there.

One imagines that, as soon as she could, Mme Rimbaud dashed off to Roche. Perhaps she went to attend Jean Charles's funeral; she must have gone looking for a reliable farmer to replace her younger brother, Charles-Auguste, whom she promptly turned out of doors. The poor wretch went off, tramping the highroads, getting work here and there as an agricultural laborer, sleeping where he could, and begging for food when he was not working. It is said that he even came back to Roche and knocked on the farmhouse door. Mme Rimbaud pretended not to recognize him, demanded to see his papers, and, when he started to make trouble, quickly slipped a coin into his hand and banged the door in his face. He ended his days on January 31, 1924. At the last moment, he refused to see a priest, but asked for a liter of red wine![2]

Meanwhile, Captain Rimbaud's adventures continued. In May 1855 he set sail on the *Zénobie* for the Crimea. There, instead of sharing in the glory of battle, his company did little more than dig trenches around Sebastopol; however, he himself did not escape the cholera epidemic.

In the summer of 1856, as his regiment was making its way back to Paris—twenty-five days of marching!—and since he had stayed at the depot at Grenoble, he asked for leave to visit his family. He saw them again at Roche, for the documents of the Charleville census show that, during that (and the following year), Jean Nicolas Cuif was still living in the Rue Napoléon, but that his daughter Vitalie had "left."

From the reunion resulted the birth, on June 4, 1857, of a daughter, Victorine Pauline Vitalie, but the child died the following month. Arthur's phrase, "that's she, the little girl behind the rose bushes" (*Illuminations—Childhood II*) would appear to be a reference to her grave, for Mme Rimbaud was rather fond of taking her children to the cemetery.

This accident was soon repaired: as a result of the captain's next visit on leave, in September 1857, another daughter, Jeanne Rosalie Vitalie, was born on May 15, 1858; but, by the time of her birth, her father had already set off for Grenoble.

By this time Arthur was nearly four. Berrichon recounts an incident from this period: one day, after the birth of his sister Vitalie, as the little fellow was hoisting himself up on to the window ledge of the Librairie Letellier to admire the red bindings and picturebooks in the window, old Letellier dashed out of his shop, and, taking the child by surprise from behind, asked him:

"What's taken your fancy so much?"

The child pointed to the beautiful pictures.

"Would you like to buy one of them?"

"I've no money."

"Ah! You've no money . . ."

"No. But you can have my little sister instead."[3]

Most of the time the captain was away, since the 47th infantry regiment was kept on the move, from Grenoble to Dieppe, and from Dieppe to Strasbourg, then from Strasbourg to Sélestat.

In late August 1859, with the harvest over at Roche, Mme Rimbaud put her children into care and was able to join her husband at Sélestat, the first holiday she had ever had. But soon the regiment was on the move again, this time for Lautenbourg and Wissembourg, and she had to go home.

One or two months later, she could no longer hide the fact that she was pregnant again. Her landlord, M. Letellier, terrified by the regular increase of his tenant's family, asked her to seek accommodation elsewhere.

Another child and no lodgings!

At Charleville tenancies usually began on the Feast of St. John (December 27). Until that date, Mme Rimbaud and her brood had to move into the Hôtel du Lion d'Argent, in the center of the town. At the end of the year she took what was on offer: lodgings in the Rue Bourbon (probably at no. 73), a working-class street without shops, consisting of small, two-story houses.

It was there, on June 1, 1860, that a second daughter, Frédérique Marie Isabelle, was born.

According to the municipal documents, Captain Rimbaud came to live for some time with his family. It was then that things began to get worse. Used as he was to giving orders, he could not bear his wife's bossy ways, and her temper was not improved by what she regarded as the sordidness and vulgarity of her surroundings. There were few comforts, and the children were kept in some kind of order by blows and punishments. It was a hellish summer. Arthur (then six years old) remembered one fight, which he later described to Ernest Delahaye: his father finally lost his temper, threw a silver bowl that stood on the sideboard in the dining room on to the floor, then, regretting his action, picked it up, and carefully put it back in its place. Whereupon his mother, not to be outdone, seized the object, flung it once more on to the floor, then picked it up, and put it back in its place.

It was shortly before September 16, 1860, the date when the 47th infantry regiment set off for Cambrai, that the marriage finally broke up (he was forty-six, she thirty-five). It was a definitive separation: there is no evidence that they ever wrote to one another again.

The captain continued on his travels from Cambrai to Valenciennes, and from there to the camp at Châlons. No doubt, in the end, Captain Rimbaud grew tired of all these comings and goings, for, on August 11, 1864, he took up his option of a pension and retired to Dijon.[4]

All we have that ever belonged to him is a grammar, by Bescherelle aîné (Paris: Simon, 1854), a thick, bound volume of 878 pages, annotated in his hand. On the end paper is written the following learned maxim: "Without a little work there is no pleasure." The title page bears the words "Grammar is the basis, the foundation of all human knowledge."

So Mme Rimbaud was left alone in the Rue Bourbon with her four children, two girls and two boys.

She was unhappy. Her dream of an ordered, dignified family life had gone forever. This regret was to pursue her for the rest of her life. Forty-seven years later, she had only to see some soldiers pass by for the wound to reopen. "Just as I was about to write to you," she confided to her daughter Isabelle on June 6, 1907, the year of her death, "a lot of soldiers went by, which deeply affected me, reminding me of your father, with whom I would have been happy had I not had certain children who have given me so much pain."

Without children, she may have been able to lead the normal life of an officer's wife. Her destiny, which she accepted, was to struggle alone against everybody, and to fail in everything. Urged on by the failures, she devoted herself with redoubled energy to the rearing of her children, determined to bring them up in the austere way of honor and duty convinced that there was no better way of getting her sons into the best professions. Then, as a grandmother, she would be able to rest at last, having avenged the affronts done to her by her two brothers and her husband.

When one compares this fine program and the lamentable results obtained, one cannot but feel some respect and pity for her.

When she grew up, Isabelle realized that her mother had sacrificed herself for nothing. This goes a long way to explaining the determination with which she set about defending her—and her brother Arthur—against historians who wished only to tell the truth. When she declared that her brother was a perfect gentleman, that he possessed all the virtues, that he died a holy death, it was the memory of her mother that she was defending. To this was added the religiosity of a schoolgirl who had refused to grow up: Arthur had become an angel, a saint, a venerated icon. This pious naïveté may raise a smile, but it does not deserve the rather heavy-handed scorn that has sometimes been poured on it: "The holy family," "Isabelle the Catholic," the tyrannical, hypocritical sister, etc.

Before pouring scorn, one should try to understand.

In the Rue Bourbon, life meant more for the children than working under their mother's strict eye. Naturally enough, they also liked to play with the local children. For that there was the staircase, the yard with its privies, and the small, drab garden. One can imagine that Mme Rimbaud disapproved strongly of all contact with these working-class children, but the two brothers, accomplices in disobedience, braved every prohibition, despite the clouts, the dry bread, the withdrawal of the dessert, and other such sanctions.

In a highly colored, vengeful poem, *Les Poètes de sept ans* (Seven-year-old Poets),[5] Arthur evoked in an extraordinary way the atmosphere of the Rue

Bourbon. Everything is there, the mother "satisfied and very proud," "the blue glance—that lies," the pitiable children

Qui, chétifs, fronts nus, œil déteignant sur la joue,
Cachant de maigres doigts jaunes et noirs de boue
Sous des habits puant la foire et tout vieillots,
Conversaient avec la douceur des idiots!

. . . . .

. . . dans la chambre nue aux persiennes closes,
Haute et bleue, acrement prise d'humidité . . .

[*Who, sickly, bare-headed, with eyes weeping on their cheeks,*
Hiding thin fingers yellow and black with mud
Under worn-out clothes stinking of diarrhea and old,
Talked with the gentleness of idiots!

. . . . .

. . . In his bare room with closed shutters,
High and blue, sourly covered with humidity . . .][6]

Still affected by a scuffle he had just had with the daughter of the laborers next door, during which he had bitten her bare buttocks, he brooded over "the taste of her flesh," then let his mind wander off to some "amorous pasture" with its "shining swells," or devoured novels that transported him to unknown lands beneath fabulous skies. The sheets of unbleached canvas on which he lay became the sails of imaginary ships that carried him off, drunk with freedom.

Alas! what little freedom he had was soon to be taken from him, for in October 1861, at the age of seven, his mother sent him, with his brother, Frédéric, to the Institution Rossat, 11 Rue de l'Arquebuse.[7]

It was a day school, founded in 1855 by a *docteur-ès-sciences* of the University of Strasbourg, François Sébastien Rossart, which, at first, had about two hundred pupils. Shortly afterward, directives from the minister, Victor Duruy, concerning modern education were implemented, and a "special" (or technical, as we would say) section was set up, with amphitheater, workshops, and laboratories. It was an immediate success: soon the Institution had over three hundred pupils (a hundred more than the Collège de Charleville). Later, when this reform had reached its height, Francisque Sarcey could write in the *Soleil* (March 19, 1866): "It is at Charleville that we find one of the finest establishments of public education in France."[8]

This Institution still exists at Charleville-Mézières, on the Place Carnot, now the Place Winston Churchill. The buildings in the Rue de l'Arquebuse that Rimbaud knew have since been demolished. Canon Mathy left the following description of them:

> *The front of the building, in the Rue de l'Arquebuse, differed little from the ordinary middle-class houses on either side of it. One entered through a large door painted dark green. One found oneself in a hall onto which opened, on the right, the parlor, where glazed cabinets contained among other things stuffed birds and a skeleton. . . . When one crossed the hall, one was in a narrow courtyard, three times longer than wide, flanked by two wings with high, crumbling walls, whitewashed in "corpse yellow," as a former pupil described it, with all the patina of an old vellum binding. Their intimidating welcome confirmed your worst fears. At the end of the courtyard was the art room, entered by going down a few steps. The wall that enclosed the courtyard on this side was so filthy that, on prize giving days, when pupils hurled their ink wells at it to break them, the stains and splashes made little difference.*
>
> *In the second courtyard, one could only play with a small ball. By way of shelter, there was a sort of washhouse, open to all weathers. Everything in the school looked poverty-stricken and dilapidated: moldy patches, huge desks, ink-stained and with deep gashes in them, walls covered with stains and irreverent graffiti. There was no chapel, and there were no religious emblems in the classrooms. Yet M. Rossat was not anticlerical: when the Blessed Sacrament was paraded through the streets of the town, it was accompanied by the music of his pupils.*[9]

Despite the appalling state of the premises, the Institution had as its pupils the sons of the wealthiest families of the town, those that had acquired their wealth in commerce and industry.

M. Taute, the librarian of Charleville-Mézières, has discovered in the *Courrier des Ardennes* for August 13, 1862, August 17, 1863, and August 9, 1864, some echo of the academic successes of the young Rimbaud at Rossat's establishment: during his first year (1861–62), he won three prizes and was commended three times (for unspecified reasons) in the prize list; in his second year (1862–63), he was awarded the *prix d'honneur* for the lower school, five prizes and seven (unspecified) commendations; and, last, in his third year, he carried off a prize in Latin grammar and translation into Latin, another for French grammar and spelling, a third for history and geography, and a fourth for classical recitation and reading, not to mention an honorable mention in arithmetic.[10]

Soon after Rimbaud's death, Paterne Berrichon rediscovered some of the magnificent volumes, bound by the Maison Mame, that were given to him as prizes: *Les Beautés du spectacle de la nature*, by the Abbé Pluche (eighteenth-century); *L'Histoire descriptive et pittoresque de Saint-Dominique*, by M. de Marlès (1858); *L'Habitation du désert*, by Mayne Reid (1861), with illustrations by Gustave Doré (a volume of 500 pages, in poor condition, owing to repeated consultation; *Les Robinsons français ou la Nouvelle-Calédonie*, by J. Morlent (1861); and Mme Fallet's *Le Robinson de la jeunesse* (1863).

It is hardly surprising if such reading inspired the young schoolboy to write stories of "marvelous travels to strange lands, through deserts and oceans, mountains and rivers" (letter from Isabelle Rimbaud to Louis Pierquin, October 23, 1892). Two documents relating to the young Rimbaud's time at Rossat's establishment have been found: first, a class photograph in which he is sitting, in uniform, in the front row, his cap on his knees, looking rather surly (*Album Rimbaud*, Gallimard, p. 40), and, second, a scribbling pad, without cover, of sixteen pages, covered with a fine, often careless and illegible handwriting. It contains dictations, translations, summaries, and notes in no apparent order whatsoever. Thus, on p. 9, we have "nam saepe, si divites sunt mali sunt, Rimbaud Athur [*sic*] de Charleville ne loqueris hominis impis nam . . . etc."

Genesis is represented, as are fables by Aesop and La Fontaine, bits of geography and the natural sciences, in all twenty-six items in French, twelve in Latin, series of words, two problems and seven drawings. This ragbag would be of little interest were it not for a curious narrative ending in a confession, with a prologue that begins thus:

Le soleil était encore chaud;
cependant il n'éclairait prés
queplus la teirre [sic].

[The sun was still warm
But now it hardly lit
the earth.]

(These texts are reprinted exactly as they appear in Mme S. Briet's article in *La Grive* no. 90, April 1956.)

In this dream ("I dream that . . . I was born at Reims in the year 1503") not everything is mere fantasy; there are also real, if transposed memories:

Mes parents étaient peu riches
mais très honnêtes; il [sic] n'avaient
pour tout bien qu'une petite
maison. . . .
mon père était officier, dans
les armées du roi. C'était un
homme grand, maigre,
chevelure noire, barbe, yeux, peau
de mem couleur. . . .
                                    il était
d'un caractère vif, bouillant,
souvent en colère et ne voulant
rien souffrir qui lui déplut
ma mère était bien diffe
rente femme douce, calme,
s'effrayant de peu de chose, et
cependant tenant la maison dans
un ordre parfait.

[My parents were not rich, but they were honest. They owned nothing but the small house in which they lived. . . . My father was an officer in the king's army. He was a tall, thin man with black hair, a beard, eyes, and skin of the same color. . . . He was a fiery, quick-tempered man, easily angered, and could not bear anything that did not please him. My mother *was very different, a gentle, quiet, timorous woman, yet she kept the house in perfect order.*]

Although he was no good at arithmetic, the story continues, and refused to read, despite the promise of money, toys, and sweetmeats, his father sent him to school as soon as he was ten years old.

Then the tone changes, the novel turns into a pamphlet, and the exercise book becomes the outlet for all the schoolboy's resentment against those who have condemned him to the prison of the classroom: "What does it matter to me if Alexander was a famous man? What does it matter to me . . . whether one knows if the Latins existed?"

The drawings (five on the penultimate page and two on the last), bearing the title *Plaisirs du jeune âge* (Pleasures of Youth), are no less curious.

1. *The Sleigh.* A schoolboy is pulling a sleigh on which a young girl is sitting. "Long live the Queen of the North," she says. "We'll be shipwrecked," he replies.

2. *The Swing.* The girl is sitting on a chair suspended from a doorknob. "Ah! I'm falling," she cries. "Hold on with one hand," her brother replies, his arms uplifted.

3. *The Siege.* The whole family, the father, the mother, and two sons are throwing all kinds of objects out of the window onto the crowd in the street. A passerby, wearing a top hat, protests, raising an arm and shouting: "A complaint should be made!"

4. *The Mass.* The two sisters are kneeling at a prayer stool. One of them is holding out a doll to her brother, who is dressed as a priest, and says to him: "You must baptize this."

5. *Agriculture* (the drawing is signed "A. Rimbaud"). The two brothers and sisters are making broad gestures in front of a box on a windowsill from which emerges a plant (a rubber plant?).

6. *Navigation* (last page). "Help!" cries a schoolboy in danger in a boat, his left arm raised. The other passenger, his brother, is lying down and also raises his arms in a gesture of distress.

7. (Untitled sketch). "It shows a woman sitting at the entrance to a copse, hiding her face with her left arm, while her right arm is waving about. A man is striding away from her with all the appearance of someone who has done something wrong" (S. Briet).[11] An allusion to the departure of his father, the captain, or to some attempt of his own to run away.[12]

These drawings, with the exception of the seventh, have been reproduced in number 21 of *Rimbaud vivant* (2ᵉ trimestre, 1982).

In the interest of completeness, we should mention that an *Atlas* by Delamanche (Edition Grosselin, 1864), which must have been used by all the Rimbaud children, also contains, on the back of the maps, drawings that are sometimes originals, sometimes obviously copied from magazines (1865–70).

On the Feast of St. John 1862, while Arthur and Frédéric were at school, Mme Rimbaud was able at last to find a suitable apartment, at 13 Cours d'Orléans, the broad avenue planted with chestnut trees that linked Charleville and Mézières. She probably let it be known in her new neighborhood that she was a widow. Understandably enough, she wanted to cut short any indiscreet questions from her neighbors, or any comments that might, for example, have expressed approval of the captain for leaving such a shrew. This became the official version: "My mother is a widow," Arthur wrote to Verlaine in 1871.

Mme Rimbaud was hardly satisfied with the Institution Rossat, approving neither of the modern, scientific orientation of the teaching nor the halfheartedness of the religious instruction. It was becoming increasingly obvious that the clergy favored the Collège.

So it was hardly surprising if, at Easter 1865, the brothers Rimbaud were withdrawn from the Institution Rossart and transferred to the Collège de Charleville.

3

The Collège

The Collège de Charleville, in the Place du Saint-Sépulcre (now the Place de l'Agriculture), housed in the former convent of the canonesses of the Holy Sepulcher, was an imposing seventeenth-century building with a facade in the shape of a Lorraine cross before a chapel surmounted by a dome and campanile. It was next to the seminary and city library.

Very much intimidated, the brothers Rimbaud first went to the school in April 1865, while their mother had yet again moved, this time to number 20 in the Rue Forest (which was later to become Avenue, de l'Empereur).

Arthur (now ten and a half) was placed in *sixième*, the class that he had been in at the Institution, and Frédéric in *septième*.[1] The younger brother was immediately noticed by the history teacher, M. Clouet, who expressed great admiration for one of his class summaries, a little masterpiece of concision and clarity, which he showed to M. Louis, who taught French and Latin.

With the new school year in October, Arthur went up into the *cinquième* class, with M. Roullier, a very quick-tempered man who had a rather surly face and an unruly forelock but who, when the fit had passed, became quite indulgent once more.

The young schoolboy managed to adapt himself, though without spectacular results: at the prize-giving on August 6, 1866, he came first in Religious Instruction (his brother came fourth), fifth in French language, but won the first prize in Classical Recitation.

When, in October 1866, he went up to the *quatrième* class, there was a new principal: M. Mallart had been replaced by a M. Desdouets.

M. Desdouets was a thin man with white hair and a contorted face. He came from the south of France and was of a restless, very active temperament. He astonished the school by his emphatic way of speaking, his extremely loose-fitting clothes, and his extraordinary hats.[2]

Arthur's class master was "Père Pérette," an old-fashioned schoolmaster who demanded high standards of work and discipline. He had been nicknamed "le père Bos" or "Jobos" because of the way in which he stressed the words *bos* or *globos* when he dictated Virgil. Pérette was quick to see that young Rimbaud was an exceptional, if disturbing, individual.

"Let him read everything, give him everything to read!" Desdouets once told him. But the old teacher, shaking his head replied: "He's intelligent, I'll grant you, but there's something in his eyes and smile I don't like. He'll come to a bad end: anyway, there's nothing ordinary germinating in that head. He'll be a genius either for good or for ill!"

Desdouets, however, already had visions of young Arthur at the Ecole Normale Supérieure in Paris, and praised him to the heights. A fellow pupil remembered Rimbaud standing up in class, blushing, yet full of self-confidence, with a touch of contempt for the others, as he heard Desdouets "analyze his compositions, making each sentence sound like the work of a genius."[3]

That year the Rimbaud brothers took their first communion. The only souvenir that has survived of that day is a rather stiff photograph: Arthur is sitting, like an angel with a round head, a pensive look in his eyes, his hair plastered down "with sweetened water" (Paul Claudel). Frédéric is standing beside him wearing his armband, his left hand on his chest, looking somewhat ordinary and surly.

At this time the younger brother made great show of a rather exalted religious faith; one day, his friend Delahaye recounts, as the bigger boys were coming out of the chapel, sprinkling holy water over one another, he rushed upon them, scratching and biting the profaners, despite the blows he got in return, until a *surveillant*, or student supervisor, appeared on the scene and reestablished order. From then on he was often called "a dirty little hypocrite."[4] But it was only a flash in the pan.

Until the school clock sounded its eight fatal blows, the Place du Saint-Sépulchre served as a recreation yard for the pupils. Like everywhere else in the world, they ran about, bumping into one another, fighting, throwing their satchels at one another or, on icy days, skating.

This square is flanked on one side by an arm of the Meuse, beyond

which rises a wooded hill ("Mount Olympus"), which, at the time, was surmounted by the rococo turret of a villa, the "tour Lolot."

Ernest Delahaye, then fourteen, had a couple of kilometers to walk from
Mézières to the school, and often arrived early. Instead of mingling with the
turbulent crowd, he preferred to saunter by the waterside, intrigued by the
activities of two boys, who, leaving their satchels on the grassy slope, were
playing around on a fishing boat—though it may have been a boat belonging
to the tannery nearby—rocking it from side to side. When it got too close to
the bank, they pulled on the anchor chain, and, with a thrust of the heel,
sent it back bobbing around in the current. They were curiously dressed, in
identical fashion, rather like English schoolboys, in slate-blue trousers and
black jackets. They wore similar small hats. Another witness describes Arthur,
for we are fairly sure that the description is of him, as "neat, with hair well
scraped and pommaded, straight backed, boots gleaming, tie perfectly knotted
under a broad, stiff collar turned down over the shoulders."[5]

They looked English, too, on account of their light blue eyes and their
rosy complexions. They did not say very much, but sometimes the younger
of the two would tell his brother to stop moving the boat so that he could
examine the riverbed. The older boy then went off to the end of the boat and
sulked, leaving the younger one lying flat on his belly, his nose almost touching the water, examining the aquatic plants rippling against a background of
pebbles and shiny fragments, potsherds or bits of glass.

The school bell soon put an end to the game; they they leaped back on
to the riverbank, picked up their satchels, and joined the throng so as to be
at the school threshold at precisely the moment when the janitor rang the
"second stroke."

"Père Chocol! Père Chocol!" the urchins would cry (they also called him
Chochol, Chouchoul, Chocoul, etc.), catching sight of the slow-moving old
fellow, who always wore a "shapeless old cap" (Delahaye) and terribly stiff
blue overalls.

One day, Delahaye, who was in *sixième*, happened to sit next to one of
the unknown "boat boys" during a German class, which was usually pretty
rowdy. Suddenly, propelled by some mysterious force, his neighbor was
thrown against him.

"Your names!" cried the master, turning round.

"Delahaye, Ernest."

"Rimbaud, Frédéric."

They each got an hour's detention, and, as they were passing the time playing cards in the corridor, the principal's wife happened to pass by and asked them what crime they had committed.

"We didn't do anything, Ma'am," said Delahaye, fiddling with his cap in his hands.

Frédéric, who was afraid that his mother would give him a box on the ears and send him to bed without supper, sobbed and sniveled.

"At least this one is sorry for what he has done," said the principal's wife, and stalked off.

Through this incident Delahaye had made a friend, "le grand Rimbaud," who was to join him the following year in the classe de cinquième, with Roullier as their master. Frédéric was a bad pupil, careless and not very intelligent: when expected to write an essay he often got no further than writing out the question. If there had been a place lower than the bottom of the class, it would have been his by right.

One Saturday the greatly feared Desdouets arrived to read out the marks for the week to his trembling pupils. When he got to Frédéric's name, at the bottom of the list, he paused, then went on:

"Poor unfortunate boy . . . and yet . . . your brother . . ."

"What about your brother?" Delahaye asked him.

"Oh, Arthur! He's brilliant!"

Unfortunately, there was a permanent obstacle to Delahaye's meeting him: the presence of Mme Rimbaud and her daughters when it was time to go home. Her proud bearing, her commanding yet irritable voice, confirmed what Frédéric had always said about her strictness. It was all very discouraging.

Every day, a disappointed Delahaye watched the majestic procession of Rimbauds move off. Louis Pierquin has left the following description of them: "In front, the two girls, Vitalie and Isabelle, holding hands, in the second rank, the two boys, Arthur and Frédéric, also holding hands; bringing up the rear, at a regulated distance, came Mme Rimbaud."[6] As they moved off, Frédéric would turn round and give a little wave to his new friend, before the procession entered the Rue de l'Eglise. Soon Arthur did the same, and this friendly gesture was enough to fill with pride the heart of his unknown admirer.

The year ended with good, if not sensational, results: a first prize for Religious Instruction and Recitation (he was, it seems, unbeatable, and the master had to cut short his recital of the Aeneid), a second prize in Latin Verse and in History-Geography, a certificate of merit in German language.

The master of the *classe de troisième* (1867–68), a thickset, hairy Burgundian called Ariste L'Héritier, known to the boys as "Père Ariste," was a good fellow afflicted by several eccentricities: first, he took snuff, and his very full moustaches were always full of the powder; secondly—a more serious defect—he could not bear the romantics, acknowledging no canons of poetic beauty other than those of Boileau. Last, he was given to appalling fits of anger that terrorized his class. But, when the fit had passed, he would offer his snuffbox, as a token of reconciliation, to pupils he had just ill-treated in the most violent fashion.

The principal, who had recognized in "le petit Rimbaud" an exceptional pupil, managed to persuade the boy's mother to allow him to have private lessons, even though he was satisfactory in every way. In an attempt to tame Père Ariste, the budding poet handed in a very detailed study of Boileau, picking out from his oeuvre the slightest contraventions of the rules of prosody. His favorite Boileau works were *Le Lutrin* and *Le Repas ridicule*: in other words, what he liked best in Boileau was the caricature. And it was this that he set about imitating; unfortunately, these writings have not survived.

There was prose, too. A *surveillant* called Poncelet boasted (to Paterne Berrichon) that he had confiscated one of the boy's adventure stories, the action of which took place among the savages of Oceania.[7]

His penchant for caricature also found expression in sketches imitated from Gill, Daumier, Le Petit, or Albert Humbert (the creator of the ineffable Boquillon). Some of these have been found in the geography book published by Delamanche mentioned earlier, but we cannot be sure of their authorship: the drawings of burghers and notaries may be attributed to Arthur, and the clumsy, spindly drawings to Frédéric; the elegant ladies, clearly deriving from fashion magazines, are obviously the work of Vitalie or Isabelle.[8]

Such juvenilia reveal the young Rimbaud's taste for exoticism and outlandish caricature, if not his tendency to mystification. This last quality appears in the Latin verses that he secretly sent to the prince imperial on the occasion of his recent first communion in the chapel of the Tuileries. We would never have known this if Mme Méléra had not found in Paterne Berrichon's papers this letter from a pupil called Joly to his brother dated May 26, 1868: "You probably know the Rimbauds; one of them (the one who's now in *troisième*) has just sent a letter consisting of 60 lines of Latin verse to the little prince imperial in connection with his first communion. He kept the whole thing secret, and didn't even show his verses to the teacher: it seems he committed a few spicy barbarisms of prosody. The prince's tutor has just replied that His Majesty's little . . . [here a word is scratched out] was very touched by his letter, and that, like him, he was a pupil, and excused his bad verses with all his heart."⁹

At the prize-giving of August 10, 1868, young Arthur Rimbauud, now fourteen years of age, proved himself to be an excellent pupil, carrying off the first prize in Religious Instruction and in Recitation, and a number of certificates of merit, in particular the second one for all-round "Excellence": M. Desdouets' predictions were beginning to come true.

As from the beginning of the school year in October 1868, Mme Rimbaud no longer collected her son at the end of the day. However, instead of taking part in the hurlyburly and exchanges of stamps after school, the two well-trained boys walked straight home. Such an attitude soon offended their schoolfellows, who were shocked by their obvious unsociableness. Soon they began to be hooted at as they left. Delahaye and his classmate, Paul Labarrière (son of the owner of a furniture shop in the Cours-d'Orléans), were not averse to joining in the booing of the two savages, who never turned round to acknowledge the jeers.¹⁰

One day, however, Labarrière managed to thaw out the two brothers by saying a few words to them. Delahaye then seized the opportunity, and dashed across the Place du Saint-Sépulcre to join the small group. From then on, the Rimbauds were left in peace. The first question that Delahaye asked Frédéric concerned his umbrella: why did it, like Arthur's, have its end missing?

"It was his fault," said Frédéric, pointing to his brother.

"No, it was yours," Arthur replied, and recounted the incident.

One Sunday recently they had gone to mass alone, and Frédéric took it into his head to poke the end of his umbrella into the hinge of the heavy church doors. Immediately Arthur moved the door and the end was snapped off. When they came out of the service, during which the guilty boy had no doubt asked forgiveness for his lack of charity, he pretended to return to Frédéric's game, and, of course, Frédéric quickly shut the door, with the result that both umbrellas were now of the same legnth. It had seemed to Arthur that the punishment that would fall upon his brother would be more easily borne if it were shared. However, Mme Rimbaud merely declared: "You will both go to school with your umbrellas shortened, and the mockery of your schoolmates will be punishment enough for your stupidity."

But far from making fun of them, Delahaye and Labarrière admired Arthur's stoicism, which they considered worthy of the heroes of antiquity.

This incident was enough to break the ice permanently, and from then on Delahaye walked home with the Rimbaud brothers before continuing on his way to Mézières. His head was filled with all kinds of questions; which authors should one prefer, the ancients or the moderns, the classicists or the romantics?

One day, he announced a delicious scandal: "Labarrière disapproves of December 2.[11] What do you think?"

Arthur, the flatterer of the Prince Imperial, laughed: "Napoleon III deserves to be sent to the galleys!"

Delahaye was astonished at this answer, as if the ground had opened up under his feet.

Labarrière often joined them, and all four walked up and down the "Allées," discussing their first attempts in poetry or fiction. According to Delahaye, Frédéric, who felt out of things, took to ringing doorbells in order to draw attention to himself, which meant that the others had to make a dash for it. They would often loiter in the bookshops, Jolly's at the corner of the Place Ducale and the Rue du Moulin, then known as the Rue Sainte-Catherine, or at Letellier's in the Rue Napoleon. Leafing through the books on display, they would try to learn bits and pieces of poems. Arthur, who had already read Hugo and the romantics, was now gorging himself on modern poetry—and at that time modern poetry meant the *Parnasse contemporain*.

Only the faintest echo had reached Charleville of the small revolution that, under the banner of Parnassus, had been brought about by a group of the best poets of the day, gathered around the publisher Alphonse Lemerre in the Passage Choiseul. Since March 1866 the sixteen-page issues of the *Parnasse contemporain, recueil de vers nouveaux* had been appearing each month. In them one could read poems by Théophile Gautier, Banville, Heredia, Leconte de Lisle, Baudelaire, Dierx, Sully Prudhomme, Verlaine, which was enough to satisfy a provincial schoolboy hungry for poetry.

He moved up into the *classe de seconde*. After the cries of Père Pérette and the outbursts of Père Ariste (L'Héritier), calm returned. The teacher, M. Duprez, was a young graduate of gentle manner and open mind. All those who knew him praised his attractive face, his curly hair, and his exquisite manners. This dreamer, the exact opposite of the curious admirer of Boileau, loved Musset, Hugo, and Lamartine. But what Rimbaud liked most of all was that a breath of liberalism had swept through the Collège: at least one could breathe.

That year (1868–69), a system was introduced in which classes would be made up of pupils from both the school and the small seminary nearby. The rector, Fleury, had imagined that this would prove advantageous, for the seminary would lend him in exchange a number of teachers (for example the history teacher, the Abbé Wuillème, who was actually only a deacon, or the philosophy teacher the Abbé Gillet). From an educational point of view, the system was disastrous, for it broke up the unity of the class: brainless, fourteen-year-old schoolboys sat on the same benches with older, more staid future priests. Inevitably antagonism broke out between the two communities (or, as Izambard nicely puts it, between the party of the cigarette—the lay party—and that of the snuff box—the clerical party).

The following year we find the two rival, enemy clans again. In *seconde*, the lay-clerical rivalry had an excellent effect on Rimbaud: he was determined to win the battle, to beat the "cassocks," so he worked extra hard. He had also made up his mind to conquer Duprez. When classes were over he was in the habit of leaving variants of his compositions on the teacher's desk. If the task consisted of turning out a piece of Latin verse on a particular subject, then he would also give another version in French verse, or translate into prose and verse Greek texts that completely stumped half the class.

Duprez, amazed by this extraordinary facility, by way of homage and encouragement, sent the Académie de Douai an excellent exercise in Latin verse, done in three hours and a half on November 6, 1868, by "Rimbaud, day boy." It was published in the number for January 15, 1869, of the *Moniteur de l'Enseignement secondaire, spécial et classique, Bulletin officiel de l'Académie de Douai*. Rimbaud had been asked to develop a passage from Horace (Ode 4, book 3) showing the poet crowned with myrtle and bay, in the midst of wonderful doves in a state of divine ecstasy. Rimbaud identified himself with the inspired poet, since he was free, he said, from a dreadful master (*diri magistri*—everyone recognized L'Héritier) he took the opportunity of wandering through "smiling countryside," sampling the delights of spring.

A swarm of white, perfumed doves crowns his head and carries him off to their shining nest. The heavens open, and Phoebus, the sun god, inscribes on his brow with a celestial flame the prophetic words: *Tu vates eris* (You will be a poet).

The whole of Rimbaud is in that first printed text of his: his hatred of discipline, his thirst for freedom, his love of the sun-drenched countryside, his dreams among luminous birds. He knows that he is marked forever by the gods.

In the course of the school year, two more of his pieces had the honor of being published in the *Bulletin de l'Académie de Douai: L'Ange et l'enfant* (The Angel and the Child), fifty-five Latin verses after an indifferent poem by J. Reboul (the number of June 1, 1869), and the *Invocation à Vénus* (Invocation to Venus), from Lucretius' *De rerum natura* (composed during the first term, 1869, published April 15, 1870).[12] In the second text, Rimbaud was content to recopy (with improvements) a translation by Sully Prudhomme that had been published in 1869 by Lemerre, but M. Duprez did not realize this.

M. Mouquet, who detected this piece of deceit, suggested that another piece, supposedly by Alfred Mabille, a day boy in the *class de seconde*, entitled *La Cloche* (The Bell) and published in the *Moniteur* of March 15, 1869, might also be by Rimbaud. Indeed the form of this piece, made up of stanzas and a refrain—"*Omnia sic pereunt, rapide per inania rapta*" [Thus all things perish, swiftly carried off to the void]—certainly recalls the technique that Rimbaud was to use later in his composition on Jugurtha. The evidence of a former pupil at the school, M. Delahaut, supports this hypothesis: "While one of us would be demonstrating some theorem in geometry on the blackboard, Rimbaud would be knocking up for you in no time at all a number of pieces in Latin verse. Each of us had one. The title was the same, but the writing of the verses, the ideas, and the way they were developed were sufficiently different for the teacher not to recognize that they came from the same hand. It was a veritable tour de force, given how little time he had to do them in. It happened quite often, I can tell you."[13]

Every coin has its reverse side; his utter inability to understand mathematics formed the negative counterpart of such remarkable gifts. He pretended that he could not do a simple division, and more than once the math teacher, M. Barbaise, was astonished to find his exercise books covered with Latin verses instead of the solutions to the problems set.

Of course, the discussions with Delahaye and Labarrière continued with renewed vigor. The former soon acquired considerable prestige in the eyes of the other two when he revealed that, in a Belgian café, he had managed to leaf through Rochefort's *La Lanterne*. One can imagine Rimbaud's excitement on hearing the few fragments of this call to revolt and vengeance that Delahaye had been able to remember by heart! Already he was playing at being a freethinker—and he could allow himself to be so since he was top in Religious Instruction. In the history class, for example, he asked the Abbé Wuillème embarrassing questions about the wars of religion, about the massacre of the Huguenots on St. Bartholomew's Eve, the Inquisition. The class was breathless with excitement, and the seminarists pretended not to be aware of what was going on around them; some of them, it seems, were not entirely averse to this indiscreet curiosity. In the street, these forbidden subjects were taken up again and argued passionately. If given an essay to write on the French Revolution, he would find a way of inserting such incendiary phrases as "Danton, St. Just, Couthon, Robespierre, the young await you!"[14]

One has to admit that although some of the pupils were excitable, the school was tolerant. Anyone was allowed to express advanced opinions in literature or religion, but there were limits: when a *surveillant* caught a glimpse of the vermillion cover of *La Lanterne* under a dictionary or some other innocent work, he protested—but only for the form: "No, no! Read what you like, but not that!"

In June 1869 the Rimbaud family took lodgings on the first floor at 5 bis, Quai de la Madeleine (now 7 Quai Arthur-Rimbaud). It was a new building of stone construction, with a wrought-iron balcony. An income-tax collector had his offices in the building. The best thing about the accommodation was its situation—one of the best in the town—very near to the Vieux Moulin, opposite the Meuse and "Mount Olympus," in an agreeably green setting.

Toward the end of the school year, the principal, M. Desdouets, suggested that Rimbaud was now ready to take the *Concours général*, a competitive examination, set by the Académie de Douai, and open to all the schools in an area comprising the departments of Pas-de-Calais, Aisne, and Somme. A former seminarist in the *classe de seconde*, the Abbé Morigny (who was to become principal of the Collège Notre-Dame at Rethel, where Delahaye and Verlaine were successively teachers), has described the series of events in vivid detail.[15]

The examination took place at Charleville on July 2, 1869, from six o'clock in the morning to noon. By half-past five, the pupils were already wondering what the subject of the competition would be.

"I bet it'll be the Universal Exposition," one of them said.

Rimbaud protested: "No, no. That would really be too obvious!"

At six o'clock, M. Desdouets entered the room, unsealing a folded piece of paper and announced: "The subject is: 'Jurgurtha.' That's all."

"But what's the outline?" he was asked.

"There is no outline."

The principal went out, followed by a number of disconcerted pupils.

Rimbaud remained impassive, preoccupied, thoughtful. By nine o'clock he had still not written a single line. M. Desdouets reappeared, surprised by his brilliant pupil's apparent failure:

"Well, Arthur? . . . Is the muse? . . ."

"I'm hungry," he said.

The principal ordered the janitor to bring him a few rounds of bread and butter. He ate his way through them, quietly, quite unconcerned at the stifled laughter around him. When he had finished eating, he picked up his pen and wrote, without stopping, and without consulting his *Gradus*, or dictionary of Latin prosody.

At noon, he handed in his work.

"But . . . you didn't have time," protested the physics teacher, who had supervised his examination.

Adjusting his prince-nez, M. Desdouets quickly read through the composition, and cried out triumphantly : "We'll get the prize, I'm sure of it!";

Rimbaud did indeed win it, and his composition was printed in the *Bulletin officiel de l'Académie de Douai* (November 15, 1869). He had treated the subject in an original way, skillfully drawing a parallel between Jugurtha, the old Numidian king conquered by Rome and condemned to die of hunger and exposure in prison, and the emir Abd el-Kader, conquered by France and held in comfortable confinement in the Château d'Amboise on the orders of Napoleon III, before being set free and pensioned off. It was a curious mixture of Roman history and contemporary history, written to the glory of the emperor in the usual style of the supporters of the régime. The poem is divided into stanzas of between twelve and fourteen lines separated by this refrain:

Nascitur Arabiis ingens in collibus infans
Et dixit levis aura: "Nepos est ille Jugurtae."

[*There was born in the Arabian mountains a child who is great,*
And the light breeze said: "This is Jugurtha's grandson."]

At the same examination, Rimbaud won only a third certificate of merit in Greek Translation—but the list of prizes awarded him at the prize-giving of August 7, 1869, must have filled him with pride: First Prizes in Religious Instruction, *Excellence* (that is, in all subjects taken together), Latin Narration, Latin Translation, Latin Verse, Greek Translation, History and Geography, Recitation.

With the new school year (October 1869), the teacher of Rhetoric was called Feuillâtre. That is all we do know about him.

A minor incident took place in November 1869 in which Frédéric (though in fact innocent) was implicated. It concerned an obscene drawing entitled "Abbé Wuillème in the bath," which was slipped under the seminary door by two pupils. It would not be worth mentioning were it not for the fact that there was some question of expelling Frédéric, and if the principal had not opposed such a course on the grounds that his glorious brother would probably be taken away from the school, which was to be avoided at all costs.[16]

Browsing in bookshops Arthur discovered about this time that the publisher Lemerre had just launched a new series of the *Parnasse contemporain*, which was to consist of ten numbers, appearing monthly, that would later be put together in a second volume. He pounced on each number as it appeared, devouring it from cover to cover. We know this because his acquisitions have been found.[17] Rimbaud sold them to his friend Paul Labarrière in February 1871. The first number contained Leconte de Lisle's *Kaïn* (a hundred stanzas of five lines each), which was read and reread since the verses are awarded in the margin with between one and seven parallel strokes. The second number was devoted to Théodore de Banville, with the 372 lines of *La Cithare*, plus ten ballads and a sonnet; long penciled lines suggest an attentive reading. Number 4 (no. 3 is missing) is more varied, with poems by Verlaine, Ernest d'Hervilly, Mme Blanchecotte—here the best lines are marked with crosses.

M. Mouquet, the author of this discovery, has noted that some poems by this Mme Blanchecotte have undergone strange interpolations. Thus, in the following lines

> *J'avais eu ma récolte pleine,*
> *Ce qu'à son pâle genre humain*
> *Dieu jette au long de son chemin:*
> *Peu de joie et beaucoup de peine.*
> *J'avais eu ma récolte pleine!*

Rimbaud altered the word "*genre*" (kind, as in humankind) to "*phoque*" (seal, i.e., the sea mammal).

In another line, "J'ai porté bien lourd mon chagrin dernier," the word "*chagrin*" (sorrow, affliction) has become "*chignon*" (bun, of hair). (*Bulletin du Bibliophile*, March 1946.)

He loved this kind of humor.

The resurrection of the *Parnasse contemporain* gave him immense hope. Why shouldn't he dare?

He was only a schoolboy, lost in the depths of the provinces. Very well, he would get himself known. He would force destiny's hand. He would get his verses printed, people would talk about him. The Parnassians would just have to move up a bit and make room for him on their Olympus.

Without more ado, he set to work on this splendid undertaking. Under the influence of poems that had appeared in the *Revue pour tous* in 1869— Victor Hugo's *Les pauvres gens* (Sept. 5) and Marceline Desbordes-Valmore's *La Maison de ma mère* (Nov. 7)—he composed a piece of over a hundred lines, *Les Étrennes des orphelins* (The Orphans' New Year's Gifts), which he sent to the *Revue pour tous*. Marcel Coulon has found this note under the heading Correspondence in the number for December 26, 1869: "M. Rim . . . at Charleville. The poem that you have sent us is not without merit, and we would print it if, by some skillful cutting, it were shortened by a third."[18]

One can only suppose that he immediately cut two passages out of his poem—indicated in the text by a row of dots—since it appears in the number for January 2, 1870.

One can imagine how proud he must have felt: his work had been printed in Paris! The gates of Parnassus were about to open!

On January 14, 1870, Georges Izambard was appointed to the chair of Rhetoric at the Collège de Charleville. He was only twenty-two and had had only one other teaching post, at Hazebrouck (Nord).

He was born on December 11, 1848, studied at Douai, and passed his *licence-ès-lettres* (humanities degree) in July 1867. Being still too young to teach, he had to wait until November 1868 before being given a job. A photograph of him taken shortly after his arrival at Charleville shows him with an "artistic" hairstyle and frightful pince-nez, which really don't manage to give him a scholarly air. The eyes are bright and sharp, the mouth has the trace of a smile; the whole face reveals an open-minded originality and a proud independence of mind: an absence of pettiness or vulgarity. His love of freedom in every domain immediately attracted Rimbaud. Certainly, something seemed to be changing in the University: Lenel, Pérette's successor, Duprez, and now Izambard, three young teachers, who loathed dull routine and had faith in the future. The last of these approached his subject with all the enthusiasm of a student. "You must see him getting down from his desk and, as a juvenile lead, acting out for us a scene from the repertoire of the Théâtre-Français," wrote one of his former pupils to a friend.[19] He had his faults (touchiness, bad moods), but Paterne Berrichon was very unfair to him—never was a teacher less of a pedagogue.

His arrival acted as a stimulus on the young Rimbaud, who was determined to trounce the seminarists in the first term. He did so well that the principal rewarded him with a copy of La Bruyère's *Caractères*, with the following dedication: "In acknowledgment of my satisfaction with the pupil Rimbaud, *classe de Rhétorique*, for his achievements in class—March 17, 1870—the Principal Desdouets." It was a sort of preprize.

A month later, on April 15, he again had the honor of appearing in the *Bulletin de l'Académie de Douai* with forty-three Latin verses entitled *Jesus at Nazareth*, a poem by an anonymous author, together with four other exercises dating from 1869 (*Combat d'Hercule et du Fleuve Acheloüs*, *Invocation à Vénus*, *De rerum natura*, mentioned above, and *Paroles d'Apollonius sur Marcus Cicéron*, an address in Latin published for the first time in the Pléiade edition of Rimbaud's works, edited by Antoine Adam).

Of course, he resumed his habit of placing extra work on his teacher's desk with the note: "*Lege quaeso*" (Please read). Among such pieces was a poem in French entitled "Ophélie," concerning a composition in Latin verse on the same subejct—or some poem of his own.

Izambard, at first intrigued, then deeply interested, did not stint either his advice or his encouragement. The young schoolboy, so reticent, so shy in class, immediately came to life, overflowing with enthusiasm, when the question of poetry arose.

Around March or April 1870, the subject for a French composition was: "A letter from Charles of Orléans to Louis XI begging him to pardon Villon, under threat of execution." In order to provide his best pupil with material, Izambard lent him a few books, in particular Hugo's *Notre-Dame de Paris* and Théodore de Banville's comedy *Gringoire*. But this was not enough: he asked, by letter, for several other works concerning historical and literary curiosities (the Feast of Fools, the Ribauds, the Francs Taupins, etc.).[20] The rather cavalier tone of this letter (it begins: "If you have and if you can lend me . . ." and ends: "I would find it very useful") indicates a certain impudence that he was to show later on many occasions.

The lending of these books was to trigger off a vigorous counteroffensive by Mme Rimbaud, who sent the following letter to Izambard via the school janitor:

> *Monsier,*
>   *I am extremely grateful to you for all that you are doing for Arthur. You give him advice, and help him with extra teaching outside school hours. All these are attentions that we have no reason to expect. But there is one thing that I cannot approve of, and that is, for instance, the reading of the book you lent him the other day* (Les Misérables, *by V. hugot)* [sic]. *You must realize, even better than I, that great care is needed in the choice of books that are put in the hands of children. And so I am forced to believe that Arthur must have got hold of the book without your knowledge. It would certainly be dangerous to allow him to continue with such reading.*
>   *I have the honor, Monsieur, to present you with my respects.*
> V. *Rimbaud*

May 4, 1870

At the same time Izambard was summoned to the principal's office: a very angry lady had come, it seemed, carrying a pernicious book that one of the teachers had dared to lend to a pupil of rhetoric.

"It's absurd, I know," concluded M. Desdouets, "but it might be a good idea if you went along and had a word with this difficult mother."

A meeting was arranged, and Izambard turned up at Mme Rimbaud's. The poor fellow could not get in a word edgeways:

"What? This 'Hugot'? This depraved author, this enemy of religion? These *Misérables*, full of dishonest things and vulgar words? Aren't you ashamed to teach such dreadful things to your pupils, Monsieur le professeur?"

An astounded Izambard was just able to mutter, before the door was slammed in his face:

"But it wasn't *Les Misérables*, Madame, but *Notre-Dame de Paris*."

For Izambard this meeting was a revelation. Rimbaud's whole attitude, his constrained manner, as well as his thirst for freedom, were obviously a reaction to the tyranny of this narrow-minded mother. "My affection for him," he said, "increased when I saw the moral distress in which he lived."[21]

So he did his best to encourage his young pupil's love of poetry, since for him it was the only escape allowed him. Their relationship became increasingly more trusting and friendly. Often Rimbaud would walk home with him and ask him advice about his latest works. One day he read him a fairly sarcastic poem, A la musique (Set to Music) depicting "wheezy bourgeois, choked by the heat," "retired grocers," "private-incomed men in pince-nez," who had come to listen to a military band on a Thursday evening, in the Square de la Gare. He also puts himself into the scene, "dressed as badly as a student," following the lively girls, and undressing them with his eyes.

Izambard liked the biting wit of the little tableau, but he did not care for the last line: "Et mes désirs brutaux s'accrochent à leurs lèvres" [And my fierce desires fasten on to their lips]. Such realism, he thought, struck a false note. So he suggested an alternative ending, taken from one of his own poems, Le Baiser du Faune:

> Extasié, le pouls battu de mille fièvres,
> Tout pâle du désir fauve qui l'enhardit
> Et qui lui fait monter des baisers fous aux lèvres,
> Il écarte à demi les branches et bondit.

> [In ecstasy, his pulse beating with a thousand fevers,
> Quite pale with the wild desire which emboldens him
> And which brings wild kisses to his lips,
> He parts the branches and leaps.]

So Rimbaud, in order not to thwart him, ended his poem with the rather nonsensical line "Et je sens les baisers qui me viennent aux lèvres" [And I feel the kisses coming to my lips].

In exchange, the young fawn presented him with the phrase "belles fièvres" from his poem ("Je reconstruis les corps, brûlé de belles fièvres" ["Burning with fine fevers, I reconstruct the bodies"], and so Izambard's line was changed to "Extasié, le pouls battu de belles fièvres" [In ecstasy, his pulse beating with beautiful fevers].[22]

Last, inspired by Izambard's Baiser du Faune and the long Faune by Victor de Laprade, which appeared in the second series of the Parnasse in

March 1870, Rimbaud composed his short, sensual, and disturbing poem *Tête de Faune* (*Fawn's Head*), which was to outclass both of them.

However, each month brought a new number of the *Parnasse contemporain*. On May 1, 1870, number 7 appeared. Three more, and the series would end. Rimbaud thought that the moment had come to make a great splash. He had prepared in secret a long poem, *Credo in unam*, influenced by Banville's *L'Exil des dieux*, which appeared in the first number of the *Parnasse*.[23] It is a vibrant hymn to infinite, universal Love and to a pantheistic nature abounding with goddesses: Venus, Cybele, Astarte, Aphrodite, Europa, Ariadne. In this profession of faith, there is no lack of passion, or beautiful lines, such as this one: "Notre pâle raison nous cache l'infini" [Our pale reason hides the infinite from us], but the rush of ideas and images betrays the breathless clumsiness of a beginner. It is his "credo," his "prayer on the Acropolis." To old Jehovah, who chased Adam and Eve from the earthly paradise, or to the other God who "harnessed us to his cross," he prefers the trinity of Sun ("hearth of tenderness and life"), Love ("splendor of flesh"), and Liberty.[24]

To this main course he attached an hors d'oeuvre, *Ophélie* (in which Rimbaud again shows the influence of Banville), and a dessert (*Sensation*), an exquisitely fresh little poem:

Par les soirs bleus d'été, j'irai dans les sentiers,
Picoté par les blés, fouler l'herbe menue.

[*In the blue summer evenings, I will go along the paths,*
And walk over the short grass, as I am pricked by the wheat][25]

with its reminiscence of François Coppée's line "Quand je vais dans les champs par les beaux soires d'été" [When I walk through the fields on fine summer evenings] and he sent the lot off to the master of the Parnassian School, Theódore de Banville: "chez M. Alphonse Lemerre éditeur, Passage Choiseul, Paris," with this letter bearing the date May 24, 1870:

Cher Maître,

We are in the months of love; I am seventeen.[26] The age of hopes and dreams, they say—and I, a child touched by the finger of the Muse—forgive me if this is a platitude—have be-

gun to express my beliefs, my hopes, my sensations, all those things dear to poets—and this I call the spring.

If I send you some of these verses, through Alph. Lemerre, the good publisher, it is because I love all poets, all good Parnassians—for the poet is a Parnassian—in love with ideal beauty. It is because I admire in you, in all simplicity, a descendant of Ronsard, a brother of our masters of 1830, a true romantic, a true poet. That is why—this is all very foolish, isn't it? But so be it! . . .

In two years, in one year perhaps, I shall be in Paris— Anch'io, gentlemen of the press, and I shall be a Parnassian too!—. . . I swear, cher Maître, *that I shall always worship the two goddesses, the Muse and Liberty.*

Do not frown too much as you read these verses. . . . You would make me mad with joy and hope if you were willing, cher Maître, *to make room for the poem* Credo in unam *among the Parnassians. . . . I would like to be in the last issue of* Parnasse: *it would become the Creed of the poets! . . . O mad ambition!*

                                    Arthur Rimbaud

After the poems comes a postscript:

What if these verses found a place in the Parnasse contemporain?

—Do they not express the faith of poets?

—I am not known; but what of that? Poets are brothers. These verses believe; they love; they hope; that is all.

—My own Master: raise me up a little, I am young, give me a helping hand.

We do not have Banville's answer, but we can be sure that he congratulated the boy. It is likely that he expressed regret that he could not publish Rimbaud's work since the second volume of *Parnasse contemporain* was full. He probably mooted the possible appearance of a third volume, at a later date. A later date . . . But for Rimbaud's "impatient genius" this was no consolation.

Of course, Izambard was told nothing of all this, either of the attempt or of the failure.

In class, meanwhile, friction was growing between the fifteen be-cassocked seminarists, starchy and well-behaved, and the twelve resentful day boys.

The rector had advised Izambard to be prudent and circumspect. But it was difficult to be impartial before such a heteroclite audience, ready to pounce on the slightest sign of favoritism. Thus, since Voltaire's tragedy *Mérope* was one of the set texts, the teacher did not hesitate to criticize Voltaire severely, as a dramatist, to the great delight of the seminarists. Had he praised the play, these same seminarists would have accused him of antireligious propaganda. The rivalry between the two clans, which was already noticeable in the *classe de seconde*, was becoming more marked, with equal bad faith on both sides.

Rimbaud, of course, had the honor of being the spokesman of the "lays"; he alone was capable of blocking the clerics' access to the first prize.

One day, during a Latin verse exercise, the whining voice of one of the seminarists called Alexandre rose from the back of the class:

"M'sieur! Rimbaud is cheating. He's passed a paper to his neighbor!"

Izambard seized the paper and showed it to the denunciator; it contained nothing suspect, but Rimbaud had already thrown his heavy Thesaurus (a dictionary of quotations from the Latin poets) at the seminarist's face. Confronted by such a strong reaction, the teacher cried out in anger, but he did not punish Rimbaud. He would have done as much himself.

It was due, therefore, to the physical presence of the seminarists in his class that the lover of the beautiful goddesses of antiquity owed the strengthening of his antireligious feelings.

Toward the end of the school year, by way of satisfying his anti-clericalism, he wrote a story of about twenty-three pages entitled *Un coeur sous une soutane* (A Heart under a Cassock), inspired by Hugo (one of the chapters of *Les Misérables* is called "A Heart under a Stone"). It purports to be the secret journal of a seminarist called Léonard, who is consumed by love for a certain Timothina Labinette, the daughter of a friend of his late father, Césarin. There is mention of a superior, given to equivocal gestures, of strong smelling socks, and dirty linen, the whole thing spiced with rather naive parodies of prayers and hymns. This minor work is too caricatural to be amusing, but it is curious in that some of its compositional techniques were to be used again in *Une saison en enfer*.

From now on, for Rimbaud, God, inseparable from his mother, the clergy, and the seminarists, was to represent duty, discipline, and constraint—in a word, as Proudhon was to say, evil. One of his sonnets, entitled *Le Mal* (Evil), depicts the greedy God of the altars who sleeps while men slaughter one another but awakes when some anguished mother offers him money.

But it wasn't only a question of killing God. "What a task," he remarked to Delahaye, "everything to be demolished, everything to wipe out in my head! Ah! how fortunate is a child abandoned to the roadside, brought up at the whim of chance, who, reaching the age of man with no ideas inculcated by masters or by a family: new, clean, without principles, without notions—since everything one is taught is false!—and free, free of everything!"[27]

These thoughts show the extent to which he was susceptible to the ideas of the eighteenth century: the noble savage, Condillac's "statue," the tabula rasa, Holbach's atheism. In this, he was at one with the Parnassian school, which placed an incorruptible art above all moral, political, or religious servitudes, despised Christianity (Théophile Gautier said he preferred the void to it), and valued only primitive cosmogonies, virgin nature, and, above all, nirvana (Leconte de Lisle).

Rimbaud threw himself enthusiastically into this current of ideas.

In politics, a single ideal: liberty. So it is hardly surprising if he found inspiration in the French Revolution: in a long, violent poem, he shows how, on June 20, 1792, in the Tuileries, a blacksmith found himself face to face with a terrified Louis XVI, and how, "with his broad hands, superb with dirt," stuck his red cap on the head of the sweating, pot-bellied king. (The fiction goes well beyond reality here, for the butcher Legendre, who spoke to the king in the Tuileries, did not treat him roughly, or use familiar language, but on the contrary treated him with respect.)

At the end of the Second Empire, France was divided into two parties: the conservative, more or less Bonapartist right, whose program could be summed up by the words *order, greatness, religion*, and the liberal left, which was preparing for the advent of the Republic, the reign of science, and the death of God.

At Charleville, one was either for or against *Le Courrier des Ardennes*, the reactionary newspaper read by Mme Rimbaud and other right-thinking people. Arthur was against.

It should be noted that although he remained true all his life to the anticlericalism of his youth, later, when in the middle of some violent crisis, he wanted to rid himself once and for all of God, he did so only with great difficulty and pain. This was because his atheism was not the result of his reason (as with many men of science), but rather an allergy due to an epidermic repulsion: he hated religion because he associated it with all the works of the monster authoritarianism, which he found everywhere, in his family, at school, in Caesar's palace, and in God's church.

Soon Rimbaud's friendships, which had hitherto been confined to Izambard, Delahaye and Labarrière, broadened: his teacher introduced him to two of his own friends, also bachelors, Léon Deverrière and Paul Auguste (also known as Charles) Bretagne. The first was a philosophy teacher at the Institution Rossat. He lived at 95 Cour-d'Orléans (Izambard lived at number 21). Delahaye describes him as "a big, cheerful fellow, energetic, practical, hard-working, full of optimism." We know very little about him. He gave up teaching in July 1871 to become a subeditor on a new regional daily newspaper, *Le Nord-Est*. It is a pity that nobody asked him about Rimbaud, whom he found "very original, very amusing" (Delahaye), and to whom he lent books and gave tobacco.

Nor did anyone question the other man, Paul Auguste Bretagne, who died in 1881, but we do know more about him.[28]

He was thirty-five years old. His father had been head of the income-tax office at Nancy, and he himself had the post of principal clerk, second class, of "Indirect Taxation" at the Petit Bois sugarworks at Charleville. He was a rather fat Fleming, with large eyes, large lips, and a large moustache. He came from Fampoux, near Arras, where he had met Paul Verlaine, who had stayed with him in 1869 before getting married. Together they had frequented the bars of the region, and, as a token of friendship, Verlaine had given him a fine glass inkstand.

With the young schoolboy, whose sense of the burlesque and forthright views amused him, he was lavish with glasses of beer, tobacco, and books (in particular, he lent him Charles Deulin's *Contes*). For his part, Rimbaud was very fond of Bretagne, because he was boisterous only in fits and starts, and could sit quietly with him for hours in a café, content to smoke his heavy meerschaum pipe. But it only needed some importunate individual to appear, and his attitude would change. Louis Pierquin relates how, one evening, in the Café Duterme, in the Place Ducale, a customs sergeant in uniform came and sat near them. They both then started to vituperate against non-commissioned officers, and other old fuddy-duddies who got in the way of the young, adding that to get rid of such individuals they would not hesitate to go as far as murder, and that their greatest pleasure would be to watch their victims die a slow death. The poor fellow looked at the two young men apprehensively, and retired to a discreet distance, leaving Bretagne's corpulent body shaking with stifled laughter.

All those who knew him praised his musical gifts: he played with equal virtuosity on the violin, the viola, the cello, and horn. His cartoons, usually drawn—to Rimbaud's delight—at the expense of the clergy—also brought him great success. He was such a clergy-hater that he was variously nicknamed Father Bretagne, the High Priest, the Magnus Sacerdos—which did not prevent him from being of a mystical turn of mind in his own way, where magic and the occult sciences were concerned. But what his young admirer liked most about him was his utter intellectual anarchism: he bristled at any form of authority—dogma, rules, discipline—while displaying the qualities of an excellent civil servant. "Faculties and academies," wrote Delahaye, who knew him well, "seemed to him to be equally oppressive forces to be combated, and, just as he calmly maintained—when he decided to take his pipe out of his mouth for a moment—that the most illustrious physicians were asses compared to certain "country bone-setters," he took great pleasures in seeing the bold, independent-minded young poet dismantling principles, demolishing what passed for accepted wisdom, trampling over tradition, overturning reputations and authorities."[29]

Bretagne played an important role in the formation of Rimbaud's mind, which, at this time, was developing increasingly in the direction of intolerance and absolutism.

He may not have appeared to have changed, but he was no longer the same. He was still a neat, polite boy. Physically, there was still something of the child about him: the sulky expression, the clear complexion, and the pale blue eyes, in turn disturbing, angelic, or pitiless. Delahaye saw them above all as angelic: "He had brown hair, and blue eyes," he wrote, "of a double blue, the areas of which, deeper or lighter, expanded or merged together at moments of reverie, or intense thought: when he was thinking, when he was staring into the unknown, he carried his mental gaze very far, his eyelids moved closer, like a cat's, the long, silky lashes fluttered slightly, while his head remained still."[30]

At the Collège, though not a rebel, he was full of self-confidence. Delahaye has stressed his shyness, for he blushed easily, but, by the *classe de première*, he had acquired enough personality to make his presence felt. "It has been said that Rimbaud was shy," one of his former schoolfriends has revealed; "we always found him very self-assured . . . even impudent; he was always very confident when speaking to the teachers, even to the principal, and was fond of playing jokes on his fellow pupils."[31]

I have already mentioned his arguments with the Abbé Wuillème, the history teacher. He also teased the chaplain, the Abbé Joseph Gillet, but with greater circumspection, for he was a very irritable man. One day, an unnamed former pupil recounts, when one of the day boys asked him if the pope was a coiner since the currency of the Papal States was not accepted in France, the priest flung his fur-collared cape around his shoulders, and, quite pale, strode towards the door, crying "I will not remain here to hear my convictions insulted!" It required all the principal's diplomacy to smooth over the incident.

Rimbaud was regarded by his schoolfriends as a "good guy," not only because of his prestige, but because he was able to hold his position at the top of the class without compromising his convictions, without "crawling" to the teachers. Moreover, one could always depend on him for a good turn. He was something of a dealer. For a small commission, he would acquire in town any books anyone wanted. Sometimes he would kill two birds with one stone: he bought a book, which he devoured in one night, without cutting the pages, then took it back to the bookseller under the pretext that he had made a mistake, and exchanged it for the one that he had been asked to buy, which he also read before handing it over to his fellow pupil.

He was able to read an incredible number of books in a few months: not only Izambard, Deverrière, and Bretagne, but also the principal lent him books. He devoured everything with equal appetite: philosophy, sociology, politics, the works of Thiers, Mignet, Tocqueville, Edgar Quinet, Proudhon, Louis Blanc—and of course the classical authors and poets, not forgetting the Bible, which he often looked into.

At school, he did not take part in such escapades—they were rather the work of the boarders—as nocturnal expeditions into the storehouse, where the apples (and the underwear of the principal, his wife, and his daughter) were kept, or the "raids" on the young ladies of the convent nearby, or the "outings" *chez* Duterme, the café owner on the Place Ducale, whose son easily obtained friendly adults to act in loco parentis for boarders wanting an outing.

Sexually, Rimbaud seemed normal enough. For him, love was a poetic theme rather than an actual experience. His exalted rhetoric in *Credo in unam*, or his first emotional disturbances expressed in A *la musique* do not betray a morbid sensuality. There is no evidence of homosexuality from this time. The fellow pupil whose evidence has often been cited here mentions "questionable practices," without coming up with anything very precise.

This is what he says: "The lads of the Meuse valley were always the ring leaders, were up to all the tricks, and were not without certain vices, grand masters of the questionable practices of boarders, both in the Collège and in the seminary. Did Arthur, like Frédéric, acquire certain habits whose stigmata were later to appear on the physique of that darling of Apollo? This would explain how he found good friends among their ranks."[32]

Delahaye is quite categorical on this subject: "As far as Rimbaud's morals or tastes are concerned, I can say this: he never had a reputation for inversion in the Collège, though it was quite common there, as in all schools. He never realized the slightest disposition to that in our conversations, which were very frequent and intimate, and in which he never concealed anything."[33]

So, in that summer of 1870, no one had realized that he had already left the normal path. His mother thought that she had tamed him ("Mme Rimbaud's naiveté," Izambard wrote, "never ceased to amaze me"). He was always there, apparently submissive, but already absent, already far away.

The die was set; the drama was about to begin; it was already too late.

The school year ended in the heat of a summer heavy with threats. The *concours académique* took place in June 1870. Rimbaud was once again M. Desdouets' supreme hope. To "warm him up," Izambard gave him free private lessons several time a week.

The subject of the Latin verse composition, "Sancho Panzas's speech to his dead donkey," had everything to excite his virtuosity; unfortunately, his composition, which was given the first prize, has not survived, since the *Bulletin de l'Académie de Douai* was not published on account of the war.

Grave dangers were emerging on the horizon. On July 15 the announcement of the famous despatch from Ems was interpreted as an affront to the French ambassador in Berlin, and the legislature reacted unanimously: it was war! The next day, July 16, *Le Pays*, the Bonapartist newspaper, published a stirring appeal by Paul de Cassagnac to the sacred union of all French people: "You, Republicans, remember that in 1792 . . . you, Legitimists . . . you, Orléanists . . . you, Bonapartists." What! One of the newspapers supporting the régime, which a few days earlier had been proclaiming the need for a war to consolidate the dynasty, was daring to mobilize the Great Ancestors and their descendants, who had never ceased to fight tyranny. An outraged Rimbaud immediately composed a vengeful sonnet:

Morts de Quatre-vingt-douze et de Quatre-vingt-treize,
Qui, pâles du baiser fort de la Liberté,
     . . . . .
—Messieurs de Cassagnac nous reparlent de vous!

[*Dead of '92 and '93*
Who, pale from the hard kiss of freedom,
     . . . . .
—The gentlemen Cassagnac are speaking again to us about you!][34]

He handed his poem to Izambard on July 18, after school, as they were walking together in the Cour-d'Orléans:

"This is for you, Monsieur," he said, without further explanation.

He also read to him a large section of his bravura piece *Credo in unam,* but without referring to his correspondence with Théodore de Banville.

Next day, war was declared between France and Prussia.

From now on reservists summoned by the decree of July 17 were flowing into Mézières and Charleville. The two towns were a hive of activity: processions of conscripts with music and flags crossed detachments of the 96th infantry regiment stationed at Mézières, on their way to defend the national frontiers. The shouting and cheering were endless: "To Berlin! To Berlin!"

The enthusiasm of the population delighted many. But it left Rimbaud quite unmoved: that stupid war, which would strengthen the régime in the event of victory, was the ruin of any hope he had of appearing in the *Parnasse contemporain!*

On July 24 Izambard left Charleville, where he had nothing to keep him: he said himself that he was under no obligation to be present at the prize-giving. His "Aunt" Caroline (in fact one of the three women who brought him up after his mother's death) had come to collect him from Douai, where she lived. She quite took to Deverrière, and so invited him— at Izambard's request—to come and spend a few days at her house.

This double departure plunged Rimbaud into the depths of despair.

"What will become of me?" he moaned. "In any case I shall not go on living here a year longer. I shall go to Paris and do journalism!"

Deverrière tried to dissuade him ("Journalism, at your age? But you have no experience, no training in the job!"), but it was no use:

"Then that's just too bad! I shall fall by the wayside, and die on a pile of paving stones, but I'm going!"

"I forbid you to go," Izambard interrupted. "You have no right to do that. At least wait until you've got your *bachot*. Surely you can wait another year! Don't upset your mother: in a few days your prizes will make her more indulgent."

"You don't know her."

"I'm telling you that you must stay, finish your studies, take your *bachot*. It serves no purpose, as Talleyrand would have said, but it leads to everything." Rimbaud shrugged his shoulders, and muttered haughtily: "You're just like everyone else!"

This was the worst insult he could find.

Izambard, who was not a vindictive man, found it in himself to forgive him. He even gave his pupil permission to use his room while he was away, and to read his books if he wished; the landlord, M. Petit-Dauchy, would give him the key whenever he asked for it. Izambard also gave him two works by Théodore de Banville, *Les Cariatides* and the *Odes funambulesques*. So, by the time Rimbaud went to the station to say goodbye to his two friends, he had considerably calmed down: he had two or three months' respite in front of him. After that he would see.

In the evening of August 2, the *Courrier des Ardennes* announced the Victory of Sarrebrücken: "Our army has crossed the frontier," said the communiqué, "and invaded Prussian territory." Pandemonium broke out: long into the night, torchlight processions paraded the streets. This meant victory: peace would soon be restored. The local youths followed the armed detachments, covered with flowers. One of them was Frédéric Rimbaud; fascinated by the military music, he could not bear to leave the soldiers, who, in the end, adopted him as their mascot. One can imagine Mme Rimbaud's consternation.

In late July the *Courrier des Ardennes* started a fund to help volunteers, war widows, and orphans. Charleville municipal council took a number of steps of this kind, and decided to turn the Collège, the seminary, and the stud farm into military hospitals. Seized with patriotic fervor, the pupils of the Collège decided to renounce their prizes: "We wanted to offer our tribute to the French army, which at this moment is defending the national cause," they wrote to the *Courrier des Ardennes*.[35]

The great day of the prize-giving—August 6, 1870—came round at last. The weather was magnificent. From among the crimson hangings, the flags, and the green plants, M. Lenel regaled the serried ranks of pupils, all spruced up in their best clothes, with an oration on Virgil, while the imperial procurator, M. Angenoux, who presided over the ceremony, launched into a eulogy of his august sovereign, who was sweeping from victory to victory.

Rimbaud's own victories consisted of the general first prize for his class and six other first prizes (Religious Instruction, Latin and French Composition, Latin Verse, Latin Translation, Greek Translation), a second prize (Recitation), a fourth certificate of merit (History and Geography), plus the first academic prize; he took home with him a great many green and gold paper crowns but, alas!, few bound books—just two superb volumes presented by the Académie de Douai.

That evening, the *Courrier des Ardennes* made a brief mention of the defeat of Wissembourg, which had occurred two days before.

That same day the disaster of Froeschwiller took place. These two cold showers, in such rapid succession, had the effect of calming down the militaristic fervor of the Ardennais.

4

The Summer Vacation

*T*hat the French army should be beaten in Alsace, that a
state of siege should be declared in the department of the Ardennes (August
8, 1870), that a curfew should be decreed in Mézières, Rimbaud cared not a
jot: safe in his lair in Izambard's room, shaded from the pitiless sun, and
protected from his mother's endless nagging, he spent whole days reading.
And in the evening, he took back home with him new books to devour! He
also did the reverse, taking books that he had bought on credit to Izambard's
to prevent his mother seeing them.

On August 25 his provision of spiritual nourishment was exhausted. So
he went off and sold his school prizes (with a few of Izambard's books to make
up the lot). With the twenty francs the bookseller gave him for them, Paris
was within reach. Paris? Had he not been there already in a sense? On August
13 a Parisian weekly, *La Charge*, edited by the artist Alfred Le Petit, had just
published one of his poems, *Trois Baisers* (Three Kisses), which he had sent
to the review on the tempting promise of a free subscription. The number in
which his eight stanzas had appeared, inside an ultrapatriotic cover—a drawing by Le Petit entitled, "Vengeance!"—was sold, such is the irony of fate,
for the benefit of wounded soldiers and sailors. What good had it done refusing to sacrifice his prizes!

On August 25, he wrote his first ("very hasty"), letter to Izambard:

Monsieur,
You are lucky not to be living now in Charleville.
My native town is the supremely stupid provincial town.
You see, on this subject I have no more illusions. Because it is
beside Mézières—a town you can't find—because it sees

wandering about in its streets two or three hundred soldiers,
this benighted population gesticulates like a bullying M. Prud-
homme, in a very different manner from the besieged of Metz
and Strasbourg! Retired grocers clothed in their uniforms are a
terrible spectacle! It is astonishing to see how lively they are,
notaries, glaziers, tax collectors, carpenters, and all the fat-
bellied dignitaries with rifles over their hearts, patrolling at
the gates of Mézières: my country is rising up! . . . I prefer to
see it seated: don't bestir yourself! that is my principle.

I am at a loss, ill, mad, stupid, astounded. I had hoped
for sunbaths, long walks, rest, travel, adventure, bohemian
larks, in a word; especially I had hoped for newspapers and
books. . . . But there is nothing! The mail delivers nothing to
bookstores; Paris is coyly making fun of us: not a single new
book! everything is dead! In the way of newspapers, I am re-
duced to the honorable Courrier des Ardennes.

He then remembers what he has been reading recently: "Three days ago
I sank as low as *Les Epreuves* [by Sully Prudhomme] and *Les Glaneuses* [by
Paul Demény]. Yes, I reread that volume!" The exclamation marks stress the
degree of famine to which he had fallen to have to feed on such mediocrities!
Still, he did have something better: "I have Paul Verlaine's *Fêtes gal-*
antes. . . . It's very odd, very funny; but it really is adorable. . . . I advise
you to buy *La Bonne Chanson*, a small volume of poems by the same poet.
Lemerre has just brought it out. I haven't read it. Nothing gets this far, but it
has been well received in several newspapers." (In fact, the review copies had
been sent out, but copies had not yet reached the booksellers.)

In this letter there is no further mention of leaving Charleville, of going
to Paris, or of becoming a journalist, but the postscript is suggestive: "Soon I
will give you revelations about the life I am going to lead after . . . the va-
cation."

Four days later, on Monday, August 29, a day of wonderful weather, the
family went out walking in the fields (between the ramparts of Mézières and
the Meuse flanked by willows), Mme Rimbaud, stiff-backed and dressed in
black, Isabelle and Vitalie in "green faded dresses," and, last, himself, Arthur
(Frédéric had still not yet come home).

What happened then?

A poem, *Mémoire*, describes the scene: leaving "Madame" to her embroidery and the two sisters to their reading, "the man" (Arthur) walks off, and makes straight for the railway station.

> *Hélas, Lui, comme*
> *mille anges blancs qui se séparent sur la route,*
> *s'éloigne par delà la montagne! Elle, toute*
> *froide, et noire, court! après le départ de l'homme!*

> [Alas, he, like
> *a thousand white angels separating on the road,*
> *goes off beyond the mountain! She, all*
> *cold and dark, runs! after the departing man!*][1]

One can understand her pain: her second son has disappeared!

When he reached the station, a surprise awaited "the man":[2] services on the Charleville-Paris line had been suspended! Indeed, we read in Jules Poirier's excellent work *Mézières en 1870:* "On August 29, German cavalry cut the railway between Amagne and Saulces-Monclin; they later repaired it. But some hours later, the rails were again removed, between the stations of Launois and Poix."

Would he just go home, looking sheepish? There was one way out: the line to Givet and Belgium, where the trains were running normally. He set off for Charleroi, with an idea at the back of his head: he was aware that the father of one of his schoolfriends, Jules des Essarts, ran the *Journal de Charleroi.* Did he try his luck? Probably not, for he was to try again later, but he was no doubt to learn at Charleroi station that the trains to Paris, via Soissons, were still running normally. In a few hours he could be in the capital! It was wonderful! What was less so was the fact that his now still further reduced means no longer allowed him to buy a ticket for Paris—on the other hand, he had enough money to get to Saint-Quentin. So he bought a ticket for Saint-Quentin! He would stay on the train and elude the ticket control at the Gare du Nord.

Meanwhile, worried to death, his mother was dashing about trying to find out where he had gone. On the evening of August 30, the units from Sedan, retreating en masse, invaded Charleville, causing indescribable disorder: horses, carriages and vans, infantrymen and zouaves without weapons, artillerymen without canons, wounded, with torn uniforms, all thirsty, repeated over and over, "We've been sold out." In the distance, one could hear the cannons; the enemy was approaching, he was there, quite near: uhlans had been seen at Les Ayvelles and Saint-Laurent, even at the gates of Mézières. Traveling operating theaters were set up in the public squares and gardens, for the flood of wounded never subsided; close on ten thousand came there.

"But what's got hold of him?" Mme Rimbaud asked herself. "What's got into his head? He's usually so sensible."

No one had seen him. Trying to find a sixteen-year-old boy in that confusion was like looking for a needle in a haystack. It was late when she got back home, heartbroken and red-eyed. Isabelle was to remember all her life that tragic night "when the tumultuous crowd sang patriotic songs under the chestnut trees of the Cours-d'Orléans" (*Mon frère Arthur*). However, at the Gare du Nord, things were not quite as easy as the runaway had imagined. When the ticket collector saw his ticket from Charleroi to Saint-Quentin, he was apprehended, and, since he had no money, the police inspector of the "Compagnie des chemins de fer de Paris à la frontière belge" took him off to the Préfecture. His report has been found: "August 31. Gare de Paris. I found at the dépôt of the prefecture of police M. Rimbaud, aged seventeen and a half, coming from Charleroi to Paris with a ticket for Saint-Quentin, without domicile or livelihood."

So he had claimed to be older and refused to give his mother's address. Later he was to give his friend Delahaye a version of the facts that does him more honor: on arrival in Paris he was subjected to such abuse by the police that to save his face he considered it more honorable to pass himself off as a political martyr than as a youth trying to swindle the railway company.

Berrichon adds that he was searched, and that certain mysterious scribblings (probably a poetry notebook), were found on him which made the police suspect that he might be a spy. For, indeed, the imperial police had been instructed to keep an eye on all trains coming from the north and east. It was not a time for weakness: the national guards from Belleville had invaded the Hôtel de Ville and tried to overthrow the government. There was anger everywhere, with people repeating that the reverses suffered by the French were the result of treason.

A victim of this psychosis, Rimbaud was "first locked up in the dépôt courtyard," writes Delahaye,[3] "with a crowd of people of every kind, he saw 'third degrees,' and had to defend his virtue against importuning neighbors. When he appeared before an examining magistrate, he answered with such contemptuous irony that the irritated magistrate sent him at once to Mazas" (according to Izambard, the contemptuous irony was more a matter of tears and "the terror of the cornered animal").

The detention center (it was not a prison) of Mazas was a fortress situated on the Boulevard Mazas (now the Boulevard Diderot), which held about twelve hundred, mainly political, prisoners.

The young Rimbaud was taken to the records office, then to the showers, while his clothes were disinfected in the sulphuring chamber. A guard then led him to his cell, a room twenty square metres large, with a hammock-type bed, a chair, and a portable lavatory. He was awakened at seven in the morning; at the second sound of the bell the day's bread and water was handed out, each prisoner had to sweep his cell, and make his bed. About 8:30 the prisoners were allowed to walk up and down a corridor; it was the only time they were allowed out of their cells during the day. Two prisoners were never allowed to meet. There were a few consolations: one could read (the library had some four thousand volumes), write (paper, ink, and pen were provided by the administration), and smoke.

As soon as he was locked up, Rimbaud wrote a letter to his mother, another to the imperial procurator, a third to the police inspector of Charleville, and a fourth to Izambard. This last has been found; it is an extremely worried S.O.S. composed of requests and orders that betray a profoundly disturbed state.

> *Paris, September 5, 1870*
>
> *Dear Monsieur,*
>
> *What you advised me not to do, I did. I went to Paris and left my mother's home. I took this trip on August 29.*
>
> *Arrested as I got off the train, for not having a centime and owing the railroad thirteen francs, I was taken to the prefecture, and today am awaiting the verdict in Mazas!—Oh! My hope is in you as in my mother. You have always been a brother to me and now I am asking for the help you offered me. I have written to my mother, to the imperial procurator, to the head of the police in Charleville. If you hear nothing from me on Wednesday, before the train that leaves Douai for Paris, take that train, come here to claim me by letter, or go to the procurator to intercede, to vouch for me and pay my debt! Do all you can, and, when you receive this letter, write,*

*you too, I order you, yes, write to my poor mother (Quai de
la Madeleine, 5, Charlev). to console her! Write also to me.
Do all this! I love you as a brother, I will love you as a father!
I shake your hand.*
Your poor
Arthur Rimbaud at Mazas
*And if you succeed in freeing me, you will take me with you to
Douai.*

"Take that train, come here, pay my debt, take me with you, do all you
can." Certainly in this letter Rimbaud has adopted his mother's tone!

Meanwhile, since he had ink and paper at his disposal, he set to work:
the manuscript of his sonnet *Morts de quatre-vingt-douze* (Dead of '92 and
'93) bears the following words: "Written at Mazas, September 3, 1870."

Izambard immediately took the necessary steps, paid off his pupil's debt,
and sent him the money for his journey home. Rimbaud was released, taken
to the Gare du Nord, and put on the train for Douai.

He arrived in Izambard's rooms on September 8. One can imagine his
state of mind: angry at the experience he had just undergone: full of gratitude,
of course, but very worried at the prospect of having to go back to his mother's, which would inevitably—perhaps very soon indeed—bring his escapade
to an end.

The house in which Izambard lived, a three-storied building with a
pleasant facade decorated in the Italian style, was situated in a quiet district
of the town, at 219 Rue de l'Abbaye-des-Prés.

It belonged to the Gindre sisters, whom I mentioned earlier, who had
taken him in and brought him up after his mother's death. The younger of
the two, Caroline, was thirty-eight; her sisters were called Isabelle and Henriette. They ran a ladies' clothes shop in the town.

The entire household, including Léon Deverrière, who was staying
there at the time, received the rescued boy like the prodigal son. "The lecture
came later," Izambard remarks.

"So you saw Paris?" the master of the household inquired.

"Pooh!" he exclaimed thinking of what he had seen through the barred
window of the prison van.

"And I supposed you applauded the proclamation of a Republic, on September 4?"

"I didn't know much about what was . . ."

They put him into a pleasant room on the third floor, where there was a well-stocked bookcase. The most urgent matter was to clean him up. First he was given a shower—he arrived covered with vermin (in spite of the "sulphuring chamber"!). He was installed in a chair in front of a window opening on to an overgrown garden ("A real tropical forest," the person who later bought the house remarked), and the "two tall charming sisters" came in to see him. He describes them in his poem *Les chercheuses de poux* (The Lice-Seekers):

> *Elles assoient l'enfant devant une croisée*
> *Grande ouverte où l'air bleu baigne un fouillis de fleurs*
> *Et dans ses lourds cheveux où tombe la rosée*
> *Promènent leurs doigts fins, terribles et charmeurs.*

> [*They seat the child in front of a wide open*
> *Window where the blue air bathes a mass of flowers,*
> *And in his heavy hair where the dew falls,*
> *Moved their delicate, fearful and enticing fingers.*]⁴

In these subtle, sensual lines, he succeeded in evoking the strange abandonment, composed of langor and unacknowledged tenderness, that took hold of him when, for the first time in his life, he was the object of women's solicitude.

Izambard informed Mme Rimbaud of her son's arrival, and asked her for instructions, while at the same time begging her to be indulgent toward him after the severe lesson that he had just been given. He made the runaway add a few words of contrition to his letter. Young Rimbaud, however, wanted only to forget Charleville and its inhabitants. In the tiny paradise that he had found he now let himself live from day to day, a spoiled child, with no concern for the future. It really was an unhoped-for dream, quiet hours devoted to reading, walking, writing poetry. Ah! How far away seemed the hustle and bustle of his native town, and the constant nagging and harsh discipline of "la mère Rimbe."

The first thing he did was to run to the bookcase, which contained among other things the twenty-one volumes of the *Magasin pittoresque* and Montaigne's *Essays*, which he enjoyed enormously. What he liked about them was not so much the subject matter, as the vivacity of style. One passage in particular amused him so much that he could not wait to tell Izambard of his discovery, and stood outside the house awaiting his return. This was the passage: "The poet, says Plato, sitting on the Muses' tripod, furiously pours forth whatever comes into his mouth, like the gargoyle of a fountain, without ruminating upon it, or weighing his words, and there comes forth from him things of diverse color, contrary substance, and uneven flow" (*Essays*, 3, chap. 9).[5] Izambard's smile redoubled his delight. For several days, they joked about it like two accomplices; "the poet's gargoyle" became Rimbaud's favorite catchphrase.

Izambard did not stop at giving him advice; he went further, and one day introduced him to a good friend of his, the poet Paul Demény, then twenty-six years old, and the author of *Les Glaneuses*, a collection of poems that had just appeared at the Editions de la Librairie artistique, in Paris. What interested Rimbaud far more than the poems, which he considered very ordinary, was to learn that Demény was in partnership with a certain M. Devienne, who ran the publishing house of the Libraire artistique, at 8 Rue Bonaparte.[6]

Immediately, without the slightest hesitation, our young poet saw Demény as a possible, nay, certain—publisher of his poems. So he asked for some large sheets of paper, and set about recopying, with devoted application and a pride that is unmistakably conveyed by the flourishes of the signatures, all the poems that he had written during the year. In the words of H. de Bouillane de Lacoste, this writing "bursts with joy." Some of the pieces (*Les Effarés*, a small masterpiece of delicate feeling, and *Roman*, lines written by a schoolboy, heart aflame) are dated with the day of the original manuscript (September 20 and 23), others with that of the final fair copy, so that it is difficult, on the basis of these autographed copies alone, to draw up an exact chronology of these poems.

Taken together they formed enough material for a slim volume.

At last Rimbaud believed that the day had come when he was going to be a journalist. Izambard was a subeditor on a new Douai newspaper, *Le Libéral du Nord*, and Rimbaud often went to see him at his office, happy to leaf through the local press and to breathe in the intoxicating smell of printer's ink. He was dying to work for this newspaper, but his teacher seemed reluctant to help him, not wishing to give him any pretext to settle in Douai, since, soon, any day now . . .

He had already had to dissuade him when he had tried to join the national guard at the same time as himself. Izambard was the plank to which he clung. Clearly he had made up his mind to stay at Douai in the atmosphere of friendship that he had found there, free, relaxed, spoiled by the good Gindre sisters. Anything was better, even if it meant military duties, than going back to Charleville!

On September 18 Izambard was entrusted with the task of composing a letter of protest against the mayor, M. Maurice, who had proved incapable of arming the national guards in a suitable manner (they drilled with broomsticks!). Two days later, as he sat down at his desk to write this letter, Rimbaud handed him a sheet of paper: "Your letter, it's here."

Izambard must have thought that this young man was beginning to make a nuisance of himself. His early shyness had given way to self-confidence verging on impertinence; he seemed to believe that everything was his due.

Each morning, the mail was awaited with apprehension, for everyone was thinking, without daring to say so, that things could not go on as they were. Indeed the boy had revealed with brutal frankness what kind of a woman his mother was, and the Gindre sisters had been so shocked that they had forbidden him to speak of his mother again.

On September 21 the dreaded letter from Charleville arrived, dated September 17: the runaway was ordered to return immediately, and not to spend a day longer in Douai. Naturally enough, Rimbaud stiffened: he would never go back to his mother's! This time Izambard lost his temper. When Rimbaud had calmed down, he refused to give him the money for his journey home, knowing only too well that he would sneak off to Paris.

At this point, Deverrière suggested shortening his holidays and accompanying young Arthur home. This was agreed on, and a reply was written to Mme Rimbaud accordingly. But, during this period of hostilities, "safe conducts" were required, which would take a few days to obtain. Rimbaud made use of this delay to practice the art of journalism.

With Izambard and Deverrière he had attended an election meeting on the evening of Friday September 23, in the Rue d'Esquerchin. He wrote up an account of the meeting that he submitted to the *Libéral du Nord*, then waited for it to be published (on September 25) before admitting what he had done to his teacher, who did not know how to react, whether to congratulate or to blame him. But Rimbaud still had a lot to learn: for example, he had called an important industrialist, well-known for his bad temper, "citizen Jeannin." The man was furious, and protested to Izambard: "It's outrageous! You're making me look ridiculous in your rag!"

When Izambard taxed Rimbaud on this matter, the boy simply replied—in all candor—that the word *citizen* was in common usage in 1789 and 1848.

About September 27 a second letter from Mme Rimbaud arrived, dated the 24. The tone was a little less harsh: "I am very anxious and do not at all understand Arthur's prolonged absence. He must have understood, from my letter of the 17, that he was not to remain another day at Douai. . . . It is impossible to understand the madness of this child, who is usually so good and quiet. How could such a wild idea have entered his head? Who could have suggested it to him? . . . Please be good enough to advance 10 francs to the wretched boy, send him away, and tell him that he must come home immediately!"

At the last moment, Izambard decided to accompany Deverrière to Charleville, because he wanted to visit the battlefields of Sedan and Balan.

Before leaving, Rimbaud ran off to Paul Demény's, 39 Rue Jean-de-Bologne, and, not finding him there, scribbled out these words across a page of one of the manuscripts that he left him:

I've come to say goodbye, but you aren't at home.
I don't know if I'll be able to come back; I leave tomorrow,
in the morning, for Charleville—I have a safe-conduct—I'm
terribly sorry that I couldn't say goodbye to you personally.
I shake your hand as violently as I can.
—Best wishes.
I'll write to you. You'll write to me? No?
Arthur Rimbaud

It was a sad return. Huddled up in the corner of the carriage Rimbaud did not open his lips, pretending not to hear Izambard telling Deverrière of his plans: "I'd like to go on to Brussels, and drop in on my old friend Paul Durand, who lives with his mother, in the Rue Fossé-aux-Loups."

They rang, and Mme Rimbaud appeared at the door.

"I've brought him back to you," said Izambard, with a forced smile.

A rain of blows immediately fell about the boy's ears, and Arthur began to yell—not so much out of pain, as rage: such a punishment in front of his teacher, who had treated him as a man, was like a branding.

When she had calmed down, the terrible woman drew herself up to her full height, and said, through her tight, "vinegary lips": "As for you, Monsieur le professeur . . ."

She dared to accuse him of having instigated her son's flight, and of sequestering him, against her orders.

Izambard listened, open mouthed, and, since she showed no signs of halting her torrent of abuse, he soon felt that he could contain himself no longer. He took the easy way out and left, banging the door in her face.

Poor Rimbaud! He was engulfed once more by the terrible boredom of Charleville. Izambard, who was busy parceling up his books, forbade him to call without his mother's express permission. He was therefore unable to tell the boy how surprised he was to find his library enriched by a number of new volumes, and lacking in a number of others, in particular a fine edition of Victor Hugo that he was very attached to. But he was wise enough to put these changes down to the profit and loss account.

One day, at a loose end, Rimbaud went out as far as Mézières with the intention of meeting up again with Delahaye. Rimbaud had always got on well with this easy-going, not to say simple soul. His mother, a civil servant's widow, a very religious woman, ran a grocer's shop at the corner of the Grand-Rue and the Rue du Faubourg-de-Pierre. For her it was an honor to receive her son's illustrious friend in her shop—her Ernest could not fail to benefit from contact with such a brilliant pupil. Naturally, she knew nothing of Rimbaud's recent escapade. Ernest himself was equally delighted: at last he had someone intelligent to talk to, the best pupil in the school, the hero who had just come out of Badinguet's prisons! Rimbaud so dazzled him when he recited to him the poems that he had written during the summer that Delahaye took two hours to walk home with him.

"And what are you going to do now?" Delahaye asked him as he was about to leave him.

"I don't know yet. I'm waiting for a favorable moment to get out of here. It's too difficult at the moment."

"Then come and see me again."

"I'll come tomorrow."

He went every day. How full of promises were those unhoped-for holidays, with no foreseeable end. Usually they arranged to meet at Saint-Julien, the Bois de Boulogne at Mézières, or at the Bois d'Amour, a charming garden with old rusty gates, planted with ancient lime trees. There they were quite safe. They would take their pipes from their pockets being careful to conceal them again if anyone walked by who might denounce them to their mothers—especially old Desdouets, whom one bumped into everywhere, and who, though a chain smoker himself, dared to forbid his pupils to do the same! Rimbaud always had a book on him—Champfleury's *Les Amoureux de sainte Perine*, Flaubert's *Madame Bovary*, or Dickens's *Hard Times*. Delahaye regarded such literature as very realistic: depicting evil, he would say, makes it easier to destroy it. But, for Rimbaud, that was not the nub of the matter: the important thing was to fear nothing, to carry revolution even into vocabulary, enlarging it with borrowings from foreign languages and from technology, creating a new language powerful enough to communicate thoughts, sensations, life itself directly. Poor Ernest did not understand much of all this, but he was proud to be the confidant of such a magician. Such self-assurance, such originality, could not fail to have a glorious future, he thought, as they gazed at the gold and purple clouds at sunset.

It would be wrong to see the two friends as aesthetes toying with sublime abstractions. They were, after all, still young, and quite liable to childish behavior. Arthur, who never wore a school cap, one day grabbed Delahaye's somewhat battered one, and tore off the loosely stitched braid.

"Hey! What you doing?" yelled Delahaye seizing Rimbaud's small boater, and flinging it into the air. But, instead of picking it up, Arthur jumped up and down on it like a thing possessed.

"Are you crazy?" cried Delahaye, picking up the battered object. "What will your mother say?"

"Oh, the sentence is fixed in advance—two days on bread and water!" he said, and set about consoling his friend, who was nearly in tears.

This incident is reminiscent of the one involving the umbrellas and the church door: there is the same deliberate will to sacrifice, the same Spartan contempt for punishment, the same pride in assuming complete responsibility for one's actions, however stupid they may be.

On other days, they would go into town, in search of amusement. Nothing ever happened. From the beginning of September a truce had been concluded with the enemy for the evacuation of the wounded, and it was still in force. At Mézières they took advantage of this respite to reinforce the fortifications, while at Charleville a Committee of National Defense had been formed to recruit national guards. But, this time, Rimbaud had no intention of signing up. The air was heavy with menace and nervous tension: at the slightest pretext the excitable crowd would cry treason; in the streets, incidents were constantly flaring up, and turning into shouting matches. Such scenes no doubt attracted the idle schoolboys, like so many attractions at a fairground.

One day, a carriage carrying British nurses was stopped:

"They're spies!" people shouted. "They're carrying weapons and ammunition to the Prussians!"

The nurses were lucky to get away without being lynched! Another day, the streets echoed to the cries of victory: a patrol of franc-tireurs presented General Mazel, commanding officer of the Mézières garrison, with about fifteen Prussians piled into four carts, stuffed with rifles and military gear.

"Now they'll be left in peace, and kept warm till the war's over," Rimbaud murmured as they passed.

But everyone was to be disappointed: they'd forgotten the truce! The military authorities had to hand the prisoners back, with apologies, and reimburse the cost of the cargo, for the convoy had been looted. But people still went on shouting: "We've been betrayed!"[7]

Mézières, with its ramparts from a former age, in which wallflowers grew between its stones, its Grand-Place turned into an entraining point, and Charleville, with its shops, its Old Mill, its little wood, its shaded quayside, saw them wandering about, sometimes in passionate conversation, sometimes mocking and amused, during that early autumn, so heavy with menace. But they were quite happy to live dangerously.

And then, one day, Delahaye waited in vain for his friend. Rimbaud must have gone off again.

Meanwhile, Izambard was visiting the sites of battle, still warm with the latest slaughter. On his return to Charleville, on October 8, as he was getting ready to set out for Brussels, he was handed an anguished note from Mme Rimbaud. Arthur had disappeared again! She had looked everywhere for him. At M. Deverrière's, at Bretagne's, at Mme Delahaye's. There was no trace of him.

"You must realize, Madame, that I have nothing to do with it this time," Izambard told her. "I haven't seen your son since he came back from Douai."

She agreed, but knowing of his intentions of going to Belgium, she begged him to help her: her unfortunate child might also have gone in that direction, for he had recently mentioned one of his school friends, Léon Billuart, who lived at Fumay, on the Route de Givet.

"Since you are going through Fumay, Monsier le professeur, could you stop there, just long enough to persuade Arthur to come back at once and to alert the police in the event of his refusing to do so."

Forgetting all his rancor, Izambard took on the mission, more out of a sense of duty and pity, no doubt, than with enthusiasm.

It was probably the night before, on October 7, that the boy had run away.[8] With money obtained by selling a few books, he had bought a ticket for Fumay, as his mother had supposed. Indeed, the date of October 7, which appears at the end of his poem *Rêve pour l'hiver*, is preceded by the words "En wagon." It is a delicate fantasy dedicated to "Elle"—an imaginary girl-friend with whom the poet sees himself "in a small pink railway carriage with blue cushions." He arrived at Fumay at about five o'clock in the evening. Billuart, whose parents ran a café, received him warmly: "You'll stay to dinner, and spend the night here."[9]

In the course of the evening, the traveler outlined his plans: first he would go to Vireux, about twelve kilometers away, and visit a mutual friend, Arthur Binard, and, via Givet, would go on to Charleroi, where he would become a journalist.

"Des Essarts' father will take me on as editor of his paper."

Next day, about 11 o'clock, he set off. Billuart gave him a little money, some chocolate, and a word of recommendation to one of his cousins, a sergeant of the *garde mobile* at Givet, who could probably put him up. He went on his way, stoped at Vireux, as planned, and called on Binard, who gave him another free meal.

Meanwhile, at Fumay, Izambard learned that the runaway had moved on to Vireux, and there that he had gone on to Givet.

On arrival at Givet, Rimbaud had no difficulty in finding the barracks of the *"mobiles"* in the Grand Quartier (destroyed by fire in 1914), dominated by the fortress of Charlemont, the work of Charles V and Vauban. But his luck was out: Billuart's cousin was on guard duty that day. Never mind! If the sergeant was absent, his bed was still there! So, without the slightest scruple, our traveler lay down on it, and promptly fell asleep, exhausted by his journey. Next day he left as evidence on the mantelpiece the recommendation that he had been given.

At Charleroi, at the offices of the town newspaper, 20 Rue du Collège, young Jules des Essarts, surprised to see him, introduced him to his father, Senator Xavier des Essarts, a solemn man, rather full of his own importance, a stickler for principles—though he was a good-hearted man, for he took in, and often helped, French political exiles. He listened to his visitor's request with sympathetic attention, but his revolutionary ideas, and the abuse he heaped on the leading French politicians of the day soon made him lose patience with him. He politely led him out, promising to give him a reply next day. According to Izambard, M. des Essarts asked Rimbaud to dinner, and it was then that the boy gave bent to his violent diatribes. The Belgian writer Robert Goffin questioned Marius des Essarts, the senator's nephew, who described the embarassment that gripped the family: Jules and his sister Léonie dared not look up.[10]

Next day, when Rimbaud, who had slept we know not where, turned up at the newspaper offices, he was told that they did not require more staff.

It seems that the young hothead had left such a disagreeable impression on M. des Essarts that he forbade his son to speak to him again. It is a pity that Rimbaud's letter to Léon Billuart describing the meeting has not been published in full. All we have is the following passage, which recounts what happened next: "I supped on the smells of roasting meat and poultry rising from the air vents of the good bourgeois kitchens of Charleroi, then went off to nibble a piece of Fumay chocolate in the moonlight."[11]

It seems that, having no particular ideas as to what to do next, Rimbaud stayed on for a few days at Charleroi, since he begins one of his sonnets thus:

Depuis huit jours j'avais déchiré mes bottines
Aux cailloux des chemins. J'entrais à Charleroi.
—Au Cabaret-Vert.

[*For a week my boots had been torn*
By the pebbles on the roads. I was getting into Charleroi.
—At the Cabaret-Vert.][12]

This Cabaret-Vert, or to be more precise "Maison-verte"—was an inn painted entirely in green, the walls outside and in, and even the furniture. M. Robert Goffin has located the building, which is incorporated in the Hôtel de l'Esperance. Was it Mia, a buxom Flemish woman—who is still remembered by a few old men—that Rimbaud describes in another sonnet, *La Maline?*[13]

Another day, a brilliantly colored Belgian engraving, representing "The brilliant victory of Saarbrücken carried off to the cries of 'Vive l'Empereur!' on sale at Charleroi for 35 centimes," inspired him to write a new sonnet.[14]

We should not forget, to complete the Belgian series, *Ma Bohème*, a little masterpiece of ironic and bitter feelings:

—Petit-Poucet rêveur, j'égrenais dans ma course
Des rhimes. Mon auberge était à la Grande-Ourse.

[Tom Thumb in a daze, I sowed rhymes
As I went along. My inn was at the Big Dipper.][15]

His failure to enter journalism does not seem to have affected him unduly, since he was still ready to make fun of himself. He must have consoled himself with the thought that a boss like M. des Essarts would not exactly have suited him, and, anyway, he still had his two mistresses, Adventure and Freedom.

Then Izambard turned up at the house of Senator des Essarts:

"Rimbaud? Yes, we did see him, but he left without saying where he was going."

Ah well, never mind! No one can be expected to do the impossible. He had more than done his duty. Few schoolmasters would have pushed professional conscience so far. Let Arthur go on his way! He had no wish to be mixed up in this business—it had already taken up too much of his time. He wrote to Mme Rimbaud that no trace of her son could be found.

Not for an instant had he realized how unwise he had been to let slip to Deverrière, in Rimbaud's presence, that he was thinking of calling on his old friend Paul Durand, in the Rue Fossé-aux-Loups, Brussels.

The address had not been forgotten, and Rimbaud, having arrived in Brussels on foot, went at once to knock on that friendly door. This excellent young man had come to announce the forthcoming visit of M. Izambard. M. Durand and his mother took pity on him, for his clothes were crumped, his shoes worn down, and his haggard face betrayed extreme exhaustion. Very generously, they took him in, and allowed him to stay—even suggesting that he should wait until M. Izambard arrived. However, he preferred to leave, with the intention of seeing something of Belgium. He would be able to look after himself, he said. As he was leaving, M. Durand gave him some money.

At Brussels, Izambard was dumbfounded to learn that his friend Durand and his mother were expecting him, and that Rimbaud had been there before him.

"What! He's been here, the animal! And there I've been running after him for over a week! Well, I hope he does see something of Belgium, and may he and his mother go to the devil!"

Forgetting Rimbaud, Izambard settled down to enjoying his friend's company.

About October 20, he must have been thinking of going back to Douai.

No sooner had he opened the door of his house than his aunt rushed up to him with the news:

"He's here!"

"Who?"

"Rimbaud."

"What the devil!"

Apparently he had got on the train, and turned up at the house of the Gindre sistes as if it was the most normal thing in the world.

"Yes, it's me. I've come back."

He was dressed in the latest fashion with wing collar, and bronzed silk tie—very much in the style of a young newspaper editor.

Izambard's patience was exhausted. This time he had gone too far! He was a pleasant enough fellow, but it was all getting too much! Not content with taking over his time, his books, and his friends, he also demanded his residences at Charleville and Douai! And, anyway, what situation did it put him in? He had promised his mother to get him to go home or to hand him over to the police. Mme Rimbaud would now accuse him of being an accomplice all along! It was intolerable! But he managed to find the words to express what he felt without hurting the boy too much: "We don't want to chase you away, but you must understand that we can't keep you here."

"Yes, I know," he said, somewhat downcast. "I'll do as you say."

Rimbaud took advantage of the few days left to him—Mme Rimbaud had been alerted of his presence there, and they were awaiting her reply—to copy out his series of Belgian sonnets, for Paul Demény, whom he no doubt saw again.

"At the slightest mistake," writes Izambard, "he began all over again, and asked for large sheets of paper. When one of his hands was black with ink, he came and said: 'I don't have any more paper,' and this happened several times a day. We gave him a few sous to go and buy more paper. One of my aunts suggested that he write on the back of the sheets. 'One never writes on the back for the printer,' he replied, obviously scandalized at the idea."[16] He had probably just learned this from Demény—for, in September, he had copied out his poems on both sides of the sheet of paper.

After a few days Mme Rimbaud's reply arrived. It was a categorical order to hand the runaway over to the police, with a strict prohibition to use any other means.

So Izambard went off to see the police inspector, who promised to do whatever was necessary. On his return Rimbaud was waiting for him, his bundle of possessions tucked under his arm. He had promised the Gindre sisters to be good. Izambard took him off to the police station; they were both on the verge of tears. They shook hands, and said goodbye.

"We won't do him any harm," said the inspector, kindly.

They never saw each other again.

Shortly after the boy had left, one of the Gindre sisters discovered an inscription in pencil on the dark green paintwork of the front door. It was a short farewell in verse, expressing sorrow and gratitude, addressed more to the house than to his hosts.

Izambard smiled, moved, but forgot to copy out the precious offering. One morning painters would come and obliterate it with an uncaring brush.

At Charleville, Rimbaud resumed his outings with Delahaye—he had little choice. The truce had been broken about October 20, and there was fighting—but quite some distance away. The town itself was quiet. The citadel of Mézières fired off its canons from time to time to remind the enemy—well out of reach—that they were something to be reckoned with. One day the two friends were walking through the suburb of Arche when a shell exploded in front of them, knocking off large bits of parapets from a nearby building. They agreed that the artillery was behaving in a particularly stupid way.

On October 28 news of the capitulation of Metz reached Charleville. The town was then filled with a disorderly influx of exhausted and demoralized French troops. Among these soldiers was Frédéric, of whom they had had no news. He had let himself be shut up in the fortress with the rest of his regiment. Mme Rimbaud welcomed him back in a pitiful state. The two brothers, the two accomplices, says Delahaye, could hardly keep a straight face. Arthur teased his militaristic brother who had volunteered for glory, and Frédéric, in a southern accent that he had picked up in the army, replied calmly: "*Ar-thu-re, tu me dégoûtes.*" The defending of the citadel had been actively carried out in October, and everything that might interfere with visibility and the canon fire had been ruthlessly razed to the ground. The orchards near the ramparts and the Bois d'Amour had been turned into frightful wastelands strewn with branches intended as a barrier.

"Quel saccage du jardin de la beauté!" [What slaughter in the garden of beauty!] Rimbaud was to write later (*Conte—Illuminations*),[17] but at the time he approved of the massacre, though he did regret the felling of the ancient lime trees.

"Some destruction is necessary," he said. "Selfishness, inequality, privilege—all that must disappear."

"But that will mean the reign of universal mediocrity," Delahaye objected.

Rimbaud then picked a yarrow, and, in the manner of Jesus speaking of the lily of the fields, replied: "Look, when all social institutions have disappeared, nature will still offer us the most perfect art." (Anarchism and ecology often consort well together.)

He had become a fervent disciple of Jean-Jacques Rousseau, Helvetius, and Baron d'Holbach. Whatever thwarted self-fulfillment—the discipline of family or school, religion with its Ten Commandments, morality and its constraints, money and its servitudes—must be destroyed like the old trees that had to make way for flag poles. Then men would be able to raise themselves, and society itself become a "Bois d'Amour."

One day, Delahaye recounts, as they were sitting on the steps of the Military Tribunal, Rimbaud took out of his pocket a booklet with a blue cover. It was Hugo's *Les Châtiments*, which was still being sold in secret. He gorged himself on the hatred and contempt expressed in that work by initials, accompanied no doubt by a wide range of obscene epithets!—but Rimbaud regarded no invective as excessive.

"It's true," agreed the candid Delahaye, "what a pack of bandits our rulers have been!"

"Make no mistake," Rimbaud replied, "the new régime is no better."

Meanwhile, the fighting that had been taking place in the surrounding country gradually seeped in between Mézières—the citadel of honor and pride—and Charleville, the good, peace-loving market town. It seemed that the defence of Mézières would prove illusory, if, as in 1815, the Germans went round it and occupied Charleville first. It was therefore important to fortify Charles of Gonzaga's city—and as quickly as possible. But the local authorities were slow to act: they were lacking in men, money, and equipment. Gambetta's proclamation of October 24 (outright struggle!) and the injunctions of General Mazel, governor of Mézières, finally won the staid citizens over. The Municipal Council agreed to fortify twenty points recommended by the sappers, but did so only under protest, "in the name of the dignity of the city, and of the respect due to the life and fortunes of its inhabitants." Barricades and small fortresses went up in the suburbs; the town became a closely observed camp, from which no one could leave. Rimbaud was caught in the trap.

If he did not take to the road, as he was dying to do, it was because he could not. But he let Izambard believe that he was staying at home out of obedience.

This is his letter:

Charleville, November 2, 1870

Monsieur,
—This is for you alone.—
I returned to Charleville the day after leaving you. My mother
took me in, and here I am . . . without occupation. My
mother will not put me back in school before January '71.
So, I kept my promise.
I am dying, I am decomposing in dullness, in paltry
wickedness, in grayness. What can I say?—in a terrible way I
insist on worshipping free freedom, and so many things that I
am to be pitied, isn't it true? I was to set out again today. I
could have done so. I had new clothes on, I would have sold
my watch, and long live freedom!—But I stayed at home!—I
will want to leave many more times.—Let's go, hat, coat, my
two fists in my pockets, and we're off! But I will stay, I will
stay. I did not promise to! But I will do so as to deserve your
affection. You told me this. I will deserve it.
The gratitude I feel for you, I could not express today any
more than any other day. I will prove it to you! If it were a
question of doing something for you, I would die in order to do
it. I give you my word.
I still have many things to say. . . .
This "heartless"

A. Rimbaud

War:—No siege at Mézières. When will it be? Nobody
talks about it.—I have carried out your errand to M. Dever-
rière, and, if there is anything else to do, I'll do it.—Franc-
tirades, here and there—Abominable prurigo of idiocy, such is

*the spirit of the population. One hears some pretty good
things. Well, better stop. Everything is rotten.*

The term "this heartless Rimbaud" is an allusion to the criticisms made
by the Gindre sisters who, scandalized by what he was saying about his
mother, reproached him for having no heart. (Delahaye heard him say:
"What makes me superior is that I have no heart.")

Izambard explains the words "I have carried out your errand to M. Deverrière" as concerning some of his books that still remained parceled up at
Charleville. In fact it was a letter to Deverrière in an envelope that also contained a note for Mme Rimbaud. But Deverrière, not daring to rub her up
the wrong way, asked Arthur to hand it to his mother, which he did. Deverrière was immediately summoned, and everything became clear. What did
that letter to Mme Rimbaud contain? A bill! Izambard was asking to be repaid
for the expenses that his pupil had caused him (railway ticket, large sheets of
paper). In a letter of November 11, 1870, to Izambard, Deverrière describes
the scene:

"Yesterday I saw Cousine Bête née Rimbaud.[18] I had previously sent her
your letter via her son."

First Deverrière had to submit to an interrogation:

*"You are M. Deverrière, who lives at . . . who has been
entrusted with M. Izambard's affairs, and it was you, was it
not, who gave my son a letter that came from Douai?"*
"Ye-es, Madame."
*"M. Izambard's demands are quite unacceptable. I re-
serve the right to settle with him, meanwhile, I shall give you
15 F 65. Can you accept this sum?"*
"Ye-es, Madame."
Then the rasping voice dictated the following:
*"Received from Mme Rimbaud the sum of 15 F 65, the
sum advanced by M. Iz. to M.R. her son."*
"For, M. Izambard, the . . . of the . . ."
*Thereupon the old bird of prey extended five claws and
snatched the receipt, while five other claws opened to let fall
three 100 sou coins and fifteen sous in small change. I examined the money, weighed it, tested it for sound (who knows).
Bonsoir, Dame Pernelle.[19]*

This letter of November 1870 was accompanied by another letter for Izambard from M. Lenel, Duprez' successor, mentioning the possible reopening of the Collège in the near future: "In the meantime it would seem that we will be reopening for the day boys, if not in all the classes at least in some. But there is no official news on this matter."

The days went by, in all their gloom and boredom; nothing ever happened. Rimbaud and Delahaye, to kill time, went out for walks despite the cold and frequent snowstorms. They had discovered a gardener's hut that had remained intact near the Bois d'Amour, and, there, read poetry to one another. Rimbaud always had a Banville or a *Parnasse contemporain* on him.

But, more often, they would be wandering the highways and byways. One day, as night was falling, they were stopped by a soldier of the *garde mobile* on sentry duty:

"Halt! Who goes there?"

"*Vif' la France!*" Rimbaud called out, in a German accent, trying desperately to suppress his laughter.

"Not before time," replied the sentry in all seriousness.

The search for spies was at its height. One day, a Muslim, who couldn't get over hearing himself called a Prussian, was brought before the authorities. On another occasion it was the turn of an old schoolmaster who had been caught examining the bombards on the citadel that dated from the reign of Louis XV. A furious mob wanted to throw him into the Meuse. Strange stories circulated: a German teacher from the Collège called Becker had been seen in the uniform of a captain of the uhlans. It seemed that one of his men had brought a young French soldier to him: the German had recognized the prisoner as one of his former pupils, Lagneaux, and had him released.[20]

One dared not to think of the future: war, cold, and despair had taken a hold on everyone. There was no more coal, the shops were empty; the invisible enemy was everywhere. A sense of the world ending fell with the snow.

In Charleville, at 22 Rue Forest, there lived a delightful old fellow, with a bald head and a long silver beard. Emile Jacoby, a photographer by trade, had once been a neighbor of the Rimbaud family and was well known to Arthur. Once the principal of an educational establishment at Tours, he had acquired a certain celebrity for presenting before the Académie des Sciences a fourteen-year-old shepherd boy, Henri Mondeux, who was capable of phenomenal feats of mental arithmetic. He was himself the author of a treatise published in Charleville, called *La Clef de l'Arithmétique*. He gained respect for being a former member of the Société d'émancipation intellectuelle of

Paris. Rimbaud warmed to him because of his political opinions: this veteran of '48 claimed to be a political victim of December 2. In October 1870 he founded a republican newspaper, *Le Progrès des Ardennes*, with the intention of counteracting *Le Courrier des Ardennes*.. Deverrière, who had been approached with a view to contributing to the paper, wrote an article for the first number that appeared in a considerably altered form. As a result Deverrière did not entertain kindly feelings toward Jacoby and his paper.

But what did that matter to Rimbaud, if he got published. He had to be. It is possible that his sonnet *Le dormeur du val* appeared in *Le Progrès*.[21] According to Delahaye, he sent some pastoral verses to Jacoby, who replied, in the correspondence column, that circumstances were unsuited to tunes played on a panpipe. So, signing himself Jean Baudry,[22] he suggested something more up to date: a tale showing Bismarck, drunk and gross, sleeping on a map of Paris and waking up with a cry, his nose stuck into the bowl of his Bavarian pipe.

In the correspondence column, again according to Delahaye (*Souvenirs familiers*), appears the following message in the number for December 29: "M. M. Baudry and Dhayle [Delahaye], I found your articles interesting, but unmask yourselves a little."

"That's all he needs?" cried Rimbaud. "Excellent, we'll go and see him."

"Capital!" Delahaye agreed. They already saw themselves as journalists.

Unfortunately, other events were in train that were to bring their expectations to nothing.

The surrender of Montmédy and Thionville had released the German 14th division, which, on December 14, was ordered to encircle Mézières, and to seize the fortifications. It took the Prussians a fortnight to install their batteries, for the ground was frozen to a depth of eighteen inches. At Mézières, the population was determined to resist. They were all aware that they would soon be bombarded, but they boasted that they did not fear it. However, as a precautionary measure, public buildings and the church had been protected. "The enemy may use up his ammunition to burn down the town, but the fortifications will resist," General Mazel proclaimed proudly.

On December 30, Rimbaud and Delahaye found themselves in the crowd that filled the Place de la Préfecture. A lieutenant of the German hussars, von Reymann, accompanied by two liaison officers, had come to demand the surrender of the town. It was a pure formality, the Prussians were politely shown the gate. The governor of the citadel had simply asked that Charleville be spared.[23]

The fireworks could now begin.

That evening, it began to snow. The canon went into action. Immediately afterwards, an alert was sounded by drum: each side was to retreat to its own quarters, and the bombardment would begin next day at dawn. Delahaye and Rimbaud parted, more worried than they let on—but quite pleased that something at last was going to happen.

On December 31, at half-past seven in the morning, in a freezing mist (–18°C), a rocket went up: that was the signal. One of the first shells fell on a house in the suburb of Pierre, quite close to where the Delahayes lived— the boy himself had taken refuge in the cellar of the former police station.

Then all hell was let loose.

The town was soon little more than a furnace, constantly shaken by new shocks that sent huge sheathes of sparks up into the air. At first some of the canon on the fortress had tried to reply, but they were soon reduced to silence.

It went on all day. At first, Delahaye found the surprising spectacle amusing: from his air vent he observed a butcher's shop in flames, where carcasses were being grilled on their hooks dripping hot fat on to pots of geraniums that had been brought into the shop ("I'll tell that to Rimbaud," he said to himself), but he soon grew tired of the monotony of the explosions: one every three minutes. Nightfall brought no respite. In the shelters, stiff with fear, cold, and exhaustion, people were thrown from one wall to the other by the impact of the explosions. One of Rimbaud's friends, Jules Mary, later to be a successful novelist, was also in a cellar: "For twenty-seven hours," he wrote in *Le Temps*, "I listened to those sinister engines of death pass over, tracing a parabola above me, with the hiss of a furious snake."

However, in the afternoon of December 31, Charleville had decided to surrender, despite the opposition of General Mazel, on the pretext that the town had suffered enough material damage. At Mézières, the defense committee was still hesitating. However, at ten in the evening, the surrender was rejected. At midnight precisely, as a greeting to the New Year, a salvo of ninety Prussian shells rained down on the town. It must have seemed like the end of the world. The church bell "began to ring out without stopping all the hours it had in its belly" (Delahaye).

At six in the morning a white flag was hoisted up into the church tower, though no one could see it for the smoke and fog. About ten o'clock, a sergeant was appointed to carry a message to the commanding officer of the German forces: it was unconditional surrender. Mézières had been hit by 6,319 shells, including 893 incendiaries; 262 houses had been totally destroyed, not one had remained unscathed. According to official figures, there were forty-three dead and many wounded.

At Charleville, only two houses had been demolished, and there were only nineteen victims: four dead and fifteen wounded. A stray shell exploded—much to Rimbaud's amusement when he heard of it—in the office of M. Desdouets, slightly wounding him, his mother-in-law, and two visitors who happened to be there.

At dawn on January 1, 1871, Mézières was a pile of ruins, broken glass, charred wood, and ash, giving off acrid-smelling smoke, while the snow tried to cover everything up. Here and there, fires were still burning, which could not be fought because the water supply was frozen in the pipes. The downcast inhabitants observed in silence the extent of the disaster.

Rimbaud had lived through a day of great anxiety. His mother had shut him up with his sisters.

"No, Monsieur Arthur, we are not going to watch the bombs fall. It is quite without interest."

However, during the evening of New Year's Day, he was able to escape, climb up to the top of the suburb of Flandre, and see Mézières, in the distance, a glowing, smoking pile of rubble.

"There can't be many people left alive in Mézières," he heard all around him.

That same evening, at midnight, the German troops, preceded by fife and drum, streamed on to the Place Ducale of Charleville, and billeted themselves in the town.

On January 2, at three in the afternoon, it was the turn of Mézières to be invested, with the same ceremonial and gayer music. But the Germans shut the city gates behind them and no one could enter the ravaged town.

There was talk of thousands of victims. One newspaper, *L'Etoile belge*, still circulated, giving a list of those who had died. Rimbaud glanced down it: the Delahaye family was on the list. No doubt he would never see his friend again—his only friend—probably blown to pieces.

"Poor fellow."

Finally, on January 4 or 5, Rimbaud was able to go and see for himself. Of the Delahayes' house in the Grand-Rue only one wall was left standing. Three Prussians in black berets with red bands were removing rubble from the cellar entrance, in the hope of finding wine and liqueurs there. Rimbaud in order to keep warm, lent them a hand. He was expecting to find his friend's corpse; he found only those of his cats. So! Perhaps there was still hope.

Suddenly, who should he see arrive, pale, under a large Auvergnat hat that a neighbor had lent him to replace his own cap, but Delahaye himself. What luck!

His friend told him about the tragic hour that he had lived through in his cellar, beneath the delulge of iron and fire. Soon, Mme Delahaye appeared, who thanked her son's friend for showing such concern about their well-being.

Rimbaud listened with a slightly ironic air, and, when he was alone with his friend, said: "This is all very well, but where are our pipes? You went off with them when we parted."

Delahaye pointed up to the second story of the house gaping into the void.

"You see the stove up there? I hid them in the oven, go and fetch them if you want them so much."

They went off on a tour of inspection on the ruins.

"It's ugly," Rimbaud murmured, "a tortoise in oil."

The lawcourts, with their mean columns and Greek pediment were still standing.

"Of course," he said, "they burn all the shops and hospitals, but the lawcourts. . . . I bet they haven't touched the prison either!"

Indeed, it was still intact, as also was the former police station—in which Delahaye had taken shelter. But, "of course," M. F. Devin's workshop, where *Le Progrès des Ardennes* was printed, was a mass of twisted girders.

But what did Jacoby matter? Though he did not show it, Rimbaud was very happy: he had refound his friend, that is to say, according to the famous definition, a pair of ears to listen to him.

A mechanic of the Mohon workshops, called Bourgeois, took the Delahaye family into his own home at Prix, a village near Mézières. Rimbaud often went there, and got on well with him, for, though a bourgeois, he had advanced ideas.

He often went to collect his friend and the two of them, braving the inclement weather, went off smoking their new pipes to tramp the sodden lanes around Warq, Evigny, Warnécourt, or La Francheville. They talked endlessly—of politics, sociology, metaphysics, and above all poetry. On every matter, Rimbaud now made no secret of his radical, absolute opinions, and heaped insults on all those who did not agree with him. As they tramped through the muddy countryside, he read out *Accroupissements* or *Oraison du soir*, and Delahaye was amazed at his audacity.

Sometimes they came across Prussians, who gave them an amused look from on top of their heavy carts, and wished them a good walk.

Rimbaud, Delahaye recounts, chuckled mockingly at the slaves.

One day, as they were crossing a thick wood, the young poet knocked his head against the trunk of a robinia, and a drop of blood stood out on his forehead.

"Are you bleeding?" Delahaye inquired.

"It's nothing," he said, "it's the thorn of thought."

Did he mean that he was ready to shed his blood for his ideas, or that they were for him like a crown of thorns? No one can say, but it's a fine phrase, which, one could say, inspired Paul Valéry (*Mauvaises pensées*) to write: "Man is on the cross of his body. His overburdened head is pierced by the deep thorns of his crown of thoughts."

When he heard of the bombardment of Paris on January 5, which, it was said, had carried off six hundred victims, Rimbaud was heartbroken. It hardly mattered if Mézières was burning: they had not even heard of Baudelaire. But Paris! The heart and brain of the world, the seedbed of the intellectual and revolutionary forces that were capable of dragging the country from the bloody mire into which despotism had plunged it! He shared in the martyrdom of the Holy City, reliving its great upheavals: the mass marches, the demonstrations, the popular uprisings. But an implacable destiny was drowning in pools of blood any attempt to loosen the grip of the enemy, whether he was called the Prussian barbarian or the conservative bourgeois. Things were going from bad to worse: January 28 saw the shameful capitulation of Jules Favre, against the wishes of the citizenry of Paris; on February 8 the elections put the republicans in the minority and, finally, the crowning insult, on February 12, the National Assembly brought M. Thiers to power!

The return to the capital of the shopkeepers, bankers, and well-fed defeatists, in short, of the "party of order"—as Eugène Vermersch in *Le Cri du peuple* (March 6, 1871) put it—inspired in Rimbaud a fierce diatribe, *L'orgie parisienne, ou Paris se repeuple* (Parisian Orgy, or Paris is Repopulated):

> *Syphilitiques, fous, rois, pantins, ventriloques,*
> *Qu'est-ce que ça peut faire à la putain Paris,*
> *Vos âmes et vos corps, vos poisons et vos loques?*
> *Elle se secouera de vous, hargneux pourris!*

[*Syphilitics, fools, kings, puppets, ventriloquists,*
What does Paris the whore care about
Your souls and bodies, your poisons and your rags?
She will shake you off, you rotten scoffers!][24]

As we can see, Rimbaud was getting angrier.
But this was only the beginning.

5

Back to School

Alas! What Lenel had hinted at to Izambard in his letter of November 11 became in February a sad reality. Since the premises of the Collège were still being used as a military hospital, and since one could not allow the youth of the town to remain idle indefinitely, Desdouets informed the parents in a circular dated around February 15 that a number of classes would take place in the Municipal Theater, which, in those troubled times, was now no longer being used for its normal purposes.

For Rimbaud, the news exploded like a bomb. He had got so used to a life of permanent holiday that he could no longer imagine how it could ever end. The world had changed, the Empire was dead, liberty had triumphed, the people had thrown off their chains, yet here they were talking once again about homework and discipline! It was intolerable! Delahaye, however, took the news calmly: "I said all along this would happen one day."

Arthur would hear nothing of it. When his mother ordered him to turn up at the theater-school, he replied that he had no desire to tread the boards! But Mme Rimbaud was not to be disarmed with a smart reply. She DE-MAND-ED that her son return to school, like his friends. The confrontation was long and bloody, worthy of two rams. But neither orders, police, nor threats ("Then get out!") had any effect on him. He had said no, and no it would be. The morning that lessons began, he stayed in bed.

Delahaye was delighted.

"Capital! We'll play hide-and-seek backstage and in the prompter's box!"

The reality was less amusing: in a small room, M. Duprez dictated a Latin translation, commented on a text of Euripides, and discussed Pascal with half-a-dozen pupils, who, to say the least, were rather lacking in enthusiasm. At the end of the day, Rimbaud arrived, in sarcastic mood, to meet his friends, "the artistes," at the stage door. He was immensely amused to hear

Delahaye's gloom-filled description of the school day, but he became serious when he confided in his friend that things were not going well at home. His mother had made up her mind to put him in a boarding school, or to throw him out. He didn't care what she said: whatever she decided, he would lead a free life, like a hermit, in the woods.

Over the next few days, Mme Rimbaud, having got nowhere with her son, and at the end of her patience, asked her son to leave. For his part, he had had enough of being called an idle good-for-nothing and had made up his mind to go: but instead of shivering in the woods, he would go back to Paris and make contacts in the literary and artistic world. To pay for his ticket, he sold his watch. This was about February 25.

According to Delahaye, he was not leaving alone; a girl, it seems, was going with him. The couple, neither of whom had any money, appear to have spent the night on a bench on one of the town's boulevards. At dawn, it is said, he gave her the last money he had so that she could go home to her parents at Villers-Cotterêts.

Much has been made of this slight incident, which has remained unconfirmed. What is certain is that Rimbaud did not like his friends to refer to his love affairs; it is quite likely that the whole thing was a practical joke. Rimbaud boasted of having had a girlfriend in Paris, and no doubt this planted the idea in his friends' minds.

One of the purposes of his trip was to find out what had happened to Paul Demény—and if possible to meet up with him. What had happened to his manuscript? Had it been accepted or not? One of the first things he did on arriving in Paris was to go to the Librairie Artistique, 18 Rue Bonaparte ("I was trying to find Vermersch's address," he was later to explain to Demény himself). But, to his great disappointment, instead of giving him news of his friend, they asked *him* for news of him. He could only reply that as far as he knew, M. Demény was still under arms at Abbeville. It is thought that he got from the Librairie Artistique the address of André Gill, whose cartoons in *L'Eclipse* and other newspapers he had long admired. Indeed he turned up at Gill's home in the Boulevard d'Enfer (now Raspail). Since the master of the house was absent and the key was still in the studio door, he went in, and, seeing a sofa there, lay down on it without the slightest hesitation, as he had already done in the quarters of the *garde mobile* at Givet. When Gill came back he found him asleep.

"Well! Well!" he said, shaking the intruder. "What are you doing in my studio?"

"I'm a poet," Rimbaud replied, "and I was having beautiful dreams."

"When I have them, young man, I have them in my own home."[1]

But Gill was a good-hearted man, and gave the boy some money, and probably shelter, too, for a few days.

When he was finally asked to leave, on what terms we do not know, the poor boy was reduced to wandering the streets, for a lot of writers and artists whom he had hoped to meet had not yet returned to Paris. However, there can be no doubt that Rimbaud lived through a historic period: on February 26 the temporary armistice had come to an end, and, to avoid new bombardments, Thiers had allowed the Germans to occupy the west of Paris and the Champs-Elysées. The people reacted violently at the news: "No to capitulation! They will not come in!" yelled the demonstrators at the Bastille, waving their red flags. But Rimbaud apparently unaffected by popular passions, wandered from one bookshop to another, discovering all the new things on display, mostly books about the siege or the war.

In the evening, he picked through garbage cans and slept in coal barges moored along the quayside. Delahaye tells how he bought a herring, which he hid in his pocket, and ate only one mouthful of it at midday and another in the evening.

Certainly there was nothing to do in this city, still stunned by the haunting memory of hunger, where people did nothing but talk about food. ("Paris is nothing but a stomach," he was to say when he saw Delahaye again.)

He came back on foot. On March 10 his mother took him in, coughing, his clothes in tatters.

That day, the National Assembly decided to move to Versailles, the first sign of the new war that was to break out between a revolutionary, patriotic Paris and the conservative provinces, which thought only of peace.

During Rimbaud's absence the Delahaye family had moved to the village of Le Theux, to the east of Mézières, which would be reached directly from Charleville through a disused railway tunnel. There the young "Parisian" won a certain success on account of the length of his hair, for he had not been to the hairdresser for four or five months. Delahaye no doubt exaggerates when he describes his hair as a silky mass some eighteen inches long that reached halfway down his back. The reason for this phantasy is quite simple: the Parnassians had been criticized for the length of their hair and beards. So Rimbaud wanted to indicate to the population of the Ardennes that he was a member of the Parnassian movement! However, the children of Le Theux and Mézières were probably not impressed by the new school, for they shouted insults after this "Merovingian," and even threw stones at him. This is why Delahaye had to tell Rimbaud of a secret way by which he could reach his house. At Charleville, Rimbaud enjoyed the same success, that is to say, was subjected to the same insults. One day, a group of young clerks were standing in the Place Ducale, before starting work, when one of them came up to the "Parnassian," holding out a ten centimes coin.

"Here, *mon petit*, take this", he said, "go and get your hair cut!"

"Thanks," Rimbaud replied, pocketing the coin, "it will buy us some tobacco."

Another day, someone yelled out behind him, "*Oh, la belle demoiselle!*" But he was ready to bear more than insults for the cause.

A week after his return, on March 18, two memorable events took place: in Paris, the proclamation of the Commune; at Charleville, the announcement of the official reopening of the Collège.

At Montmartre, the assassination of Generals Thomas and Leconte, who had tried to seize cannons from the National Guard, was the last straw that broke the camel's back.

The news reached Charleville only the next day.

On March 20, according to Delahaye, Rimbaud turned up, looking particularly excited. "Well, that's it!" he said. At last, the thread of history, cut in 1794, had been retied. The stay of execution granted the bourgeoisie was coming to an end, as the warnings issued in 1830 and 1848 had suggested. This time, "this was it," the people were on the march again. This time it would be the coup de grace. "We walked on into Charleville, to see how people were taking it," Delahaye goes on. There was consternation everywhere; after the horrors of foreign war, were they now to slip into civil war? Bright-eyed and defiant, Rimbaud walked in front of the terrified shopkeepers and bourgeois talking of apocalypse, calling out: "That's it! Order is vanquished!"

He poured out an endless stream of inflammatory comments and predictions, while Delahaye, excited by contact with him, "found it fun." Mankind, freed of its material tasks, was about to take flight, the age of Science and Poetry would replace that of Money and Obscurantism. Nature would be at the disposal of all in freedom. The ideas of Rousseau, Proudhon, Louis Blanc were fermenting in his feverish head. Delahaye, good fellow that he was, could not get over his amazement. Rimbaud, usually so uncommunicative, would stop passersby and ask them if they had news from Paris. According to Delahaye, Rimbaud harangued a stonebreaker in the following terms: "The people are rising up for liberty and bread, tomorrow they will be victorious. All workers must rise up in solidarity!" The good fellow listened to him, rather skeptically, then spat into his calloused hands before resuming work with his hammer, and muttered: "There's something in what you say!" (*Souvenirs familiers*).

The second piece of news was less exciting. The following notice had been stuck on the walls of the town: "At its meeting of 4 instant, the Management Committee of the Collège decided that the work of repair and cleaning made necessary by the extended presence of wounded was to begin immediately. Thanks to the zeal and active supervision of the commission appointed to direct it, this work is well under way, and will be completed shortly. The return of the boarders and the regular organization of lessons will take place on Wednesday April 12"[2]

It could be said that this announcement came at an odd moment. As if there were still such things as prisons and schools! What was the point of studying literature and philosophy when the future was being created on the Paris barricades!

Fortunately the pupils of the Collège still had three weeks' liberty left. Delahaye announced that the classes in the theater had been suspended until the reopening of the Collège itself. Mme Rimbaud loosened her grip: "You'll be going back to school on April 12, won't you?"

"We'll see when we get there."

Delahaye and Rimbaud had been in the habit of meeting in a small wood near Romery and Le Theux.[3] There, among the fir trees, the robinias, or false acacias, they had discovered an abandoned quarry shaft, about ten or twelve feet deep, lined with ferns and moss, a veritable haven of peace. Then, one day, in the hollow of a rock, Rimbaud found a cave in the hillside.

"This will be my retreat," he said, "just bring me a piece of bread every day. I won't need anything else."

Meanwhile, they talked through the afternoons, excitedly devouring Rabelais, Rousseau, Helvétius. They lived immured in their world of ideas, far from the crass stupidity of the "Carolopolitans" and Mme Rimbaud's nagging. How marvelous their retreat was! In the grass one found tiny calcarious balls which were in fact the petrified excrement of owls and which, when broken open, shone with the tiny remains of bones and fragments of insects.

But the fateful date of April 12 was approaching. Mme Rimbaud let her son know that, if he persisted in refusing any work, she would no longer feed him. He could not see himself as a clerk or a pen-pusher in a solicitor's office. So, once more, they reached an impasse.

However, by what miracle we do not know, Jacoby had been able to revive *Le Progrès des Ardennes*. With Deverrière's help, Rimbaud started work, on April 12, in the newspaper offices—the only possible job that could have suited him in the two towns. His work amounted to going through the mail, filing papers, writing short news items. It was not a great deal, but since it was paid, he was able for a time to shut up his mother's "shady mouth." Furthermore, he expected to improve his position, to become editor, and perhaps one day to replace old Jacoby.

It was natural that, to avenge his failure at the *Journal de Charleroi*, his first action was to inform his old friend Billuart of his promotion. Indeed, in a letter from the Abbé Gillet, the philosophy teacher, to Izambard, one reads: "Of the day boys, only Rimbaud is missing—he is greatly disposed to being a newspaper editor, from what Billuart tells me."[4] He was dearly missed, for the other pupils would like to have had him in discussion with the Abbé Gillet, who was not always in agreement with the principal; what jousts, what assaults they were missing!

But disaster was not far off! On April 17, Rimbaud had to tell Paul Demény that Jacoby's journal had just been suspended on the orders of the occupying authorities.

His letter to the poet from Douai is somewhat cold; it opens on a note of bitterness: "As for what I asked you, was I stupid! Knowing nothing of what has to be known, determined to do nothing of what has to be done, I am condemned, forever. Long live today! Long live tomorrow!" Such a reaction seems to show that Demény had replied evasively to a precise question from Rimbaud: what does one have to do to be a journalist? Demény no doubt replied that he must not expect too much, that it takes experience, references, connections. Perhaps Demény's reply also was equally negative concerning the Douai manuscripts: if Rimbaud says nothing about them, it is because the question is already settled. He refers only to his last stay in Paris and to the titles of books that he saw in the bookshop windows. The letter ends in total indifference: "And may Belgian literature carry us off under its arm—au revoir."

Unemployed once again, Rimbaud's thoughts returned to the cave at Romery. But the desire to participate in the Great Cause then rising on the reddening horizon of Paris had not left him. Living as a hermit came to seem more and more an act of cowardice. His place was on the battlements of Paris, or on the barricades, where the fate of liberty was being played out.

The *Fédérés* were recruiting troops at thirty sous a day—a minimum

wage. After all, being a soldier of the revolution was as good as being a journalist! He set off on April 18, on foot, of course.

Delahaye has recounted how he shortened his journey. It is what we
would now call hitching. He would hail a cart, ask to be taken to the nearest
town, and pay for his journey by recounting more or less imaginary episodes
based on the inexhaustible wealth of subjects provided by contemporary
events.

Getting to Paris was a dangerous undertaking at that time: the capital
was under strict surveillance by government troops, and the Prussians were
everywhere. With each step one took one ran the risk of stumbling on some
patrol, or being arrested as a suspect. As he crossed the forest of Villets-
Cotterêtes at night, he had quite a shock: suddenly horses were galloping
furiously towards him. He had to stand flat against a tree: apparently, they
were German cavalry amusing themselves by charging into the darkness.[5]

We presume that he reached the gates of Paris on April 23 or 25. At the
post he declared proudly that he had come from the Ardennes on foot. He
was congratulated, and, as he was without money, a cap was passed round
among the soldiers; the collection amounted to 21 francs and 13 sous. To
show what a good fellow he was, he bought drinks all round.

He was sent off to the Babylone barracks, a former guards barracks. He
was then attached to a group of *francs-tireurs* volunteers, probably the
"*francs-tireurs de Paris.*"[6]

At that time the government in Versailles was preparing to make a final
attack, but nothing had happened yet. Each side was spying on the other. A
few sporadic engagements had taken place near Vanves or Issy, while a truce
spared Neuilly. Paris bristled with barricades, and was plastered with white
posters issuing brief orders. The only recent demonstration had been that of
the freemasons on the Champs-Elysées. But this apparent calm failed to conceal a profound apprehension. The atmosphere was not unlike that of Mézières under the siege of 1870. Civilians who became inflexible as soon as
they put on military boots and belt, sergeants who couldn't tell the difference
between authority and brutality, groups of soldiers wandering about without
orders, everywhere a complete breakdown in discipline—all this presaged an
imminent catastrophe.

Terrifying disorder reigned in the barracks: soldiers from various regiments that had been dissolved for fraternizing with the people, national
guards, sailors, zouaves—all were thrown together pell-mell. There was no

question of clothing them, arming them, or even providing them with blankets.

So, one fine morning, Rimbaud woke up in a room stinking with tobacco smoke and wine, surrounded by rough fellows, all sporting tatoos, like so many volunteers for death.

There was nothing to do but await orders. Since no one forbade them to go out, we may presume that our poet did not refrain from doing so. Later, he told Delahaye how he went for long walks with a former member of the 88th regiment of the line (now dissolved), a highly intelligent, dreamy, idealistic young man. This friend, he believed, must have been shot later, like all those who were caught and recognized. It is possible that Rimbaud, wandering about here and there, may also have met Jean-Louis Forain—unless it was the second time that he had seen him, having perhaps met him first in André Gill's studio, where he was a frequent visitor at the time. Berrichon says that he met him by chance,[7] and Fernand Gregh confirms this in his memoirs (*L'Age d'or*): "He [Forain] told me about his youth when he was known as Gavroche.[8] He had 'knocked around' during the Commune with Rimbaud—there was also a priest, whose name I can't remember, who was very interested in Rimbaud."

On the subject of these outings, perhaps we should mention the incredible information provided by Delahaye concerning once again the girl from Villets-Cotterêts mentioned earlier. It appears that Rimbaud was astonished to see her in the crowd, and imagined that she had come to Paris to join him. But she seems to have vanished under his very eyes, and he never saw her again. This "meeting" has no doubt as little basis in fact as the previous one in February-March, and need not detain us here.

But Rimbaud did not spend all his time tramping the streets—he also worked. It was during this time in Paris that he wrote his *Chant de guerre parisien*, and his *Constitution communiste*. The essay has not been found, but Delahaye was to read it in July. It is a utopian dream: money and central government are to be abolished, the communes are to be independent, and federated under the control of elected leaders with limited, temporary powers, executive power is to be based on the referendum.

Rimbaud's contact with the undisciplined soldiery was soon to go sour; it was more than he could bear. So deep was his disgust that it destroyed all his enthusiasm for the revolution. The poem that refers to this disgust was given three successive titles: *Le cœur supplicié*, *Le cœur du pitre*, and *Le cœur volé*. Yes, it was certainly that, torture, foolery, and theft: he had been hurt, he had been made fun of, his heart had been stolen.

> *Mon triste cœur bave à la poupe,*
> *Mon cœur est plein de caporal:*
> *Ils y lancent des jets de soupe,*
> *Mon triste cœur bave à la poupe:*
> *Sous les quolibets de la troupe*
> *Qui pousse un rire général,*
> *Mon triste cœur bave à la poupe,*
> *Mon cœur est plein de caporal!*

> [*My sad heart slobbers at the poop,*
> *My heart covered with tobacco-spit:*
> *They spew streams of soup at it,*
> *My sad heart drools at the poop:*
> *Under the jeering of the soldiers*
> *Who break out laughing*
> *My sad heart drools at the poop,*
> *My heart covered with tobacco-spit!*][9]

Colonel Godchot, noting certain evocative words (*"poupe,"* *"ithyphallique"*), has suggested that some incident of a sexual order (attack? attempted rape?) was the key to this chiaroscuro poem.[10] Without going as far as that, the disgust and disillusion of these lines might also be explained by the sordid materialism of his fellows in the Babylone garrison: their horizons were limited to a world of soup, tobacco, drink, and obscenity. How could such brutes be made to understand the greatness of the cause that they were defending? In any case there can be no doubt that real experience lay behind the poem: clearly there was a wound, and a deep one. Izambard implies that it was all fantasy, and that Rimbaud never came to Paris under the Commune. In that case, how could the Commune have come into his poetry? The great social drama had brought the dregs to the surface. The Versaillais claimed that it was alcohol that killed off the Commune. There must be something in that, for the *fédérés* themselves were constantly telling their troops to behave correctly.

The truth is that Rimbaud, a son of the bourgeoisie, was in love with the revolution, but not with revolutionaries "with dirty hands."

His brief stay in the barracks inspired in him a terror and abhorrence of military service that was to remain with him till the end. If he did end up as a soldier in Africa, it was because his wanderlust and love of adventure were stronger in him than anything else.

It was all over. A page in his life had been turned. His only wish now was to go back to Charleville: they could carry on with the revolution without him.

Again it took a good deal of cunning to avoid the ambushes in the Parisian suburbs, which were constantly being combed by patrols of cavalry looking for suspects. At Villers-Coterêts (decidedly a fateful locality!), he had one small adventure that he recounted to Delahaye with a smile. He had stumbled upon an abandoned hut, and decided to spend the night there. Unfortunately, it happened to be the love nest of a young couple. The young man turned Rimbaud out, and, as he left, the girl said to him with a kindly smile: "Go to the woman next door, my lad. She's called Mme Lévêque. She's a charitable old body, and would be only too pleased to take you in."

As soon as the key was turned, Rimbaud heard stifled laughter and a mocking voice behind the door: "Mme Lévêque, uh? Don't forget. It's only a few steps away!"

That night he had to be content with a ditch to sleep in.

Like every hardened vagabond, he knew the tricks of the trade; thus, whenever he came to a village, he presented himself to the mayor, passing himself off as a demobilized soldier on his way home. This provided him with a travel warrant, a barn to sleep in, and, with a little luck, a meal at some farmhouse.

He reached Charleville in early May. When he saw Delahaye again— he had been away on his return—he did not boast of imaginary exploits. He told the truth. On May 8 the bloody repression of the Commune by the Versaillais troops began: the news aroused in him a final burst of passion. On May 13, he wrote to Izambard: "I will be a worker: this idea holds me back when mad anger drives me toward the battle of Paris—where so many workers are dying as I write to you!"

Clearly, the poetic fever had driven out from him the political fever, as we shall soon see.

Before we leave the question of the Commune, it should be said that his brief incursion into Paris at that time does not merit the defamatory label of *"Rimbaud-le-communard,"* which he was made to bear for the rest of his life. About 1887–88, at Obok, people heard him say that he had been in prison in Paris with the *Communards*[11] (he made no distinction between barracks and prison). In 1891 Dr. Baudoin heard an inhabitant of Charleville say as Rimbaud walked by: "There's old Cuif's grandson, the well-known ragamuffin and *Communard*, a good-for-nothing who painted the town red!"[12]

Rimbaud's "participation" in the Commune was to become a part of his legend. It was not strictly true, but if intentions are taken for facts, the legend is truer than reality.

At the emotional level, Rimbaud had hardly developed from the time when he peopled his poems with somewhat mischievous imaginary "beloveds." He had done little more than flirt with the "forward girls" of the Square de la Gare, and the buxom serving wenches of Belgian taverns. His eroticism was nourished on imagination.

In the spring of 1871, "stripping his heart bare," he tried his hand at the poem in prose, in the manner of Baudelaire. The result was two rather melancholy texts, in which a serving girl and a society woman make a brief appearance, and their disappearance brings on a flood of tears in the poet. In an introductory Notice, Rimbaud explains what he is doing thus: "Not having loved women—although passionate!—his soul and his heart and all his strength were trained in strange, sad errors. From the following dreams—his loves!—which came to him in his bed or in the street, and from their continuation and their ending, pleasing religious considerations may perhaps be derived. Remember the continuous sleep of the legendary Mohammedans— brave nonetheless and circumcised!"[13]

Such imaginary loves soon came to seem rather thin nourishment. Soon after his return from Paris, he summoned up the courage to approach a girl of more or less his own age and handed her a note (in verse?), begging her to meet him in the Square de la Gare. According to Delahaye (who, he says, received a letter, while in the Eure, from Rimbaud describing this adventure), the Chosen One had eyes "beyond praise," and looked for all the world like Psyche. She arrived at the Square, curious and amused, but chaperoned by her maid! Rimbaud, blushing madly, his heart beating violently, was incapable of saying two words to her. He took to his heels at once, to the great amusement of the girl and her maid. He had been terrified out of his wits.[14]

According to Berrichon, Mme Rimbaud received a letter from an industrialist whom she did not know—the girl's father—suggesting that she keep a tighter control over her son.[15]

Who was the heroine of this abortive idyll? One researcher, M. Alain Goldie, has suggested that she was a certain Marie Henriette, known as Maria

Hubert, born, like Rimbaud, in 1854, who, if her photograph is to be believed, does bear a striking resemblance to the Psyche in Baron Gérard's painting *L'Amour et Psyché*.[16] This is not impossible, but Louis Pierquin, who says that he suspected who the young lady was, was not thinking of her: indeed he says quite specifically that she was still alive in 1924 (whereas Maria Hubert died in 1875). Furthermore, her father, who died in 1864, could not have been the author of the letter received by Mme Rimbaud.

Anyway, first one door, politics, and now another, love of women, had slammed in his face. The sluice gates of his hate were now open.

To avenge himself for the affront to which he had been subjected, he turned, in an acidulous poem, *Mes petites amoureuses*, to furiously trampling underfoot his fantasies of the night before:

> *O mes petites amoureuses,*
>   *Que je vous hais!*
>
>   . . . . .
> *Et c'est pourtant pour ces éclanches*
>   *Que j'ai rimé!*
> *Je voudrais vous casser les hanches*
>   *D'avoir aimé!*
>
> [*O my little lovers,*
>   *How I hate you!*
>
>   . . . . .
> *And yet it is for these mutton shoulders*
>   *That I have made rhymes!*
> *I would like to break your hips*
>   *For having loved!*][17]

Soon afterwards, in a less violent but more desperate poem, *Les sœurs de charité*, he complained that the young man who desired a "sister of charity" will never find her in woman, who is too weak and too alien ("But O Woman, heap of entrails, sweet pity"). Then, condemned to solitude, all that is left to console him is the "green Muse" (absinthe),[18] and "ardent Justice," until the arrival of his true sister of charity, mysterious death.

Indeed, that was to be the shape of his destiny, for it was only on his deathbed that he was to meet his sister of charity, his own sister, the gentle Isabelle, who had come to help him die.

He had become impatient and irritable with everything. Izambard was soon to realize this. In early February, while awaiting transfer to a new job, Izambard was sent a tempting offer from his brother, who was living in St. Petersburg: the post of tutor in the family of a Russian prince. He hesitated for some time, feeling that his proud character would ill fit him for servitude, however gilded—and, in the end, he turned down the offer. Deverrière and Rimbaud were kept informed of the affair. In April, a temporary vacancy occurred in the Lycée at Douai (a *classe de seconde*), so he returned to teaching.

Then Rimbaud, disappointed in his teacher (how could he refuse a trip to Russia, and a life of luxury!), no longer confided in him and, since he was unable to feel anything but extreme emotions, moved from wild gratitude to ironic contempt.

They had not yet broken off relations, but there was a serious cooling, with some acidulous touches. Thus, because Izambard had not liked his *Petites amoureuses*, Rimbaud told him in a letter that has not survived, that he had shown them to him *on purpose* in order to catch him out. And he fell for it![19]

There were other subjects of disagreement between them: when Rimbaud told him of his decision to leave school and to launch himself as a poet, his reaction was condemned as the worst kind of bourgeois conformism. His sermons were as good as those of his mother: you'd do better to pass your *bachot* first. If you can't bear family life, get a job as a *surveillant*, a grocer's boy, or a cleaner, but don't abandon your studies.

The letter from his former pupil dated May 13, 1871, is certainly the most important that he ever wrote to him. In it he reveals himself for the first time.

He launches an attack at once:

> *Cher Monsieur!*
> *You are a teacher again. You have told me we owe a duty to Society. You belong to the teaching body: you move along in the right track. I also follow the principle: cynically I am having myself kept. I dig up old imbeciles from school: I serve them with whatever I can invent that is stupid, filthy, mean in acts and words. They pay me in beer and liquor. . . . My duty is to Society, that is true—and I am right.—You too are right, for now. In reality, all you see in your principle is sub-*

jective poetry: your obstinancy in reaching the university
trough—excuse me—proves this. But you will always end up
a self-satisfied man who has done nothing because he wanted
to do nothing.

After these pleasantries, he informs him of his decision: "Work now?—
never, never, I am on strike."
And then the great secret:

> *Now, I am degrading myself as much as possible. Why? I*
> *want to be a poet, and I am working to make myself a seer:*
> *you will not understand this, and I don't know how to explain*
> *it to you. It is a question of reaching the unknown by the de-*
> *rangement of all the senses. The sufferings are enormous, but*
> *one has to be strong, one has to be born a poet, and I know I*
> *am a poet. This is not at all my fault. It is wrong to say: I*
> *think. One ought to say: people think me. Pardon the pun*
> [penser, *"to think"*; panser, *"to groom"*].
> *I is someone else. It is too bad for the wood that finds*
> *itself a violin and scorn for the heedless who argue over what*
> *they are totally ignorant of!*
> *You are not a teacher for me. I give you this: is it satire,*
> *as you would say? Is it poetry? It is a fantasy always.—But I*
> *beg you, do not underline it with your pencil or too much*
> *with your thought:*
> THE TORTURED HEART
> *My sad heart drools at the stern . . .*
> . . . .
> *This means nothing.*
> *Answer me care of M. Deverrière, for A.R.*
> *Warm greetings, ARTH. RIMBAUD*[20]

Believing the poem to be a gratuitous fantasy, Izambard maintains that
Rimbaud's poem recounted the adventures of a cabin boy sickened by the
orgy that had taken place on board during the ceremonies that traditionally
marked the "crossing of the line."
The great turning point had been made. Another Rimbaud had just
been born—one so different from the old one that he was unrecognizable.

Delahaye recounted to the poet's first biographers: "In fact, about that time, I began to be struck by certain oddities; several times I had seen Rimbaud in the streets of Charleville, walking straight ahead, with a mechanical step, his body proudly erect, head held high, cheeks flushed, his eyes staring into the distance."[21]

It was certainly a case of visionary possession. His prolonged silences, his automatonlike movements, his fixed gaze, his feverish complexion, everything seemed to indicate that he was no longer there, that someone else had taken his place.

"When he was at home," Paterne Berrichon adds, "we found him too gloomy, too irascible; his movements were jerky, his manners crude. His mother was desperate about him: at one point, he seemed so strange that she thought he was mad."[22]

Since poor Izambard was incapable of understanding anything, Rimbaud had no alternative—hopeless as the task must have seemed—but to expound the details of his new doctrine to Paul Demény. This he did on May 15, 1871—and this has given us the most extraordinary text by the young seer, at once a literature lesson and a revolutionary manifesto. The thesis may be summed up in the form of four propositions:

—Fate has made me a poet
—To be a poet is to be a seer
—To be a seer one must derange all one's senses and make oneself hideous
—Until now, no poet has attempted the experience of complete vision

Fate is the fulfillment of the mysterious oracle of Phoebus-Apollo: "TU VATES ERIS" ("YOU WILL BE A POET"). To be a poet is to awake inside someone else's skin ("I is someone else.") It is to become, unknown to oneself, an instrument: the wood that finds itself a violin has no say in this metamorphosis. It is not a question of regretting or rejoicing, but simply of stating.

Seer. The word *seer* was very widespread in the late nineteenth century: Mallarmé said of Gautier that he was a seer, Gautier said the same of Baudelaire, Nerval said it of himself. But Rimbaud took the word in its biblical sense: he who sees beyond the things of God. The seer dives into the depths and brings back from the unknown the new (Baudelaire—*Le Voyage*). Beauty, ugliness, art, morality, filth, ignominy, are terms devoid of meaning. Whatever comes from *over there* is sacred!

The Conditions. The ascesis of the seer is "the rational derangement of all the senses," voluntary self-soiling. The seer "exhausts all poisons in himself, and keeps only their quintessences." He must become "the great patient, the great criminal, the one accursed—and the supreme Scholar!—Because he reaches the *unknown!*" He can then say, like Victor Hugo's deep-sea diver: "I have experienced, I have seen. I am a diver, and I bring back the pearl, the truth" (*L'Homme qui rit*).

No one has yet done it. Poetry up to Casimir Delavigne, including Racine, has been nothing but rhymed prose, again, "degradation and glory of countless idiotic generations." The poets of the past may be categorized as innocent, dead or fools. No one has had the courage to become a seer. Baudelaire nearly became one, but he lived in too artistic a milieu; Paul Verlaine ("a true poet"), and Albert Mérat are the only two seers in the Parnassian school.

Rimbaud has decided to be the first complete seer. He will clear the ground, he will lead "other horrible workers," men and women, he will be their standard bearer. His pride did not take long to catch up with his stubbornness.

He advanced with all the determination of the martyr into the circle of fire that was to devour him. The way that he had chosen, in all lucidity, was a true "way of the cross," as Verlaine was later to say—but he was ready to endure torture, every kind of torture, which he knew to be necessary and inevitable.

To begin with, Izambard had to be liquidated. We do not have the text of Izambard's reply to Rimbaud's letter of May 13. "I was content," the teacher admits, "to regard as youthful folly the filth that he revealed to me of his new life in Charleville." He regarded the *Cœur supplicié* as a sickening piece of work. "I wouldn't say you are mad—that would merely put you in your seventh heaven—but if you think you've done something extraordinary, I can only prove to you that on the contrary being absurd is within the reach of everybody." And Izambard enclosed in his letter a piece of largely nonsensical verse. "Here is the recipe," he added. "You put together some incoherent and heteroclite thoughts, from which is born a small monstrous fetus, which you then put into a glass jar. . . . And be careful, with your theory of the seer, that you don't end up in the jar yourself, a monster in the museum."[23]

Izambard claims that Rimbaud would have accepted this lecture with a smile, but Berrichon is surely closer to the truth when he says that the young seer responded to it with a volley of insults. Moreover, he tells us, things did not stop there: apparently Izambard sent the inflammatory letter to Mme Rimbaud asking her to be the judge of it, and suggesting that she take every precaution in view of her son's mental state. When his mother demanded an explanation of the letter, it seems that Arthur replied with two specific epithets, which Berrichon leaves his reader to imagine.[24] Isabelle remembered this memorable scene. Mme Méléra, who knew her well, writes: "Arthur's two younger sisters did not breathe a word about it in front of their mother, but they certainly discussed this incident between themselves, and never forgot it."[25]

As for Paul Demény, he did not reply to the seer's long letter, since, as we shall soon see, Rimbaud sent him on June 10, 1871, three new poems, adding: "Please say something, by way of reply, to this and my earlier letter." I shall explain later why Demény could not reply.

So all that remained to Rimbaud was to continue, ax in hand, with his work of demolition.

One can observe at this period a recrudescence of his antireligious passion. It is certain that his contacts with Charles Bretagne had something to do with this: indeed Rimbaud was a frequent visitor at his home and there, before a few friends, enjoyed great success, reading his recent, violent works, such as *Accroupissements*, or *Les Primières Communions*, a poem inspired by Isabelle's first communion, which took place on May 14, 1871. There is a good deal of sarcastic abuse thrown at the priest who was preparing the children for the ceremony: "Un noir grotesque dont fermentent les souliers" [A grotesque priest whose shoes stink]; at the girls: "contentes / De s'entendre appeler garces par les garçons" [happy / To hear themselves called sluts by the boys] with their "languor," and their "filthy compassion"; and, last, at Christ: "Christ! O Christ, éternel voleur des énergies" [Christ! O Christ, eternal thief of energy].[26]

His hate-filled mockery really does make him look like an "adolescent Satan," to use Verlaine's term.

On walls or on public benches, he would write in chalk: "Death to God!" The very sight of a priest was enough to bring a torrent of insults to his lips. He even went so far as to throw lice at them which he had especially cultivated for this purpose in his hair.[27]

Other victims of his corrosive fury were Ernest Delahaye's teachers. He wrote an idiotic letter to Henri Perrin, Izambard's successor, supposedly from Ernest's uncle, who lived at Remilly-les-Pothées. The principal, Desdouets, recognized the authorship of the letter at once by the handwriting. There was pandemonium in class when the letter was read out.

This Perrin was a "red" (militant radical), the author of a political pamphlet (*Le Fouet*, The Whip), who had caused some scandal at Nancy, where he had previously been living. In fact he was to leave the Collège after the Easter break to take up a post as editor—with Deverrière—on the new daily, *Le Nord-Est*, the first number of which bears the date July 1, 1871: a new and serious opportunity for Rimbaud to become a journalist! So, through the school janitor, Rimbaud sent Perrin a few light-hearted verses, of a somewhat caustically humorous vain for publication in the new paper. One of them depicted the panic of the grocers before the advance of the "reds"; another was a monologue by a patriotic army veteran who swears to oppose the new organ.

Perrin found these caricatures to be in bad taste, and forbade the janitor in the future to accept any of the effusions of "the young man with long hair."

Rimbaud also tried to play a few tricks on Perrin's successor, Edouard Chanal, but we do not know what his reactions were. In any case, his name, like that of his predecessor was doomed to be execrated by future generations. "Merde à Perrin" became the final ritual phrase of Rimbaud's letters—and Verlaine found it amusing enough to imitate him.[28]

Another inevitable victim, another butt, was the librarian of Charleville, Jean-Baptiste Hubert, a former "regent of logic and rhetoric" at the Collège de Charleville, the author of worthy works on the history of the Ardennes.

The library was housed in the former monastery next door to the Collège, and Rimbaud spent a great deal of time there. Almost every day, while waiting for the library to open, he would walk up and down in front of his school, delighted at scandalizing old Desdouets, smoking his pipe with the bowl upside down, his hair unacceptably long, making provocative faces. Old Hubert had little patience with young ragamuffins who entered his temple and caused trouble. Louis Pierquin, as a pupil in the *classe de seconde*, was once thrown out when he had the temerity to ask for La Fontaine's *Contes*. Ever since the old grumbler had been known as "Saint Hubert *cul*." One imagines that he did not have a very high opinion of Rimbaud: he was always there, poking around in the catalogues and reference books, never satisfied, constantly asking for new books—and they were always the most inaccessible ones, lying on the top shelves under a thick layer of dust, treatises on sorcery, the occult sciences[29], or novels, tales, or licentious verse (Restif de la Bretonne, *Parnasse satyrique*, etc.). The regular visitors to the library finally lost patience with this turbulent, insatiable boy, and one day old Hubert was forced to eject him: if he was so thirsty for knowledge, why didn't he go next door, to the Collège, and study the authors of his own age, Homer, Cicero, Zenophon, Horace, and leave serious researchers in peace.

Those "men who sit" could not have known that the young intruder would put them in the pillory in a poem written to their glory, showing them

> Noirs de loupes, grêlés, les yeux cernés de bagues
> Vertes, leurs doigts boulus crispés a leurs fémurs,

> [Black with wens, pock-marked, their eyes circled with green
> Rings, their swollen fingers clenched on their thighbones],

making "one tress with their seats," and "trembling with the painful tremble of the toad" (June 1871).[30]

Thus turned out of doors, Rimbaud, with Delahaye still at his side—he would get him to miss certain classes—resumed his walks in the countryside. It was there that he would now have to pour out his sarcasm and black humor.

One day, as they were walking past the stud farms at Mézières, which had been turned into a hospital camp, they caught sight behind the barbed wire of some pitiful cripples in greatcoats, some with legs missing, dragging themselves from one wooden shed to another. It was an image of a war that had been lost, of the low tide when the sea of patriotic enthusiasm has receded. Delahaye had to give vent to his feelings of disgust: "A conquered country is as noble as a victorious one. Why does the public, which showered those soldiers with flowers, wine and sweet words, now turn its back on them in their misfortune?"

The "heartless" Rimbaud replied that it was quite normal: "Those fellows were simply the instruments of the defunct regime. As long as they were thought to be the stronger, they were feted. Today they wear cotton caps and are half dead, what do you expect to be done with them."

Another day, they attended a German military parade on the Place de la Préfecture. Delahaye admired the impeccable turn out and discipline of the troops. "Ah!" he sighed, "those people are certainly superior to us!"

Rimbaud turned on him angrily: "They are certainly inferior to us! They'll die from their victory! They'll swallow all the poisons of glory, force an iron discipline on themselves, to hold ranks, hold on to their prey, and increase their prestige. Then, in the end, they'll be crushed by some coalition, as Napoleon was punished for ruining the hopes born in the great Revolution! Bismarck is as stupid as he was: by cultivating the vanity of his people, he is driving it to suicide!"

The "pointed helmets" goose-stepped by: "No, look at those brutes, drunk with victory, and tell me if we aren't better than they!"[31]

However the ills of the time had not dampened their taste for childish pranks. One day they were standing outside the church of Mézières, watching the workmen repairing the tower. Suddenly they noticed that a low side door, usually kept closed, was open. Without hesitation, they went in and clambered up the narrow staircase. At the top, while Delahaye stroked the enormous bells, and tried to make out their Latin inscriptions engraved in the bronze, Rimbaud noticed in the corner of the loft an object, surrealistically, shall we say, unexpected in that place, a superb white china chamberpot, brought there no doubt for the use of those on guard during the hostilities. Two minutes later the object, decreasing in apparent size, was to smash to the ground, after describing a graceful parabola through the air. Much to their delight, a passerby stopped, picked up a fragment of china, examined it carefully, and looked up with some perplexity to the sky.

"What if it's Desdouets!" they both exclaimed together.

In order to exorcise an evil fate, Rimbaud scribbled on the ledge of the louver window the following eight lines, which Delahaye managed to memorize:

> *Oh! si les cloches sont de bronze,*
> *Nos coeurs sont pleins de désespoir!*
> *En juin mil huit cent soixante et onze,*
> *Trucidés par un être noir,*
> *Nous, Jean Baudry, nous Jean Balouche*
> *Ayant accompli nos souhaits,*
> *Mourûmes en ce clocher louche*
> *En abominant Desdouets!*

> [*Oh! Though the bells are of bronze*
> *Our hearts are filled with despair!*
> *In June one thousand eight hundred and seventy-one,*
> *Slaughtered by a black being,*
> *We, Jean Baudry and Jean Balouche*
> *Our wishes fulfilled,*

Died in this shady tower
Abominating Desdouets.][32]

However, Rimbaud suffered from the frustration of not having been able to extend his reading, as a result of his mother and old Hubert—she because she refused to give him any money, he by chasing him from his temple.

As it happened, a book had just appeared that interested him enormously: it was *Les Rébellions et Apaisements* by Jean Aicard, a young poet of twenty-three who was beginning to make a name for himself. How could he get hold of a copy? Or, to be more precise, how could he get a copy without paying for it? Well, after all, all poets are brothers, are they not? A poem would serve as currency. So, through the publisher Lemerre, Rimbaud sent Aicard his poem *Les Effarés*, with the following laconic note:

June 1871—Arthur Rimbaud
5 bis Quai de la Madeleine, Charleville, Ardennes.
One copy, Rébellions, *if the author would be so kind.*
                                                    A. R.[33]

We do not know whether Jean Aicard agreed to the swap. We do know that Rimbaud continued his dealings with the booksellers of Charleville. Sometimes he managed to borrow a volume secretly, then take it back after reading it. But since the restoration proved as dangerous as the borrowing, he sometimes omitted that stage of the dealing, fear of punishment not always being the beginning of wisdom.[34]

With sublime trust in the future, he also bought books on credit. As a result, one day, his mother was sent an injunction to pay the sum of 35 francs, 25 centimes, incurred by her son.

"Very well, then, you'll go to prison," was Mme Rimbaud's reaction.

After thinking about the problem, he had a brilliant idea. It will be remembered that in July the previous year he had left for safe keeping some of his books in Izambard's rooms to avoid his mother's prying eyes. Among them were Banville's *Florise* and *Les Exilés*, Louis Veuillot's *Les Couleuvres*, Armand Renaud's *Les Nuits persanes*, Paul Demeny's *Les Glaneuses*, and a few other titles. Very well, he would go and ask for those books back from Izambard, and then, of course, sell them to pay off his debts. That was the purpose of his last letter—dated July 12, 1871—to his former teacher, who then occupied the chair of rhetoric at the Collège de Cherbourg.

A short opening sentence wipes out the past: "The Boyars, that was ages ago, don't hold it against me." Another sets out his present predicament: "I'm terribly bored, and I really can't put down anything on paper." Not a word about seers and their visions. He soon comes to the point: "I've landed myself with a huge debt, and I haven't a sou in my pocket." He is successfully negotiating the sale of the books that he is asking back, and reveals a glibness worthy of a market–stall keeper: "Do you really want *Les Glaneuses?* . . . I could demonstrate to my contact that the buying of such a collection would bring him enormous profit. I would dangle the unseen titles before his eyes. I'm getting quite a dab hand at this sort of dealing, I assure you."

Coming to practicalities, Rimbaud asks for the parcel of books to be sent to M. Deverrière—he has been told to expect them. "I would reimburse you the cost of the freight, and I'd be overflowing with gratitude!"

Rimbaud adds as a postscript: "I have seen, in a letter from you to M. Deverrière, that you were concerned about your chest of books. He'll send them to you as soon as he has your instructions."

So Izambard's books—and among them those that Rimbaud was asking for—were still at Charleville! That being the case, Rimbaud would probably have to wait a long time![35] And, without delaying still further, Izambard, or so he says, sent Deverrière, on Rimbaud's behalf, the 35 francs 25 centimes that he so desperately needed.

That was the last contact that Rimbaud had with his former teacher.

Izambard was now out of the way, but there were other mandarins that deserved to be punished. To begin with, the amiable Théodore de Banville, that demigod of Parnassus, whose elegent and facile verses had once so captivated him. What exactly was this versifyer? A florist? A salon florist, for his poems were so filled with cut flowers that they resembled for all the world a bride's bouquet: so he would teach M. Théodore de Banville "What is said to the poet concerning flowers": "Lilies, clysters of ecstasy," "Lilacs—O seesaws!" "Violets, / Sugary spit of black nymphs."

Toujours les végétaux Français,
Hargneux, phtisiques, ridicules,
Où le ventre des chiens bassets
Navigue en paix, aux crépuscules;

Toujours, après d'affreux dessins
De Lotus bleus ou d'Hélianthes,

Estampes roses, sujets saints
Pour de jeunes communiantes!

[*Always the French vegetables,*
Cross, phthisical, ridiculous,
Where the bellies of basset dogs
Navigate peacefully in the twilight;

Always, after frightful drawings
Of blue Lotuses or Sunflowers,
Rose prints, holy subjects
For young girls making their communion!]

These "droolings from shepherds' pipes" are to be vomited out:

—Tas d'œufs frits dans de vieux chapeaux,
Lys, Açokas, Lilas et Roses!

[*—Pile of fried eggs in old hats,*
Lilies, Asokas, Lilacs and Roses!]

The poet should show true flowers; not the decorous contents of suburban gardens, but exotic, intoxicating, monstrous flora. Better still, he should give up the shoddy world of flowers altogether:

—En somme, une Fleur, Romarin
Ou Lys, vive ou morte, vaut-elle
Un excrément d'oiseau marin?
Vaut-elle un seul pleur de chandelle?

[*—In short, is a Flower, Rosemary*
Or Lily, alive or dead, worth
The excrement of a sea-bird?
Is it worth one single tear of a candle?]

To conclude, if the poet must include vegetables in his verse, let them at least be useful, modern ones:

Surtout, rime une version
Sur le mal des pommes de terre!

[*Above all, put in rhyme a tale*
On the potato blight!][36]

It should be noted that the insolence of this diatribe (the recipient is called a Juggler and Joker) is tempered by the fact that it is aimed not only at Banville but at all those poets like him: what he said to the poet is what is said to the poets.

Nevertheless, from beginning to end, the tone is caustic and unpleasant. The accompanying letter is in keeping with the poem:

> *Sir and cher Maître*
> *Do you remember receiving from the provinces, in June 1870, a hundred or a hundred and fifty mythological hexameters entitled* Credo in unam? *You were kind enough to answer!*
> *The same imbecile is sending you the above verses, signed Alcide Bava—I beg your pardon.*
> *I am eighteen.—I will always love the verses of Banville.*
> *Last year I was only seventeen!*
> *Have I made any progress?*
> *Alcide Bava*
> A. R.[37]

No more begging appeals, no more outstretched hands: "Have I made any progress?"

Banville must have been flabbergasted.

Having emitted his venom, Rimbaud had nothing more to do but to wander around Charleville and Mézières, in the company as always of Delahaye, now officially on holiday. They wandered the woods of La Culbute and La Havetière, declaiming till their throats were sore Villon, Baudelaire, Gautier, Dierx, Verlaine. Sometimes they held their recitals in an inn, Chez Chesnaux, where, for two sous, they were given a tankard of beer, which they shared as brothers, and two hours of quiet. Rimbaud, eyes aflame, was carrying the torch of revolution into the temple of the muses. Nothing could resist his destructive fury.

When they were short of tobacco, they organized a supply expedition to the Belgian frontier. Via La Grand'Ville and Pussemange, it took them a three hours' walk (nearly nine miles as the crow flies). An unexpected trial awaited them on their arrival: they were put into a sulphuring chamber, for, to protect Belgian livestock from the foot-and-mouth disease raging in the Ardennes, Leopold II's underlings disinfected all travelers crossing the border from France. So the two friends were shut up in a gas chamber, from which they emerged choking and weeping. But, once they had gone through this purgatory, they were free to enter the grocery shops full of all the good things that were so scarce at home, or the bright inns, where, for three sous, they could purchase a packet of tobacco. The return through the woods was dominated by the fear of seeing some customs officer pop up with a fierce–looking mastif on the leash: "No tobacco, no coffee, chicory, gunpowder?"

They innocently showed their packet of tobacco, some of which they had already consumed. The customsman went through the motions of frisking them. "All right. Off you go!"

Later, Rimbaud wrote a sonnet about the good customsmen, most of them old soldiers, who, in former times, made or unmade frontiers, and who now were reduced to frisking travelers.

Night had fallen when they finally reached home.

But each day that passed seemed to Rimbaud to tighten the net in which he was caught. It was already August, and the heavy threat of the new school year was already looming up. In October—it had been settled—his mother would send him to a boarding school, whether he liked it or not.

Where had all his anger got him? Twice Paris had disillusioned and rejected him. Izambard had made fun of him, pretending not to understand what he wrote; Demény had kept a disapproving silence. (In fact, Demény had been deeply shocked by Rimbaud's excesses, but, deep down, he thought that he was right.)[38]

He had no need of him now, except for practical, down-to-earth advice. This was the purpose of his letter of August 28 1871.

> *Sir,*
> *You make me begin my prayer over again: so be it. Here is the entire complaint. I am looking for calm words: but my knowledge of the art is not very profound. But here it is.*
> *Situation of the accused: For more than a year I gave up*

*ordinary living for what you know. Closed up without respite
in this unmentionable Ardennes country, seeing not a single
man, engaged in an infamous, inept, obstinate, mysterious
work, answering questions and coarse evil apostrophes by silence, appearing worthy in my extralegal position, I provoked
at the end frightful resolutions of a mother as inflexible as
seventy-three administrations with steel helmets.*

*She tried to force me to perpetual work, in Charleville
(Ardennes)! Get a job by such a day, she said, or get out—I
refused that life; without giving my reasons: it would have
been pitiful. Up until now I have been able to avoid these
terms. Her only constant hope is for me to take it into my
head to run away! Poor and inexperienced, I would end up in
a house of correction. And from then on, I would sink without
trace!*

*This is the disgusting handkerchief that has been stuffed
into my mouth. It is all quite simple.*

*I am not asking for anything, but I am asking for some
information. I want to be free when I work, but in Paris,
which I love. You see, I'm a pedestrian, nothing more than
that; I've come to the huge city without any material means:
but you said to me: the man who wants to be a worker at
fifteen sous a day comes here, does that, lives in this way. I've
come here, do that, live in this way, I beg you to tell me of
work not too absorbing, because thought demands long
stretches of time. Absolving the poet, this sort of material nonsense is agreeable. I am in Paris: I need a positive economy!
Don't you find this sincere? It seems so strange to me that I
have to argue with you about my seriousness! . . .*

*So, not knowing what you might write to me about, I cut
short all explanations and continue to trust your experience,
your kindness, which I have blessed, in receiving your letter,
and I engage you somewhat with these ideas . . . if you
will. . . .*

*Would you accept without too much dismay some samples
of my work?*

A. Rimbaud

One can gauge Rimbaud's instability: a month earlier, he had declared to Izambard that he would never work, never, and now he is asking for advice as to how to get work at fifteen sous a day. He also reveals his naiveté, since he seems to imagine that a paid job will leave him "long stretches of time" to write poetry. In any case, as far as his poetic career was concerned, it would seem that Rimbaud no longer expected any help from Demény.

His way was blocked, whichever direction he turned.

One day, when, as usual, Rimbaud was complaining to him that nobody understood him, Charles Bretagne deigned to open his mouth and remark that, in his last job at Fampoux, near Arras, he had been very friendly with the poet Paul Verlaine, who might . . .

"I'll send him some of my verses!" cried Rimbaud, leaping at the opportunity.

When he learned that Bretagne would be willing to add a few words of recommendation, he leaped out like a prisoner from his cell. He met up with Delahaye and took him off without further ado to the Café Duterme, and got him to copy out several of his poems.

"They're for Verlaine!"

And, while his friend transcribed in his best handwriting *Les Effarés, Accroupissements, Les Douaniers, Le Coeur volé, Les Assis,* he composed, on manilla paper, to cut down on the postal charges, a long letter in small handwriting, explaining his ideals, his anger, his enthusiasms, his distress, begging his correspondent, with much wheedling and insistence, not to reject the hand that was being so trustingly extended to him. The whole packet—letter, poems, Bretagne's note—was sent off to Verlaine, in care of the publisher Lemerre, 47, Passage Choiseul, Paris.

Verlaine has said of this letter, which has not survived, that it swarmed with bizarre information and curious turns of phrase. Its author's intention was to come to Paris to write poetry, because he could no longer work in the suffocating atmosphere of his provincial town. Furthermore, he had no money: his mother, who was extremely religious, only gave him ten centimes every Sunday to pay for his seat in church.

Two days later, Rimbaud, bubbling over with excitement, was already knocking at Bretagne's door. No, no news yet.

"Be patient for a time," said his phlegmatic friend.

But Rimbaud, quite beside himself, sent off a second, even more pressing letter to Verlaine, to which were added *Mes petites amoureuses, Paris se repeuple,* and *Les premières Communions.*

For some days, he lived on his nerves—or rather he had given up living. Paris was within reach, and he was free of servile labor for thirty sous a day. He was doubly lucky! But on his arrival he would have to present a poem of indisputable quality. Now, a fairly original theme had just been treated by Léon Dierx, a poem, *Le vieux solitaire*, published in *Le Parnasse contemporain*. The poem describes a sort of phantom ship adrift, haunting the oceans and terrifying ships' crews. Rimbaud turned himself into that "solitary old man," after decorating him with dazzling elements borrowed from Hugo's *Les Travailleurs de la Mer*, Jules Verne's *Vingt mille lieues sous les mers*, and also, no doubt, from the *Magasin pittoresque* of his childhood. But it was his own genius alone that was responsible for the magnificent lines of this poem, which unfolds like a symphony rising up from the green depths of the sea to the virginal immensities of the interstellar ether, falling back at the end into a void of bitter despair: truly an image of his own destiny. It would have been understandable if the victory that lay within his grasp had inspired him to write a sort of hymn, beginning in chiaroscuro, then rising, opening to the light, and bursting forth in an apotheosis of triumph; instead of that, he did the reverse. The old ship, drunk with fantastic visions, calls out in a great cry to the shipwreck in the void: "O que ma quille éclate! O que j'aille à la mer!" [O let my keel burst! O let me go into the sea!].[39]

Like a meteorite, it is consumed in the lightning of its own dizzy fall. This *Drunken Boat*, which was intended to be a prelude, already contains his swan song.

According to a well–established tradition, this masterpiece is associated with the old mill at Charleville, near which it was composed, and with the small arm of the Meuse that sweeps past the Quai de la Madeleine, where at the time there was a tannery, which colored the water of the river. "He loved to paddle on the damp, sandy water's edge," writes Delahaye, "among the weeds and bits of wrecked boats."

At last, on the fourth or fifth day, the response, so impatiently awaited, arrived from Verlaine.

The great poet apologized for not replying sooner to the two letters, which arrived one after the other, but he had just got back to Paris after a visit to the country, and he had not had time to prepare a proper welcome for the poet whose verses had won him over. He did not say that his friends—Léon Valade, Charles Cros, Philippe Burty, Albert Mérat, Ernest d'Hervilly,—had been variously repelled, disturbed, and enthusiastic.

One small phrase of Verlaine's is to be noted: "I have something like a whiff of your lycanthropy." It is important, for it throws light on the rest of this story. According to Georges Zayed, lycanthropy is "above all the revolt of a maladjusted person against a society that he regards as shameful, and on which he piles every anathema he can think of."[40] Littré, however, defines lycanthropy as "a sort of mental illness in which the patient imagines that he is being turned into a wolf." Verlaine's diagnosis is correct—but he does not conceal his sympathy for the lycanthropists, or young wolves, affected by this disease: he was Rimbaud's accomplice even before he met him.

Now, while the lycanthropist of the Ardennes was torn between impatience and joy, Jacoby was in the process of getting permission to revive his *Le Progrès des Ardennes*. Indeed, one researcher, Jules Mouquet, has discovered in *Le Nord-Est* of September 16, 1871, an article signed Jean Marcel, which bears all the marks of Rimbaud's manner. It is a fanciful, slightly farcical commentary on contemporary politics entitled, "Letter from Baron de Petdechèvre to his secretary at the Château de Saint Magloire."[41] On September 7 and 8, 1871, two events stand out: first, the condemnation to deportation to a fortified place of Georges Cavalier, known as Pipe-en-bois, after being found guilty of passing the plan of the Paris sewers to the Executive Committee of the Commune, and, second, the rejection of Baron Ravinel's proposition that the government departments should move from Paris to Versailles. These events, not at first sight an obvious target for humor, inspired Rimbaud to write a lively, mischievous commentary.

> *Versailles, September 9, 1871*
> *France has been saved, my dear Anatole, and you are right to say that I have greatly contributed to saving it. . . .*
> *We have reorganized an army, bombarded Paris, crushed the insurrection, shot the insurgents, tried their leaders, established constituent power, mocked the Republic, paved the way for a monarchist ministry, and passed a few laws that will be repealed sooner or later. . . .*
> *Did you see how they condemned Pipe-en-bois? We have our revenge, citizens of the Commune!*

This article reveals Rimbaud bursting with joy: Verlaine's response had transformed him. What a contrast with the desperate tone of his last letter to Paul Demény!

Then Verlaine's second letter arrived, just as admiring as the first ("You are prodigiously well armed for battle"). This time, everything was arranged, everything was ready for him. "Come, my dear, great soul. We are calling for you. We await you."

A money order was attached, for his traveling expenses, raised by a collection among the Parnassians. This time, "that was it." The holidays would go on, the dictatorship of "la Mère Rimbe" was coming to an end, the gates of the celestial Parnassus were opening as if by magic.

But a deep apprehension took the gilt off his triumph. It was the same apprehension that broke the onward rush of his glorious *Bateau ivre:*

> *Mais, vrai, j'ai trop pleuré! Les Aubes sont navrantes.*
> *Toute lune est atroce et tout soleil amer.*

> [*But, in truth, I have wept too much! Dawns are*
> *heartbreaking. Every moon is atrocious and every sun*
> *bitter.*][42]

On the very very threshold of the world of artists and intellectuals, a sudden paralysis froze him: would he be able to overcome his peasant's awkwardness, his schoolboy's shyness? Delahaye recounts the circumstances:

> *The day before his departure, he wanted to go for a final walk into the countryside around Charleville. It was in September, the light was glorious, yet gentle, the air deliciously mild, with a slight breeze, everything seemed to encourage hope, everything was associated with the joy of that conquered liberty. We sat down on the edge of a wood [the Fontemps or Fortant wood, near Evigny].*
>
> *"This is what I've done," he said, "to present to them when I get there."*
>
> *And he read to me Le Bateau ivre. On hearing such a dazzling marvel, I celebrated in advance the extraordinary entrance that he would make in the literary world: who could fail to admire such a work at once, without any reservations? There seemed to be no doubt that immediate success and fame in the near future awaited him.*
>
> *After the temporary excitement that this reading had given him,*[42] *Rimbaud became sad and downcast once more.*

"Ah yes!" he went on, "nothing like it has been written
yet, I know. . . . And yet . . . that world of literary, artistic
people! . . . Those elegant salons! . . . I don't know how to
behave. I'm awkward, shy, I don't know what to say. . . .
Where thought is concerned, I fear nobody. . . . But . . . Ah!
What am I going to do there?"[44]

The great day had arrived. Bretagne shook his hand for the last time, and wished him good luck. Deverrière gave him a fine louis d'or. Delahaye insisted on seeing him off. "Départ dans l'affection et les bruits neufs!" [Departure into new affection and sound.] (*Départ, Illuminations*).[45]

"When I got to the station for the final handshake," he writes, "he had been there for a long time, watching the hands move round the station clock, and he seemed to be in much better spirits. . . . I was so pleased for him and said: 'You'll shoot in there like a bullet. . . . You'll show Hugo and Leconte de Lisle!' "

And Delahaye made sarcastic remarks at the expense of the small provincial town, with its narrow-minded outlook, the Square de la Gare, with its mean lawns, which he had the good fortune to be leaving!

Rimbaud smiled calmly.

"Passengers for Balzicourt, Poix, Launois, Rethel, Reims, and Paris. Please take your seats!"[46]

Delahaye waved his hand, and the train of the Great Adventure moved off.

6

Paris: Disillusion

When he received Rimbaud's letter, Paul Verlaine was twenty-seven years old. He had been married for thirteen months, and his wife was expecting a child.

His father, a native of the Belgian Ardennes and a captain in the Engineer Corps, had died six years before. His mother was a countrywoman from the Artois region. When his parents decided to settle in Paris on his father's retirement, Verlaine spent his childhood in the Batignolles district. He first attended a small local school, then became a boarder in an institution whose pupils attended classes at the Lycée Bonaparte (now Condorcet). He was not a particularly good pupil, somewhat lazy and inattentive in class, and cared only about poetry (at fourteen he had sent some of his verses to Victor Hugo). However, as a result of sustained efforts, he attained his baccalauréat with quite good results. He went on to the Sorbonne to study law, but spent more time in the cafés of the Latin Quarter than in the lecture rooms. He moved from one job to another before finally passing an entrance examination for a minor local government post. At twenty, his character was already formed: he was indecisive, overemotional, oversensitive. If one adds that he was easily susceptible to infatuation, one can see how vulnerable he was. Among friends, he could be a cheerful, sensitive, and witty companion, but, when faced with disappointment and difficulties, he fell into a neurasthenic melancholy, from which he emerged only by doping himself with alcohol. He would then become self-confident again, authoritarian, and violent, ready for anything.

His two collections of poems, *Poèmes saturniens* (he claimed to be born under the sign of the star of misfortune) and *Fêtes galantes*, had brought him to the forefront of the Parnassians. In the name of this young school he had gone off to Brussels to congratulate the exiled Victor Hugo on the triumphant revival of *Hernani*.

He had fallen unhappily in love with his cousin Elisa—"his big sister"— who, unfortunately, was already married, and the mother of two children. His homosexual tendencies were already to the fore, but he kept them hidden: in any case, they had not yet been the cause of any scandal. Just before the war, he had thrown himself enthusiastically into the frantic festivities and noisy meetings of the literary and artistic youth of his day.

In August 1870 he married a girl of sixteen, of good upper-middle-class background, the half sister of his friend Charles de Sivry, a musician and singer. For her he had written a series of exultant love poems under the title *La Bonne Chanson*, but the work, which had been ready in July 1870, could not be distributed to the bookshops because of the war.

At first the young couple rented an apartment on the Quai de la Tournelle, but, as a result of the tragic circumstances of that terrible year, the lease had to be terminated. Indeed, after the Commune, Verlaine was terrified that he might be arrested for having stayed at his post, in the Hôtel de Ville, during the insurrection. He had done so more out of patriotism (he had been born at Metz!) than out of political or social conviction. As the repression got worse during the summer of 1871—and as his wife was pregnant—he had taken refuge with his wife's family, in the countryside, near Arras. It was only on his return to Paris, at the beginning of September, that he found, at his publisher's, the double letter from Rimbaud and Bretagne.

At that time Verlaine and his wife were staying with her parents, who lived in a three-story detached house on the side of the Butte Montmartre, in the Rue Nicolet. His father-in-law, Théodore Jean Mauté—who liked to call himself Mauté de Fleurville—was a white-bearded, thick-set bourgeois, fairly well off, with an income from rents, and sat on the local school board. He had agreed with some reluctance to his daughter's marriage to a poet. The mother-in-law, who had first been married to the marquis de Sivry, was herself artistic, musical, and of a very happy disposition. She was able to calm the first conflicts that began to disturb the happiness of the young couple.

It can be said, then, that Rimbaud's request for hospitality did not come at a particularly good moment. But Verlaine did what he could. He asked his mother-in-law, Mme Mauté, to take in this highly talented young poet—a new Baudelaire, but somewhat wilder, as someone had described him—lost in his native province. Attending to the most urgent matter first, the good lady suggested putting him into the "linen room," a small room on the third floor, where her son Charles de Sivry had more than once taken in friends in need. This was a temporary solution; they would decide what to do next on the return of M. Mauté, who was away hunting in Normandy.

Rimbaud's arrival in the Rue Nicolet on a fine September afternoon has been recounted many times. We know that Verlaine and his friend Charles Cros, a poet and inventor, went to collect him at the Gare de l'Est (then known as the Gare de Strasbourg), but failed to recognize him by the mental picture they had of him. They expected to find a tall young man, between twenty-five and thirty, with dark, feverish eyes. Finding nobody who corresponded to this description, they had to leave empty-handed.

When they got back, they found Rimbaud sitting on the edge of a chair in the small Louis-Philippe drawing room on the ground floor, opposite two women—Mme Mauté and Mathilde—who were beginning to find the wait rather long, since the young man was not very "talkative." Rimbaud could not get over it. How could it be that the seer Paul Verlaine lived in this undistinguished setting, in the company of these very ordinary women? It was not to be believed!

At first, he had replied with bored monosyllables to the battery of questions concerning his family, his mother, his sisters, his friends—if he went to school, if he had already been to Paris. In short, the usual resources of polite conversation. But the ladies soon grew tired of this, and they were almost dying of boredom when Verlaine—a sprightly figure, with receding hair, and a short goatee, and Charles Cros, a thick-set figure with rather heavy features—appeared, and started the interrogation all over again.

He knew that he was being observed and judged pitilessly. Quite obviously, they regarded him as a country bumpkin. Ah yes! What was he doing there, in that ridiculous drawing room?

"He was a tall, well-built boy, with a red face, a peasant," Mathilde wrote in her *Mémoires*. "He looked like an overgrown schoolboy, with his trousers a bit too short and showing his blue cotton socks, obviously knitted by his mother. His hair was long and untidy. He was wearing a cord tie, and looked generally unkempt. His eyes were blue, and rather beautiful, but they had a cunning look that, in our indulgence, we took for shyness."

He had a slight Ardennais accent, that of the Meuse valley, a bit sing-song, quite close to the Walloon—but he soon lost it.[1] For his part, Verlaine was as surprised as Rimbaud had been. He had certainly not expected a shy youth, with angelic features, but eyes of steel. How could such dark poems as *Accroupissements* or *Les premières Communions* have germinated in that choirboy's head?

History has recorded only one thing that Rimbaud said during this interview. As the family was talking to the household pet, a huge dog called Gastineau, by allusion to Benjamin Gastineau, a well-known red agitator, Rimbaud remarked: "Dogs are liberals," meaning no doubt that liberals are always ready to "beg" for a piece of sugar.

The clock chimed seven, and they all passed into the dining room. The guest accepted the soup, and remained as uncommunicative as ever. On the pretext of tiredness, he retired to bed early.

He was bitterly disappointed. He, who had dreamed of revolutionizing the world of poetry, had fallen into this vilely bourgeois milieu, the very antithesis of poetry. He had imagined everything except that. Without a shot being fired he had become the enemy's prisoner.

Well, he would not give in to the conventions of polite society. Mme Mauté and her daughter would soon get acquainted with filth, moral and physical, the precondition of the seer's vision. An ivory crucifix, one of M. Mauté's hunting knives, and other objects disappeared. "The soul must be made monstrous," he had written to Paul Demény. So away with prejudice, politeness, cleanliness, decency. He would behave like a wild boar, to the consternation of his hosts, saying neither good morning nor good evening, not washing, not combing his hair, taking no care of his clothes, lying full length at the foot of the steps leading up to the front door whenever a ray of sunshine appeared. Without going into details, Verlaine refers to a few eccentricities of this kind, and other such excesses, "the latter not entirely devoid, I fear, of sly malice and straightfaced humor."[2]

Mme Mauté warned her son-in-law that all this was most regrettable, that the young man would not be thrown out, but that steps should be taken immediately to find him other accommodation, for M. Mauté, who was about to arrive back home, would certainly not tolerate such behavior.

During the first few days Verlaine showed his young friend something of Paris: first the Butte Montmartre, then the Latin Quarter with its cafés. But this tourism did not interest Rimbaud—any more than the Louvre was to interest him when Forain took him there some time later. Forain went there to copy pictures, because it was heated! Rimbaud just sat there, looking out of the windows.

Obsessed by his mission, the young poet became more and more excited, determined to turn Verlaine into a complete seer. It was his imperative duty: nothing else mattered. Of course, he realized that it would be an uphill task, but that merely stiffened his resolve. He would struggle on to the end with the faith of a martyr; the idea of failure never crossed his mind; his very life was in question; he would succeed or disappear.

To start with, everything must be demolished—beginning with the Parnassian movement, which was already in ruins. There would be no more prosody, no more rules, no more constraints, since it was the task of the seer to invent a universal language capable of expressing all sensations and all ideas. Nothing must be allowed to oppose this renewal: so that the flowers of tomorrow might bloom, the ground must not only be leveled, it must be plowed deeply in order to rid it of the old rotten layers of the state, the family, culture, the worship of money, so that the new seeds of fraternity and science could be sown. The *Communards* had made a good start, but they had been stopped too soon: the Napoleonic triumphal arches, Notre-Dame de Paris, the Bibliothèque Nationale, the Musée du Louvre, those piles of stone should have suffered the same fate as the Tuileries palace, so that future generations might learn that poetry was first and foremost action.

Verlaine was certainly given a good lesson in lycanthropy!

This apostle of a new gospel reminded him of another lycanthropist who had once interested him: Petrus Borel, the author of the *Contes immoraux d'un lycanthrope*.[3] At first amused, then interested and conquered (the *Communard* that he had been in spirit surfaced), he came to share the view of this young man whose sole ambition was to give poetry its rightful place, that is to say, the first place, for it alone was capable of purifying and regenerating the world. Of course, there were excesses in the theory of the seer, but these excesses, like the acne of adolescence, would disappear with time. The true foundation of poetry—the only serious thing in his eyes—was still emotion and music. And that was not incompatible with the search for the unknown. Indeed Baudelaire had already opened up this way.

The Parnassians met each month over dinner at a sort of club that came to be known as the "Vilains ou Affreux Bonshommes" (an insult that had been addressed to them), during which they recited poetry in an atmosphere of warm, light-hearted fellowship. The war had interrupted this agreeable tradition, but it was to begin again in September 1871: this was to be an important meeting, for the war and its aftermath had dispersed many of its members; many had not seen one another for a year. The reunion would take place with a certain solemnity.

It was a memorable evening, highlighted with a certain surprise, for, at the dessert, the unknown young man sitting next to Verlaine—who introduced him as a very promising poet from the Ardennes—rose and recited in a rather emphatic voice his *Bateau ivre*. The diners were paralysed with admiration, surprise, astonishment.

Fortunately for us, Emile Blémont was absent from that evening. As a result, his friend, Léon Valade, a poet from Bordeaux, immediately wrote off an account of the meeting in a letter dated October 5, 1871:

> *You certainly missed out by not being present at the last dinner of the* Affreux Bonshommes. *A most alarming poet, not yet eighteen, was exhibited by Paul Verlaine, his inventor, and indeed his John the Baptist. . . . Big hands, big feet, a completely babyish face, like that of a child of thirteen, deep blue eyes, a temperament more wild than shy, such is the boy, whose imagination, compounded of great power and undreamed of corruption, who has fascinated and terrified all our friends.*
>
> *"What a fine subject for a preacher!" Soury exclaimed. D'Hervilly said: "Behold Jesus in the midst of the doctors." "More likely Satan!" replied Maître, and so the most apt description occurred to me, "Satan in the midst of the doctors." I cannot give you the life history of our poet. Suffice it to say that he has just come from Charleville, with the firm intention of never going home again.*
>
> *Come and you will be able to read his verses and judge for yourself. Were it not for the millstone that Fate so often keeps in reserve to hang about our necks, I would say that we are here beholding* the birth of a genius. *This is the statement of my considered opinion, which I have reached after three weeks of reflection, and it is not merely a passing whim.*[4]

But Valade's enthusiasm was a flash in the pan. He was never again to speak of Rimbaud, who, however, gave him an autographed copy of one of his poems (*Oraison du soir*), which was found among his papers. As for Emile Blémont, who also possessed an autographed copy of one of Rimbaud's poems (*Voyelles*), he certainly did not share his friend's enthusiasm. We shall see how he ignored him in April 1872 when he took over the editorship of a literary review.

Verlaine was quite clear when he wrote: "When he [Rimbaud] came back to Paris, a year or more later, he was not popular, believe me. Except for a small group of independent Parnassians, the Great Parnassians (Coppée, Mendès, Heredia) had little or no admiration for the new phenomenon. Apart from Valade, Mérat, Charles Cros, and me, then, he received no welcome in the Capital on his return."[5] And again: "This time, Cros was enthusiastic, Cabaner charmed, a crowd of others disturbed and delighted, a number of fools appalled, even, it is said, grieving families which, we are assured, later returned to their settled ways." (In this entry on Rimbaud in *Hommes d'Aujourd'hui*, Verlaine is referring to his wife's family.)

The success due to his curiosity value soon wore off. His new friends expected a poet, and what they saw emerging was a visionary given to hallucinations. His credit soon fell, and he came to be regarded as a crank, and a not very pleasant one at that, who held erroneous and unhealthy views about poetry. The more indulgent among them saw him as a failed genius, a shooting star that shone brightly before landing in a cloud of dust. Parnassian poetry was well-built, impassive, marmorial; when confronted by the delirious outpourings of this apprentice, the masters shrugged their shoulders, and they were soon joined by Rimbaud's earliest supporters, Valade, Cros. Only Verlaine retained his belief in his protégé, defending him unconditionally against all comers, and began to collect his works with a view to later publication. Copies of several poems, notably of the *Bateau ivre*, in addition to those sent from Charleville, were found in his papers.[6]

During the brief spell that Rimbaud was the star of the Latin Quarter, he had to submit to the demands of fame. He was taken and shown to the masters—and to the photographer.

One has to be Théodore de Banville to receive the impertinent author of *Ce qu'on dit au Poète à propos de fleurs* with a smile. Léon Valade declared to one of his friends: "That young Rimbaud is astonishing! Did he not declare to Banville that the moment had come to demolish the Alexandrine! You can imagine our surprise at this rebellion, followed by an exposition of his theories. We listened to him attentively, struck by the contrast between the youthfulness of his face and the maturity of his ideas."[7]

This was confirmed by Banville himself, who noted that one day "M. Arthur Rimbaut" had asked him if it would not soon be time to suppress the Alexandrine" (*Le National*, May 16, 1872).

Delahaye adds: "Verlaine told me how, when Rimbaud read his poem (*Le Bateau ivre*) to Banville, the latter objected that it would have been better to say at the beginning: 'I am a boat that . . . ' etc. The young savage said nothing, but as he went out he shrugged his shoulders and muttered '*Vieux con!*' "[8]

It is also said that Rimbaud was introduced to Victor Hugo, who appears to have welcomed him with the words: "Shakespeare *enfant*," but Verlaine confirms neither the visit nor the words. Rodolphe Darzens, who was the first to recount this incident, added the reservation: "Or so legend has it." In fact, it would seem that the words were said to Albert Glatigny, a poet and actor. They certainly suited him better than Rimbaud, who, apart from his poem on Ophelia, has nothing in common with the great Will.[9]

However, he met neither Théophile Gautier nor Leconte de Lisle—in fact he was received only by the small circle of the Latin Quarter Parnassians. There was one exception: he seems to have spent an evening in a café with Jules Claretie, a highly esteemed critic; Delahaye, who reports the fact, adds that he called him a "good lad," which, on his lips, was praise indeed.[10]

He also renewed some old acquaintances: the draughtsman André Gill, who did a drawing of him on the prow of his drunken boat,[11] and Jean-Louis Forain, as poor and passionately devoted to art as ever, who earned a living as an advertising artist, or painting fans.

He was also taken to see Etienne Carjat, a photographer who specialized in celebrity portraits, a man with a goatee, a poet in his spare time, whose studio was at the end of a courtyard, at 10 Rue Notre-Dame-de-Lorette. His photograph of Rimbaud is extraordinary: the clear gaze of the seer, fixed on the far distance, an air both of defiance and resignation, "and that quite virile disdain for a good wash, which would have been useless to that literal beauty of the devil" (Verlaine).

On October 10, M. Mauté returned from Normandy. Verlaine summoned a few friends and suggested that they offer Rimbaud "Circular hospitality," each of them taking charge of him in turn. But Rimbaud himself did not appreciate this generous initiative. Not that he regretted the bourgeois atmosphere of the Rue Nicolet, but he could not bear to be separated from Verlaine: he needed to have him permanently near him to help him free himself of the rut into which he had fallen. Indeed, Rimbaud suddenly became aware of his weakness, an unacceptable fault in a seer, who must be capable of superhuman courage. The journey up river would be difficult; it would demand an unflagging effort: he would make that effort; it was his duty to do so. Meanwhile, he would sleep here or elsewhere, the guest of this or that fool.

Charles Cros was the first to contribute. The studio in which he made synthetic precious stones was in a former townhouse in the Rue Séguier, a narrow street in the Saint-Michel quarter. A young painter, Pénoutet, known as Michel de l'Hay, was already living there. Théodore de Banville got his wife to provide for the young poet a folding bed, sheets and blankets, and a washstand. These attentions merely exacerbated Rimbaud's resentment: he was being placed in the category of those who lived off public charity! No doubt his benefactors expected thanks and gratitude. It was intolerable that his life depended on their good will. At least in his cave at Romery he would have been free, owing nothing to anybody!

This horror of dependence coexisted inside him with its exact opposite, which he revealed to Izambard on May 13, that of getting himself "cynically kept." If he met some good soul willing to entertain or clothe him, he would go along with it. Rodolphe Darzens, who, twenty years later, carried out research on this period, provides the following details:

Henri Mercier, the founder of a fine review that, unfortunately, lasted for only three numbers (La Revue du monde nouveau), met him at Antoine Cros's, while he was staying with his brother, Charles.[12] Rimbaud was introduced to him, but throughout the whole evening he remained surly and uncommunicative in his corner. Some days later Rimbaud came to see him, bringing a number of articles for the Figaro, then in the Rue Rossini, including among others "Les nuits blanches," "Le bureau des cocardiers" (neither of which has been found). But he was too wretchedly dressed to present himself at the office of the editor of a newspaper like the Figaro. Mercier, who was well off, offered to take him to a tailor's, and to give him some money. Arthur Rimbaud took himself off at once to the Carreau du Temple and selected a blue suit with a velvet collar. At that time he was a tall, thin young man, with large, clumsy hands, with a peasant's thick, red fingers. That evening, he went to the first night of Théodore Barrière's La Boîte à Pandore at the Folies dramatiques.[13]

At intermission, Arthur Rimbaud bought a clay pipe, and Mercier saw him go up to one of the coach horses in such *a way as not to be seen, and take great pleasure in blowing into the poor animal's nostrils.*

It would seem that cruelty gave him real pleasure. This was not a mere pose with him, as he often maintained . . . but the result of a truly and profoundly evil nature. (Preface to the Reliquaire)

It was at this time that Charles de Sivry, Verlaine's brother-in-law, the son of Mme Mauté's first marriage, who had been in some political trouble, was freed from the camp at Satory. Verlaine, who was very fond of him, wanted very much to introduce Rimbaud to him. So he invited Rimbaud to a small gathering at the Rue Nicolet to celebrate the prisoner's return. But Sivry, a warm-hearted, spontaneous individual, did not get a very good impression of the young poet, who, that evening, did everything he could to make himself unpleasant. Then, of course, old Mauté was there, wearing his skull cap, with his constrained, severe eye, and Rimbaud was in no mood to accommodate the old man. The idea of having such a father-in-law! That's all that was needed to complete the picture!

Soon afterwards, on October 28, Mathilde gave birth to a boy, who was given the name Georges. "That day," she wrote in her *Mémoires*, "Verlaine set out in the morning and did not get back until midnight: he seemed pleased to have a son, kissed me as one would a child, and went off to bed in his room, which was next to mine."

One can imagine that this birth made Rimbaud all the more anxious, for it constituted one more link binding Verlaine to his family. It was a link that had to be broken, for the seer must be free.

That was not all. To the obstacles that piled up on the road to freedom, each day brought new occasions of disappointment and disgust: to think that he had believed in the myth of Paris, the capital of liberty, poetry, and the revolution, "holy city, foundation of the Occident!" What a joke! Paris, Delahaye was to say, is a handsome provincial town. He who had seen in poetry a sacred vertigo and Parnassus as the residence of the gods, "stealers of fire," had fallen into a group of versifiers worthy of a subprefecture, all clerks in this or that government office, who teased the muse as suburbanites tend their gardens on Sundays! So that was what the awesome *Parnasse contemporain*, which had so quickened his heartbeat, amounted to: bearded burghers, more bourgeois than the burghers of Charleville! So that was the Olympus where he had begged a little room for himself. Such mediocrity, such self-satisfaction! And if he opened his mouth to contradict the received wisdom, he was snubbed with a "Be quiet, kid!"

So he shut himself up in bitter silence, spat on the floor, and scowled. Soon, reviled by all, he attained what Berrichon called "the felicity of opprobrium."

The stay with Charles Cros was of short duration. Is it true, as Gustave Kahn maintained, that Rimbaud was thrown out for tearing up a collection of the review *L'Artiste*, "for hygienic purposes"? It is quite likely. In any case, he disappeared. Verlaine heard of his absence only some days later, for since the birth of his son he had spent more time at home. There, Mathilde, who had become increasingly nervous and jealous, regaled him with a constant stream of reproaches: why did he have to consort with that boy, of whose existence he was totally unaware two months ago, and follow him for days on end from café to café. Was he such a delightful individual?

No one had seen Rimbaud for three or four days. Verlaine was overcome with emotion and remorse: was it not all his fault? He had not done his duty: he should have taken care of him, personally, instead of handing him over to others, abandoning him in the literary jungle!

So he summoned his friends with the aim of guaranteeing him a decent existence, so that he could go on working. It was unlikely that he had gone back to his mother's: he had repeated often enough that he would never do that!

The Latin Quarter, and the surrounding districts were explored methodically. There was no trace of Rimbaud.

Then, one day, Verlaine bumped into him near the Place Maubert, wandering about, pale, covered with dirt and vermin, dying of hunger and cold, desperate—but determined not to give in: "The suffering is enormous," he had written to Izambard, "but one must be strong if one is born a poet." He had slept in filthy hostels with vagabonds, like them, picking over the contents of garbage cans for food.

Two decisions were then taken. First, as a matter of urgency, Banville, whose kindness was inexhaustible, was asked to get him an independent room in his building, then a collection was made for him from among the writers and artists of the Latin Quarter, to make sure he had enough to live on. A letter has been found from Charles Cros, dated November 6, 1871, to a playwright, Gustave Pradelle, asking him to contribute to this fund for the "foster child of the Muses," as Camille Pelletan, Emile Blémont, and he himself had already done.

Banville gave Rimbaud a fatherly, generous welcome. Mme de Banville, rivaling her husband in kindness, offered to set the young man up in a maid's room attached to their apartment in the Rue de Buci. She herself saw that the room was prepared suitably: good, clean, cretonne curtains, and new bed linen soon gave the room a pleasant, welcoming air. Of course, it was only to be temporary accommodation. Verlaine had other ideas. In the event, it was not to last more than a few days.

Rimbaud, irritated no doubt at having to take the backstairs to get to his room, felt all his resentment rising up inside him. He was no sooner in his room than he undressed, for his shirt was full of vermin, to the great indignation of the neighbors, who could see him naked through the open window. This minor incident turned into a terrible scandal. Later, when Rodolphe Darzens made inquiries in the Latin Quarter about these events, he was told: "On the first night, he slept in his clothes, his feet unwashed, between the sheets! Next day, he amused himself smashing the china—a water jug, bowl and chamber pot—then, shortly afterwards, since he needed money, went off and sold the furniture" (Preface to Le Reliquaire). This consorts well enough with Rimbaud's legend. However, there is a more plausible version: Banville, informed that same evening of his tenant's behavior, summoned him, and Rimbaud explained to him that having had to sleep rough for several nights, he had to take off his lice-infested shirt. The good man, moved by the boy's wretched plight, had clean linen sent up to him, and cordially invited him to dinner.

It is thought that Rimbaud did not stay more than a week at the Rue de Buci.

In late October, at the instigation of Charles Cros, a club—known as the Cercle Zutique—was founded. Its meetings were held at the Hôtel des Etrangers, which still exists, on the Boulevard Saint-Michel, at the corner formed by the Rue Racine and the Rue de l'Ecole-de-Médecine. There, in a fourth-floor room, in the cut off corner overlooking the boulevard, the "Vilains Bonshommes" were free to smoke, drink, read, shout, recite verse, and even hammer out tunes on a piano.

The barman was Ernest Cabaner (his real name was François Matt), a bohemian musician who had arrived in Paris around 1850 from his native Roussillon; he had never left the capital since. He had become a friend of Cézanne, and of many other painters. A tall, thin individual, afflicted with a stammer, he had acquired a legendary reputation. Verlaine described him as "Jesus Christ after three years of absinthe." His naive remarks and eccentrici-

ties went the rounds of the Parisian bohemia: during the siege he asked someone if it was still the Prussians who were besieging the city, or if they had
been replaced by some other nationality. "To render silence in music," he
once remarked, "I would need three military bands." When he inherited
some money from an elderly relative, he gave away half the money to the
poor, and, for his own use, bought an enormous porte-manteau, a barrel
organ, and a life-size plaster copy of the Venus de Milo. He collected shoes,
in which, it seems, he grew flowers. He was the gentlest, sweetest, most frugal
of men; he was a café musician, and, on occasion a poet.

Verlaine's idea was to get Rimbaud a job helping Cabaner in his work as
barman to the Cercle Zutique. This job would give him a bed, and enough
money to live on. Moreover the angelic Cabaner was the ideal partner for
Rimbaud's moody, violent character (Rimbaud's sally, quoted above—"It is
important to kill Cabaner"—was a measure of the feelings that he had for
him). The advantage of this solution was that it would reintegrate Rimbaud
into the milieu of poets and artists, who regarded him as off his head, and
were turning away from him.

The golden book of the Cercle, embellished with a fantastic drawing by
way of frontispiece by Dr. Antoine Cros, has been found.[14] It consists of about
a hundred pieces, parodies, or fantasies, and a number of drawings and
sketches. The most frequently recurring authors are Léon Valade, Charles
Cros, and Rimbaud (about twenty pieces), followed by Verlaine (fourteen
pieces), Germain Nouveau, Raoul Ponchon. Four dates appear in the album:
October 22, November 1, 6, and 9, 1871.

When asked why he was staying on in Paris, Rimbaud would reply: "I'm
waiting, I'm waiting!"

He was waiting to be taken seriously, waiting for the true power of poetry
to be recognized, and above all waiting for the companion in vision whom
he had chosen to have the courage to break off the bonds that paralyzed him.
He was waiting for "the real life." He would be patient, however long he had
to wait. (In May, while still in Paris, he was to group several poems together
under the general title, *Fêtes de la patience*.)

The famous sonnet *Voyelles*, composed in Paris, is a reflection of the
piano lessons that Cabaner gave Rimbaud at the Hôtel des Etrangers. Of
course, none of Cabaner's ideas were new; musical chromaticism, or seeing
colors when listening to music, was a phenomenon that had long been
known: as early as the seventeenth century, Father Castel had conceived of
an "ocular harpsichord" for beginners on which the keys were colored with

the colors associated with the notes. Like him, Cabaner colored the keys, and attributed to them the sound of a vowel. It was using this method that Rimbaud acquired the rudiments of piano playing. In Félicien Champsaur's *roman à cles Dinah Samuel*, Cabaner, disguised under the name of Rapanès, explains to Richard de Boishève (Villiers de l'Isle-Adam): "There is a relationship between the gamut of sounds and the spectrum of colors. Long study has brought me to the conclusion that white must correspond to *do*, blue to *re*, pink to *mi*, black to *fa*, green to *sol*. When the relationships between colors and sounds have been found, music may be translated into landscapes and portraits by replacing the colors, and by marking the halftones with sharps and flats."

One can imagine Rimbaud reciting his lesson: "*Mi* black, *do* white, *mi* pink, *re* blue, *sol* green."

With a slight transposition (A—black)—and the breath of genius—the sonnet "Voyelles" was born. This hypothesis is certainly more probable than that of the colored ABC, as if, in 1871, Rimbaud gave a thought to the child that he had been some ten years earlier. What then interested him was to find a complete, universal language—as he wrote to Paul Demény on August 15 1871: "This language will be of the soul and for the soul, embracing everything, scents, sounds, colors, thought catching thought and pulling." Scents, sounds, colors. If Cabaner had suggested seeing colors and smelling scents when listening to music, he would have grabbed at the idea. Anyway, the piano teacher wrote a *Sonnet des sept nombres*, dedicated to his pupil, "Rimbald," which colors the keys by linking them to vowels. The autograph copy is illuminated, and the keys drawn on a musical stave.[15]

Thus all those who have tried to elucidate *Voyelles* in the light of metaphysics, psychoanalysis, sexuality, etc., have fallen into a trap. Rimbaud cared nothing for such word-spinning. Only one thing was of passionate concern to him: to enlarge the vocabulary, to find a universal language, in a word, the alchemy of the word.

While Rimbaud was officiating at the Cercle Zutique, Ernest Delahaye, who had come to Paris for the first time in his life, was anxious to call on his childhood friend, whom he believed to be still staying with Verlaine, in the Rue Nicolet. He was somewhat intimidated when the maid led him into the large drawing room on the second floor. But his embarrassment was dissipated when the master appeared with a warm handshake and a friendly: "*Bonjour, cher ami.*"

Delahaye made painful efforts to bring out the words that he had learnt by heart, begging Verlaine to excuse him for allowing himself, without having the honor of knowing him, to come and ask for news of his friend Rimbaud, who . . . Verlaine briskly interrupted him: "Rimbaud? . . . Perfect! . . . Where's he hanging out? Let's see . . . everywhere and nowhere. . . . Today, I know where he is to be found. What if we go off together and look for him? Shall we do that?" (*Souvenirs familiers*).

They went out. A stop off at the Café du Delta was absolutely necessary. As he drank his bitter-curaçao, Verlaine, maintaining the light conversational tone, sang the praises of the "exquisite being" that he was, complaining only that he had no mistress: she would cure him, he claimed, of "the intercostal rheumatism" from which he suffered.

It was obviously a joke, but Delahaye listened, wide-eyed. Many more surprises awaited him!

After a trip on the top of a horse-drawn omnibus, they arrived in the Boulevard Saint-Michel, before the Hôtel des Etrangers.

"This is where the tiger has his den!" Verlaine cried.

In a large smoked-filled room, set up as a café, with tables and arm-chairs, various bearded individuals shook Verlaine's hand. Rimbaud, who had been asleep on a sofa, stretched himself, and got up, pulling a face. He had grown so much that Delahaye hardly recognized him. He was wearing a crumpled, threadbare mackintosh that was too big for him; his tie was awry and his hair unkempt. He had been taking hashish, he said, but all he had seen in his visionary ecstasy were black and white moons chasing one another. Since he complained of pain in his stomach and head, Delahaye took him outside. Rimbaud showed him the bullet holes on several houses and on the columns of the Panthéon from the recent fighting in May. He was exhausted, and when his friend asked him, "where's Paris from the point of view of ideas," he replied in a tired tone of voice: "Nothingness, chaos, reaction of every possible and even probable kind."

There were still *Communards* determined to fight to the death. He would be with them, such was his ideal.

Delahaye was utterly crushed to see how much Paris had changed him.

"Paris, city of light . . . What a joke! A heap of cupidity and vulgarity, a warren of garrisoned fools, the least intellectual place in the world."

Then he talked about the Cercle, of the "bonshommes" whom he frequented there, of Cabaner, who was one of his best friends.

Delahaye then recounts how, as they walked down the Boulevard Saint-Michel, they stopped in front of a *"beuglant,"* a sort of low-class music hall,

Le Boeuf à l'huile, outside which a patriotic song, "Reischoffen's Cuirassiers," was posted up.

The war . . . the long, hot summer of '70 . . . the prize-giving . . . the crazy dreams . . . *Le Parnasse contemporain* . . . how quickly time passed!

The Cercle Zutique had an ephemeral existence: it disappeared, it is thought, because there were fears that one day the tax man might take an interest in it. Rimbaud may well have lost his job if it had gone on, a victim of his own hoaxes, and of his jokes, practical and otherwise, perpetrated at Cabaner's expense.[16]

So new accommodation had to be found for him. Once more, the four remaining members of the faithful, André Gill, Charles Cros, Banville, and Michel de l'Hay, met and decided to rent a furnished room for him, where he would be totally independent. So, about November 15 or 20, Rimbaud was living in an attic of what was more or less a hotel at the corner of the Boulevard d'Enfer (Raspail) and the Rue Campagne-Première, opposite the Montparnasse cemetery. On the first floor was a shop, "Vins et Boulangerie," run by a certain Trépied; its customers were mainly omnibus drivers whose depot was nearby.[17]

Rimbaud's attic room, "filled with dirty light and spider's webs," with its ceiling rising up "in distressing cones" (Verlaine), was lit by a skylight.

An old artisan of the district told a journalist, Michèle Le Royer: "That's where I saw Rimbaud and Verlaine—Rimbaud was just a lad then, Verlaine had something pure, almost diabolical about him—sitting for a quarter of an hour without saying anything, in front of a drink, then going off arm in arm, along the street here."[18]

They no longer had much to say to one another. Rimbaud was ready to begin the adventure of freedom at once, but an exhausted Verlaine would not go beyond vague generalities: yes, of course, he was still thinking of their great journey together, he would free himself of his fetters, but they must be prudent, and wait patiently for the right time. In that late November, he was between the devil and the deep blue sea, determined not to abandon Rimbaud, yet subjected to the sarcasm and nagging of Mathilde, who, with growing bitterness—though she denies it in her *Mémoires*—dared to accuse him of unavowable feelings toward his young friend. He shrugged his shoulders if he was sober, and struck her if he was drunk, the second being more frequently the case. Almost every evening saw violent scenes—and one would probably be right to suspect Rimbaud of pushing Satanism as far as to drag

Verlaine from café to café, and only to let him go late into the evening when well and truly drunk, knowing that then he would be violent and dangerous.

At this point, Mathilde believed herself capable of mounting a counter-attack that would open her husband's eyes: where her reproaches had failed, perhaps public rumor would succeed.

On Wednesday, November 15, Verlaine and Rimbaud were attending the first night of *Le Bois*, a one-act idyll by Albert Glatigny at the Odéon. Mathilde reports that her husband was wearing an old, crumpled jacket, muddy boots, and one of those frightful neckties that he was so fond of. As for Rimbaud, he was "horribly dirty." She alerted Edmond Lepelletier, a journalist, and an old friend of Verlaine's from *lycée* days, confided her fears in him, and begged him to teach her husband a good lesson for his incomprehensible behavior. Of course, he should do this in the name of their old friendship.

Next morning, November 16, under the signature of Gaston Valentin (Edmond Lepelletier's pseudonym), an item appeared in *Le Peuple souverain:* "The whole of Parnassus was out in force, moving around and chatting in the foyer, under the eye of its publisher Alphonse Lemerre. One noticed here and there the fair-haired Catulle Mendès, arm in arm with the even fairer Mérat. Léon Valade, Dierx, Henri Houssaye chatted here and there. The saturnine Paul Verlaine was arm and arm with a charming person, a certain Mlle Rimbaut."

The venomous allusion must have raised more than a smile. Next day Lepelletier, who was an honest friend, tried to apologize to Verlaine for this "joke," but he did not find him in the Rue Nicolet. M. Mauté and Charles de Sivry were pleased to learn from Lepelletier that Verlaine had been seen holding Rimbaud tenderly around the neck.

A few days before, on November 14, Verlaine had attended the first night of François Coppée's *L'Abandonnée* at the Théâtre du Gymnase. He got back home, drunk, at about three in the morning, and woke up his wife, shaking her and shouting: "There she is, the abandoned woman! It's disgusting this success of Coppée's!" A tragicomic scene ensued: Verlaine took it into his head to blow up the cupboard in which his father-in-law kept his ammunition for hunting, and Mathilde succeeded in forcing him away only by brandishing fire tongs that had been made red in the fire. Next day, she summoned one of her women friends, a journalist, and, on November 18, there appeared in *Le XIXe siècle*, under the heading News Items, a paragraph

beginning thus: "*Ils sont gentils, les petits poètes du Parnasse contemporain.*"
The writer went on to relate that the success of Coppée's play had made one
Parnassian so furious that he had tried to kill his wife and newborn son. "If
M. Coppée continues to be so successful," the article concluded, "we will not
be able to answer for the life of these two individuals."

Did these warnings bring Verlaine to heel? They had the opposite effect.
He behaved like Oscar Wilde who, when warned (in 1893) of the danger he
was running by frequenting young Bosie, paraded their friendship all the
more.[19] The two cases are parallel, and both led to prison. Verlaine replied
to his friends' advice to act more prudently with this quatrain from *Jadis et
Naguère:*

> *L'injure des hommes*
> *Qu'est-ce que cela fait?*
> *Va, notre coeur sait*
> *Seul ce que nous sommes.*

> [*The insults of men,*
> *What can they do?*
> *Go, our hearts alone*
> *Know that we are.*]

However, Lepelletier was determined to be forgiven for what he had
written. Quite fearlessly he invited Verlaine and Rimbaud to dinner.

As far as Rimbaud was concerned, this Lepelletier was nothing more
than an evil-minded fool. Did that "old foot slogger," that "hack" imagine
that for a plate of soup they would start bowing and scraping before him?

First he said not a word during the first half of the meal; then, under the
effects of the Burgundy that Verlaine liberally plied him with, he became
aggressive, launching by way of provocation a few outrageous quips, accompanied by direct attacks. "In particular he tried to please me," writes Lepelletier, "by saying that I 'bowed and scraped before the dead,' because he had
seen me raise my hat as a funeral procession passed. Since I had just lost my
mother,[20] I insisted that he remain silent on the subject, and looked at him
in a way that did not please him at all" (*Paul Verlaine*, 1907).

After another remark in the same vein, which was immediately
squashed, Rimbaud picked up a dessert knife, and began brandishing it
about. Without losing his sang-froid, Lepelletier declared that, since he had

not been intimidated by the Prussians, he was certainly not going to be pushed around by a young puppy like him, and advised him to watch his language if he did not wish to descend the stairs with a boot in his backside. Verlaine then intervened, and, from then on, Rimbaud kept quiet, isolated in a cloud of tobacco smoke, while Verlaine recited poetry. As one might discern, Lepelletier never cared very much for Rimbaud.

So, as 1871 came to an end, things seemed to be at an impasse. Rimbaud was waiting, Verlaine was waiting. It looked like going on for a long time like that. However, Verlaine was ruined, for the upkeep of the "muses' foster child" was getting very expensive; so he went off to Paliseul in Belgium to collect the share of an inheritance due to him on the death of an aunt in 1869.

In her *Mémoires* Mathilde recounts how, the day before he left, he brought back with him two companions, Rimbaud and Forain, on the pretext that they lived too far away to walk home. "He asked me to make sure that they were given a bowl of onion soup on waking," she says. "So I ordered the said soup from the cook, but when she went up with it, she found the room empty."

During a stop-off at Charleville, Verlaine saw Delahaye and Bretagne again at the Café de l'Univers, near the station, in the early evening and met Deverrière.[21] Then he went on to Sedan, visited the village of Bazeilles, famous for its *"maison des dernières cartouches,"* a house in which French soldiers resisted the invading Prussians down to their last cartridge. From there, he sent word to Edmond Maître, a member of the "Vilains Bonshommes," and a great friend of the painters of his day, asking him to pass on his good news "to Rimbal," suggesting that Valade should write a note to him.

Having picked up his share of the inheritance, Verlaine was back in Paris to celebrate the end of that terrible year.

His trip had alerted his wife and mother. If he needed so much money, the two women concluded, it was because he was wasting far too much of it with Rimbaud. If he went on like that, he would be ruined, they thought, and this anxiety increased the ill-feeling and tension that were tearing his marriage apart.

Of this time when Rimbaud lived isolated from the Latin Quarter, and saw nobody except Forain, who had become attached to him with the idea of setting up a studio in his new home (they quarreled one day when Rimbaud refused to open the door of his room), we have a bad portrait of him by Alfred Jean Garnier. The face looks sullen, puffy, more suited to an unhappy *valet de chambre* than to an inspired poet. And yet there can be no doubt of its authenticity, for the back of the drawing bears the yellowed inscription: "Portrait of the poet Arthur Rimbaud. I drew it in 1872 in Paris, Bd d'Enfer, opposite the gates of the Montparnasse cemetery. Garnier." It is tempting to conclude that this Garnier made a drawing of Rimbaud in 1872, a sketch that he later overlaid with heavy color, which had the effect of altering the model's face, for the painting is dated 1873 on the back.[22]

Toward the end of 1871, on the occasion of the fiftieth anniversary of Baudelaire's birth (April 7, 1821), the painter Fantin-Latour conceived of the idea of composing, as a pendant to his *Hommage à Delacroix*, a large painting bringing together, beneath Baudelaire's portrait, the most celebrated poets of the day (Hugo, Gautier, Leconte de Lisle, Banville). However, these masters rejected the idea, so Fantin had to be content with less famous sitters, and, instead of a majestic fresco, the setting of his painting was reduced to a homely dinner table—a meeting of the Vilains Bonshommes—without Baudelaire. It is thought that Verlaine and Rimbaud came to pose in his studio, at 8 Rue des Beaux-Arts, separately at first, then together. The first study of Rimbaud's face is a gouache of extraordinary freshness: quite clearly, the artist was attracted by his model's youthfulness, which was certainly in marked contrast with the other rather dull, conventional figures. The picture is, it has to be said, terribly academic; it would have very little interest indeed if it merely depicted such insignificant individuals as Aicard, Valade, Pelletan, d'Hervilly, Bonnier, and Blémont. Verlaine is stiff, expressionless; beside him, Rimbaud, his disheveled head resting on a thick, red hand, his elbow leaning on the table, sulks, his back turned to the other diners. It is a magnificent evocation of a certain atmosphere: Rimbaud is unrelenting, Verlaine looks preoccupied, the other "Bonshommes" hardly exist at all—they are so many extras.

Indeed, Verlaine had every reason to be preoccupied, for, whenever he returned home, there was a row. It was useless apologizing next morning. This time he had gone beyond all reasonable limits, he could not go on neglecting his wife and son, spending all day trailing from one café to another with his alarming friend.

In the background, Rimbaud was not entirely displeased with the way things were turning out: at last something was happening, Verlaine was on the right path. One day Verlaine turned up to tell him that after a particularly violent scene, his wife and son Georges had gone off to the South of France, without leaving an address (in fact they were at Périgueux, M. Mauté's hometown).

Things were getting better and better: the fruit was falling from the tree. Victory was near—soon they would be able to fly off in freedom!

But Verlaine added: "My wife is talking of a separation. We must avoid such a catastrophe at all costs. She must come back at all costs. And if she makes it a condition of her return that you leave Paris, you will have to understand."

Leave Paris? It was out of the question! To satisfy the whim of that idiotic woman! He was not in tutelage. He had chosen to come to Paris, and he would stay there—even if nobody gave him any money to live on. It is quite possible that, to prove his independence to everybody, he spent some time as a street vendor. Indeed, Berrichon declares that in 1872 he saw him selling rings and keyrings in the Rue de Rivoli.[23]

It was in this atmosphere of high tension that the traditional banquet of the Vilains Bonshommes took place in late January 1872. That evening the meeting took place at a brasserie in the Saint-Sulpice district, on the corner of the Rue du Vieux-Colombier and the Rue Bonaparte—the building is still standing. They ate well, and, as usual, among the cigar smoke and brandy, they read poetry.

Rimbaud was in a filthy mood. To his personal troubles was added the exasperation of having to listen to the painful outpourings of totally un-talented rhymers. According to Verlaine, as Auguste Creissels launched into his *Sonnet du combat*,[24] Rimbaud, unable to contain himself any longer, punctuated each line with a resounding "Merde!"

He was ordered to shut up—to no avail. Uproar broke out.

"*Petit crapaud!*" ("Little toad!"), cried Carjat, rising to his feet.

"*Sale bête de comédie!*" yelled Ernest d'Hervilly.

Rimbaud spat some obscenity in his face. Carjat, who was tall and strong, got hold of the troublemaker, and dragged him outside. Calm re-turned to the dining room, but Rimbaud stayed in the anteroom, near the cloakroom, waiting for the club members to emerge. When he saw Carjat appear, he flung himself at him, brandishing an unsheathed sword-stick.[25] Carjat managed to feint the blow, muttering, between clenched teeth, "*Petit misérable!*"[26] Nevertheless, he was slightly wounded on the hand and in the groin. One can imagine the commotion. Verlaine appeared, snapped the sword stick (it was no doubt his) over his knee, and begged Michel de l'Hay to take Rimbaud back to his room in the Rue Campagne-Première.

The incident went the rounds of the Latin Quarter.[27] Forain drew the moral by writing under the sketch of the angelic-looking Rimbaud the follow-ing warning: "Qui s'y frotte s'y pique" ("Stings on contact"). Carjat, it is said, smashed the photographic plates that he had taken of his "murderer." As for Verlaine, he was told that he would still be welcome at the dinners of the Vilains Bonshommes, but that he was not to bring his friend.

Meanwhile, Fantin-Latour's painting was not finished: the portrait of Albert Mérat was still to be done. Outraged by the incident, Mérat warned Fantin-Latour that he would withdraw from company that had dishonored itself by such unacceptable acts of violence. This attack was directed not only at Rimbaud, but also at Verlaine, who did not have the courage to deny it. "On my part there was boredom, disgust, perhaps, disavowal of what after all was a rather minor incident," he wrote on September 14, 1900, to Ernest Raynaud, "a fit of sudden anger at the friend who was dearest to me, that was all there was to it. I regret that I do not appear in such a fine picture, beside my friends, in the place I ought to occupy."[28]

On March 18, 1872, the Goncourt brothers noted in their *Journal:* "On an easel [in Fantin-Latour's studio] there is a huge canvas representing the apotheosis of the Parnassians, in which there are great gaps, because, the painter tells us, this or that individual does not wish to be represented beside colleagues whom they call *m . . . deux* and thieves."

At the last moment, Fantin had to replace the absent Mérat with a bouquet of flowers. At the salon of 1872, which opened on May 10, the picture was received with amused curiosity: the gentlemen depicted therein were not very well known by the public at large. A cartoonist in *Le Journal amusant* of June 1, 1872, replaced the heads of the poets with those of dogs. In *L'Artiste*, Dubosq de Pesquidoux evoked Rembrandt. Everyone avoided any mention of Rimbaud. However, in *Le National* of May 16, Théodore de Banville was able to avoid any rancor. "Beside them, M. Arthur Rimbaut, a very young man, a child of the age of Cherubino, whose pretty head peers out with some surprise beneath an inextricably wild mop of hair, and who one day asked me if it would not soon be time to abolish the Alexandrine!"

Meanwhile, relations with Verlaine were at a standstill. Mathilde refused to come home. They were gradually moving toward a legal separation. A hard–pressed, tearful Verlaine then turned up, on his mother's advice, to beg Rimbaud to have pity on him, and to leave Paris, at least temporarily, since his presence was the only obstacle to the reconciliation that was indispensable from every point of view.

In Rimbaud's eyes this was proof that, when given a clear choice, Verlaine preferred his odious bourgeois existence in the bosom of his family to the destiny that had been assigned him: to become a seer. What a failure! What a disappointment!

Rimbaud certainly did not spare Verlaine that day! He was nothing but a contemptible coward, incapable of abandoning his home comforts, a poor wretch who crawled about his wife's feet, a small boy who had to do what his father-in-law told him.

Verlaine endured it all, begged, wept, repeated his promises: yes, one day, he would be free of his chains, but they had to avoid scandel, and, for the moment, bend before the storm, pretend; the fruit was not ripe, one day it would fall of its own accord. Since Rimbaud absolutely refused to go home to his mother's, a temporary solution was found: he would spend some weeks at Arras (with a friend of Verlaine's? A relative? Perhaps simply in a hotel?), until things settled down. As soon as things were back to normal, Verlaine would send for him.

About this time, according to Paterne Berrichon, Mme Rimbaud received an anonymous letter informing her of her son's wild behavior in Paris, and begging her to recall him at once. (Such a letter served Verlaine's purposes so well that one cannot but suspect him of being its author.)

One can imagine that Arthur received an imperative order to return home, perhaps with threats of resorting to the police—and that this letter helped to persuade him to leave for Arras. We know nothing at all about his stay there; Mathilde, who gained access to the correspondence between her husband and Rimbaud in the spring of 1872, claims that Rimbaud did indeed go to Arras. Rimbaud, his heart filled with hate, bent on revenge, and determined to make someone pay for this humiliation, left Paris.

7

Exile at Charleville and Return to Paris before the Great Departure

In Paris, everything was smoothed over as if by magic as soon as Verlaine had announced his victory. Mathilde returned from Périgueux on March 15, and everything seemed to go well. The couple enjoyed a new honeymoon: he, sober and punctual, was forgiven for his previous behavior. Everyone could breathe again. It is true that M. Mauté was sensible enough to remain at Périgueux. One day, when he was in a confidential mood, Paul declared to his wife: "When I go off with the little brown cat [Forain], I'm good, because the little brown cat is very gentle, but when I'm with the little blonde cat [Rimbaud], I'm bad, because the little blonde cat is fierce." Mathilde was very struck by these words, since she remembered them. She did not see the (somewhat provocative) humor that her husband had intended, telling the truth while making fun of himself.

The proceedings for a separation were forgotten; the marital barometer was set fair.

Rimbaud's stay at Arras was of short duration. One presumes that it came to an end when Verlaine refused to continue the subsidies that he had been paying him: after all, the young man did have a family of his own!

The young seer, his tail between his legs, had to return to his mother's, deeply mortified by this defeat.

Charleville was still the same, but, purged of his illusions, he now regarded it as another Paris, but on a smaller scale, with the same self-satisfied fools, the same puffed-up bourgeois, the same poverty of thought, the same nonentities. Fortunately, Delahaye was still there. The two young men resumed their walks, but they no longer tired themselves declaiming Hugo or Banville. They were finished with all that! Now they were quite happy to sing simple popular tunes or silly refrains from operettas—Lacocq's *Cent Vierges*, which Rimbaud had seen at the Variétés, for example. Often they would call in at some village inn, or just drop in at the Café Duterme, on the Place Ducale. Occasionally, they met old schoolfriends.

"Hey! Rimbaud! What have you been doing?"

He would get them to sit down at their table, and, resorting to an old trick, take great delight in retailing the demeaning trades that he had practiced, the unspeakable acts that he had performed. The young gentlemen "whinnied like goats," and took their leave in a dignified fashion. One day he was sitting with his friend at a table in the café of the Petit Bois when six or seven German officers wearing sabers sat down and started to recount their feats of bravery, mentioning the names of several villages in the Ardennes.

Rimbaud, staring at the speaker, suddenly burst out into convulsive laughter and slapped his thigh gaily. It might have ended badly. Fortunately the unexpected entrance of one of Delahaye's friends, who came up to shake Rimbaud's hand, caused a diversion and calmed him down.[1]

That stay in the Ardennes proved to be quite a fruitful one in terms of work.

In Paris he had written little (*Voyelles*, *Oraison du soir*, perhaps the *Chasse spirituelle*, and a few poems, including lighthearted verses for the *Album Zutique*). In the peace and quiet of the provinces, he was able to write again.

Two things are striking about the work of this period: its lucidity and its formal experimentation.

He was rediscovering life, and looking back at a few episodes of his own—his first escape from home (*Mémoire*), his walks during the sinister winter of the war (*Les corbeaux*)—or he looked at himself in the mirror as he had been when he disfigured himself in order to accede to the seer's vision. It is not a self-satisfied portrait:

> *l'enfant*
> *Gêneur, la si sotte bête,*
> *Ne doit cesser un instant*
> *De ruser et d'être traître*

Comme un chat des Monts-Rocheux;
D'empuantir toutes sphères!

[*the troublesome*
Child, the so stupid animal,
Must not stop for an instant
Cheating and betraying,

And like a Rocky Mountain cat
Making all spheres stink!][2]

As Antoine Adam correctly observes, "Now he is no longer concerned to boast of his vices, and to proclaim his revolt," and the poem ends with these two surprising lines:

Qu'à sa mort pourtant, ô mon Dieu!
S'élève quelque prière!

[*Yet at his death, O Lord,*
May some prayer rise up!][2]

"It is in the humility of his shame," the critic adds, "that he expects that at his death a prayer will rise up for him toward God—a God in whom he does not believe, but whom he does not wish to mock."[3]

It is clear that his exile in the Ardennes made a healthy break, in fact, a "drying out."

It is quite likely that he went back to the library—old Hubert no longer being there—and also likely that he became friendly with two younger pupils at the Collège who were already passionate readers, Louis Pierquin, the future historian-archaeologist, and Ernest Millot, a tall, gentle, kindly boy.

This period also saw the astonishing debut of Rimbaud as a prose writer. There were evocations of the past ("Photographs of times past," he called them), which have not survived, but of which Delahaye gives us some idea. Then he began his "Chasse Spirituelle," noting down memories and impressions of his walks. The most striking example is the poem *Enfance*, from *Les Illuminations:* "L'essaim des feuilles d'or entoure la maison du général. Ils sont dans le midi.—On suit la route rouge pour arriver à l'auberge vide. Le château est à vendre; les persiennes sont détachées.—Le curé aura emporté la clef de l'église.—Autour du parc, les loges des gardes sont inhabitées. Les palissades sont si hautes qu'on ne voit que les cimes bruissantes. D'ailleurs il n'y a rien à voir là-dedans." [A swarm of gold leaves smothers the general's house. They're in the south.—You take the red road to reach the empty inn. The château's up for sale and the shutters are coming loose.—The priest must have taken away the key of the church. Around the park, the keepers' cottages are uninhabited. The fences are so high that you can only see the tree tops moving in the wind. Anyway, there's nothing to see there.]⁴

According to Verlaine (*The Senate*), he also conceived the idea of a collection of *Etudes néantes*. To his mother, who asked him why he wrote in that way, since "it would lead to nothing," he answered one day: "Too bad, I write, I have to!" (Berrichon).

Poor Mme Rimbaud! Her children were a torture for her: one spilt ink on paper to no purpose; the other (Frédéric), in order to earn some money, had become a newspaper vendor in the town!

Sometimes, from Paris, letters arrived from Forain or Verlaine. Of the latter, three have been published out of a total correspondence of about ten. They are living documents that throw a striking light on their relationship in that difficult period. Verlaine feels guilty, even though it is not his fault: alluding to Holofernes' Judith and Marat's Charlotte Corday, he writes: "They are angry with you, furious—the Judiths and Charlottes."

At first these letters from Verlaine revived all the hatred that he was beginning to forget. After betraying him, Verlaine was now treating him with contempt, suggesting that, if he was bored, he should look for a job. He responded to these pleasantries with a broadside of insults. We do not have his answers, but Mathilde, who got hold of them one day, was horrified. She quotes these brief passages in her *Mémoires*: "Work is further from me than my fingernail is from my eye. Shit for me" (repeated eight times), or again: "When you see me positively eat shit, only then will you find how little it costs to feed me!" (Verlaine must have made some reference to his financial difficulties.)

It is clear that Verlaine had had to put up with a great deal of rancor and contempt. So he turns all contrite and submissive. In a letter of April 2, written at the Closerie des Lilas, he begins with effusive thanks to Rimbaud for sending him the score of an "Ariette oubliée" by Favart (1710–92), from the *Caprice amoureux ou Ninette à la Cour*:

The "Ariette oubliée" is quite charming, words and music! I've set about deciphering and singing it.⁵ Thank you so much for sending it! [He is overcome with remorse, so he grovels.] And thank you for your good letter! The "little boy" accepts the just spanking, the "toads' friend" withdraws everything and, never having abandoned your martyrdom, thinks about it, if possible—with still more fervor *and joy, as you know very well, Rimbe.*

So there we are, love me, protect, and trust me. Being very weak, I have great need of kindnesses. And just as I will have nothing more to do with my little boyishness, so I will no longer bother our venerable priest [Bretagne] with all that— and promise him at the soonest a real letter, with drawings and other such nonsense.

. . . But when the devil are we to begin that way of the cross—Uh?

He is busy removing his "things," etchings, etc., from the "Rue Campe."

At last we are doing things for you, you are desired. See you soon—for us—either here, or elsewhere.

And we are all yours.

P. V.

Still same address.

Shit to Mérat-Chanal-Perin-Guerin! and Laure!⁶ The late Carjat embraces you!

Tell me about Favart.

Gavroche is going to write to you ex imo.

The reader will no doubt have recognized certain allusions to Carjat and to the famous dinner of the Vilains Bonshommes.

Verlaine's second letter—undated—tries to calm an impatient Rimbaud, now anxious to get back to Paris.

Of course, *we shall see each other! When? Bide awhile! Harsh necessities! Lack of means!—So be it! And shit for the former and shit for the latter! And shit for Me!—and for you! But send me your "bad" (!!!!) verses, your prayers (!!!),*

anyway be sempiternally communicative—as we wait for bet-
ter days, after my touched up ménage.
   . . . *And never think that I have abandoned you—Re-*
member! Memento!

Your P. V.

And write to me soon! And send me your old verses and
new prayers—Won't you Rimbaud?

Verlaine's third and last letter, of late April, must have arrived shortly
before the exile's return:

> *Saturday, then, still around 7 o'clock?—Anyway, have*
> *means, will send at right time.*
>   *Meanwhile, all martyric letters to my mother's, all letters*
> *concerning reunions, prudent steps, etc., c/o M.L. Forain, 17*
> *Quai d'Anjou, Hôtel Lauzun, Paris, Seine (pr. M. P. Ver-*
> *laine).*
>   *Tomorrow I hope to be able to tell you that I've got a job*
> *at last (insurance clerk).*

As one can imagine, this news did not give Rimbaud any pleasure: here
was Verlaine forging one more bond for himself, and embarking on the life
of a clerk!

> *Didn't see Gavroche yesterday, though arranged to. I'm*
> *writing this at the Cluny (3 o'clock), waiting for him. We're*
> *plotting against you-know-who some merry acts of revenge.*
> *As soon as you get back, tigrish things will take place, if that*
> *will amuse you. They concern a certain gentleman [M.*
> *Mauté] who has not been without influence on your 3 months*
> *in the Ardennes, and my 6 months of shit. You'll see!*
>   *Write to me at Gavroche's, and inform me of my duties,*
> *of the life you expect us to lead, the joys, the pangs, the hypoc-*
> *risies, the cynicisms that will be required: I all yours, all*
> *you?—to know that!—this at Gavroche's.*
>   *To my mother's, your martyric letters, with no reference*
> *whatsoever to seeing me again.*
>   *Final recommendation: when you get back, grab me at*

once so that no one may sunder us,—and you will be able to so well!

Prudence:

Behave, at least for a time, less terrible-seeing than be-fore: linen, waxing, combing, facial expressions: *this necessary if you participate in tigrish plans: anyway I linen maid, brusher, etc. (if you like).*

(Which plans, indeed, if you participate, will be useful to us because "someone very important in Madrid" *is interested in them.*[7]*—hence* security very good! [*in English in the original*].

Now, greetings, reunion, joy, waiting for letters, waiting for You.—I last night dreamt twice: You, child martyrizer,— *You all goldez* [*presumably, Verlaine's idea of the English* "golden"]*: I forgot that you know as little of that language as I do. Odd, isn't it, Rimbe!*

Before ending this I await Gavroche. Will he come?—or would he stand me up?—(at, in a few minutes!)—

4 *o'clock in the afternoon.*

Gavroche arrived. Will talk 'bout safe houses.[8] *He'll write to you.*

Your old

P. V.

Write to me all the time from your Ardennes.

Write to you all that of my shit.

Why not shit to H. Reynault?[8]

These letters show the evolution of Rimbaud's thinking over a few weeks: from bitter recrimination to impatience to embark at last on what Verlaine called—little knowing how accurate the term was to be—their "way of the cross." What drove him on, too, was a violent desire for vengeance: he would come back, head held high; he would confound the woman who had so shamefully chased him away; he would resume control over her husband, he would force him to drop everything, and to follow him to the ends of the earth.

It was probably to Saturday May 4 that Verlaine was referring in his last letter, for, on that day, he returned home drunk, snatched his son from his wife's arms, and took him off to his mother's in the middle of the night. Three days later, a scene of rare violence broke out: losing all control, he resorted to "tigrish things," struck Mathilde on the face, and tried to set light to her hair, by way of indicating that the truce was over.

It was then that his relations with Rimbaud took a new turn. Hitherto they had remained Platonic; they now ceased to be. That is why Verlaine, in a sonnet (written in 1874), entitled *Le Poète et la Muse*, and dedicated to the sordid attic in the Rue Campagne-Première, was anxious to exculpate himself from a suspicion that had crossed many people's minds. Retrospectively, he no doubt was right:

> *Vous ne comprenez rien aux choses, bonnes gens,*
> *Je vous dis que ce n'est pas ce que l'on pensa.*

> [*You understand nothing of things, good people,*
> *I tell you it is not what people thought.*]

In another sonnet, *Le bon disciple*, dated May 1872, he comes clean, even crudely so. Rimbaud had replied to his request, "As soon as you get back grab me at once."

> *Je suis élu, je suis damné!*
> *Un grand souffle inconnu m'entoure.*
> *O terreur. Parce Domine!*

> *Quel Ange dur ainsi me bourre*
> *Entre les épaules, tandis*
> *Que je m'envole aux Paradis?*

> *Fièvre adorablement maligne,*
> *Bon délire, benoît effroi,*
> *Je suis martyr et je suis roi*
> *Faucon je plane et je meurs Cygne!*

> *Toi le Jaloux qui m'as fait signe,*
> *(Ah!) me voici, voici tout moi!*
> *Vers toi je rampe encore indigne.*
> *—Monte sur mes reins et trépigne!*

[I am chosen, I am damned!
A great, unknown breath of air surrounds me.
O terror. Parce Domine!

What hard Angel rams me in this way
Between my shoulders
As if I fly up to Paradise?

Adorably wicked fever,
Good delirium, blessed fear,
I am a martyr and a king,
Falcon I soar and I die a Swan!

Thou the Jealous One who beckoned to me,
(Ah!) I am here, all of me!
Towards thee I crawl ever unworthy
—Mount on my back and stamp!]

M. André Fontaine has some difficulty persuading one that this sonnet describes a stained glass window in which the Archangel Michael is—temporarily—brought to the ground by the devil.

It seems quite clear that these lines celebrate the beginnings of a new experience. Indeed it is curious to note that in 1874, when Verlaine had a "mystical experience" while in prison, he was similarly deeply moved and was to use the same tone and the same words to describe it:

J'ai l'extase et j'ai la terreur d'être choisi.
Je suis indigne, mais je sais votre clémence.
Ah, quel effort, mais quelle ardeur! Et me voici
Plein d'une humble prière, encor qu'un trouble immense
Brouille l'espoir que votre voix me révéla
Et j'aspire en tremblant . . .

Sagesse, II.4

[I feel the ecstasy and terror of being chosen.
I am unworthy, but I know thy clemency.
Ah, what an effort, but what ardor! And here I am
Filled with a humble prayer, though an immense fear

Disturbs the hope that thy voice reveals to me
And, trembling, I long . . .]

What I have just said is strictly in line with the logic of the character of the two individuals. Verlaine, the old faun, felt awakening within him, on seeing Rimbaud again, the homosexual tendency that had found some timid expression at school and which he must have later repressed (his friend Lucien Viotti had tried to seduce him, if a scarcely disguised admission is to be believed.)

For his part, Rimbaud had no taste in that direction, no leanings, but he had agreed to it in the interests of "the rational deranging of all the senses," which was one of the seer's "keys." By giving into Verlaine he killed two birds with one stone: he revenged himself on Mathilde ("I was unfaithful to my wife in a strange way," Verlaine was to admit to Jules Rais),[9] and he would tighten his grip on his weak friend, thus holding him at his mercy. As far as he was concerned, vice played no role in his decision; he always kept a cool head—"So I loved a pig," he was to write in *Une saison en enfer*, and, "Anyway I must help others [to become Seers], it is my duty. Though it is hardly tempting . . . dear soul."

His duty. . . . One can almost hear his mother!

In fact it was Mathilde who was to make the "way of the cross" promised by Verlaine. In the Rue Nicolet violent scenes were a constant occurrence.

Rimbaud was fixed up in an attic in the Rue Monsieur-le-Prince—perhaps at number 41, at the Hôtel d'Orient—but, more probably, at the top of an old abandoned building, where distressed painters and inveterate Bohemians had set up their studios. The fauna was rather odd: Jolibois, a painter, known as "The apple," because he specialized in painting apples; Kretz, a bearded Alsatian, illuminator, and church decorator; Raoul Ponchon, a celebrity of the Cercle Zutique, the author of drinking songs, who had built a cell for himself out of boxes. Forain, too, was there—if one of his biographers (Knustler) is to be believed. It was at Jolibois's that Jean Richepin met Rimbaud for the first time, or so he says, but his memory is not very reliable, since he places Jolibois's studio in the Rue Saint-Jacques.

It is to be doubted whether our wild Ardennais, who had no liking for painting, enjoyed such company. In June he wrote to Delahaye:

Last month, my room, in the Rue Monsieur-le-Prince, looked
out onto a garden of the Lycée Saint-Louis. There were huge

trees under my narrow window. At three in the morning, the
candle went pale: all the birds cry at once in the trees: it is
over. No more work, I had to look at the trees and the sky,
seized by that unspeakable hour, the first in the morning. I
saw the lycée dormitories, absolutely silent. And already the
jerky, sonorous, delightful noise of the carts on the boulevards.
I smoked my hammer-pipe, spitting on the tiles, for my room
was a garret. At 5 o'clock I went downstairs to buy bread; it
was the time. Workmen were walking everywhere. For me, it
was the time to get drunk at wine merchants'. I returned to
my room to eat and went to bed at seven in the morning when
the sun makes the woodlice come out from under the tiles.
What has always delighted me here is the early morning in
summer and the December evenings.

Meanwhile, Verlaine, once more back on the strait and narrow, after a threat to resume the precedings for separation at the slightest backsliding, was behaving himself; every morning he turned up at the offices of the Lloyd Belge insurance company, and returned to his parents-in-laws' house for dinner at 7 o'clock.

A letter from Forain addressed to him in 1885 has been found: "What has happened to the time when Rimbaud and I would sit waiting for you in a little café in the Rue Drouot, smoking our clay pipes, which we moistened with innumerable bitter-curaçaos, thirteen years ago!"[10]

It did not take Rimbaud long to become convinced that he was being made a fool of, that he had been brought back in order to neutralize him the better in the Parisian desert. He was seized with fury—he would have blood. Verlaine was the first victim of his knife. One day, on May 23, 1872, to be precise, Verlaine was invited with his wife to Victor Hugo's. The master expressed surprise at seeing him walk with a limp: Verlaine explained that he had boils on his legs—he could hardly reveal that Rimbaud had amused himself carving up his thighs. Dr. Antoine Cros, for his part, recounted the following to Mathilde:

The three of us (Rimbaud, Verlaine, and myself) were in
the Café du Rat Mort (Place Pigalle), when Rimbaud said:
"Lay your hands on the table. I want to show you an experi-
ment."

Thinking it to be some kind of joke, we stretched out our hands. Then, drawing an open knife from his pocket, he made a fairly deep cut in Verlaine's wrists. I had enough time to withdraw my hands, and wasn't wounded.

Another day, I was in the café with Rimbaud. I left the table for a moment, and, when I came back, I saw that my beer contained a sulphurous liquid that Rimbaud had just poured into it.

And Mathilde concludes: "The recital of these unhealthy pleasantries, and others that disgust—O Poetry!—prevents me from relating here, were hardly reassuring."[11]

Thereupon Verlaine took it into his head to play the same game at Nina de Villard's—so much so that people got into the habit of hiding any sharp knives when he had been drinking. Mathilde, too, experienced some strange scalp dances from her husband, whose eyes on such occasions shone like a wolf's.

All that Rimbaud could get was a change of residence. Verlaine rented a tiny room for him in the Hôtel de Cluny, Place de la Sorbonne, overlooking a small courtyard. It was from there that in June he wrote to Delahaye an extraordinary letter, part of which I quoted above. It is a crucial document on the life he was leading and on his state of mind at the time.

Parshit, Junish 72

My friend,

Yes, surprising is existence in the Ardennes cosmorama. The province where you eat flour and mud, where you drink local wine and local beer, is not what I miss. You are right to keep on denouncing it. But this place: distillation, compromise, all narrowness; and the oppressive summer; the heat is not continuous, but seeing that good weather is in everyone's interest, and that everyone is a pig, I hate the summer, which kills me when it shows itself even a bit. I am so thirsty that I fear gangrene: what I miss are the Belgian and Ardennes rivers and caves.

There's a drinking place I'm very fond of. Long live the Academy of Absinthe, in spite of the ill-temper of the waiters! It is the most delicate, the most tremulous of garments—this drunkenness induced by virtue of that sage of the glaciers, ab-somphe [absinthe]! in order to recline in shit afterwards!

Always the same whining! What is certain is: shit on Per-rin. And on the bar of the Café de l'Univers, whether it faces the square or not. Yet I don't curse the Univers. I strongly hope the Ardennes will be occupied and pressed more and more rigorously. But all this is normal enough.

What is bad is you have to torment yourself so much. Perhaps you'd do well to walk a great deal and read. A reason in any case not to be confined in offices and homes. Degrada-tions must take place far from such places. I am far from ped-dling balm, but I think that habits do not offer consolations on wretched days.

I work at night now. From midnight to five in the morn-ing. Last month . . .[here follows the passage quoted above].

But at the moment, I have an attractive room, on an endless courtyard, three meters square—the Rue Victor-Cousin forms a corner on the Place de la Sorbonne with the Café du Bas-Rhin and opens on to the Rue Soufflot at the other end.—There, I drink water all night. I don't see the morning, I don't sleep, I stifle. So, there you are!

Your claims will certainly be honored! Don't forget to shit on La Renaissance, *review of literature and the arts, if you come across it. So far I've avoided being pestered by Charleshits* [Carolopomerdés]. *Shit on the seasons.*

Courage.

A. R.

At night he wrote spare ballads, imbued with a gentle melancholy, "using only assonances, vague words, childish or popular phrases" (Verlaine). Some of his songs are grouped together under the title *Fêtes de la patience*, scribbled with a trembling hand, suggesting drunkenness. A resigned lassitude and a "gentle fatalism" (Delahaye) are to be read in counterpoint to these sad verses:[12]

> *Oisive jeunesse*
> *A tout asservie,*
> *Par délicatesse*

J'ai perdu ma vie.
Ah! Que le temps vienne
Où les cœurs s'éprennent.

(Chanson de la plus haute tour)

[*Idle youth*
Enslaved to everything,
Through sensitivity
I wasted my life.
Ah! Let the time come
When hearts fall in love.]

(Song of the Highest Tower)[13]

Or again:

Je veux bien que les saisons m'usent.
A toi, Nature, je me rends;
Et ma faim et toute ma soif.
Et, s'il te plaît, nourris, abreuve.
Rien de rien ne m'illusionne;
C'est rire aux parents, qu'au soleil,
Mais moi je ne veux rire à rien;
Et libre soit cette infortune.

(Bannières de Mai)

[*I am willing that the seasons wear me out,*
To you, Nature, I give myself over;
And my hunger and all my thirst.
Nothing at all deceives me;
To laugh at the sun is to laugh at one's parents.
But I do not want to laugh at anything!
And may this misfortune be free.]

(May Banners)[14]

A physical thirst—which according to Delahaye he had always had—devoured him, and "darkened his veins" in that torrid summer; and he felt hunger, too. He would dream of the cool rivers of the Ardennes, the Semoy or Oise, the waterway at Roche.

Non, plus ces boissons pures,
    Ces fleurs d'eau pour verres;
Légendes ni figures
    Ne me désaltèrent;
Chansonnier, ta filleule
    C'est ma soif si folle,
Hydre intime sans gueules
    Qui mine et désole.
                            (Comédie de la soif)

[No, no more of these pure drinks.
    These water flowers for glasses;
Neither legends nor faces
    Slake my thirst;
Singer, your god-daughter
    Is my thirst so wild,
A mouthless intimate hydra
    Who destroys and afflicts.
                            (Comedy of Thirst)[15]

The Académie d'absinthe, referred to in the letter of Delahaye, was in the Rue Saint-Jacques (no. 176, according to the directory of the period). This drinking establishment was run by a certain Prosper Pellerier. "Tradition has it that at its foundation, in the late eighteenth century," write F. A. Cazals and G. Le Rouge, "the walls of the establishment were lined with forty barrels of brandy. At the time when Alfred de Musset frequented it, it was the custom, when one of its members had just died, to pierce one of the forty barrels after decorating it with a black mourning band" (*Les Derniers jours de Paul Verlaine*). The clientèle was made up of students, street traders, street singers, local painters, and artisans. The "green" cost only three sous there.[16]

One day, to his great surprise, Rimbaud met there a former pupil of the Collège de Charleville, Jules Mary—who was later to become a successful journalist, but who, at the time, was a poor student, wandering the streets of the Latin Quarter. "In his broad, constant gaze," he wrote of Rimbaud, "there was a touch of embarrassment and hesitation, but always that gentle mockery that might lead someone to believe that he hardly took anyone seriously, either himself at that troubled time, or others" (*Littérature*, October 1919). He jotted down his address, then, one morning, turned up at his residence,

in the Rue des Grands-Degrés, between the Place Maubert and the Seine)—
though, he adds, it might have been in the Rue Saint-Séverin. "He was then
living," he explains "in a vast room, the only furniture in which was a table
and a bed stuck in a shady alcove at one end of the room."

"Is this where you work?" he asked.

"Yes, yes," said Rimbaud, and, with an ironic smile, he showed him the
table; there was neither pen nor paper, just a lead inkwell, with, at the bottom, a greenish, dried mud. That day, Mary invited him out for a meal in a
restaurant, where, for forty centimes, one got a portion of boiled beef and a
ladleful of soup.

Rimbaud reciprocated shortly afterwards, by inviting his friend to a dinner that consisted of a bunch of watercress that he had bought from a green-
grocer's stall near the Place Saint-Michel.

Rimbaud's last poem, entitled *Jeune Ménage* (Young Couple), is dated
June 27, 1872. It describes a young couple's bedroom and the view out of the
window:

> *La chambre est ouverte au ciel bleu-turquin;*
> *Pas de place: des coffrets et des huches!*
> *Dehors le mur est plein d'aristoloches*
> *Où vibrent les gencives des lutins.*

> [*The room is open to the turquoise blue sky;*
> *No space; coffers and chests!*
> *Outside the wall is full of birthwort*
> *Where the gums of elves vibrate.*]

He imagines the various characters that come and go, but often

> *le ménage s'absente*
> *Peu sérieusement, et rien ne se fait.*

> [*the family is out*
> *For no serious reason and nothing is accomplished.*][17]

This descriptive poem shows clearly that he had nothing more to say. If
he did work—and it was more and more rarely—it was, as he was to say later,
for "vaguely hygenic reasons." Why should he have bothered? No one was

interested in him, not a single editor or publisher. So what was the point? He was constantly made to feel that he was in quarantine, like some plague victim. On April 27, 1872, Emile Blémont, Jean Aicard, and Richard Lesclide had founded a review, *La Renaissance littéraire et artistique*, which refrained from publishing *Voyelles*, of which Blémont had the autograph copy. He had dropped to the rank of those one did not see and did not publish. (In September 1872, this same *Renaissance* was to publish one of his poems, *Les Corbeaux*, without comment: by this time, the author, who was away from Paris, was no longer compromising.) Similarly, in February or March, Nina de Villard had reopened her celebrated salon (82 Rue des Moines). Verlaine did not dare to take Rimbaud along.

This absurd existence—sleeping and getting drunk—could not go on. The breaking point was not far off. The fine promises, the "way of the cross," the "tigrish things," a life that would be at last free, it was all lies! They had all got rid of him and stifled him. Verlaine was once more under the discipline of his wife and her family, his pathetic attitude evidence that he lived under the constant threat of a legel separation. This separation, which he ought to have desired with all his heart, and done everything he could to bring about if the instinct for freedom had really lived in him, he feared like the worst misfortune. Nothing could ever be done with such a slave.

Then, on Sunday July 7, Rimbaud wrote a letter of farewell: he now realized that he had been made a fool of, and had made up his mind to go away, first to Belgium and then on to hot, distant lands, with no intention of ever coming back. (We do not have the text of this final message, which must have been packed with suppressed anger and biting sarcasm.)

To be on the safe side, he decided to deliver the letter himself to Verlaine, at the Rue Nicolet.

8

Belgium and England

*I*t is tempting to believe in the existence of a god called Chance. Logically, Verlaine should have found in his letterbox, on Monday July 8, the final farewell from his friend, who would already have been on the road bound for Antwerp or Rotterdam. As it was, the night before, a Sunday, Mathilde was ill: she had a headache and a slight fever, and she begged her husband to go and fetch a doctor, who lived nearby. Their relationship had become more or less normal since the eruptions in May. No doubt the relative peace that reigned in the household was due to the fact that Verlaine was in regular work, and had become sober and punctual once again. There was no more question of consorting with Rimbaud than if he had gone back to the Ardennes.

So, before going out, Verlaine gave his wife a perfunctory kiss, and left the house in perfect peace of mind.

He had no sooner gone a few yards than—surprise! surprise!—he saw Rimbaud, who stopped him, and, blurted out that he could no longer bear the life that was being forced upon him, and had made up his mind to leave Paris. One can readily imagine that the rest of the conversation took place in a café, where Rimbaud confirmed that he was at the end of his tether, and that no promises or assurances whatsoever could make him change his mind. He was leaving that very day for Belgium, and, from there, he would travel the world.

Verlaine suddenly found himself at the crossroads: a clear alternative lay before him, and his choice would decide the kind of life he would live thereafter. In a flash, he saw before him an endless succession of boring days, divided between the discipline and habits of office and home, a life lived in a joyless rut, with nothing better to look forward to. On the other side lay adventure, the unexpected, freedom, danger. Shade or sun. It was now that he had to make up his mind; in a few seconds it would be too late: the everyday gloom would descend once again on his tired shoulders. Suddenly he blurted out: "I'll go with you!"

The dice were thrown.

Quickly he thought of the alibi that might justify this sudden act of madness: prudence dictated that he should go abroad for a while, for, every day people often less compromised than he were being court-martialed for collaborating with the Commune. And it was certainly true that as he read the lists of victims in the newspapers, he had begun to dream of an exile outside France, until such time as an amnesty had been declared. So, since the opportunity had cropped up, he would leave and take shelter in Belgium . . . temporarily, of course. Afterwards, they'd have to see.

As neither of them had any money, their first steps were to approach Verlaine's mother—to whom Paul explained that he was about to be arrested—and to beg for an advance to cover the expenses of the first few weeks. No sooner had he got a bit of money in this way, than the two companions were at the Gare du Nord.

No doubt long discussions were required before travel plans could be drawn up, since they took the night train for Arras, the first stage in their trip to Belgium. Perhaps Verlaine had insisted on thanking the person who had put Rimbaud up in February. However, they arrived too early to visit anyone. They were sitting in the refreshments bar of the station having breakfast, about seven in the morning, when a simple old fellow sat down next to them. After digging one another in the ribs, the two conspirators nodded to the newcomer, then, in the most natural way in the world, embarked on "Bretagne's game," that is to say, talked at length of the murders, thefts, and rapes, that they had recently committed, with no details spared. After a while, the fellow sneaked off. However, their ensuing merriment was short-lived: before long two policemen turned up, like jack-in-the-boxes, and arrested them.

Their protestations were met with a curt "You can save all your explanations for the station chief."

The office of the assistant procurator was in a wing of the townhall, so they had to cross the town, and one can imagine that, flanked by two policemen, with passersby turning round and staring at them, our two heroes were not in the best of spirits. As they waited to be received by the magistrate, Verlaine was preparing his defense (I am a Frenchman by choice, having been born at Metz, I am a republican), and Rimbaud wiped away a tear: it reminded him only too well of Douai in 1870, when the police, at his mother's request, put an end to his marvelous adventure in Izambard's house. Similarly, no doubt, he would be sent back *manu militari* to Charleville. There could be no doubt about it. Fortunately, the assistant procurator, realizing that he was simply dealing with two practical jokers, released them with no more than a brief lecture. The good police officers led them back to the railway station, and refused the brandies that Verlaine insisted on offering them as they awaited the Paris train.

From the Gare du Nord, they crossed over to the Gare de l'Est, for the aim was still the same—Belgium—with, as an additional spice, a stop at Charleville.

So, on the morning of July 9, "Father" Bretagne was astonished to find them at his door. They drank and talked at length, like old friends. They probably had lunch at the refreshment bar of the station, their presence in the town not passing unperceived, as we shall see. That evening, Bretagne woke up one of his neighbors, a coachman by trade: "Jean, my brother, I have two fellow priests with me who need your services. Bestir yourself and harness the Beast of the Apocalypse!"[1]

"Father" Jean's carriole took them through the night to the Belgian frontier. We do not know how, but, avoiding the rounds of the customs men and the police checks (a passport was necessary), they were able to get over the frontier without hitch.

Next day, Mme Rimbaud learned that her son had been seen near the station, in the company of Bretagne and another man. Without hesitation, she went off and demanded an explanation from Bretagne, and, when she had confirmation that Arthur had dared to come to Charleville without visiting her, she went immediately to the police, ordering that a search be made for her son, who had probably caught a train for Belgium.

At last, the two fugitives, having set foot on Belgian soil, suddenly realized that the impossible had become reality, that they were free! No more surveillance, prohibitions, suspicions, nagging. No more cares. An endless holiday! The "real life" was opening up before them, an intoxicating, carefree, unpredictable life.

They whistled through Walcourt, then through Charleroi, whose coal fields and tall chimneys left a sinister impression on them. Then, following the Senne and the canal, on foot and by rail, they arrived at last in Brussels.

They moved into the Grant Hôtel Liégois, which Verlaine already knew, since he had stayed there with his mother when he went to greet Victor Hugo in 1867.

One may doubt the alarmist statements made by Mathilde, who, in her *Mémoires*, saw fit to dramatize her husband's flight, and to describe the state of acute anxiety into which it had thrown her. There can be no doubt that her mother-in-law, Mme Verlaine, reassured her very quickly. Paul had gone away because he was afraid of being arrested—there was nothing to worry about. Paul really had been in danger.

One can imagine that Verlaine's letters to his wife were full of mystery and rather short on facts: "It has been a nightmare, I shall come back one day." In those that he wrote to his mother, on the other hand, he told the truth, that his marriage had been the worst mistake in his life, that his existence had become that of a galley slave.

One day, Mathilde, who was not excessively concerned, went to visit her and found her in tears, which highly intrigued her: What had she learned? What fearful secret? What were they hiding?

Now, while these ladies were questioning one another in Paris, the two exiles lost no time in resuming contact with the proscribed supporters of the Commune, whose group comprised about two hundred and fifty members and published an incendiary newspaper, *La Bombe*. They met the most famous of them, Jean-Baptiste Clément, Henri Jourde, Léopold Delisle, Arthur Ranc, Benjamin Gastineau, and Rimbaud was especially pleased to meet Georges Cavalier, familiarly known as "Pipe-en-bois," whom Verlaine had known for a long time and to whom he himself had referred in an article for *Le Progrès des Ardennes*.

It was then that Verlaine, in contact with the heroes of the great tragedy, conceived of the idea of writing a *History of the Commune*, which would be easy enough for him, since his work at the Hôtel de Ville had placed him at the epicenter of the movement. So he asked his wife to send him a file on the subject, which she would find in an unlocked drawer of his desk. This request, harmless enough in itself, was to trigger off a series of catastrophes. For Mathilde, rummaging around in another drawer (one that was probably locked), came across Rimbaud's replies to the secret letters sent to him from her husband between February and May 1872. So, while Paul was declaring that Rimbaud had definitively returned home, he had been secretly planning his return! Could one imagine a more flagrant lie, a more patent betrayal? M. Mauté, who chose that unfortunate moment to come into the room, confiscated Rimbaud's letters, handed them over to his daughter's lawyer, and tore up the rest, including Rimbaud's other writings. This action no doubt explains the disappearance of the *Chasse spirituelle*, the manuscript of which could not have been very thick, since, according to Verlaine, it was contained in a sealed envelope.

More and more anxious, Mathilde went off to her mother-in-law's in order to know precisely what had been troubling her on her previous visit. She asked after Paul, and the good woman fetched the last letter that she had received from him. A mere glance was enough to convince Mathilde that Rimbaud was in Brussels! Everything was becoming clear; fear of arrest was merely a pretext.

Then, since she was a dutiful wife, she made up her mind to go herself and snatch her husband from the claws of his diabolical companion. If Paul did not feel safe in Paris, then the two of them would go off for a time and settle in New Caledonia, where there were plenty of *Communards* who could provide him with all the information he needed concerning the tragic events of May 1871.

So, around July 20, Verlaine alerted Rimbaud of his wife's imminent arrival, accompanied by Mme Mauté. This was bad news for him: Mathilde was quite capable of casting a spell on Paul and getting him back. If the marvelous adventure that had only just begun were not to be aborted, he would have to play his cards very close to his chest. Indeed things very nearly did turn out badly, for, as one can well imagine, Mathilde began at once to pull out all the stops: kisses, mingled tears, and laughter, in short, *love*. As far as she was concerned, the battle was won.

Verlaine, disoriented, pulled in two directions at once, could only come up with vague objections to his immediate return to Paris—objections that Mathilde did not immediately grasp. I'm not free, he wanted to say, but he could not bring himself to do so. Among the reasons he gave for delaying his departure were unfinished business, a situation to be clarified, replies to letters expected . . . in short, pitiful stammerings. Mathilde realized that she would have to strike while the iron was hot, and arranged to meet her husband in a public garden near the Gare du Midi, at 4 o'clock, one hour before the Paris train was due to leave.

Rimbaud, aware of the way events were going, reacted at once, declaring that, if that was the case, he too would go back to Paris on the same 5 o'clock train. That would be impossible, Verlaine objected; if he were in Paris, the hell would begin all over again, the office, the servitude, the teasing of his colleagues, everything that he had rid himself of. But what could he do against Rimbaud's obstinacy? Indeed, Rimbaud would not be moved. That was why, when Verlaine turned up to meet his wife, at 4 o'clock, he was no longer the same man; he dragged himself along, almost tottering, a hang-dog look about him. Mme Mauté and her daughter each took one of his arms, and turned him in the direction of the station. When they had got him into the train, they believed the victory to be theirs. Verlaine himself was gloomy and bad tempered.

At the frontier station of Quiévrain, all the passengers had to get off the train in order to go through customs.

Verlaine caught sight of Rimbaud in the crowd, and let Rimbaud take his hand.[2] The train was about to leave. Mathilde and Mme Mauté went back to their compartments, and peered up and down the platform in search of Verlaine. Finally they caught sight of him: "Hurry! Get on quickly!"

"No. I'm staying," he said fiercely, knocking his hat down over his eyes. He then ran off to join Rimbaud who was hiding.

Mathilde, mortified, deeply wounded, returned to Paris in tears, her heart overflowing with contempt for her husband, whom she was never to see again. Her temperature rose, and she had to retire to her bed. Some days later a note from Verlaine was the final blow: "Miserable ginger-fairy, princess mouse, bug awaiting two fingers and the jar, you have done everything you can to me, you may even have killed the heart of my friend. I'm going off to join Rimbaud if he will still have me after the betrayal you have forced me to subject him to." (Our only source for this message, probably written while half drunk, is Mathilde's *Mémoires*.)

The procedure for a legal separation was reactivated, of course; it would be resumed after the summer holidays. Rimbaud was triumphant; like Caesar, he had come, seen, and conquered. The sky had cleared.

A police report dated August 1, 1873, concerns these events:

> *The scene takes place in Brussels.*
> *. . . Relations between husband and wife were quite*
> *good, despite the infatuations of Verlaine, who had long been*
> *off his head, when misfortune brought to Paris a lad, a native*
> *of Charleville, who had come on his own to present his works*
> *to the Parnassians. From the point of view both of morality*
> *and of talent, this Raimbaud, aged between fifteen and six-*
> *teen, was and is a monster.*

*He possesses a rare gift for verse making, but his words
are absolutely unintelligible and repulsive.*

*Verlaine fell in love with Raimbaud and they went off to-
gether to Belgium to enjoy their love in peace, etc.*

*Verlaine had abandoned his wife with unparalleled
blitheness of spirit and yet, it is said, she is a very likeable and
well-brought-up woman.*

*The two lovers were seen in Brussels openly indulging
their love. Some time ago, Mme Verlaine went to find her
husband with a view to bringing him home. Verlaine replied
that it was too late, that a reconciliation was impossible, and
that in any case he was no longer his own master. "Married
life is hateful to me," he cried, "our love is that of tigers!"
Thereupon he showed his wife his chest, which was tatooed
and slashed with a knife, which, he said, was his friend's,
Raimbaud's, work. Those two individuals fought like wild animals, just for the pleasure of making it up afterwards.*

Mme Verlaine returned to Paris, defeated in her object.

(Verlaine's admissions are pure phantasy; the knife duels belong to May-
July 1873, as we shall see later.)

The danger over, the honeymoon could begin. Verlaine expressed his
happiness at this time in the light verse of "Laeti et errabundi" from *Paral-
lèlement:*

> *Car les passions satisfaites*
> *Insolemment outre mesure*
> *Mettaient dans nos têtes des fêtes*
> *Et dans nos sens, que tout rassure,*
>
> *Tout, la jeunesse, l'amitié,*
> *Et nos coeurs, ah! que dégagés*
> *Des femmes prises en pitié*
> *Et du dernier des préjugés.*
>
> [*For passions satisfied*
> *Insolently, to excess,*

Put in our heads festivities
And in our senses, reassured by everything,

Everything, youth, friendship
And our hearts, ah! freed
From women trapped in pity
And from the last of the prejudices.]

Rimbaud, too, had developed. His poetry, abandoning the sad, resigned tone of the Hôtel de Cluny period, now exploded with joy:

O saisons, ô châteaux!
Quelle âme est sans défauts?

O saisons, ô châteaux,

J'ai fait la magique étude
Du bonheur, que nul n'étude.

O vive lui, chaque fois
Que chante son coq gaulois.

[*O seasons, O castles,*
What soul is without blame?

O Seasons, O castles,

I carried out the magic study
Of happiness that no one eludes.

Oh! May it live long, each time
The Gallic cock crows.][3]

"Happiness!" he was to cry in *Une saison en enfer.* "Its tooth, sweet to death, warned me at the crowing of the cock—*ad matutinum,.* at the *Christus venit*—in the darkest cities."[4]

Mais! Je n'aurai plus d'envie
Il s'est chargé de ma vie.

Ce charme! il prit âme et corps,
Et dispersa tous efforts.

Que comprendre à ma parole?
Il fait qu'elle fuie et vole!

O saisons, ô châteaux!

[But I will have no more desires,
It has taken charge of my life.

That charm! It took my soul and body
And dispersed every effort.

What can be understood from my words?
It makes them escape and fly off!

O seasons, O castles!][5]

In another poem, *Bruxelles*, he lets his imagination run along the Boulevard du Régent, that great shaded thoroughfare, from which one could see the royal palace ("the delightful palace of Jupiter"). It was pleasant to walk there in the sunshine between the "calm houses," several of which were schools, noisy with the "chatter of children in cages." Then, he stops:

C'est trop beau! trop! Gardons notre silence.

—Boulevard sans mouvement ni commerce,
Muet, tout drame et toute comédie,
Réunion des scènes infinie,
Je te connais et t'admire en silence.

[It is too beautiful! too beautiful! let us keep silent.

—Boulevard with no movement and no business,

Mute, every drama and every comedy,
An endless joining of scenes,
I know you and admire you in silence.]⁶

He repeats the phrase "it is too beautiful!" in another poem of the same period, *Est-elle almée?* It really is too beautiful, unimaginable, like a dream or fairy tale.

Could he suspect that in the shadows, dangers, black clouds were gathering that would overshadow his clear sky? In a secret file belonging to the Belgian police a letter has been found from an informant to his boss showing that Mme Rimbaud's request had been implemented.

> *I have the honor of sending you a letter from a M. Rimbaud [Mme Rimbaud always signed herself V.—Veuve (widow) or Vitalie—Rimbaud—hence the confusion: V. was assumed to be the father's initial] asking for a search to be carried out for his son Arthur, who left the parental home in the company of a [the words* young man *have been crossed out] called Verlaine, Paul.*
>
> *From information gathered it appears that [the word* young *is crossed out] Verlaine is staying at the Hôtel de la Province de Liège, Rue de Brabant, Saint-Josse-en-Noode. As for M. Rimbaud, my office has not so far been informed of his presence [the words* Rimbaud's residence has not yet been discovered; however one may suppose that he is living with his friend *are crossed out].*⁷

This document shows that if an obscure policeman had not confused the Grand Hôtel Liégeois and the Hôtel de la Province de Liège, the adventure would have come to an abrupt end: Rimbaud would have been escorted home and, in all likelihood, Verlaine charged with corrupting a minor. But the gods were watching over them. As if they sniffed danger, they decided to leave Brussels and travel around the kingdom. Like good tourists they visited Malines, Ghent, Bruges—though without taking over much interest in old stones, or aldermen's houses, markets, cathedrals, churches, and convents.

It was at Ostend, on Saturday, September 7, 1872, that they saw the sea for the first time—and they were stunned into silence; it was the real image of their dream of endless freedom. Of course they embarked immediately on a steamer bound for Dover. To Rimbaud, this came as an emotional shock. In the poem *Marine*, which he wrote on board, he compares the boat, land-lubber that he and his ancestors were, to a plow cutting into the liquid surface, and raising foamy waves on each side of the furrow:

> *Les chars d'argent et de cuivre—*
> *Les proues d'acier et d'argent—*
> *Battent l'écume,—*
> *Soulèvent les souches des ronces.*
> *Les courants de la lande,*
> *Et les ornières immenses du reflux,*
> *Filent circulairement vers l'est,*
> *Vers les piliers de la forêt,—*
> *Vers les fûts de la jetée,*
> *Dont l'angle est heurté par des tourbillons de lumière.*

> [*Chariots of silver and copper—*
> *Bows of steel and silver—*
> *Beat the foam—*
> *Raise up the stumps of bramble.*
> *The currents of the moor*
> *And the huge ruts of the ebb tide*
> *Flow circularly toward the East,*
> *Toward the pillar of the Forest,*
> *Toward the poles of the pier,*
> *Whose angle is struck by whirls of light.*][8]

The seven- to eight-hour crossing was "fairly rough," said Verlaine, but they both had their sea legs. At dawn on that Sunday morning, the White Cliffs of Dover appeared in the sunlight. Unfortunately, all the "public houses" and restaurants were shut. It was with great difficulty that they managed to get a meal of eggs and tea.

They got to London. They felt totally at a loss, surprised, delighted: the Thames, that "huge whirlpool of mud" (Verlaine), the enormous bridges with their blood red piers, the "incredible" docks, the streets swarming with feverish activity, the green, open spaces, the "Babylonian" buildings beside neo-Gothic houses, the factories, the smoking chimneys, the poor districts—a permanent din. Beside bourgeois, staid Paris, London seemed a vibrant modern metropolis, open to the world.

Taking the most urgent matters first, they could not dream of living in a hôtel; so Verlaine, who had the address of a few exiled friends, began to do the rounds. As a result Vermersch, a faithful friend and colleague from the *Hanneton*, who was about to get married, gave up his room to them at 34 Howland Street. Félix Régamey, a painter and a draughtsman for popular magazines, received them on September 10 in his studio in Langham Street. Of that meeting—and of others that followed in October—valuable souvenirs have survived: a portrait of Verlaine, with a rather Socratic cranium, a sketch of Verlaine strolling with Rimbaud through a London street under the suspicious eye of a policeman. Presenting these documents (in *Verlaine dessinateur* [Paris: Floury, 1896] Régamey writes: "We spent some delightful hours. But he [Verlaine] was not alone. He was accompanied by a silent companion. This was Rimbaud."

One imagines that Rimbaud did not feel obliged to set out to please, and went to sleep in a corner of the studio, on a chair—which is how Régamy drew him—wearing a top hat! Meanwhile, Verlaine picked up a pencil and sketched out an amusing scene: on the terrace of the Académie d'absinthe, in the Rue Saint-Jacques, a flower girl tries to seduce Carjat, who in turn is pointing a finger—to show that he is mad—at an angelic Rimbaud, who is crowning him, while the Parnassians (Leconte de Lisle, Catulle Mendès), on the left, seem to be darkly plotting their revenge.

So we find our Londoners set up in an eighteenth-century former townhouse, now fallen to the status of a mere rooming house. Their days were well filled: expeditions to every part of "the incredible city," and interminable discussions with the *Communards* in exile, who all welcomed Verlaine as one of themselves (had he not been head of the press bureau of the Hôtel de Ville under the insurrection?). Among them, one might mention, in addition to Eugène Vermersch, Jules Andrieu, a fine writer, Pierre-Olivier Lissagaray, author of a *History of the Commune*, Camille Berrère, a contributor to the newspaper *La Sociale*, ex-colonel Matuszéwicz. This small group indulged in a great deal of activity, organized lectures (Verlaine gave two) and debates, publishing newspapers—but Verlaine soon gave up seeing them because he felt in his bones that there were a number of police informers among them, and, for obvious reasons, Rimbaud and he had no wish to live their lives under the eyes of the police—in fact, they were under permanent observation. So they preferred the street, delighting in the passing show, constantly amused by the pecularities of the natives: women wearing red shawls, the boot blacks, the Negroes, the coachmen (Rimbaud drew one wearing a romantic box-coat), the drunks, the beggars, the prostitutes. Of course, they also frequented, as far as their means allowed, the pubs, the coffee houses, and the theaters, where they saw operettas in English: Hervé's *Le Roi Carotte* or *L'Oeil Crevé*, with music by Offenbach, and no doubt several Shakespeare plays. They also visited the international exhibition in Kensington Gardens, the focus of which was the enormous Albert Hall, the size of the Coliseum and, out in the suburb of Sydenham, the famous Crystal Palace, with its impressive structure of steel and glass. These strange, grandiose monuments of an industrial civilization in full expansion provided fine subjects for Rimbaud's "Chasse spirituelle": they are to be found in *Les Illuminations* (*Villes*),[9] and Underwood is no doubt right to regard the "burning aquarium" of *Bottom* as a memory of the gas-lit aquarium at the Crystal Palace, a "scientific marvel," it was said at the time, and a great attraction for visitors.[10] Life was a succession of festivals: the picturesque procession of dummies for Guy Fawkes Night, the inauguration of the Lord Mayor of London, Madame Tussaud's wax works, the visit of the shah of Persia, the "Metropolitan Railway," the "Tower subway" (a tunnel under the Thames), fireworks displays with jets of colored water. They were amused spectators at all these celebrations. Rimbaud was enthusiastic about the industrial progress, the vitality, the confidence in the future of the whole nation, which, there could be no doubt, was the first in the world. And all this took place in a setting that was at once delicate and barbarous, beneath "Gray crystal skies."

A *strange pattern of bridges, some straight, some arched, others going down at oblique angles to the first, and these shapes repeating themselves in other lighted circuits of the canal, but all of them so long and light that the banks, heavy with domes, are lowered and shrunken. Some of these bridges are still covered with hovels. Others support masts, signals, thin parapets. Minor chords cross one another and diminish, ropes come up from the shores. You see a red jacket and perhaps other costumes and musical instruments. Are they popular tunes, bits of castle concerts, remnants of public hymns? The water is gray and blue, as wide as an arm of the sea.*
    —A *white ray, falling from the top of the sky, blots out this comedy.*

    Les Ponts (*Bridges*), Illuminations[11]

Meanwhile, Verlaine, who had not written a line for two years, took up his pen again, urged on by his companion's excitement. The poetic era, the era of the seer's vision was about to begin at last. The *Romances sans paroles*, which are also bathed in the unreal English light, express gentle melancholy and langorous regret.

But there is a big gap between poetry and reality—and reality was soon to spread its poison, an ever blacker poison over their carefree lives. Verlaine could not hide the fact that his wife had opened legal proceedings for a "separation of bed and board" (divorce not yet having been reestablished in law), on ten grounds, including acts of violence perpetrated on her by her husband when drunk, his desertion, and his strange behavior in Brussels. Even if he had wished to forget this offensive, which he regarded as unspeakable, the stream of hateful blue Court papers constantly revived his anxiety: the issuing of the writ, the summons (with a view to attempting a reconciliation), the serving of the court order of October 13 allowing Mathilde to reside with her parents, and forbidding her husband "to frequent his wife in the said house," lastly the serving of the claims for maintenance amounting to 1,200 francs a year, with provision for an immediate payment of 1,000 francs.

This continual harassment so enraged Verlaine that he altogether lost his self-control: he talked of cracking the skull of Maître Guyot-Sionnest, his wife's lawyer, and of putting in a counterclaim—for he, too, he thundered, had "proof!" He was made to understand that all this would serve no purpose, and that he would do better to abide by the rules if he wanted to defend himself. So he appointed a lawyer, a Maître Pérard, of the Rue Rossini. In a letter dated November 8, he informs his friend Lepelletier that he is drawing up his defense, pulverizing, he says, the unspeakable accusation (of homosexuality): "In it I expound, in a psychological, but very clear and sober analysis, the highly honorable and commendable motives for my very real, very deep, and *very persevering* friendship for Rimbaud—I shall not add *very pure*—for shame!"

It is certainly a pity that this document has not survived (Maître Pérard's files were destroyed in 1919). Incorrigible artist that he was, Verlaine imagined that a well-written analysis, in which he gave himself the best role, would prevail over stamped paper and the tenacity of the lawyers! In much the same spirit, he conceived of the idea of grouping together under the title "La Mauvaise chanson" the poems denouncing his wife's treachery and his own martyrdom, but Rimbaud persuaded him against it. The idea struck him as being in bad taste—and, anyway, was that creature worth the trouble?

These vexations and the approach of winter had somewhat diminished the joyful enthusiasm of the early days, and then the lack of money (Verlaine could not go on forever asking his mother for subsidies) placed them on a level with the disinherited—and, God knows, there were enough of them in London!—whom they came into contact with every day: "In the dives where we used to get drunk, he [Rimbaud, the "Infernal Bridegroom," as seen by Verlaine, the "Foolish Virgin"] would weep as he observed the herd of poverty-stricken people about us" (*Une saison en enfer*)

Such a climate was not very inducive to literary creation: for that, both needed a relaxed, carefree atmosphere. Their high point, they realized, was behind them; their fates were grinding to a halt.

Yet Rimbaud went on noting down in his seer's notebook sensations, landscapes, and dreams, in a poetic prose, which for him represented so many stylistic exercises: that is why the *Illuminations* are so fragmented and disconnected. Perhaps he intended one day to bring these notes together in a properly constructed work that would be one of the summits of French literature, but that would take years of labor in a sort of permanent state of grace. And the fact was that he lived in a permanent state of discord. His relationship with Verlaine went on declining. Mathilde's husband, overcome with regret and remorse, was in a constant state of anguish, forever sighing and on the verge of tears; his constant feelings of bitterness verged on hypochondria. Rimbaud regarded him with irritated pity; the poor fellow did not understand that the seer is a superman, impervious to discouragement, because his will and energy are capable of overcoming failure, emotional ties, contempt, and sarcasm. And there he was dragging around with him a poor, lost individual, paralyzed by fear of the courts and regret for the wife, child, and parents-in-law that he had lost.

> *Poor brother! What terrible nights I owed him! "I had no deep feeling for the affair. I played on his weakness. Through my fault, we would return to exile and slavery." He believed I had a very queer form of bad luck and innocence, and he added upsetting reasons.*
>
> *With a jeer I answered my satanic doctor, and left by the window. Along the countryside, streaked with bands of rare music, I created phantoms of a future night parade.*

After that vaguely hygienic distraction, I lay down on
straw. And almost every night, as soon as I was asleep, my
poor brother would get up, his mouth dry and his eyes pro-
truding—just as he dreamed himself to be—and would drag
me into the room yelling his dream of a sad fool.
  In deepest sincerity, I had pledged to convert him back
into his primitive state of a sun-child,—and we wandered,
sustained by wine from caverns and traveler's crust, with me
impatient to find the place and the formula.
(Vagabonds, Illuminations)[12]

Rimbaud makes his self-criticism at the beginning of this revealing piece: he accuses himself of lacking firmness. "I played on his weakness" means: I had underestimated his weakness; he should have been treated more harshly ("Through my fault, we would return to exile and slavery").

At this time, therefore, Rimbaud was partly aware at least that the experiment had failed. It was a failure of which he would be the principal victim, for he would not go unscathed by that legal business: in accusing Verlaine of having run away with a young man, Mathilde was aiming at him, and her lawyers would unmask him; the authorities would probably intervene, since he was still a minor. Inevitably, one day or another, his mother would learn of the unspeakable insinuations being leveled at him. On top of everything else, it would be the ruin of his literary career.

So he had the courage to forestall matters by admitting everything to her. "Rimbaud recently wrote to his mother," Verlaine informed Lepelletier on November 14, 1872, "to warn her of what was being said and done against us, and I am at present in proper correspondence with her. I have given her your address, and those of my mother, the Mautés, M. Istace, and the two lawyers."

Mme Rimbaud received the news as an attack on the honor of her name. Her son involved in a legal case, and suspected of some abominable vice, it was more than she could bear! So, dropping everything, she informed Paul's mother that she was about to descend on her. Mme Verlaine, naturally enough, talked of calumnies, and blamed her son's family-in-law: they wanted to ruin him, the evil-minded people.

Not to be put off, she turned up at the Rue Nicolet. There she was received in a supercilious, tight-lipped manner—"We don't know what to believe"—and had to beat a retreat without being able to get back any of her son's letters and manuscripts, for which Verlaine would have paid dearly.

"We don't have anything any more, some of the items are in the lawyer's file, and no doubt he would hand them back after the court hearing."

So the danger was real, serious, urgent. Mme Rimbaud demanded Arthur's immediate return. Verlaine, who considered that their separation would amount to an admission of guilt, refused at first to give in—no doubt urged on by Rimbaud, who was not looking forward at all to a period spent in the Ardennes.

In the end, at the urgent demand (accompanied by threats) of his mother, Rimbaud had to obey, much against his will.

"My life is about to change," Verlaine wrote to Lepelletier at the beginning of December. "This week, Rimbaud must go back to Charleville, and my mother is coming here."

It is in this letter that he says that he has seen himself—and Rimbaud—again in Fantin-Latour's painting, which was in an exhibition. They must have had a good laugh at the sight of those impassive, bearded Parnassians!

9

Interlude at Charleville

and Roche:

Reprise before the Drama

For some days Verlaine seemed relieved at Rimbaud's departure, which, in the end, might have a beneficial effect by cutting short the Mautés' calumnies and malevolent insinuations. He glimpsed the prospect of a peaceful future, in the company of his mother—who had just had a very violent scene with M. Mauté, after categorically refusing to accede to the demand for alimony. He was planning on renting a small house—or so he said to Lepelletier—and there find what peace and quiet he could; if not—who knows—a ménage. The hearing could now take place. He feared it no more than if it did not concern him.

Mme Rimbaud, too, was relieved. Verlaine was a nice enough man, but Arthur must understand that he must not see him again, since there must be no question of his being involved in a matrimonial lawsuit.

Rimbaud felt betrayed. Still dazzled by the lights of the huge city, his head filled with the din of carriages and ship's sirens, he found his native town gloomier than ever—when night fell, around 5 o'clock, the streets were deserted. Furthermore, it was still occupied by the Prussians—they did not leave until July 24, 1873. Good old Delahaye was still there, but he was working in an office. And even he was still so provincial.

Delahaye tells us that Rimbaud read to him some of the poems written between May and August 1872. "Now," he said, early in 1873, with that smile of mock-resignation that he often had, "now I am composing songs, childish rustic, naive, pleasant songs."[1]

Deep down, he was boiling with impatience and rancor: the coalition had reformed. For the second time, Paul, Mathilde, the Mautés, and "la mère Rimbe" had ganged up against him.

Then, as he was still chewing over his grievances, about January 10, 1873, a letter arrived from Verlaine. He was, he said, gravely ill, "ready to pack it in." To prove that this was not a lie, he enclosed a note that Rimbaud was asked to send on to Emile Blémont: "I am *dying* of grief, sickness, boredom, desertion. Rimbaud will send this on to you. Excuse my brevity—I am *very ill*. Hail, or perhaps farewell!"

What had happened? After the Christmas festivities, Verlaine had got very depressed. As he wrote to Lepelletier, "Very sad, however, very lonely. Rimbaud (whom you don't know, whom only I know) is no longer here. What a terrible void! The others mean nothing to me. They're all riff-raff. Q.E.D. But hush! Shit!"

Suddenly, he had sunk into the deepest depression, thinking that his last hour had come.

His desperate letters had the result of bringing his mother, accompanied by a female cousin, over to England to see him, and of bringing Rimbaud back.

The gates of Rimbaud's Carolopolitan prison opened a little. He could not let such an opportunity go by, nor, of course, abandon his friend, his only friend, when he was seriously ill. Mme Rimbaud was up in arms when he asked her for money to go back to London.

"Never! You'll stay here!"

But Verlaine's mother sent him the fifty francs necessary, via Delahaye.

Two days later, Rimbaud was in London.

Verlaine received him with open arms and was happy to announce to Emile Blémont that, thanks to his companion, he felt much better: "Listening only to his friendship, he came here at once, where he still is, and where his good care may help to extend less painfully the poor existence of a damned soul."

Rimbaud arrived in the middle of a family council: something had to be done. Paul could not be left in that state. Since the accursed proceedings that Mathilde was subjecting him to were the source of his misfortunes, he should not be allowed simply to bury his head in the sand, and remain paralyzed before such a threat, but, on the contrary, he should react bravely, take the

bull by the horns, go to Paris, and offer Mathilde a sincere, total reconciliation. If she accepted, the problem would be solved: if not, he could go to the
court, head held high, with good arguments and a good lawyer, and with
every chance of winning the case. Verlaine admitted that he had everything
to gain and nothing to lose by taking such a determined stance. But, once his
mother had left, he fell back into apathy and anxiety.

As for Rimbaud, he doubted whether Paul would ever have the courage
to act in such a way; indeed, he saw no reason to look for trouble. Better to
keep quiet and carry on living. The poor fellow should stop complaining and
realize that his troubles would end as soon as he forgot that he had ever been
married! The obvious fact was that the two of them must stay in England, in
independence and liberty. They must find a "positive economy," as he had
once said to Paul Demény: first, they must make a thorough study of English
in order to be able to teach it, earn some money, and owe nothing to anybody.
Verlaine wrote to Emile Blémont:

> We are learning English apace, Rimbaud and I, in Edgar
> Poe, in collections of popular songs, in Robertson, etc., etc.
> Also in shops, public houses, libraries, etc., we are applying
> mouth glue to ourselves, in order to aid our pronunciation.
> Every day we go for long walks into the suburbs and country-
> side, Kew, Woolwich, etc., for we've known London for a long
> time now. Drury Lane, Whitechapel, Pimlico, Angel, the
> City, Hyde Park, etc. no longer hold any mysteries for us.
> . . . For the moment, we're trying to earn a few sous.
> Very soon we'll be able to jabber enough English to give
> French and Latin lessons, etc.

Long walks and study were excellent distractions. Reading was another.
On March 23 and 25, they applied for reader's tickets to the British Museum.
We do not know who their sponsors were. Rimbaud signed to the effect that
he was acquainted with the rules of the library and that he was over twenty-
one (in fact he was nineteen).

What did they read, sitting, perhaps, beside Karl Marx, an assiduous
reader at the time? No doubt Poe, Longfellow, Swinburne. Delahaye says
that Rimbaud was refused permission to consult the works of the marquis de
Sade, since a special authorization was necessary to consort with this resident
of hell.

But these occupations and this work did not prove to be enough to contain Verlaine's anxieties: before long he was obsessed once more by his marital drama. He had now become convinced that he would have to act, and that he would never be at peace if he did not do so. For days on end he haunted Victoria Station, no doubt consulting the timetables. Finally, on April 3, he made up his mind and set off for Newhaven with the intention of sailing to Dieppe. But, as he was waiting for the boat, he was horrified to overhear two very suspect gentlemen talking between themselves about the *Communards* and the fate that awaited them in France. The police were everywhere! So he went on to Dover, and, on the morning of April 4, boarded the *Comtesse de Flandres* bound for Antwerp. He had previously written to Mathilde a begging, tender, touching letter: she must be reasonable, give up this stupid case, which was ruining both their lives, think of young Georges, come to Namur, where he was alone, and where she would find reconciliation, and they would go back to Paris together, once they had forgiven one another.

Having thus unburdened himself, he confidently awaited her response. Could she be so stony-hearted as to remain unmoved by his loving supplications?

He was quite unaware that the police had long been on his trail: the day before he left London, the Paris police were alerted by the following note: "Verlaine, ex-clerk at the Hôtel de Ville before and during the Commune, friend of Vermesch [*sic*], Andrieux and Co. . . . left for Paris (to settle family business.)"

On April 8, a second note stated: "He has spread the rumor that he is staying at Namur; he is living quietly at his mother's"—proof that Rimbaud had been kept informed of his stop-off at Namur.

On April 17, Lombard, an officer from the Paris police, was given the task of providing all possible information concerning his past record, his morality, his conduct during the insurrection, and above all the real purpose of his trip to Paris.

One can now see how dangerous was his attempt to regain Mathilde; at the very least, she was exposing him to ten years in jail.

All this vexed Rimbaud considerably, but did not worry him unduly: he was sure that Verlaine would come back discomfited and furious. Actually, he was not very far out. Mathilde had replied that her husband's letter merely betrayed his fear of losing the case; that, for her part, she knew that she could not lose; that, consequently, he should cease importuning her, for she would not open any more of his letters.

So, once again, it was he, Rimbaud, who would suffer—indeed, Verlaine, exhausted by the effort, had gone off to rest at his Aunt Evrard's at Jehonville (Belgium). He found himself alone once more, not knowing enough English to give lessons, and therefore unable to pay rent or keep himself.

He knew that, from April 5, all his family had left Charleville for Roche—not to get a breath of country air, but because serious trouble had struck their relations: a barn and stable had burned down, with the loss of the harvest, and the departure of the tenant farmer, who had shown little interest in the running of the farm. "Wild hops and nettles covered the ruins," Paterne Berrichon remarks.

Arthur arrived unexpectedly on Good Friday, April 11 (which shows that he remained in London for only a few more days). His sister Vitalie (then fifteen) described the event in her diary.

> That day was to mark an epoch in my life, for it saw an event that deeply moved me; without any warning, as it were, the arrival of my second brother completed our joy. I can still see myself in our room, where we were arranging some of our things; my mother, my brother, and my sister were with me, when there was a gentle knock on the door. I went to answer it and . . . imagine my surprise, when I found myself face to face with Arthur. When we had got over the first shock of surprise, the newcomer explained to us the object of his visit; we were delighted, and he was very happy to see our pleasure. We spent the day together, showing Arthur the farm, which he did not know, so to speak.[2]

On Easter Sunday, April 13, the whole family attended High Mass at Chuffilly, and, in the afternoon, they all went off for a long walk. One can imagine the country scene: Mme Rimbaud giving orders to the masons and farmer, Isabelle and Vitalie chasing the chicks in the farmyard, Frédéric cleaning out the paddock.

Poor Arthur! What a hole he had fallen into! That desolate part of the Vouzinois was the very image of his mother, gloomy and austere. "Nothing distinguished that spot from total insignificance," writes Julien Gracq, "a landscape of boredom and deep rural slumber: not a hill, not a stream, not a forest" (En lisant, en écrivant). "Only the sky matters," adds André Dhotel.[3]

How could he spend his exile? Rimbaud soon guessed what kind of a life awaited him: that of a beclogged peasant, without a penny, without a friend, without the slightest entertainment. So he decided to write a book that would describe his spiritual adventure, and thanks to which he might earn enough money to set off again, without having to beg it from his mother, or call on the generosity of Mme Verlaine. It would be a slim volume comprising a few chapters; it would not take him long to write it. The great work that he was planning, the exploration of a hitherto unknown, barbarous world in the light of his seer's vision could wait.

He had brought back from London ("What a city of the Bible!" said Verlaine) a few pages on which he had written a commentary of three scenes from St. John's Gospel, the first miracles of Jesus in Galilee, Samaria, and at the pool of Bethsaida. As paper was in short supply at Roche, he wrote on the back the first draft of a few chapters of the "Pagan Book," or "Negro Book," which he was planning, namely, "Bad Blood," "False Conversation," "Alchemy of the Word."

He was in constant correspondence with Verlaine, who, at Jehonville, was as bored as he was, and he had renewed contact with Delahaye, who was still in Charleville.

On Sunday, April 20, a pleasant tradition was established: the three friends would meet around a restaurant table near the frontier.

About May 15 Rimbaud wrote to Delahaye an illustrated letter, which is a valuable document concerning his life at Roche, and his literary and other projects.

> *Dear friend, you can see my present life in this enclosed draw-*
> *ing.*
> *O Nature O mother of mine!*

> [*Here there is a drawing well described by Berrichon: "In*
> *the sky there is a little fellow holding a spade as if it were a*
> *monstrance, with the following words coming out of his*
> *mouth: 'O Nature, O my sister!' On the ground is a larger*
> *fellow, wearing clogs, a shovel in his hand, a cotton cap on his*
> *head, in a landscape of flowers, grass, and trees. In the grass*
> *is a goose, which is saying: 'O Nature, O my aunt!'"*]

> *What a tough shit! and what monsters of innocence these*
> *peasants are! At night, to have a drink, you have to walk two*

leagues or more. The mother [in English] has put me in this sad hole of a place.

[Here there is another drawing: a landscape, bearing the legend "The hamlet of Roche, canton of Attigny, seen from the house of Mme Rimbaud."]

I don't know how to get out of it, but I will. I miss that vile Charlestown, the Univers [Café], the library, etc. . . . . Yet I work quite steadily; I'm writing little stories in prose, general title: Pagan Book, or Negro Book. It is crazy and innocent. O innocence! innocence; innocence, innoc . . . , scourge!

Verlaine must have given you the wretched commission of arguing with Monsieur Devin, printer of the Nord-Est. I think this Devin could do Verlaine's book [Romances sans paroles] reasonably and quite satisfactorily. (If he doesn't use the shitty typing characters of the Nord-Est. He would be capable of sticking an illustration on it or an ad!)

I have nothing more to tell you, the contemplation of nature completely filling my ass. I am yours, O Nature, O mother!

I shake your hands, in the hope of a reunion I am activating as much as I can.

R.

I reopen my letter. Verlaine must have suggested a rendezvous for Sunday the 18th in Bouillon. I can't go. If you go, he will probably give you a few fragments of my prose or his to return to me.

Mother Rimb. will return to Charlestown sometime in June. This is certain, and I will try to stay in that pretty town a little while.

The sun is strong and it is freezing in the morning. The day before yesterday I went to see the Prussians in Vouziers, a subprefecture of 10,000 souls, seven kilometers from here. This cheered me up.

I am absolutely thwarted, not a book, not a bar within reach, not an incident in the street. How horrible this French countryside is! My fate depends on this book for which I still

have to invent a half-dozen atrocious stories. How can I invent atrocities here? I am not sending you any stories, although I already have three. It costs too much! *That's all for now!*
Goodbye to you. You'll see it later.

RIMB.

The allusion to the rendezvous for Sunday the 18th at Bouillon refers to a letter from Verlaine to Delahaye dated May 15, asking him to cancel the planned meeting at Sugny, and mentioning that quite by chance he would be at Bouillon on May 18.

Indeed he went there and saw nobody: "Arrived here at noon, in pouring rain, on foot," he wrote to Rimbaud. "Found no Deléclanche. Will leave again by the mail coach—dined with Frenchman from Sedan and a tall pupil from the Collège de Charleville. A somber feast!"

This letter, obviously written after a meal during which he had drunk deep, contains, apart from a few heavy jokes, an announcement of good news to come: "You'll be pleased." The words are repeated twice. They meant that the way to England was free, for Verlaine's mother, who was not in favor of her son returning to London, was going home to Arras.

On Friday May 23, two days before the decisive reunion of the following Sunday at Bouillon, Verlaine confided his plan to Lepelletier: he would leave for Liège, Antwerp, and finally London, after a reunion of the "comrades of Charleville-Mézières."

This is exactly what took place on May 25. On that day Verlaine was so late at the Hôtel des Ardennes that he still remembered it two years later (in a letter to Delahaye dated July 1, 1875). Delahaye himself provided an account of the historic lunch fifty-five years after the event (*La Grive*, October 1928), which contains too many manifest errors and improbabilities to be taken seriously.

Rimbaud, no doubt, was delighted at this resumption of the "way of the cross," especially as Verlaine appeared to be calmer, if not cured altogether. His decision to organize his life without further concern for his wife seemed irrevocable. And, anyway, for him anything was preferable to Roche in May and Charleville in June!

A rather sad Delahaye took the stagecoach back to Sedan alone.

After visiting Liège on Monday, May 26[4] and Antwerp on the 27, the two travelers embarked that same evening on the steamer of the Great Eastern

Railway, which, lifting anchor at four o'clock, did not reach Harwich until the following day at 6:40. "An incredibly beautiful crossing," Verlaine told Lepelletier, in a letter dated Friday May 29 (in fact it was May 30).

Rimbaud admired the seascape and wrote a poem in free verse, *Mouvement* (Motion) in a very different tone from that of *Marine*, which celebrated his discovery of the sea. The two travelers had set out to conquer the world (*A youthful couple withdraws into the archway*):

> *Ce sont les conquérants du monde*
> *Cherchant la fortune chimique personnelle;*
> *Le sport et le confort voyagent avec eux . . .*
> *Repos et vertige*
> *A la lumière diluvienne*
> *Aux terribles soirs d'étude . . .*
> *Eux chassés dans l'extase harmonique*
> *Et l'héroïsme de la découverte.*

> *[They are the conquerors of the world*
> *Seeking a personal chemical fortune;*
> *Sports and comfort travel with them . . .*
> *Repose and dizziness*
> *To the torrential light*
> *To the terrible nights of study . . .*
> *Themselves driven into harmonic ecstasy,*
> *And the heroism of discovery.]*[5]

They rented a room in the house of Mrs Alexander Smith, 8 Great College Street, in Camden Town (N.W.), a very lively district, not far from Highgate, where a great many artists lived.

At first everything went perfectly. Verlaine, at last, was behaving sensibly. "I shall no longer bother anyone with my business," he wrote on May 30, 1873, to Emile Blémont. "The lawcourts will settle all that."

Rimbaud would have been justified in thinking that the game was won. His mind at rest, he got down to work on the sketches of his *Livre Païen;* Verlaine sketched him writing in a public house, adding by way of a legend, "How *Saison en enfer* was written, London 72–73." This drawing, mentioned by Charles Houin, belonged to the publisher Léon Vanier. It has not been rediscovered.[6]

Verlaine, similarly carefree, was a frequent visitor to the Reading Room of the British Museum, and his powers of literary creation recovered. He realized that Rimbaud was right when he insisted on their need for financial independence. Since they contemplated a long stay in England, they could not decently continue to live on the generosity of Mme Verlaine. French lessons would bring in enough money to pay for their current expenses, and to put a little by. After all, was not money the source of freedom? They already saw themselves traveling comfortably, two dilettantes, in the southern seas. In any case, far, very far from the Rue Nicolet!

Underwood has found two almost identical advertisements that appeared in the popular newspaper *The Echo* on June 11, 12, and 13, 1873, and in the *Daily Telegraph* on June 21.

"French, Latin, Literature Lessons, conducted in French by two Parisian gentlemen; moderate fees—VERLAINE, 8 Great College St., Camden Town."[7]

On June 25, Verlaine was able to announce triumphantly to Emile Blémont that he had found a pupil! It is quite likely that he did better, since both very soon were giving two lessons a day at three shillings—which would give them pocket money (tobacco, drinks). To the question asked of him by the examining magistrate at Brussels, on July 12, 1873, "What did you live on in London?" Rimbaud replied: "Mainly on the money that Mme Verlaine sent her son. We also had French lessons, which we gave together, but they did not bring in very much, about 12 francs a week toward the end."

They expected to improve, so they set about learning English, this time more seriously, spending whole days at it. Verlaine read the poets—Swinburne, in particular—and Rimbaud copied out words from whatever magazines he could lay his hands on, mainly from the sports or farming pages. They already knew enough English to carry on a conversation: they now deepened their knowledge by acquiring the technical terms of various activities. They also went to the theater again.

Now, just as they were beginning to feel that they would soon be self-sufficient, that is to say, free, everything collapsed around them.

Why?

To begin with, because of the gossip, smiles, and insinuations concerning their relationship current among the exiled *Communards*. This must have been going on for some time, but they had been unaware of it because they no longer consorted with the exiles. However, Verlaine still saw some of his old friends, Vermersch, Régamey, or Andrieu. It was inevitable that, sooner or later, the scandal would break.

One day, Rimbaud went to visit Jules Andrieu, a highly cultured man, whose company therefore Rimbaud enjoyed. To his great surprise, Delahaye writes, Rimbaud was received "very badly, not to say roughly."[8] In fact, Rimbaud was thrown out, perhaps in front of witnesses. Andrieu had learned what was being whispered about Rimbaud and Verlaine.

For Verlaine, this was a catastrophe. Suddenly all his wounds reopened. Only on June 25 he had written to Blémont: "My morale and health have returned." Now he collapsed again. The rumor of his "unspeakable relations" with Rimbaud confirmed everything the Mautés had said. Not only would he lose the case, but he would emerge from it dishonored.

So he tried to mend the damage by going to see those who might help him. He called on Camille Barrère, who later recounted the incident to Mr Underwood, in order to plead his innocence. "I'm accused of being a homosexual, but I'm not!"[9]

The Andrieu-Rimbaud incident did the rounds of the small *Communard* world of London, and did not escape the attention of police informers who always frequented their circles. On June 26, 1873, a note was transmitted to the Paris police prefecture: "A liaison of a strange kind links the former employee of the Prefecture of the Seine (who remained at his post during the Commune), sometime poet on the *Rappel*, a M. Verlaine, and a young man who often comes to Charleville, and who, under the Commune, was a member of the Paris *francs-tireurs*, young Raimbault. M. Verlaine's family is so sure of the authenticity of this degrading fact that they are basing part of their case for a separation on this point."

Verlaine may have been furious; Rimbaud's reaction was no less violent. The reputation that he had acquired in London would follow him everywhere. It was the end of an entire literary career: his name would be forever besmirched, and his mother would soon know of it.

Each could blame the other for ruining his life. An irreparable split had just taken place.

It is likely that Verlaine returned to his excessive drinking habits, which was usually the case whenever he was thwarted in his wishes. One can imagine how violent their relationship became. In a conversation with Underwood, Camile Barrère has described their arguments, which, very often, degenerated into fisticuffs or the brandishing of knives (*Verlaine et l'Angle-terre*). Ernest Delahaye has spoken of German-style duels: "Sharp blades are wrapped in towels and grasped in the hand, only the tips showing, and one aims at the face or throat."[10] Rimbaud confirms that such fights took place: "On several nights, his demon seizing me, we rolled on the ground and I fought with him!" (*Une saison en enfer*).[11]

Soon they could no longer hide the violence in which they lived; it was all too apparent in bruises and cuts. A police report dated August 1, 1873, declares: "These two individuals fought and tore at one another like wild beasts, just for the pleasure of making it up afterwards."

Things could not go on like that.

10

The Dramatic Events of July 10

*I*n early July, Verlaine had made up his mind to have done with it. He would have another shot at the Namur tactic, summon his wife to Belgium, and if, by some misfortune, she refused to join him, he would kill himself. In the greatest secrecy, he set to work planning his scenario and preparing for his flight, noting in his secret diary (found by Underwood) the steps to be taken: put all his manuscripts in a safe place here, his linen and clothes there, etc. He had made inquiries, and knew that on Thursday July 3 at midday a boat was leaving the London docks for Antwerp.

In the morning, as he was coming back from shopping, serious and determined, holding a bottle of oil in one hand and a herring in the other (Cazels says that it was a mackerel wrapped up in newspaper, and Delahaye adds that the fish was spoiled—but no matter!) Rimbaud caught sight of him from the window, and called down: "You don't know how silly you look with your oil and your fish!"

Since he needed a pretext, this uncomplimentary remark was to be the signal for setting his great plan in motion. Verlaine rushed into the room like a madman: threw his acquisitions down on to the table, and, his face purple with anger, yelled: "No! This is intolerable! It must cease!"—and since, on top of everything else, he had to put up with being made a fool of, he was leaving!

He quickly grabbed his case, which, as if by magic, was all packed, stalked out, and banged the door behind him. Rimbaud, taken completely by surprise, watched him stride away, then, realizing that this was no joke, decided to follow him.

At this point, there is a gap in our story. Rimbaud definitely saw his companion embark at St. Catherine's Wharf on a boat bound for Antwerp.

But it is nearly four miles from Great College Street to the docks,[1] so they could hardly have walked there. Verlaine must have taken a cab or some form of public transport (the underground? an omnibus?). Did some final, bitter argument take place between them? We shall never know, but, at noon precisely, as the siren roared and the ship lifted anchor, Rimbaud, standing on the quayside was gesticulating wildly, not to say goodbye, but to make a desperate appeal.

Now it was the end. The boat disappeared. Rimbaud was alone, without a penny, lost in the huge city.

Next day, in the afternoon, he wrote a letter intended for Verlaine, without having very much idea as to where to send it.

> *Come back, come back, dear friend, my only friend, come back. I swear I'll behave myself. If I was surly with you, I was only joking. I couldn't stop myself. I'm more repentant than I can say. Come back, everything will be forgotten. How terrible that you took that joke seriously. For two days now I haven't stopped crying. Come back. Be brave, dear friend. Nothing is lost. You have only to make the journey again. We will live here again, courageously and patiently. Oh! I beg you. It is for your good, too. Come back, you will find all your things here. I hope you realize now there was nothing serious in our argument. What a terrible moment it was. But why didn't you come when I signaled you to get off the boat? Have we lived two years together to come to this! What are you going to do? If you don't want to come back here, do you want me to come to you?*

In a postscript he adds:

> *Answer quickly: I cannot stay here any later than Monday evening. I haven't another penny. I can't put this in the mail. I have given your books and manuscripts to Vermersch to take care of.*
>
> *If I am not to see you again, I will enlist in the navy or the army.*

He imagined that Verlaine had acted in a fit of anger, as he so often had before, and that it would be followed before long by a reconciliation.

Next day, a letter from Verlaine marked "very urgent" arrived, written "at sea." It must have made Rimbaud think again.

First came reproaches: "My friend—I don't know whether you'll still be in London when this reaches you. However, I feel that I have to tell you that you really must understand, *at last*, that I had to leave, that I could no longer put up with our violent life together, and all those pointless *scenes!*"

Now came the key to the riddle: he was going to Brussels, and had summoned his wife to join him. "If three days from now, I'm not back again with my wife in perfect conditions, I'll do myself in."

Rimbaud probably shrugged his shoulders. But what angered him above all was the final sentence: "We won't see each other again in any case."

He then continued the letter that he had begun the day before (he now had Verlaine's address, a *poste restante* in Brussels):

I have your letter dated "at sea." You are wrong this time, very wrong. First there is nothing positive in your letter: your wife is not coming, or she will come in three months, three years, who knows?

As for packing it in, I know you. So, while waiting for your wife and your death, you'll be flailing around, wandering about, boring people. What! Don't you see that our anger was phoney on both sides! But you were wrong up to the last because, even after I called you back, you persisted in your phoney feelings. Do you think life will be happier with others than it is with me? Think about it!—Oh! Indeed it won't!

Only with me can you be free, and, since I swear I'll be good in future, I'm sorry for my part in the wrong, since my mind is clear at last, since I really am fond of you, you'll be committing a crime if you don't want to come back or don't want me to join you, and you'll be sorry for LONG YEARS to come, because you'll lose all your freedom, and find yourself in even more terrible trouble perhaps than any you've already known. After this, think of what you were like before you knew me!

This was a bit much: before knowing him, Verlaine was a highly respected poet, a happy husband and father (a few painful scenes had taken place between his wife and him, but in August 1871, while staying in the country, they had had a second honeymoon)—and now he was almost forgotten, his wife was suing him for separation, and he was being openly accused of unspeakable morals!

The rest of the letter is taken up with domestic details ("I've had to sell all your clothes, but they haven't called for them yet"), and plans ("I expect to leave on Monday for Paris; Forain will have my address"). Last, a threat: "Believe me, if your wife comes back, I will not compromise you by writing to you. I will never write to you."

However, in Brussels, Verlaine was already convinced that Mathilde would not come. He already regretted his impetuous action, of which Rimbaud had been the victim. On July 5, in order to get news of him, he wrote to Matuszewicz, a former colonel of the *Fédérés:* "I had to leave Rimbaud rather stranded, to be frank, in terrible difficulties! (And whatever one may say) it means to me—leaving him my books and things to sell off in order to get home. . . . Have you seen him since I left? Let me know how he is. I'd be very interested! (No, seriously!) This is no time for jokes, for God's sake!"

His mother, Mathilde, and Mme Rimbaud had been warned of his deadly decision: if by Monday at noon his wife was not at his side, he would blow his brains out!

However, on the advice of the son of a former friend of his father's—and his mother's godson—Auguste Mourot, whom he met quite by chance, he altered his plans: instead of committing suicide (I'm beginning to find the idea of killing myself like that altogether too stupid, he wrote to Matuszewicz), he would enlist instead in the Carlist army.

His mother dashed to Brussels and begged him not to do anything silly, and Mme Rimbaud, in a magnificent letter, urged him to be brave: "Monsieur, I don't know anything about your unfortunate life with Arthur, but I always said that your relationship could not be a happy one. Why? you may ask. Because acting without the authorization and approval of good, honest parents cannot bring happiness to the children. You young people may laugh at everything, but it is true nevertheless that we have greater experience of life, and whenever you do not follow our advice you will be unhappy."

She ends with an admirably elevated lesson in morals: happiness consists in doing one's duty; therefore, work, give your life a purpose, do not despair in God, who alone can cure and console. Truly a letter worth framing!

As for Mathilde, she did not deign to reply—let alone go to Brussels.

As soon as he realized the inevitability of his failure, Verlaine wrote to his landlady, Mrs. Smith, asking her to look after his things until he got back to London. It was the most sensible solution: quite simply the abandonment of great, empty, historical decisions, and the return to everyday life with its mundane problems. Mrs. Smith hastened to show the letter to Rimbaud, who thought it his duty to bring his friend back to some sense of reality (July 7): "So you want me to come back to London! You don't know how everyone will receive you! And the way Andrieu and the others would treat me, if they saw me with you."

Obviously, London was out of the question. And, anyway, there was nothing left ("Everything has been sold, except for one overcoat," said Rimbaud).

Verlaine was rather taken aback, and anxiously began to reflect on his situation. As far as he was concerned, things were quite clear and final: he would enlist in the Spanish royal army and would shortly be transferred to the front. God alone knew what the outcome would be. He had a bad conscience where Rimbaud was concerned. The good lady of Charleville was right: one should always do one's duty. Now, he had not done his duty by Arthur, abandoning him in cowardly fashion on the London streets, sacrificing him to the illusion of a change of attitude by his wife, who had just reminded him that she had a heart of stone. Ah! What a good friend he had, a friend who did not reproach him, and who was still calling out to him.

Without further reflection, on July 8, at opening time, Verlaine went to the post office and composed this telegram, which he sent to Rimbaud: "[I am a] Volunteer [to fight in] Spain. Come here [to Brussels]. Hôtel Liégeois. [Don't forget to call at the] Laundry [and collect the linen, shirts, etc. that you left there. Also bring] manuscripts if possible."

Everything was now settled. Rimbaud would come with the manuscripts, and, after a tender farewell, he would set off to try his luck elsewhere.

Verlaine now turned to the main job in hand: enlist in Don Carlos's troops.

About noon, that same July 8, Verlaine, accompanied by Mourot, went to the Spanish Embassy.

Catastrophe! They did not accept foreigners.

J'ai voulu mourir à la guerre
La mort n'a pas voulu de moi

[*I wanted to die in battle*
Death did not want me],

Gaspard Hauser (Verlaine) was to sing in *Sagesse.*

The situation was getting clearer: London was out of the question, because of Andrieu and the others—in any case, Rimbaud would be arriving soon. Nor could there be any question of a romantic suicide, or enlistment in some army. The only solution was to try, as best he could, to settle his marital problems. He would therefore go to Paris, demand an interview with the woman who was still his wife, and try to come to some arrangement with her: either she would give up the case, and agree to resume married life with him, or blood would flow. Whose blood? His perhaps: since he had sacrificed his life, the cause of his happiness was certainly worth that of the pretender Don Carlos. Hers? She would have been quite willing. Her father's? Why not, if he got in the way of what, after all, were his legitimate wishes?

He understood at last that his hesitation and his natural generosity were responsible for his repeated failures, and that a more determined, implacable, and, if necessary, violent attitude would force the hand of fate.

In case Mathilde changed her mind, he booked two rooms on the second floor of the Hôtel de la Ville de Courtrai, in the very center of the city, on the Grand-Place, on the corner with the Rue des Brasseurs.

Later that evening, Rimbaud arrived, after having first gone to the Grand Liégeois. [2]

Next day, Wednesday July 9, in the fiercest manner he could summon up, so as to deprive Rimbaud of any temptation to smile or to doubt his intentions, Verlaine explained to him his plans, then asked him what he intended doing.

"I'm going to Paris, I told you so in my letter," Rimbaud replied.

But that was impossible! Last year, in Brussels, in this very place, he stubbornly insisted on going back to Paris. He wasn't going to start all over again!

Rimbaud, with a stubbornness worthy of his mother—Ah! What a Cuif he could be at times!—would hear none of it. He was free, wasn't he? Free to do as he liked—and to begin with, to satisfy his thirst for revenge against the bitch who had humiliated him, and who was quite capable of falling into her husband's arms. Circumstances had made him the arbiter of the situation: nobody wanted him around, everyone was trying to get rid of him because he was in the way. Very well! He was at nobody's beck and call, he would not give in. Verlaine could do what he liked, but *he* was under no obligation to serve as a stepping stone to the happiness of the Mauté woman; she had better not expect him to sacrifice *his* life.

"Listen . . ."

"Whatever happens, I'm telling you. I'm going to Paris, and you won't stop me."

"Very well, you'll see."

The rest of the day was taken up with bitter argument, each side refusing to give an inch. Gradually, Verlaine's position hardened: his place was with his wife: and whoever got in the way of his decision would be ruthlessly destroyed. He was in a position of legitimate defense.

Now, as Verlaine, much the worse for drink, was arguing his case step by step, it never occurred to him that, on that July 9, an informer from London was conveying the following note to Paris: "Paul Verlaine, close friend of Vermersch and Andrieu, has left London and arrived in Brussels, where he receives his letters *poste restante.*" He was in grave danger, and he never realized it.

At dawn—6 o'clock!—of July 10, he went out, apparently for a stroll, in fact waiting for Montigny's gunsmith's shop, which he had noticed in the Passage des Galeries Saint-Hubert, to open. No one was going to make a fool of him! For twenty-three francs he bought a 7mm, six-cylinder revolver, with a patent leather case, and a box of fifty cartridges. He got the shop assistant to explain to him how the weapon worked, then went off to the café to give himself some Dutch courage. It was in the toilets in the café of the Rue des Chartreux that he loaded the revolver.

Around noon, back in the hotel, he showed Rimbaud his acquisition.

"What do you intend doing with that?"

"It's for all of us," he replied, "for me, for you, for everyone!"

In actual fact, he had nothing particular in mind. He simply wanted to show that he wasn't joking, that he had a decisive argument in his pocket, and let no one forget it!

They then went off for a drink—it was already very hot—and they did not get back to the hotel until two o'clock.

There they continued their argument with redoubled vigor, neither seeing the other's point of view. The Paris train would be leaving at ten to four. Rimbaud packed his things; all he needed to leave was some money for his ticket. Mme Verlaine would not have refused him the 20 francs he asked for, but his son forbade her to give him the money. She was torn between fear of contradicting Paul, who was in none too good a mood, and her desire to bring this painful scene to a speedy end. Minute by minute, as the fateful hour approached, Verlaine became more and more nervous, more and more overexcited. He was defending his home, his happiness, like a tigress. He started to shout. He would do anything! He was afraid of no one! Several times he had to go off for a few minutes for a drink in the hotel bar, his throat was so dry (he probably locked the room door each time.)

The time had come. The comedy had gone on quite long enough. Rimbaud had made up his mind: he would leave, even without money. Verlaine put a chair against the door, which he locked, and, taking out his revolver, pointed it at his friend, yelling: "This is for you if you leave!"

Rimbaud, looking very pale, was standing against the wall opposite. Two shots were fired: the first bullet hit him in the left wrist, the second hit the wall a foot from the floor. On hearing the shots, Mme Verlaine banged on the door: her son let her in, and she ran up to the wounded boy, whose hand was dripping with blood. A dazed Verlaine threw himself on to his mother's bed, sobbing. When he came to himself again, he handed Rimbaud the revolver, saying: "Here, unload it in my temple."

They tried to calm him down. Rimbaud's wound was not very serious, the artery had not been cut, but the blood was flowing freely, and it would be better to have it bandaged.

So all three of them went off to St John's Hospital (it was, of course, an accident, the gun went off while he was cleaning it), and the patient had his wound treated and bandaged, and was told to come back the following day.

They went back to the hotel, where no one appeared to have noticed anything. Each of them realized that they had been very close to catastrophe but that nothing irreparable had been done.

Nothing had been settled, however. The argument resumed. Rimbaud stuck to his decision to leave at any price. Verlaine's "argument" had been ineffective.

Was it all going to start again? Mme Verlaine, beside herself, finally gave Rimbaud the twenty francs for his ticket, and, as he was dashing to the door, Verlaine stopped him! "I'll go with you!"

So all three of them set off for the Gare du Midi. For Verlaine, it was capitulation, defeat all along the line, his happiness destroyed. No! He would be brave: he would make one last attempt to take fate by the throat.

It was ten to eight when they got to the Place Rouppe. Verlaine strolled ahead a few yards, then turned round, and, facing his mother and Rimbaud, declared that he was going to blow his brains out, there and then. At the same time, he put his hand into his pocket (no one had thought to disarm him). Then, panic-stricken, Rimbaud jumped to one side, in the direction of a policeman, and, pointing to Verlaine, cried out: "Arrest him! He wants to kill me!"

The trio was led off to the central police station, at the Hôtel de Ville. There, after a considerable delay, Assistant Inspector Delhalle began his examination. Calmly and precisely, Rimbaud described the scene that had taken place that afternoon. As for the motive of the quarrel, he blamed Verlaine. "His company had become impossible, and I expressed a desire to return to Paris." On the other hand, Mme Verlaine showed no tenderness for Rimbaud: "For two years, M. Rimbaud has lived off my son, who has often had to complain of his cantankerous nature." She did not say what the argument was about. As for Verlaine himself, he was so disturbed that he made one blunder after another, declaring that his wife was suing him for a sepaaration, and accused him of "immoral relations" with Rimbaud; then explaining that Rimbaud, who had arrived in Brussels two days before, had wanted to leave him. "I don't know what came over me—I just took a shot at him."

It was quite clear: the fight was all about one lover threatening to leave the other. It was a case of the classic "He wanted to leave me, so I shot at him." This thesis has been adopted by almost all the biographers. In fact, the reasons were quite different. The truth was that, because he felt he could no longer go on with the dissolute life that he had been leading, Verlaine had decided to return to a normal married life. If he had fired at Rimbaud it was not because he was leaving him but because he was getting in the way of his plans; in fact, there was an incompatibility between the simultaneous presence in Paris of Mathilde and Rimbaud.

The police officer arrested the accused on a charge of assault and battery, seized the revolver, and the case, which contained forty-seven cartridges—which proves that the weapon was still loaded—and asked Rimbaud and Mme Verlaine to remain available in case they were called upon to assist the royal prosecutor.

Verlaine was escorted to a cell in the police station, while his mother and Rimbaud returned to the hotel, by which time the evening was well advanced. The painter Mourot, whom we have already met, was waiting for them; he embraced his godmother, who was so upset that she was incapable of uttering a word. It was left to Rimbaud to recount the stupid incident.

Next day, July 11, the owner of the Hôtel de la Ville de Courtrai, Verplaëtz, intrigued by Rimbaud's bandage, asked him: "Have you hurt yourself?"

So he had heard nothing.

"It's nothing," Rimbaud replied.

When Mme Verlaine and Rimbaud returned to the hospital, the patient was examined and it was decided to remove the bullet. He was admitted into ward 11, bed 19.

Mourot was there. Mme Verlaine went back with him to the hotel, paid her bill, and went off to rent a room at Ixelles.

Next day, Saturday July 12, Rimbaud was visited by a small gentleman wearing pince-nez, the examining magistrate, Théodore S'terstevens, accompanied by his clerk, who had come to take his statement. He had to go over his account of events again. The beginning was left vague: "Last year, after disagreements with his wife and her family, he [Verlaine] proposed that I should spend some time abroad with him. Our quarrels began after we had been in London for some time. I criticized him for his laziness and his behavior toward certain people we know." At Brussels, Verlaine had "no particular plans," he did not want to stay in that city, since he had nothing to do there. "I wanted to go back to Paris. Sometimes Verlaine said he would go with me, in order, as he said, to get justice from his wife and her parents; sometimes he refused to go with me, because Paris had too many sad memories for him. He was in a very excited frame of mind. However, he tried very hard to persuade me to stay with him: sometimes he was in the depths of despair, sometimes he would lose his temper completely." This is what is called throwing up a smoke screen. An account of such incoherent behavior could not fail to arouse in the magistrate the suspicion that the young man was hiding something.

The clerk of the court went off with Rimbaud's papers, some of which were of great interest for the investigation: Verlaine's letters of April and May 1872, the sonnet *Le bon disciple*, and various documents.

The bullet was extracted on July 17.

Predictably enough, the magistrate had to come back the following day to make further enquiries. He was familiar with the broad outline of the affair. However, one point remained obscure, namely, the exact motive for the revolver shots: one does not buy a weapon without some definite intention of using it.

"Verlaine had tried all kinds of things to make me stay with him," Rimbaud declared. "It is true that at one point he expressed the intention of going to Paris to attempt a reconciliation with his wife, and tried to stop me going with him; but he was always changing his mind, he never stuck to one plan, so I can't think of any serious motive for his attack on me."

Rimbaud was becoming concerned at the judge's insistence: the whole affair was beginning to assume dangerous proportions. Would an investigation be carried out in Paris perhaps—or even in Charleville. So, thinking that this would bring all legal proceedings to an end, he made a statement to the magistrates, on July 19, to the effect that he was dropping "all criminal, correctional, and civil action," and waived "any compensation that might accrue from proceedings instigated by the crown against M. Verlaine for the actions that he has committed." In other words, he was dropping his civil charge, but this was insufficient to stop the criminal proceedings, since the state had already instigated them.

On the same day, the director of St. John's Hospital sent the examining magistrate the bullet that had been removed from Rimbaud's wrist, informing him that the patient had demanded to be released from the hospital.

So Rimbaud was now free, alone, still suffering from the shock of recent events, and already full of regrets and bitterness. He was no longer interested in going back to Paris. His wound was healing; in a few weeks it would no longer be visible. But his psychological wound remained. Verlaine would be found guilty, there could be no doubt of that; he himself would be involved (reference would also be made to him during the other case, the one concerning the separation), his name would appear in the newspapers, the scandal would spread to Paris, and his whole life might be ruined by this stupid business. And all because of his own stubbornness: by trying to punish Mathilde, he had merely punished himself.

Ernest Delahaye tells us that he came back to the Ardennes after a few weeks.[3] It is likely that he stayed in Brussels to hear the sentence of the court. Indeed this has been confirmed by the discovery in 1947 by M. Matarosso of a painting on mahogany in which a feverish young man is lying on a bed covered by a red eiderdown. On a fourfold shutter in the top left-hand corner of the picture is written: "Epilogue à la française. Portrait of the Frenchman Arthur Rimbaud wounded after drinking by his intimate, the French poet Paul Verlaine. From life by Jef Rosman, at the shop of Mme Pincemaille, tobacco merchant, Rue des Bouchers, Brussels."

This André Marie Joseph Rosman, born on January 31, 1853, and Mme Pincemaille, née Anne Porson, "shop girl" between 1872 and 1874, have been traced.[4]

Rimbaud, then, had ended up in a small, cheap furnished room over a tobacco shop.

On July 28, an order in chambers summoned Verlaine before the court of summary jurisdiction for "assault and battery on the person of Arthur Rimbaud, who, as a result, has been unable to work" (article 399 of the Belgian Penal Code). However, in Paris, the police had been alerted and were investigating Verlaine's attitude during the Commune and his relationship with Rimbaud. As a result, we have a report, written in a deliciously typical policeman's prose, by an individual called Lombard. This has already provided us with some of the information concerning the drama, which, says Lombard, "caused a great commotion in Brussels" (in fact, there was no mention of it in the press). The report is as follows: "A week or two ago, in the presence of his mother, Verlaine had an argument with his friend [*amie*, the feminine form, in the original] Raimbaud, concerning money, and, after indulging in a stream of unimaginable insults, fired a pistol shot at Raimbaud, who called for help. Verlaine's mother, knowing who the author of this attempted murder was, also cried for help and Verlaine was arrested, and taken to the Carmes prison, where he is awaiting trial. . . . The facts are correct, as you will discover in Brussels. It is possible that Raimbaud fired the pistol at Verlaine, for I have been unable to ascertain who handled the said revolver."

On August 8, Verlaine appeared before the judges of the sixth Court of Summary Jurisdiction. Rimbaud and Mme Verlaine had also been sent a summons (to the Hôtel de la Ville de Courtrai), but, since they had both left, they did not attend the hearing.

Despite the efforts of his lawyer, Maître Nelis, of the Brussels bar, the accused was condemned to two years' imprisonment and ordered to pay a fine of 200 francs. It was a normal sentence: there had been intent to wound, and things might well have taken a more serious turn.

Appeals were lodged by both prosecution and defense. The decision of August 27 was to confirm the sentence.

Verlaine was led out, handcuffed, and was taken off to the "Maison de sûreté civile et militaire," known as the Petits Carmes.

Rimbaud, with nothing more to do in Brussels, set out for Roche.

11

England with Germain Nouveau

*H*e arrived at Voncq station, near Roche, one day about noon. His mother was there to meet him. One can imagine her bitter triumph: "I said all along that it would end badly. God always punishes disobedient children."

She had a horror of scandal: she felt deeply humiliated. He, with his bandaged hand, could not have looked very proud of himself.

According to Berrichon, Isabelle, then thirteen, had a clear memory of the scene: Arthur, she said, collapsed on to a chair, repeating, between sobs: "Oh, Verlaine! . . . Verlaine."

Perhaps he had begun to realize the degree of his own responsibility, for it was certainly he who, out of diabolical stubbornness, had sent him to prison. Since everything was finished between them, would he not have done better to stay in Belgium, and then to embark at Antwerp for some far-off land? There he would have lived free—whereas now he, too, was back in prison, at Roche.

"Oh well, that's all over with now."

"And what about your papers? They gave them back to you I hope." He had brought back with him a few pages of his book, which he now hoped to finish. It is unlikely that he did not breathe a word about the compromising items seized by the magistrates.

Without further delay, the family got back to work: the harvest was due.

The "sad hole" was deeper than ever. Exactly how boring life in Roche could be is suggested by the fact that, in her diary, Vitalie says how she cannot wait for the gates of the convent of the Holy Sepulchre at Charleville to open and for a new school year to begin.

More than ever Arthur had to depend on his pen as his only means of escape. His recent experiences had provided him with a wealth of memories that were to give his work sharper relief. Then, abandoning Frédéric in shirt-sleeves, manipulating the hayfork, or his mother tirelessly collecting the sheaves, he would go off to the high farmhouse attic, the only oasis of peace in that bustling world. "My brother Arthur," writes Vitalie in her diary, "did not take part in the farmwork; for him the pen was a serious enough occupation to allow him not to share our manual labors."

(It should perhaps be noted in passing that Vitalie says nothing about her brother's departure in May and his return in July; did some secret instinct warn her perhaps that certain things would be better not mentioned?)

Rimbaud returned to his *Livre païen*, or *Livre nègre*, crossed out these titles, and replaced them by the much more suggestive *Une saison en enfer* (A Season in Hell).

The character of Verlaine provided suitable inspiration for one of the most successful chapters, entitled *Délires* (Delirium), with its two subtitles, "Vierge folle" and "L'Epoux infernal" (The Foolish Virgin and The Infernal Bridegroom). Mathilde's unfortunate husband turns up disguised as a foolish virgin, seduced and terrorized, complaining, in a long, fearful, sniveling monologue of the harshness, cruelty, and cynicism of his seer-companion, strangely persisting in wishing to "change life."

> *Lui était presque un enfant . . . Ses délicatesses mystérieuses m'avaient séduite. J'ai oublié tout mon devoir humain pour le suivre. Quelle vie! La vraie vie est absente. Nous ne sommes pas au monde. Je vais où il va, il le faut. Et souvent il s'emporte contre moi,* moi, la pauvre âme. *Le Démon!—C'est un Démon, vous savez, ce n'est pas un homme.*

> [*He was almost a child . . . His mysteriously delicate feelings had seduced me. I forgot all my human duty to follow him. What a life! Real life is absent. We are not in the world. I go where he goes. I have to. And often he flies into a rage at* me, poor me. *The Demon! He is a Demon, you know. He is not a man.*][1]

All that was missing now was an introduction. This did not take long: "Or, tout dernièrement m'étant trouvé sur le point de faire le dernier *couac!*

j'ai songé à rechercher la clef du festin ancien, où je reprendrais peut-être appétit." [But recently, on the verge of giving my last croak, I thought of looking for the key to the ancient banquet where I might possibly recover my appetite.][2]

A few paragraphs, illuminated by the tall flames of hell, by way of conclusion, and it would be finished.

This *Saison en enfer* is not a meditation conducted according to stated principles, a logical development and a conclusion; it is a breathless monologue, a permanent questioning of the author's instincts, tendencies, and choices, in a seething mass of antinomies and contradictions: the lure of evil and innocence, the desire and hate of God, the attraction of the primitive peoples and of industrial civilizations, a preoccupation with, and a rejection of, the East. It is a Manichean struggle between the forces of darkness and the forces of light, waged with stubborn pride and accompanied by grimaces, dances, and pirouettes.

One of the constant themes is that of failure. He is the first to mock his ambitions, his illusions, and his pitiful achievements. The chapter "Alchimie du verbe" (Alchemy of the word) opens with the ironic words. "A moi. L'histoire d'une de mes folies" [It is my turn. The story of one of my follies].[3] This is how he describes what he sacrificed his life for: poetry in the light of vision.

Each evening, in a feverish state, he rejoined his harassed family, and took refuge in silence when everyone seemed to be against him. Now that his wrist was better, did he imagine that, instead of working, he could stay up in the loft, sucking his pen!

He consigned his anger to paper: "I hate all trades. Masters and laborers, all peasants, ignoble. A pen in one's hand is worth one's hand on a plow. What a century of hands! I shall never have my own hand."

Looking down from his perch at his family, bent over mother earth, he noted: "Life flourishes through work, an old truth. My life is not weighty enough, it flies off and floats above action, that dear point of the world."

If, in his retreat, he sometimes gave vent to his rage, it was, in my opinion, as a way of expressing the resentment aroused in him by the criticisms of his family. Paterne Berrichon, however, favors a more romantic interpretation. "During his working hours," he writes, "one could hear, through the floor, repeated, convulsive sobs, alternating with groans, derisive laughter, cries of anger, curses."[4]

This is probably just as much a legend as the cross supposedly carved with a penknife into his desk—a detail that was passed on to Paul Claudel, and gave him great pleasure.

The conclusion of the work may be summed up in the words: "My life was used up."

It is an astonishing piece, full of lightning flashes and sparks, with passages that are among the most perfect in French literature:

> *Quelquefois je vois au ciel des plages sans fin couvertes de blanches nations en joie. Un grand vaisseau d'or, au-dessus de moi, agite ses pavillons multicolores sous les brises du matin. J'ai créé toutes les fêtes, tous les triomphes, tous les drames. J'ai essayé d'inventer de nouvelles fleurs, de nouveaux astres, de nouvelles chairs, de nouvelles langues. J'ai cru acquérir des pouvoirs surnaturels. Eh bien! je dois enterrer mon imagination et mes souvenirs! Une belle gloire d'artiste et de conteur emportée!*
>
> *Moi! moi qui me suis dit mage ou ange, dispensé de toute morale, je suis rendu au sol, avec un devoir à chercher et la réalité rugueuse à étreindre! Paysan!*

> [*Sometimes I see in the sky endless beaches covered with white joyous nations. A huge golden vessel, above me, waves its multicolored flags in the morning wind. I have created all celebrations, all triumphs, all dramas. I have tried to invent new flowers, new stars, new flesh, new tongues. I believed I had acquired supernatural powers. Well! I have to bury my imagination and my memories! A fine reputation of an artist and story-teller lost sight of!*
>
> *I who called myself magus or angel, exempt from all morality, I am thrown back to the earth, with the duty to find, and rough reality to embrace! Peasant!*][5]

At dawn, when the nightmare had left him, he staggered out, his forehead bathed in cold sweat and "dried blood." No one was there. The fantasies and demons had vanished. Still weak, but determined, he was like the sick man cured by Jesus beside the pool at Bethsaida referred to in one of his Gospel-inspired pieces: "The Paralytic who had remained lying on his side, stood up, and the Damned saw him cross the gallery with an unusually firm step and disappear into the city."

Soon he had to admit that, although he had emerged from Hell, he had not ceased to be one of the damned.

The summer had been unusually hot. On the trees and on the ground dried leaves heralded the end of the long, sunny days.

Autumn already!

Reread and corrected, the manuscript was now ready. The author dated it "April-August 1873."

The harvest was in.

He held—or thought he held—the key that would open the door of his prison, so he could sink back into dreams and idleness: "I envied the happiness of animals—caterpillars representing the innocence of limbo, moles, the sleep of virginity!" He was now wanted by his family to help in the fruit picking (in the country, one's work is never done!), but, yet again, they had to do without him, as Vitalie suggests in her diary: "The time of the fruit picking arrived. Almost all of us set our hands to it."

The most difficult, the most urgent task remained: finding a printer, if not a publisher. One can imagine that he had to fight hard to get out of his mother even so much as an advance on the expenses to be incurred. She could not understand why one should waste one's time writing stories that had neither rhyme nor reason, and she must have loved her Arthur a great deal to allow herself to be swayed.

"My book will sell well, it will bring me in 500 francs. If you advance me the initial expenses, I'll be in a position to pay the printer myself."

In the end, she gave in, with a shrug of her shoulders: it was money wasted, that would have been better employed buying a piece of land.

According to Isabelle, she asked to look at the manuscript. She couldn't make head or tail of it.

"What are you trying to say?"

"I tried to say what it says, literally and in every sense."

With whom should he try his luck? He had kept the name of a printer in Brussels, Jacques Poot, 37 Rue Aux-Choux, manager of the Alliance typographique, which published a periodic collection of legal articles, *La Belgique judiciaire*. Perhaps Rimbaud had read his name while leafing through this periodical when, in the courthouse, he had waited anxiously to know what Verlaine's fate was likely to be. Perhaps, too, he had already been in contact with this Jacques Poot for a contract involving generous payment. Whatever the reason, he sent him the manuscript. It was agreed that the author would receive complimentary copies on account, and that the printing (five hundred copies, selling at 1 franc each) would be payable on delivery.

Let us return for a moment to Brussels, where the unfortunate Verlaine had still not realized what had happened to him. Having neither learned nor forgotten anything, he was still dreaming in his cell of returning to Mathilde, without leaving Rimbaud. Incidentally, Rimbaud resurfaced in a very fine poem, *Crimen amoris*.

Or le plus beau de tous ces mauvais anges
Avait seize ans sous sa couronne de fleurs.

[*Now, the most beautiful of all those wicked angels*
Was sixteen under his crown of flowers.]

His sin was to exalt life and pleasure, while sheltering behind a God that he would create: "O je serai celui-là qui créera Dieu!" [O I shall be he who will create God!].

But God, after throwing him into hell, changed him into a statue of ice. Verlaine sent this poem to Rimbaud, who copied it out by hand, which proves that they had not broken off relations.[6]

A reconciliation with Mathilde was to prove more difficult. Nevertheless Verlaine redoubled his attempts: for example, he assured Lepelletier that he was ready to forget the enormity of his wife's conduct, and to take her back with open arms if she begged his forgiveness.

It is reasonable to believe that Rimbaud did not go to Brussels to supervise the composition and printing of his book, as Paterne Berrichon maintains: his mother's generosity did not stretch to indulging such whims. It is also unlikely that he was given proofs to correct, for he would not have let pass such misprints as "J'ai songé à rechercher *le* clef" or "Cette inspirations prouve que je n'ai pas rêvé," or again "Et où puisser le secours."

On the other hand, it has been established that, around October 23, on being summoned by Poot, he went to Brussels to collect his author's complimentary copies. On this occasion he stayed at the Hôtel de la Ville Courtrai, of sinister memory, as is shown by the following report made by the Belgian secret police and found in his file: "RIMBAUD, Arthur, aged 19, *born* at Charleville (France)—*Profession:* man of letters: *domicile:* Rue des Brasseurs, No. 1, *change of domicile:* October 24, left furtively."[7]

At the conciergerie of the prison of the Petits Carmes he left a copy for Verlaine. He was just in time! For, on October 25, the prisoner was transferred to the "Maison de sureté cellulaire" at Mons. This copy, which bears the laconic dedication "To P. Verlaine—A. Rimbaud," was to remain one of Verlaine's most cherished possessions throughout his life, and was bequeathed to his son Georges.

In a letter to Lepelletier, dated November 28, 1873, we learn that Verlaine sent his former companion, no doubt by way of thanks, several poems composed in prison: *Impression fausse (Dame souris trotte* . . .), *Autre* (la ronde des prisonniers dans la cour), and two narrative poems, *La grâce* and *Don Juan pipé.* These "diabolical" compositions are Verlaine's "Saison en enfer," and this exchange of gifts is a good example of their fraternal methods.

Rimbaud, back at Roche, thoroughly enjoyed his status as published author, and got everyone to admire his name displayed on the white cover of his book. He had twelve copies with him.

Instead of arranging to send out copies in a rational and efficient way, worthy of a man of letters, to individuals who might encourage the book's fate, he amused himself, like a child, handing out his precious copies to friends who were quite incapable of helping him: thus Delahaye received one (which Rimbaud asked back at a later date), as also did Ernest Millot (he, too, was to give it back, it seems.)

Forain, who was not at all interested in literature, was entrusted with a number of copies and told to distribute them at his discretion. These particular copies ended up with various friends (Jean Richepin, Raoul Gineste—if Charles Maurras is to be believed—and perhaps Raoul Ponchon). In short, no serious attempt was made to publicize the book.

Being fully aware of their hostility toward him, Rimbaud could hardly send copies to the Parnassians (Mendès, Blémont, Valade). He was persona non grata in those quarters.

However, he placed too much value on his freedom, which was tied up with the fate of his book, not to neglect any opportunity that was offered. Something had to be done. So he set off for Paris with a few copies in his pocket.

Colonel Godchot maintains that he paid for his trip with the money that his mother had given him to pay the printer.[8] This is not out of the question, for she had a horror of debts, while he, for his part, needed at all costs to get himself known, but this is no more than a supposition.

In the Latin Quarter, the story of the ignoble events that had taken place in Brussels was there before him. Jean Richepin has written that at this time he was much better known for his adventures with Verlaine than for his works.[9] (Quite spontaneously, everyone was against him: people had not forgotten his ill-tempered provocations of the winter of 1871–72, and everyone regarded him as responsible for the accident that had befallen their dear friend Verlaine. He was certainly beginning to reap what he had sown.)

The few former acquaintances whom he contacted turned their backs on him, and made it quite plain that he was not wanted. Berrichon recounts the following incident: Alfred Poussin, a young Norman poet, was sitting one evening in the Café Tabourey, near the Odéon, and everyone was talking about the Brussels scandal. Suddenly, people began to point their fingers at a pale young man sitting at a table, saying nothing. Poussin, who had recognized him, went up and offered him a drink. Rimbaud did not respond, but looked at him with so much sadness in his eyes that Poussin remembered it all his life.[10]

Such silence certainly accords with his character. He was both all-of-a-piece and highly emotional; when faced by adversity, he would close up in silence, and, as one says, "crack up." At that point, one can be fairly sure, he had thrown overboard both literature and writers.

Another evening, also at the Café Tabourey, he unexpectedly met a Provençal poet called Germain Nouveau, who had taught at the Lycée de Marseille (Lycée Thiers). Perhaps they had originally met at the Cercle Zutique, a year before, for Nouveau had written and sketched in the *Album*, and it is difficult to imagine his making these contributions after the event. He was a friend of Raoul Gineste, Jean Richepin, Léon Cladel, and Maurice Bouchor, who also attended Nina de Villard's celebrated salon. He had been greatly struck by Verlaine's adventure: in his eyes, the prisoner of Mons was a sort of hero who had had the courage to despise fate before being brought low by it. So it was probably Verlaine that they talked about most.

Ernest Delahaye, who knew them both well, has described the contrast in their appearances: Rimbaud, tall, with fair hair and blue eyes, and a surly, sulky expression, and Nouveau, short, broad-shouldered, as dark skinned as a Spaniard, bubbling with enthusiasm. When Rimbaud told him that he was disgusted with all literature, and intended to travel the world—beginning with London—because it was important for him to get a proper command of English, his companion's eyes lit up: "Would you mind if I went with you? I'd like to travel, too, and I don't know a word of English."

Rimbaud, who had not forgotten the cold fog of the Thames, replied that he would not be setting out until the following spring.

"Very well, it's a promise!"

So, suddenly in a happier mood, reconciled to life, he set out, on November 2, in short stages, for Roche, still carrying his remaining complimentary copies: his life was to find a meaning once more.

His season in hell was now no more than a far-off, unpleasant memory. As for the printer, he would, if he so wished, keep the edition of his book.

(It is very likely that Jacques Poot sent his bill to Roche, where it was torn up. Long afterwards, in 1901, the stock of the slim white volumes was discovered in the storeroom of the Alliance typographique by a Belgian literary critic, Louis Piérard, who alerted a bibliophile, Léon Losseau, who bought the lot for a pittance in 1911.)

Literature? What a filthy joke! He never wanted to hear another word about it again!

Mme Rimbaud could not believe her eyes when she saw him throw the books that he had brought back into the fire, together with piles of rough drafts, letters, and other paper. (However, he spared his seer's notebook, which contained his poems in prose, which were to become *Les Illuminations*.) All this paper produced a fine show in the big fireplace at Roche, to the delight of Isabelle, then thirteen, who could not understand why this purificatory fire made her brother look so happy. Mme Rimbaud was happy to see her son cured at last of his madness, and become a reasonable human being once more. A whole past, heavy with misery and suffering, was in a moment reduced to ashes.

He spent the winter at Roche, where it was warm, though he did make a few excursions to Charleville, early in 1874. There he saw a few old friends, Ernest Delahaye, Louis Pierquin, Ernest Millot.

Pierquin recounts:

After the Brussels affair, the bourgeoisie, flogged by Rimbaud, was happy to spread the most infamous rumors about him; neither Delahaye, nor Millot, nor I—his three best friends, I would even go so far as to say his only friends— ever believed in these calumnies. I always avoided questioning him on the matter, knowing how much it had affected him. One evening, he was waiting for me at the Café Duterme, sitting alone in front of a tankard of beer, which he had not even touched. He was quite capable of sitting for hours on end like that, silent, absorbed. I went up to him and said: "Well! And what has happened to our repugnant contemporaries?"

I don't know whether it occured to him that I was alluding to Verlaine and the Brussels affair; he looked at me, his eyes veiled with sadness, and replied with a shrug of the shoulders. Some time later, Millot, less timid than I, was more specific: "Don't stir up that pile of filth," said Rimbaud, "it's all too disgusting!"

Millot did not pursue the matter.[11]

One may presume that, in accordance with the promise exchanged in October 1873, Rimbaud went to Paris around mid-March 1874.

On March 26, Germain Nouveau informed Jean Richepin that he had left Paris at the moment when he least expected to and that he was now in London with Rimbaud. One can only presume that Rimbaud, turning up without warning, had come to fetch him; this hasty departure, writes Richepin, looking very like an abduction.

"We have rented a room with a family in Stamfort Street," Nouveau goes on. "The young man of the household, who knows a little French, converses with us for an hour every day. . . . As for Rimbaud, he must improve his English though he knows enough for our everyday needs."

Then follow Nouveau's impressions of London: on arrival, London produced in me an impression of physical and moral suffocation: the thin daylight, the smell of tar and coal in the streets, the expressionless faces of the English, a great deal of bustling about, without any sound of voices. The cabs are charming!"

Underwood tells us that their landlady, Mrs. Stephens, nicknamed by Nouveau Mme Polichinelle (Punch), lived at 179 Stamfort Street, near Waterloo Station, on the south bank of the Thames.[12]

As in the time of Verlaine, the days were spent studying English, looking for French lessons, and going for long walks. They soon found out where, for a few pence, they could get a large plate of fish and chips in an English-style French restaurant. They also went, but only occasionally, to the music hall at the London Pavilion (jigs, songs from *Mère Angot*, minstrels). They saw little of their compatriots: Rimbaud had good reason to avoid the *Communard* émigrés.

But the most serious problem and also the most urgent was to find pupils, for Mme Verlaine was no longer there to subsidize their idleness. So they put advertisements in various newspapers (*The Times, The Echo*), but it seems, from the researches carried out by Underwood on this matter, that perhaps, out of consideration for their landlady, or distrust of the political exiles, they concealed their names and addresses.[13] Do the initials N.A. mean Nouveau, Arthur? Silvy, on the other hand, clearly refers to Nouveau (it was his mother's maiden name), especially as this Silvy offers lessons in literature—French, ancient, classical, contemporary, and Provençal. But there is even more solid evidence: in *The Echo* of April 29, 1874, one finds the following ad: "Two Parisians, one of whom speaks *passablement* [in French in the original], seek conversation with English gentlemen—TAVANT, NOUVEAU—30, Argyle Square—Euston Road—W.C." Since a certain M. d'Harcourt often offered lessons at the same address, it is possible that Rimbaud and Nouveau used the services of an agency.

On the matter of work, it should be mentioned that, according to Delahaye's very vague memory, the two Londoners worked for a Mr. Dry Cup (or, more probably, a firm of that name), makers of cardboard at Holborn, or, again, that Nouveau found a job as a tutor and Rimbaud took a job as supervisor-janitor in a boarding school, from which he was kicked out for bursting the drum that was used to summon the pupils. Underwood has shown that these various stories amount to little more than hoaxes, jokes, or legends.

To return to more serious realities. From the beginning, Nouveau realized that his best chance lay with his pen. On March 26, 1874, shortly after his arrival, he suggested to Jean Richepin a few articles for the *Renaissance:* "This will give me a few sous," he says, "which you could send me, deducting the cost of postage."

Curiously enough, the day after, on March 27, Verlaine, from his prison, made a similar approach to his friend Lepelletier: "Meanwhile I have here, already for the *Renaissance*—SINCE IT PAYS—a delicious story, as yet untranslated, by Dickens."

In its April 1, 1874, number the *Revue du Monde nouveau* (managing director Henri Mercier, editor Charles Cros) published a poem by Germain

Nouveau, *Rêve claustral,* which is reminiscent of Rimbaud's *Les premières Communions"* and *Les Chercheuses de poux.*

At this period, Nouveau had not yet found his own style: he had imitated the Verlaine of *Fêtes galantes;* now he underwent the influence of Rimbaud (which is even more obvious in his poem *Les Hôtesses*).

At last, on April 4, Rimbaud and Nouveau took out reader's cards at the British Museum (out of love of mystification, no doubt, they had given their respective Christian names as: Jean Nicolas *Joseph* Arthur and *Georges* Marie Bernard).

So both of them were gradually returning to literature—largely under the impetus of economic need, considering it easier to write than to teach. Rimbaud, in particular, had a treasure to be exploited, his poems in prose, which might well make up a slim volume that could be sold in Paris. It is quite likely that Nouveau urged him in this course of action. Rimbaud agreed and set about revising his drafts. Nouveau lent him a hand (the beginning of *Villes,* the end of *Métropolitain*) with its final recopying, which was done onto odd pages of white or pale blue paper, further proof that they were in a hurry.[14]

Another aspect of their collaboration at this time is that Rimbaud re-copied Nouveau's sonnet *Poison perdu,* which for a long time was attributed to him.

We do not know whether the collection of poems in prose then in prep-aration was entitled *Illuminations* (with the subtitles mentioned by Verlaine: Colored plates, or Printed plates), but we do know that it was ready in June. They had certainly both succumbed to the literary fever.

Then, suddenly, everything collapsed. Germain Nouveau, dropping everything, went back to Paris. There must have been some serious reason. What had happened, for there had been no disagreement between them and they were both full of hope?

It is easy to imagine. Nouveau had resumed contact with Parisian liter-ary circles, and they had made it quite clear to him that any work he did for reviews or newspapers would come to an abrupt end if he continued to con-sort with Rimbaud. Jean Richepin does not mince matters: "Subjected to Rimbaud's direct influence in a foreign country, without any counterinflu-ence, we believed that Nouveau was lost, or very near it."[15] It had been enough to seal Verlaine's fate!

In those days one did not tangle with morality. A year and a half later,

Verlaine, having emerged from prison, was to be subjected to the same prohibition, when, in October 1875, he dared to send a few poems to the publisher Lemerre for his new *Parnasse Contemporain*. "The author is unworthy" was one of the reasons given by Anatole France, a member of the jury, for his negative vote.

What reinforces this thesis is the fact that from that time on Nouveau did not dare to write Rimbaud's name in his private letters: he calls him "Chose" ("Thing"), "l'Autre" ("The Other"), or is content with the initial R. At last, on January 27, 1876, in a letter to Verlaine, he lifted the prohibition that he had imposed upon himself: "No news of Rimbaud (why should I be afraid to write all his name?)." The danger had then passed; it had not yet done so in June 1874.

It is understandable that Nouveau, at twenty-three, had no wish to ruin his career, and to sink into oblivion and contempt.

It might be added that it was quite normal for his friends to be concerned, for Rimbaud then had the deplorable reputation of having dragged Verlaine into a life of debauchery. Indeed many biographers have suspected Nouveau of having taken Verlaine's place in a second "drôle de ménage."

One must be prudent here, for we have no hard evidence. One can hardly base such an accusation on the innocuous *Poison Perdu:*

Des nuits du blond et de la brune
Pas un souvenir n'est resté,
Pas une dentelle d'été,
Pas une cravate commune.

[*Of the nights of the fair-haired man and the dark-haired woman*
Not a souvenir remains,
Not a piece of summer lace,
Not an ordinary necktie.]

Nor can one bring up as evidence a few jokes in rather dubious taste on the same subject that are sometimes to be found in his work.[16] In any case most of his poems are addressed to women, to whom he was not indifferent.

As for Rimbaud, I have already stressed that, for him, debauchery (homosexuality) was the precondition of the seer's vision. It was not motivated by inclination. If he succumbed to it, he did so voluntarily, and the enemies that he made on his way (scandals and mockery, first in the Latin Quarter, then in London, the Lepelletier and Andrieu incidents, the failure of *Une saison en enfer*) had been painful enough to deprive him of any desire to return to that kind of life.

About this time—to be precise, on April 24, 1874—the civil court of the Seine delivered its judgment on the proceedings for separation between Verlaine and his wife. One of the reasons adduced in the judgment concerned him: "Considering that it transpires from Verlaine's correspondence that he abandoned his wife and home to go and live in Brussels, where he gave himself up to his old habits of drunkenness; that this correspondence establishes moreover that Verlaine had immoral relations with a young man; that he was condemned on August 8, 1873, by the criminal court of Brussels to two years in prison and to a fine of 200 francs for assault and battery against that person, which acts he appears to have committed in a jealous rage."

Germain Nouveau's departure left Rimbaud at a loss to know what to do. Any future as a writer was closed to him; he did not even have the right to be in the company of a friend without that friend immediately being suspected of every vice. Solitude would be his eternal companion. He tried bravely to confront adversity, and put new advertisements in the newspapers.

Underwood has found some of these; the following appeared in *The Times* for June 8, 1874; "A French Gentleman (twenty-five years of age), excellent family, highly educated, possessing a French degree, excellent knowledge of English, knowledge of many branches of learning, seeks post as Private Secretary, traveling companion or tutor. Excellent references: Address: A.R., 25, Langham Street, London, W." (The address is probably that of the painter Felix Régamey.)

Another advertisement appeared in *The Echo*, on June 9, 10, and 11. "A YOUNG PARISIAN speaks *passablement* [in French] seeks conversation with English gentlemen; in his own home; preferably afternoons—Rimbaud, 40, London Street, Fitzroy Square, W."[17]

The text of this advertisement gives rise to two observations: First, it is strangely reminiscent of the earlier advertisement signed TAVANT, NOUVEAU, and, second, it is very possible that Rimbaud did in fact live at the address he gives, 40 London Street, Fitzroy Square. Underwood suggests that this accommodation must have been fairly modest, good enough for clients that might come to him from the popular *Echo*, but not for those of *The Times*— which is why he asked Régamey to lend him his studio, or a room in his apartment.

It is likely that these advertisements led to nothing. Indeed, one can imagine the unhappy Rimbaud sinking into despair, convinced that fate was against him. In the grip of a nervous depression comparable to the one experienced by Verlaine in 1872, he acted in a similar way: by letter or telegram he begged his mother to come and spend a few days with him.

Believing this to be her duty, Mme Rimbaud set off with her daughter Vitalie, now sixteen years old (Frédéric had meanwhile signed up in the army).

We have first-class evidence concerning their stay in London: to begin with, Vitalie's diary (corrected by Isabelle on her return),[18] and, second, three letters from Vitalie to Isabelle, who remained at Charleville, dated July 7, 12, and 24, 1874.[19]

From their departure from Charleville (Sunday July 5, at dawn) to their departure from London (Friday July 31), the trip lasted twenty-seven days. It could have been shorter if Arthur had found a post more quickly, and would have been pleasanter if the weather had not been so unbearably hot.

At first Vitalie recounts her more or less naive impressions: she cannot believe her eyes when she sees the railways "on top of the houses" (she means overlooking them). Arthur was there to meet them on Monday July 6 at 10:10 A.M. at Charing Cross Station ("A dozen times bigger than the one at Charleville"). He took his family to a suitable hotel ("There are carpets everywhere!" Vitalie observes) in 12 Argyle Square ("Under the windows of our apartment grows an infinity of flowers in the shade of enormous trees"), where he booked two rooms. The girl is astonished by everything. The gardens in front of the houses, the intense traffic, the noise, the "American omnibuses" (trams). During her first walk she is so disturbed that she takes Nelson's column in Trafalgar Square to be a huge fountain! On the evening of July 8, Arthur took his mother and sister off to hear a sermon in English at St. John's (Anglican) church, and next day to evensong in St. Paul's Cathedral. Vitalie is struck by the fervor of the congregation ("What good Catholics they would make!").

Arthur spends most of his time in the British Museum, where Vitalie, allowed to accompany him one day, admired the prehistoric animals and the antiquities. He experienced moments of exaltation, followed by painful depressions. On July 11, a letter proposed three different posts to him—then nothing more: on the eighteenth he had to put new advertisements in the newspapers.[20]

The stay went on for too long. Boredom turned to gloom, and gloom to a vague anxiety. Even the shops no longer held any interest for Vitalie ("What is the point, if one doesn't buy anything?").

They had already done the usual tour of the sights (the Tower of London, the Tower subway, the docks, the Houses of Parliament, Leicester Square, the Horse guards, and St. James's Palace ("The walls, blackened with time, have no carvings on them. And the windows? They are just like any windows, but very small.")

On July 27, Arthur took his family to the British Museum to see an exhibition devoted to Theodoros, emperor of Abyssinia, who had died in 1868, showing his crown, his ceremonial dress, his weapons, his jewelry. In glass cases there were manuscripts and illuminated books, which the catalog refers to as "Illuminations."

But now it really was time for the trip to come to an end, for the atmosphere was growing worse: Vitalie was missing Charleville, which now seemed to her more and more "a place of delight," and Mme Rimbaud was permanently sunk in gloom. Finally, on Wednesday July 29, there was good news: at nine o'clock, a depressed and nervous Arthur declared that he would not be back for lunch; however, he reappeared at ten o'clock with the news that he would be leaving next day. There was universal relief. Mother and daughter hastily bought presents and souvenirs. But they had to wait another twenty-four hours because the laundress had not brought back the linen.

Finally, the trip came to an end:

"Friday 31, half-past seven in the morning. Arthur left at half-past four. He was sad."

In the afternoon, Mme Rimbaud and her daughter also left London. It was a sad return. "I think of Arthur, of how sad he is," Vitalie notes, "and of Maman who weeps and writes."

Her brother had worked out their itinerary for them: Folkstone, Ostend, Bruges, Alost, Brussels, Namur, Dinant, Givet, and Charleville.

Where did Rimbaud go on July 31, 1874, at half-past four in the morning? His sister Isabelle told her brother's first biographers, in 1897: "He left London for Scotland."[21]

His latest advertisements requested "a post in London or elsewhere as tutor or traveling companion."

Scotland? Miss Starkie and Underwood have researched the question, studying railway timetables, examining the records of schools in Edinburgh and Glasgow, but without result.[22]

The only serious possibility is Scarborough, a port and fashionable seaside resort in Yorkshire, some two hundred and forty miles north of London—and it is Rimbaud himself who provides the clue in his poem

Promontoire (*Illuminations*). Some of the details are disturbing, for example, Rimbaud writes "Scarbro," an essentially local abbreviation; the name of the town was usually pronounced "Scarboro." Furthermore, the descriptions in the poem apply perfectly to that town. There are the "fanums," that is to say, Roman temples; and indeed, a building of rounded shape does crown the landscape. There is mention of "Royals" or "Grands," and there were indeed two grand hotels in Scarborough at the time, the Royal Hotel, with its ten floors and three hundred and forty rooms, opened in 1867, which corresponds to the colossal, elegant construction described by Rimbaud, and the Grand Hotel, which was run by a Frenchman, Auguste Fricour, which indeed did have a semicircular façade, as can be seen in the engravings reproduced in Underwood's book[23], from which I have borrowed these details. The Grand Hotel, built on a promontory, would seem, then, to be the "promontory palace" referred to at the end of the poem, which, in addition to Scarborough, also mentions Epirus, the Peloponnese, Carthage, Venice, Germany, Japan, Brooklyn, Italy, America, and Asia—ingredients that help to give the text its dreamlike dimension.

It is reasonable to suppose, then, that Rimbaud had received a reply to one of his advertisements asking for a post as tutor in a rich family, which took him to Scarborough—perhaps in a yacht, for the poem begins thus: "L'aube d'or et la soirée frissonnante trouvent notre brick au large en face de cette villa et de ses dépendances, qui forment un promontoire aussi étendu que l'Epire et le Péloponnèse, ou que la grande île du Japon ou que l'Arabie!" [The golden dawn and the chilly evening find our brig out at sea, opposite this villa and its dependencies, which form a promontory as extensive as Epirus and the Peloponnesus, or as the large island of Japan, or Arabia!].[24]

The dependencies referred to are villas with stepped terraces, lighted and decorated, on which drinks were served and where people danced (the "tarantellas of the coast"), for the place is a resort of high society.

"Promontoire" is such a precise description of Scarborough that it is inconceivable that Rimbaud did not stay there.

What happened to him then? Here there is another abyss of obscurity, in the depths of which shines a tiny light, namely, the rough draft of an advertisement in Rimbaud's hand, corrected by someone else (certainly not Verlaine, who was then languishing in prison). This document was discovered in 1937, among the papers of the painter F. A. Cazals, a friend of Verlaine's. The corresponding advertisement was located by Miss Starkie in *The*

Times for November 9, 1874. Underwood also discovered it in the November 7 edition. Here is the text:

"A PARISIAN (20), of high literary and linguistic attainments, excellent conversation, will be glad to *accompany* a *Gentleman* (artists preferred) or a family wishing to travel in the southern or eastern countries. Good references.—A.R. no. 165, King's Road—Reading."

Rimbaud's draft contains several incorrect terms, as Underwood shows, which proves that his knowledge of English was still superficial.

So we are now in Reading, a small town nearly forty miles from London, on the Oxford road. The address given was that of a Frenchman, Camille Le Clair, a university graduate, who, on July 25, 1874, had set up an Institute of the French Language in a fine three-story building. There lessons were given in French language and literature. Miss Starkie has discovered in the local press (the *Reading Mercury*), advertisements for the Institut Le Clair.

Since Rimbaud gives his address as the Institute, we may presume that he taught and lived there. Perhaps he regretted the luxury and comfort of Scarborough. A cruise in the South seas was a tempting prospect.

But an unexpected event put all such plans in question.

12

Travel: Liquidating Verlaine

"This month [December] has begun with certain serious events," Vitalie Rimbaud notes in her diary on Tuesday December 1, 1874. About that time, according to the same diary, a great many letters were passing between Arthur and his family.

What was happening? Since he was now twenty years of age, Arthur had been summoned by the army authorities for the drawing of lots for military service. It was a serious matter. So he decided to return immediately to Charleville. Vitalie tells us that he arrived on Tuesday December 29 at nine o'clock in the morning—it was snowing and icy. And that the very same day, at nine o'clock in the evening, Frédéric turned up to spend his New Year's leave with his family.

Arthur, having made inquiries concerning his own situation, learned that the mayor of Charleville had picked his number for him (probably a bad number). He then made representations to the effect that, according to article 17 of the recruitment law of July 27, 1872, his brother's enlistment for five years exempted him from military service—though not from the periods of instruction. His claim was upheld. All this is clearly summarized in the "Tableau de recensement" of the class of 1874 preserved in the Charleville-Mézières Archives:

"RIMBAUD—JEAN NICOLAS ARTHUR—Height: 1.68m, teacher of the French language in England. Exempted on claim. Can read and count. Number drawn at the ballot, 24—the mayor drew for him" (there then follows Mme Rimbaud's signature).

On January 10, 1875, Frédéric set off to rejoin his unit.

Arthur, disappointed by the poor response to his advertisements, and considering that he now knew enough English, decided not to go back to

England, and, anyway, he did not see himself teaching for the rest of his life. What he wanted to do was to prepare himself for the future, and to make up by a knowledge of foreign languages, what he lacked in academic diplomas. To get a good post in commerce or industry, he would need a knowledge of German. So he now went off to Germany.

He was looking for a post as tutor living with a family, and found such a post with Herr Lübner, Wagnerstrasse, Stuttgart. This, at least, is what his earliest biographers say,[1] but this name has been challenged for it is not to be found in the official records of the city. D.-A. de Graaf proposes a certain Wilhelm Luebke, an art historian and teacher at the Polytechnic of Stuttgart. As we shall see later, his hypothesis is very plausible.[2]

Mme Rimbaud, delighted at seeing her son becoming reasonable and concerned with serious matters, did not refuse to advance him the traveling expenses. (Isabelle was angry because Delahaye later wrote, somewhat insensitively, that he "extorted this money.")

When everything was ready, he set off for Stuttgart, according to Vitalie's diary, on Saturday, February 13, 1875.

He plunged at once into an enthusiastic study of the German language, devouring newspapers, books, and reviews (he sent Vitalie a thickly illustrated magazine), rummaging in libraries and picture galleries, copying out lists of German words, attending evening classes, and talking as much as possible in his host's family. But he did not find the atmosphere there very congenial. Was this young "Französe" made to feel perhaps that he belonged to a conquered nation?

He was unaware that on January 16 an important event took place in Belgium, at Mons: Verlaine was freed after eighteen months in prison. He emerged a very different man: in June 1874, after the governor of the prison had read to him the judgment of the court, confirming the separation from his wife and condemning him, he underwent a profound religious crisis. After a few days at his mother's home, he had returned to Paris in order to make representations to his wife's lawyer concerning his right to see his son; but the official concerned did not deign to see him. Then, in some distress, he took part in a retreat at the Carthusian monastery of Notre-Dame-des-Prés, not far from Montreuil-sur-Mer. On his return to Arras, at his mother's, a letter from Delahaye was waiting for him. "I recently saw Rimbaud at Charleville," this excellent friend informed him, "but he has now left for Stuttgart."

For Verlaine, faithful to the logic that was his at the time, Rimbaud, too, had been baptized and redeemed by the Cross of Jesus Christ, but his soul was overgrown with sin, like a neglected garden with weeds: pride, unbelief, selfishness, and other vices. To snatch this poisoned flower, to pull the unfortunate soul out of the rut into which he had sunk, and to show him the true light, that which comes from On High—such seemed to him to be the mission that God had entrusted to him. So they could both take to the road together, in a purified friendship, not now toward perdition, but toward sanctity. So he handed Delahaye a letter, to be sent on to Rimbaud, the contents of which, he said, he had been thinking over for the past six months. It was moving and categorical; according to Delahaye, it could be summed up in four words: *Aimons-nous en Jésus* (Let us love one another in Jesus).

After a few days, the reply arrived: it was a page of sniggerings and insults at the expense of the "new Loyola." Verlaine, who had expected this reaction, did not give in so easily. He was aware of the difficulty of the undertaking, and knew what humiliations he would have to submit to—but they would be his justification and glory. Determined to pursue this new "way of the cross," he urged Delahaye to give him Rimbaud's address. Delahaye consulted Rimbaud, who in the end agreed to it: "I don't care any more. If you like, yes, give Loyola my address."

Three days later, Verlaine was in Stuttgart.

One can imagine Rimbaud's amazement when he saw Verlaine appear, wearing a voluminous Inverness cape and looking for all the world like a highwayman. But his surprise must have been far greater when he realized how changed Verlaine was: instead of the suave, polite manner that came naturally to him, he affected a seriousness that was positively frightening and an unction worthy of a prelate.

First they talked about literature. Verlaine gave his companion a few copies of his latest works, in particular the poem *O mon Dieu, vous m'avez blessé d'amour*—which was later found in the latrines at Roche, and which Isabelle thought to be by her brother.[3]

In exchange, Rimbaud gave him, or rather left him, his "Poèmes en prose," which he had revised in London, asking him to send them to Germain Nouveau, who was then in Brussels, with a view to trying to get them published in Belgium. Their first contact, then, was not unfavorable—but Verlaine had not come to indulge in literary chit-chat. As soon as he got to the main point, that is to say, religion, Rimbaud suggested that they go for a tour around the city, and in one of several bars, got him to drink a great deal of beer, knowing that it disagreed with him. And, inevitably, after a while, Verlaine, irritated by his sarcastic remarks, began to get heated. Then, since Rimbaud did not give up making fun of him, his old devils resurfaced, and the holy man began to swear in the most atrocious manner, banging the table, totally unaware of the ironic twinkle in his companion's eyes. In order to calm him down a bit, Rimbaud took Verlaine out into the open air, to a small wood outside the city, where the argument resumed as violently and as bitterly as ever. By this time, Verlaine could hardly stand on his feet, and, clinging to Rimbaud, begged him to think of his soul. Rimbaud only had to make a move with his arm, and Verlaine fell into a ditch.

Verlaine never referred to this scene, which was really only a minor incident, but a number of biographers have elaborated it, describing it in lyrical terms as the collision between the angel of light and the angel of darkness,. as a struggle between Jacob (Rimbaud) and the angel of God (Verlaine) at the ford of the river Jabbok: Delahaye, for example, adds that Verlaine, who was left unconscious on the ground, was found next day by kindly peasants, who tended him in their cottage. This is pure imagination, for Delahaye had proof that the two friends had not left one another on bad terms—this proof is the letter that Rimbaud sent to him on March 5, 1875 (dated in error February 5, since the postmark bears the date March 6):

Verlaine arrived here the other day, a rosary in his hands. . . . Three hours later we had denied his God and made the 98 wounds of O.L. bleed. For two days and a half, he remained very reasonable, and at my urging went back to Paris, with the intention, later, of finishing off his studies over there in the island.

I have only a week left of Wagner [strasse], and I regret this money paid in hatred, all this wasted time. On the fifteenth I will have Ein freundliches Zimmer anywhere, and I'm frantically lashing the language so that I'll have finished in two months at the most.

Everything is inferior here, except one. Riessling. . . . The sun is shining and it's freezing—it's very tiresome.
(After the fifteenth poste restante, Stuttgart),
Yours,
Rimb.

This letter is illustrated at the top left-hand corner with a drawing vaguely representing Professor Luebke's house with the following legend: WAGNER VERDAMNT IN EWIGKEIT (May Wagner be damned in eternity). It should be said that Rimbaud had heard enough of the great composer, for, from February 27 to March 5, the *Wagnerwoche* (the Wagner week founded by Liszt) had taken place at Stuttgart. At the foot of the letter, another drawing gives an impression of the old city of Stuttgart: it is a jumble of landscape, bottles, glasses, bearing various inscriptions (RIESSLING, FLIEGENDE BLATTER (the name of a local newspaper), street cars, small figures, obscene graffiti.[4]

As soon as he could, probably from Arras, Verlaine sent the manuscript of *Les Illuminations* to Germain Nouveau (2.75 F postage! he observes in a letter to Delahaye, of May 1, 1875). He then went off to England, where he soon found a post as teacher in a private school, the "Grammar School," at Stickney, a village near Boston (Lincolnshire).

On March 17, Rimbaud informed his mother and sisters of his new address, 2 Marienstrasse, 3 tr. "I have a very large furnished room in the town center for ten florins, that is, 21 francs, 50 cent., service included; and I'm offered full board for 60 francs a month: I don't need it anyway: those little arrangements are always a trick and an enslavement, however good a deal they seem."

So Rimbaud preferred to lead an independent life—though he went on giving private lessons. And it is here that M. de Graaf's discovery becomes interesting, for it shows that the house in which Rimbaud lodged, situated in fact in the *Mariensbadstrasse* (now Urbanstrasse, 34), a sort of *pension de famille*, belonged to Professor Luebke.[5]

In this letter he does not hide the fact that his finances are somewhat precarious: he has only fifty francs left, and on April 15 he will need fresh advances. He concludes: "I'm trying to infiltrate myself into the ways things are done here by every possible means, I am trying to get informed; though one really does suffer much from their ways. Greetings to the army [Frédéric], I hope Vitalie and Isabelle are well, please let me know if there is anything you want from here, and I'm your devoted A. Rimbaud."

In April, as expected, his money was at its lowest ebb, and, worse, he had got into debt (perhaps on account of the visiting cards that he had had printed). Furthermore, he had had an idea: he would make an appeal to Verlaine, who, in the name of Christian charity, could hardly refuse to help him. So he asked him, quite openly, through Delahaye, for an "advance" of a hundred francs.

At this time their relations were not bad. When Rimbaud had complained of being bored in Stuttgart, Verlaine (again through Delahaye) had replied, in a friendly enough way, amuse yourself, go to the bars a bit, then you've got the theater.[6] But he gibbed at the request for money. Oh, no! The joke had gone on long enough! The goose that laid the golden eggs was dead! He refused curtly, even though he had discerned vague threats of blackmail in the event of a negative reply. Before long he received a letter full of insults, written, Rimbaud was to say later, while drunk (he quoted as evidence a few bizarre turns of phrase).

The break had finally come.

All that Verlaine could now do was to weep on Delahaye's shoulder (about April 22 1875): "To begin with, I didn't *break it off*. I'm waiting for an apology, without promising anything. And if he is sulking, very well! Let him sulk! After all, he hasn't done me much good, that philomath! Eighteen months of you-know-what [prison], my son taken from me, my marriage destroyed, my advice rejected, lastly the grossest ill-treatment: no thank you!"

Then, after declaring that, in all seriousness, he is still very fond of him, and that he is ready to receive him if ever he comes back (ready, in a *Christian* sense, of course, he stresses), he nevertheless gives way to his resentments, and goes on to draw a really black portrait of Rimbaud: "When one takes grossness for strength, evil for craftiness and swindling—his own word—for cleverness, then damn it! One really is a bore and a swine. He'll be a horrible, vulgar bourgeois by the time he's thirty—unless he is given a good lesson, as I have given him. . . . It's all over. But remember what I've said. You'll see. Anyway, I'm whispering this in your ear."

This letter of April is the prose version of the poem *Malheureux! tous les dons . . .* , which was to be composed three months later:

Malheureux! Toi français, toi chrétien, quel dommage! . . .
Seul l'orgueil est vivant, il danse dans tes yeux,
Il regarde la Faute et rit de s'y complaire.
Dieu des humbles, sauvez cet enfant de colère.

(Sagesse)

[Wretch! You a Frenchman, you a Christian, for shame! . . .
Only your pride is alive, it dances in your eyes,
It looks at the Sin and laughs in delight at it.
God of the humble, save this child of anger.]

Delahaye, the confidant of two old friends tearing one another apart, caught between Stickney and Stuttgart, received from Verlaine an imperative reminder not to give his address to anybody. Indeed he issued the same order to all his friends: very serious reasons, he said to one, "beware of the leeches," he said to another—proof that he was afraid of some counterattack from Rimbaud. This fear was to haunt him for a long time to come.

Thus, for Rimbaud, Verlaine was now no more than a Jesuitical skin-flint, from whom he could no longer expect anything except lessons in morality.

"You're no longer good for anything," Verlaine replied from his side. So they thought exactly the same about each other. And yet, for a long time to come, Verlaine was to show interest and concern in what his old friend was doing, constantly asking Delahaye for news of "Stuttgars" or "Stuttgarce" (*gars* = lad, *garce* = bitch), or "*l'Oestre*" (a parasitical insect).

But what Verlaine regretted above all was letting go of the manuscript of *Les Illuminations*. What had become of it? Had Nouveau found a publisher for it? To ease his conscience, Verlaine did everything he could to get this Nouveau's address—and to find out something about him: "What sort of a moral gentleman is he?" he asked Delahaye. After much beating about the bush, he found out that he was in England, and arranged to meet him in London, at King's Cross Station. One can imagine that, if he traveled a hundred and twenty-five miles (13 shillings, 3 pence) to meet him, it was with a precise aim in mind. On May 7, he wrote to Delahaye about this trip: "I shall take advantage of this very brief stay in town (one or two days at most) to meet Nouveau, and to get to know him a little better: really I believe him to be a good young man who believes that philomathy has arrived: you can see that from here."[7]

The meeting took place around May 20. Nouveau promised, it is thought, to hand back Rimbaud's manuscript, which he did not have on him (in fact, he did not do so until 1877).

Meanwhile, Rimbaud had left Stuttgart, leaving behind him nothing but bad memories and probably a few debts. He felt drawn to the south, and duly set off for Italy. The sale of his trunk had paid for his "railroad" tickets to Altdorf, the beginning of the Saint-Gothard pass, and he had continued on road by his own means. Though the weather was now good (late April, early May), the crossing of the Gothard was not as easy as he had expected. We have no details about this journey, which must have been very hard. In November 1878 he was to repeat this exploit in worse conditions, but, in his very detailed and very vivid account of this performance, he made no reference to his earlier crossing, except perhaps at the end, where, in reference to Lake Como, he writes: "crossing known." Did he stop off at the famous Benedictine Abbey of Disentis (which had become a civil hospice)? This is suggested by one of Delahaye's drawings, which shows a disheveled Rimbaud, dressed *à l'italienne*, falling back, tears in his eyes, before a plump monk firmly entrenched on his legs. The title ("Le Capucin folâtre"—"folâtre" means playful, spritely, but there may well be a suggestion of "folle," a "queen"—Translator's note), and the legend ("Is it true or isn't it?") refer to some incident that Delahaye recounted to Verlaine. But the situation of this abbey in Grisons, in the Rhine valley, makes this hypothesis improbable.[8]

Then, about May 5 or 6, Germain Nouveau informed Verlaine that Rimbaud was in Milan, intending to travel eventually to Spain. Verlaine immediately transmitted the news to Delahaye: "Thing is in Milan, expecting money for Spain." Thus the roles were reversed: Verlaine is now informing Delahaye, proud to suggest that he, too, has his informers. This letter of May 7 is illustrated with a sketch showing Delahaye, Nouveau, and himself, as grave academics, while "Thing," wearing a Piedmontese hat, turning his back to the group, is plunged in a "*traduzione.*"[9]

At Milan, the traveler must have wandered about for some time, exhausted and without money, waiting for luck to smile on him at last—which it did: "A charitable lady," writes Delahaye, "took an interest in him, and nursed him for a few days. She must have recognized, by his conversation, that he was a man of letters, and asked him what he had written, for her guest, who no longer had any manuscripts on him, has remembered that he once gave me *Une Saison en enfer*, and now wants it back."[10]

One can imagine that Verlaine, kept informed, was furious at the incident. Twice in *Les Hommes d'aujourd'hui*, and in a letter of November 17, 1883 (to Albert Max?), he referred to this "*vedova molto civile*," hinting at some amorous adventure on Rimbaud's part. In fact, it would appear that it was simply a question of disinterested pity and pure charity. This is what Delahaye had to say about the incident:

> *When Rimbaud told me about the episode, he did so with all the punctilliousness of detail that he put into his writings. I asked him: "What kind of a woman was she?"*
> *"A good woman," he replied.*
> *"Young?"*

He shrugged his shoulders, as if I had asked some absurd question:
"Er . . . no."
I did not pursue the matter.
(Unpublished note preserved in the Doucet Collection)

It should also be mentioned that Delahaye received a visiting card from Rimbaud (it has been rediscovered), bearing, in his hand, his Milanese address: "39 (not 2) Piazza del Duomo, terzo piano." The building was long since demolished, and the good widow has never been identified.

Milan was only a stage. Rimbaud had other plans, either to join the Carlist army (an idea stolen from Verlaine), or to go to Brindisi, on the Adriatic, with a view to sailing to one of the Cyclades islands (Ceos, Naxos, or Syra?), where Henri Mercier would be able to get him a job in a soap factory of which he was part-owner.[11] In any case, he crossed Lombardy, stopping at Allessandria, Genoa, and Livorno in Tuscany. But, on the road from Livorno to Sienna, he fell ill with sunstroke. The French consul at Livorno had him taken to the town hospital, and, on his recovery, took steps to have him repatriated to Marseille.

There is an entry in the consular register: "1875—June 15, repatriation of Sr. Raimbaud, Arthur, son of Frédéric and Catherine Cuif, native of Charleville (Ardennes), aged 20, to travel to Marseille by the steamer *Général Paoli* and embarcation, 12.50 F. Given in money, 3.20 F. Two days at the Stella of Sr. Raimbaud, 2.00 F. [Total,] 17.70 F."[12]

At Marseille, Rimbaud, who had still not fully recovered, must have been treated in a hospital—which one we do not know—for several weeks. It was no doubt from there that he recounted his latest adventures in a letter to Delahaye, who immediately informed Verlaine: "Rimbe is at present in Marseille, having it seems, made a tour of Liguria on foot. After sundry weird and wonderful adventures, he appears to have got himself repatriated administratively, by a consul. However, he declares his intention of going off and joining up with the Carlists! Some story of going to learn español, and is continuing his attempts to swindle money out of the few friends he has left."[13]

From Stickney, Verlaine hastened to convey the news to Germain Nouveau, who was staying at Pourrières (Var), and he in turn informed Jean Richepin, who was visiting London. "I have news of P.V. You might meet him in London over the next few days; he is passing through on his way to

France. Rimbaud appears to be at Marseille! But I have neither address nor news: joining the Carlists!" (July 27, 1875).

Delahaye gave two somewhat different versions of this attempt: "He is enlisting in a band of Carlists, and is coming back to Paris with his bounty,"[14] and, "He then decided to enlist in one of the Carlist bands, which was being formed on this side of the Pyrenees, when the end of the insurrection caused the recruiting offices to be shut down."[15] In support of the first thesis, Charles Maurras writes in *La Gazette de France* of July 21, 1901: "My friend the poet, Raoul Gineste, was to meet Rimbaud in Marseille. He had just joined in a Carlist band."[16]

Let us now return to Verlaine and Delahaye. The latter, now a civil servant in the Charleville townhall, remained in continuous correspondence with Verlaine, who, curiously enough, told him (July 1, 1875) that he was beginning to learn Italian and Spanish—but with Dante and Cervantes.

Then came the holidays. In August, Verlaine invited Delahaye, who had at last passed the first part of the *baccalauréat*, to spend a few days with him at his mother's house in Arras. It was there that, one day, leafing through a photograph album, he suddenly put a loose photograph against the portrait of his wife, and shutting the album, said: "I thus unite the two beings who have caused me the greatest suffering!" "Sacrilege!" Delahaye exlaimed. "No, justice!" he replied fiercely.[17]

Of course, a great deal more was said about Rimbaud, none of it being complimentary, as one can imagine.

Then, a little later, Germain Nouveau was leaving Paris to return to Pourrières, with the intention of passing through Marseille, and was given the mission of locating Rimbaud! In his letter to Verlaine of August 17, he admits, with the help of drawings, how little success he has had: we see him, for example, in the Old Port at one o'clock in the morning, wondering, on seeing a shadowy figure enter a café with the sign "Vermouth" over it: "Who knows? . . . No, it was nothing."[18]

Now, at Pourrières, a letter from Forain was waiting for him from which he passed on the following information to Verlaine: "Rimbaud in Paris, according to Forain. Adds that he's living with Mercier and Cabaner."

We know very little about this stay in Paris. The few pieces of information that we do have we owe to Delahaye; thus, in a letter to Verlaine: "The wretch boasts with rather astonishing volubility of his part in kicking everybody up the ass."[19]

For her part, Isabelle Rimbaud told Paterne Berrichon that her mother,

her sister Vitalie, and herself made a trip to Paris "in June, July and August 1875," so that her younger sister could be treated by a specialist for the synovitis that was to carry her off six months later. They had left Charleville on Wednesday, July 14, at four o'clock in the morning. We know this from Vitalie's *Mémorial*, preserved in the Musée Rimbaud at Charleville-Mézières: "Tuesday, 13 [July]—We leave tomorrow for Paris. What joy and what emotion! . . . Last year, we were in the capital of England, this year it is to be the capital of France. . . . It is eight o'clock in the evening and tomorrow morning at four o'clock we set off. How many different thoughts I have!"

Unfortunately, the *Mémorial* ends with these words. Isabelle told Berrichon: "When we left him [Arthur, in Paris], he had just obtained a post as assistant teacher at Maisons-Alfort."[20] Was it some kind of holiday school? Or just some project? The mystery has never been solved.

Meanwhile, on August 24, Verlaine sent Delahaye a letter for Rimbaud—which has not been found: "Am sending you the enclosed letter for Rimbaud. Give it him or send on if gone. I think it's what's required. Perhaps, who knows?" To this letter was added a "coppée," "Ultissima verba," ten lines of comic verse, illustrated by a sketch showing Rimbaud slumped over a table covered with bottles and glasses.

Rimbaud, it seems, did not reply, but only intended to reply, for, shortly afterwards, Delahaye asked Verlaine: "Have you received the epistomph expected from The-man-with-the-Spanish-grammar? Has your heart cried out? If you do slit his throat in some tavern, don't let him die in too much pain."[21]

About the Spanish, it should be said that we have found in the papers of the draftsman Cazals a list of Spanish words, in Rimbaud's hand, that Verlaine had given him—but we would be hard pressed to say how Verlaine got hold of them.[22]

Delahaye tried to give Verlaine some hope: "But, you know, I still think L'Oestre will grow sweeter in time." Still on tenterhooks, Verlaine replied to him on September 3 from Arras: "What news (in any case) of L'Oestre? Has he grown any sweeter?"

Now, about this time, Delahaye went off to take up a job as assistant master at a school in Soissons, much to Verlaine's chagrin—he had now lost his only informant. So he decided to write directly to Rimbaud, *poste restante* at Charleville, giving a choice of two addresses, one in Paris—12 Rue de Lyon, c/o M. Istace—the other at a *poste restante* in London.

Finally, around October 6, Rimbaud reappeared in his native city. The correspondence from Verlaine, which he found at the *poste restante*, put him in a fury. What? Did Loyala have the audacity to try to start things up again with him? To put an end to it, once and for all, he decided to write (Delahaye made a sketch of him, writing this letter in a bar), and chose the Paris address in the Rue de Lyon.[23] Unfortunately, this letter did not reach Verlaine, or was lost, which was why Verlaine, still anxious, was to ask Delahaye: "Try to find out what sweet things were addressed to the Rue de Lyon." One may be sure that the "sweet things" were well laced with vinegar!

Rimbaud then wrote to Delahaye, at Soissons, and, this time, we are fortunate in having the letter: "Received the postcard and letter from P.V. eight days ago. To simplify everything, I have told the poste restante to send his restantes to me, so that you may write to me here, and not to the restantes. I have nothing to say about Loyola's latest enormities, and I no longer have any activity to spare in that direction at present!"

In the same letter, he asks Delahaye to send him "according to circumstances any relevant 'Loyolas'—and ask him for information concerning the *'bachot' ès sciences*, part classics and mathematics. Above all I want precise details, since I'll be buying those books soon. Military training and *'bachot,'* you see, will provide me with two or three pleasant seasons! To hell anyway, with that 'gentle labor.' Be so kind as to let me know the best possible way of tackling it."

Finally, on October 18, Delahaye, who had left the school at Soissons, on account of the poor pay he received there, was astonished to meet Rimbaud in a street in Charleville. He sketched the scene, which took place in front of Hudréaux's grocery shop: an enormous Rimbaud, dressed impeccably, with wing collar, is poking a rather stout Delahaye with his index finger.[24] On the back of this sketch is part of the letter giving Verlaine news of L'Oestre: ". . . that this *end* we talked about over there [at Arras, in August] will be some madhouse. It strikes me he's going that way now. The reason is simple enough: alcohol."

To please Verlaine, Delahaye blackened Rimbaud as much as he could, though in fact he had been very pleased to see him. He goes on: "But note this, Nouveau's conduct inspires anxiety and suspicion in him, he knows that he went to his home and is going to write to him to demand an explanation. You'd do well to warn him." What was it all about? Apparently Nouveau, under the name of M. Germain, had come to take up a post as teacher at the Institut Barbadaux (formerly Rossat) at Charleville, at the beginning of October, and Rimbaud was annoyed that he had not looked him up. In any case, Nouveau was soon dismissed on account of his eccentricities.[25] To Verlaine, who had warned him, he replied on October 20: "Complete ignorance as to what has aroused Rimbaud's anger. No correspondence in Paris."

And Delahaye goes on: "As for you, you're just an old skinflint—it's 'cunning or hostility.' He called at your mother's in Paris. The doorkeeper told him she was in Belgium. He (the monster) knows that you went to somewhere called Boston, but supposes that you are in London at the moment. I, of course, know nothing about all that, I've completely lost sight of you."

It is a pity we don't have the whole of Delahaye's letter, which must have recounted Rimbaud's "weird and wonderful" adventures in Italy. There is also the question of Rimbaud's health (already in 1872, he declared: "I've only got five years left"), the climate of France did not suit him, and he dreamed of hot countries, Africa or Asia. This gave him a rather original idea: he might join the Brothers of the Christian Schools in order to be sent to China or some distant land. "And why not," Delahaye adds, "at least for as long as it takes him to get there."

Verlaine replied with two letters. The first around November 20, of which we have only a fragment: "As for his entry into religion, inform me of the beautiful mysteries thereof!"[26] With this letter was enclosed a (lost) "coppée" on Rimbaud entitled: "Chanson du Gars pas poseur" (Song of the lad who is not a poseur, an allusion to Gaspard Hauser). The second letter, of November 27, has survived. It is very vindictive. It begins with a little threatening couplet in case Rimbaud's "little projects" (blackmail) materialized. And, anyway, Rimbaud's letter, sent in care of M. Istace, and since lost, intrigues Verlaine, who now unleashes a torrent of quite unjustified anger on the subject of his friend's intention of continuing with his education—right up to the Ecole Centrale or the Ecole Polytechnique, roundly abusing those who could have been so stupid as to put such an idea into his head.

Incidentally, without being aware of it, Verlaine was putting his foot into it here, for Delahaye was one of those who had encouraged Rimbaud in this course of action.[27] Furthermore, it struck him as odd that Rimbaud should live at 31 Rue Saint Barthélemy—which fact sent Verlaine off into another torrent of abuse: Was he living outside his family, perhaps, or with some relation? And Verlaine goes on to imagine him coming back late at night, on all fours, "and the vomitings—I've seen a few of them!" He was quite simply unaware that the Rimbaud family had moved—to be precise, on June 25, according to Vitalie's *Mémorial*. Then greetings to "la Daromphe" (Mme Rimbaud): "What does she say to that? Is it still my fault? I would have to communicate with this mother of the Gracchi about my separation proceedings." Last, Verlaine asks Delahaye to send him a copy of the "Being's" old verses—if there are any (the free sonnets suggested to him by Delahaye didn't interest him for the moment.)

"Verses by him?" Delahaye was to reply, "it's a long time since the Muse visited him. I don't even think he remembers ever having written anything."[28]

Too bad, but Verlaine was not put off so easily: "Send news of Homais," he would ask, almost out of habit.

Rimbaud resumed his walks with Delahaye, both relaxed and delighted at being able to return to the habits of their youth. A drawing by Delahaye shows Rimbaud clambering with two friends up a steep hill at the top of which shines the sign of a bar: "Pêquet" (a brandy made from juniper berries).[29]

At this period the piano became one of Rimbaud's passions. It is said that when his mother refused to buy him one or to hire one, he carved the dining-room table into the shape of a keyboard instrument in order to practice his fingering (an anecdote which Louis Pierquin places much earlier). Young Lefebvre, referred to above, later declared when he had become a doctor: "At that time [late 1875], I took German lessons from Rimbaud, and I remember seeing him tap out sometimes on his table a few scales or a score in front of him, as he explained some piece of German literature or corrected one of my translations."[30]

Then, in the course of that winter, he frantically set about learning foreign languages—Russian, Arabic, Hindustani, Amharina. "So as not to be disturbed," Louis Pierquin recounts, "he shut himself up on several occasions in an old chest, and stayed there sometimes for twenty-four hours on end, without eating or drinking, totally absorbed in his work."[31] "Henri Pauffin, a member of the Paris bar, relates how he met him in a wood near Charleville, learning Russian with the help of an old Greek-Russian dictionary, the pages of which he had cut into pieces and stuffed into his pockets."[32]

On Sunday December 12 Verlaine, irritated at receiving no reply to his letters, decided to send Rimbaud a final message. It contained nothing new: "Still the same, strictly religious, because it's the only intelligent, good thing to be. The rest is swindling, wickedness, stupidity. The Church created modern civilization, science, literature: it made France, in particular, what she is, and France is now dying for having broken with her."

He then confesses, and regards himself as having been "punished" for "*our* absurd and shameful life three years ago."

"So still the same. The same (modified) affection, for you. I would so much like to see you enlightened, thoughtful. It's a source of great sorrow to me to see you persisting in such idiotic ways, you are so intelligent, so *ready* (though that may surprise you!). You have only to notice your disgust for everything and everyone, your perpetual anger against everything—which really is justified, though unconscious of its *true cause.*"

He would not encourage him in the way that he had chosen, and would not help him financially: "Where would my money go? On drinks and prostitutes! Piano lessons? What a bore! Won't your mother pay for them, then?"

There then follows a reminder that any attempt at blackmail would be answered "*legally*, evidence in hand." The letter ends on a rather cool note:

> *Come now! Show a little kindness, consideration, and affection for someone who will always remain—and you know it— very cordially yours*
>
> P.V.
>
> *I shall explain my plans—they are so simple—and the advice that I would like to see you follow, religion apart, though it is my great, great, great piece of advice, when, via Delahaye, you have replied to me properly.*
>
> *P.S.—Useless to write here* till called for [*in English*]. *I leave tomorrow on a long journey, very far . . .*

Of course Rimbaud did not reply to this rather clumsy letter. The surprising thing is that he did not tear it up.

He must have received it on December 14. Now, four days later, on the eighteenth, his young sister Vitalie, whom he was very fond of, died at the age of seventeen, from tubercular complications following an attack of synovitis (hydrarthrosis). Her suffering at the end deeply moved her brother Arthur (who was himself to die from the sequellae of a similar disease). With her blue eyes, her fair hair, and her fresh complexion, she also looked very like him. Her death affected him so much that his health suffered. "This shock," writes Delahaye, "even more than the long, intense hours of study, must, I think, have been responsible for the violent headaches that afflicted him at that time. Attributing them to his excessively thick hair, he applied an odd remedy: he had his head shaved, I mean shaved . . . with a razor, which the wig-maker agreed to only after many cries of astonishment and protest." So Rimbaud had to attend his sister's funeral with a head as white as new parchment, and those placed in the church at some distance from them, said among themselves, "the brother already has the hair of an old man"[33] This heroic decision was taken—need one say?—against the furious opposition of his mother. Delahaye sketched his friend's curious profile, with the cranium shaven like an egg, and sent the drawing ("La tronche à Machine [Thing's Nut]") to Verlaine, who was about to come back to France for the Christmas holidays.[34]

And so that year of 1875, so rich in events, ended with the grief of a bereavement and the bitterness of a broken friendship.

Now, for both Rimbaud and Verlaine, the dice were thrown: for one, a future of travel and adventure, for the other, a continuous, determined attempt to rehabilitate himself in literary circles.

13

Long Journeys: Discovery of the Orient

The year 1876 began with music: Mme Rimbaud had agreed at last to hire a piano, hoping perhaps to keep Arthur at home.

"Are you making progress with the piano?" Delahaye asks Verlaine, who had also taken up playing. "Man has just got his hands on one at last and beats on it from morning till night. But this conquest was accompanied by a little amusing incident that I will tell you about next time."[1] Elsewhere Delahaye suggests that Rimbaud, tired of waiting, went off one day to hire a piano in town, giving the name and address of his mother, without first telling her. When the piano arrived, a tenant in the building protested: the landlord had assured her that no piano would ever enter the building.

"Who's it for?" she asked.

"For Mme Rimbaud."

Whereupon hearing her name, Mme Rimbaud came out on to the landing and declared haughtily that no one would ever stop her playing the piano day and night if she so wished![2]

Louis Pierquin adds the following detail: the instrument had to be carried up a common staircase and through a boarded-up door. When the delivery man had finished, Mme Rimbaud banged her door in their faces without giving them a sou by way of a tip.[3]

Arthur took lessons with a young man of his own age, Louis Létrange, whose great delight in life was running a choir and playing the organ. He earned his living as head clerk to M. Lefebvre, Mme Rimbaud's landlord, and a dealer in nails.[4] He was later to marry Ernest Millot's sister. M. de

Graaf tells us that his son, Ernest Létrange, found the following note in his father's account book: "1875 . . . La Méthode de Mlle Carpentier, for Rimbaud."

Verlaine illustrated this musical apprenticeship, depicting Rimbaud mistreating an upright piano before a copy of the Méthode Carpentier, to the great despair of his mother, who rushes out terrified, as the landlord, on the first floor, lifts his eyes up to heaven. "Music soothes the savage breast" is the title of this caricature.

Piano (exercises, improvisations) and foreign languages occupied his days, as he waited for the spring to come round.

In February 1876 an event of some importance took place: Delahaye left for the Collège Notre-Dame at Rethel, where he had been given a junior teaching post. From then on he illustrates his letters to Verlaine with truculent sketches, sometimes involving Rimbaud. "I have had no news of Thing since my last," he wrote to Verlaine in late February. "I shall write to him at once and, as you are no doubt aware, it has been raining here perpetually for over a month. Has it been the same over there? What at least is sure is that in such weather Philomathy is forced to keep to its room. So, nothing new until the weather turns drier."[5]

And, in fact, as soon as the weather did get dry and the sun came out (early April), Rimbaud dropped his dictionaries, opened the doors of his old cupboard, and flew off to central Europe, with the intention of setting sail at Varna (Bulgaria) for the Near East.

As soon as he was informed of Rimbaud's departure, Verlaine scribbled a sketch, whose proverbial legend, "Travel broadens the mind," serves as a pendant to the one accompanying the piano sketch. It depicts a lively Rimbaud, wearing new clothes, his hat still draped with a mourning band, striding toward the railway station, crying delightedly: *"Merde à la Daromphe, j'fous l'camp à Wien!"* ["Shit to *la Daromphe*, I'm off to Vienna!"—"La Daromphe" was one of the nicknames given to Mme Rimbaud by her son and Verlaine].[6]

He visited the Austrian capital, with the help of a rather battered map of the city that is now in the Musée Rimbaud. As he had rather overindulged in beer, or brandy, he was imprudent enough to fall asleep in the coach in which he was seeing the city, and the coachman took the opportunity to rob him of his overcoat, which contained his wallet and all his money. It has been said that, having fought with his thief, he was picked up unconscious, on the pavement, and taken to a hospital, from which, it seems, he wrote to

Delahaye announcing the arrest of the ungrateful coachman and the recovery of his property.[7] However, when informed of the incident, Delahaye did not confirm this version of the facts. He says that, in order to earn some money, Rimbaud became a street hawker, which enabled him to keep an eye on all the coachmen in the city—but he never saw his thief again. This precarious situation was not to last for long: after an altercation with a policeman, he was taken to a police station, and, since he could produce no identity papers, he was expelled as a foreigner with no means of support. He was taken to the Bavarian frontier, then thrown out from one German state to another, until he finally reached Charleville, via Strasbourg and Montmédy.

Delahaye made a magnificent illustration for Verlaine of the unglorious return of the "new wandering Jew." Rimbaud, striding through the Black Forest to Charleville, is greeted by Austrian and Bavarian customs officers and peasants; he is wearing a battered hat, a "passe-porc" is sticking out of his pocket, while a "collosal cockchafer" flies before him.[8]

Verlaine returned the compliment in verse and a drawing depicting the Viennese escapade. Rimbaud is shown stripped to the waist, scratching his head in the "Vingince strasse," as the accursed coach disappears into the distance.[9]

We do not know whether Rimbaud was back in Charleville on May 6, 1876, the date on which the Collège de Charleville was burnt down.

Did this stupid adventure spoil his spring and summer? Those few days of freedom had whetted his appetite. No, he would not be staying in Charleville! Soon after his return, he set off on foot for Brussels and Rotterdam. Had he heard—perhaps in London, according to Isabelle—of the advantages to be obtained by signing up in the Dutch colonial army, which was recruiting foreigners, or did he meet in Belgium some recruiting sergeant—or some former deserter—who painted for him the delights of the sea voyage and the charms of Java? We do not know, but the fact remains that he went through Utrecht to the port of Harderwijk, on the Zuyderzee. Whether as a mercenary in the Spanish cause, or a mercenary in the Dutch cause, he was still a volunteer for adventure.

On May 18, he turned up at the colonial recruiting office. Next day, he was informed that his request to enlist for six years had been accepted. He would be joining a force being sent to put down a revolt in the former sultanate of Achin—or Atjeh—in Sumatra. He was given his bounty of 300 florins (a fortune at the time!), and his outfit, consisting of a blue serge uniform, grey greatcoat, and a cap trimmed with orange.

Dr. Marmelstein has provided the following description of Rimbaud, from the records of the war department at Bandung: *"Face:* oval. *Forehead, nose:* normal. *Eyes:* blue. *Chin:* round. *Hair and eyebrows:* light brown. *Height in meters:* 1.77 (5 ft 8 ins.). *Distinguishing marks:* none.[10]

A few days later, he was one of a line of volunteers who, preceded by music and flanked by guards sporting bayonets in their rifles, marched toward Utrecht and the port of Den Helder.

A section of the *Illuminations, Democracy,* depicts the scene so precisely that it deserves inclusion here:

> *The flag's off to that filthy place, and our speech drowns the sound of the drum.*
> *In the town centers we'll feed the most cynical whoring. We'll smash all logical revolts.*
> *To the peppery dried-up countries!—in the service of the most gigantic industrial or military exploitation.*
> *Goodbye to this place. No matter where we're off to. We conscripts of good will are going to display a savage philosophy; ignorant in science, rakes where our comfort is concerned; and let the world blow up! This is the real march. Forward, men!*[11]

The steamer *Prins van Oranje* of the Dutch shipping lines set sail on June 10 from Nieuwe Diep, the port of Den Helder, with fourteen officers, including Captain Aukes, twelve sergeants, three corporals, and a hundred and ninety-two troops, including six Frenchmen. With the help of the newspapers of the time[12] we are able to follow the course taken by the ship. On June 11, at ten in the evening, it stopped off at Southampton to take on fresh meat. The first desertion, that of a Frenchman, Louis-Joseph Marais, aged twenty-nine, born in Paris, previously of London (was it, perhaps, he who gave Rimbaud the idea?), took place on that day. On the thirteenth, at two in the afternoon, the ship lifted anchor, and, on the seventeenth, passed Sagres (Cape Saint Vincent—southern Portugal). In the afternoon of the twenty-second they arrived at Naples, and left that evening. A few days later, in the waters of the Red Sea, the desertions increased (Delahaye tells us that Rimbaud saw several of his comrades throw themselves into the water and swim for the coast): on the twenty-sixth an Italian, on the twenty-eighth six others (one of whom was recaptured), on July 2 a German (it is thought that he drowned). In the Red Sea tropical gear was issued: white linen jackets, blue and white striped trousers, tartan berets.

Thanks to the patient researches of a Dutch writer living in Indonesia, M. Van Dam, we have a sufficiently detailed picture of the life of the Dutch colonial troops to give us some idea of what Rimbaud experienced in his floating barracks. Reveille was at 5 A.M. The day was divided between fatigues, games (cards, lotto, dominoes, music), and relaxation on the deck chairs. There was only one hour of military training per day, which took place after lunch. Alcohol was forbidden; however, the quartermaster's stores provided tea, tobacco, and, on Saturdays, a small glass of brandy. On Sundays, the menu included fresh meat and cakes. Lights out was at 9 P.M. As one can see the routine was almost touristic.[13]

On Wednesday, July 19, the *Prins van Oranje* finally berthed at Padang (Sumatra), and, twenty-four hours later, the ship set sail for Batavia (Djakarta), on the north coast of Java, where the army depot was situated.

They landed by canoe, assembled and marched to music. The barracks had been situated (since 1848) in the so-called Meester Cornelis quarter, nearly four miles from the port, in the southeast of the city. They had been set up in a former tea factory.

Rimbaud was attached to the 4th company of the first battalion. He was in barracks for only a week or so, and—according to M. Van Dam—was one of a contingent of 160 men who, on July 30, embarked on a coaster bound for Semarang. From there, a train took him to Tungtang, near Fort William I, and the company set out on foot, for Salatiga, at an altitude of two thousand feet, in the heart of the island.

Rimbaud was only waiting for a suitable opportunity (a day off, like August 15), to resume his liberty. It may be that the death of a Frenchman, Auguste Michaudeau, aged twenty-eight, on August 3, hastened his decision. On the fifteenth, he was missing at rollcall. In accordance with regulations, he was declared a deserter twenty-eight days later, and his name struck off the rolls on September 12. His military effects were sold by the quartermaster's department and the money raised (1 florin 81 cents), given to the orphanage at Salatiga. This equipment was listed as follows: one pair of lanyards with shoulder straps, one greatcoat, three ties, two shirts, underwear, two police caps, two pairs of blue trousers, two fatigue jackets, one briefcase, one wooden chest.[14] He had no weapons.

It is in fact Isabelle who is correct when she refers to a stay of one month:

"For one month we wandered through the burning hot atmosphere of Java" (*Mon frère Arthur*).

If he had been caught he would not have risked hanging, as has been said, but only several months' imprisonment.

Meanwhile Verlaine and Delahaye exercised their imaginations on the possible fate of the traveler: perhaps he had ended up with the savages of Central Africa. This gave rise to a flood of nicknames for Rimbaud:—the Senegalese, the Hottentot, the Kaffir, etc.—and also to a flowering of amusing sketches by Delahaye (intended for Verlaine), showing Rimbaud in Kaffir dress, as a missionary of some special kind, as a king of the savages (*Cahier Doucet*). In July 1876 Verlaine was asked by Delahaye to come and spend a few days with him at Mézières. Over and over again they asked one another the same questions: where, to which continent, had the animal fled? Soon, Germain Nouveau was adding his own graphic fantasies to the subject: Rimbaud's profile in the depths of the ocean—an allusion to a possible drowning—or running after his hat in the midst of a "negro landscape."

The summer came to an end, and still the silence continued. "Still no news of the Hottentot," Delahaye wrote to Verlaine. "What has become of him? Perhaps, at this very moment, his bones are whitening on some magic pyramid. . . . Anyway, not my fault!"[15]

By the end of November they could both feel that they had heard the last of Rimbaud, that the jungle, the desert, or the ocean had finally swallowed him up. He did not return to Charleville until December 9, 1876. The date is given in a letter from Delahaye to Ernest Millot of January 28:

> *Dear Friend,*
>> *I've kept you waiting, and I'm even rather ashamed of having to be told so, but, by way of compensation, I bring you great news:*
>> HE HAS COME BACK!!!
> *from a short journey—nothing very much, really. This is the itinerary: Brussels, Rotterdam, Den Helder, Southampton, Gibraltar, Naples, Suez, Aden, Sumatra, Java (a stay of two months), the Cape, St. Helena, Ascension Island, the Azores, Queenstown, Cork (in Ireland), Liverpool, Le Havre, Paris, and, to conclude . . . Charlestown. By what series of astonishing tricks he has performed these acrobatics would take too long to explain: I'll content myself with enclosing a few abso-*

lutely authentic ham-men. He has—to spoil it all—been at
Charlest. since December 9: enough said!
   Anyway, it isn't over yet, and we shall see further adven-
tures, it seems. Though not for the time being. The illustrative
debauchery enclosed says more than any words.
       See you soon,
              ta vieille

                        Delahaye[16]

   The sketches enclosed are in a rather poor state. Three of them have
been reproduced (*Album Rimbaud*): Rimbaud on board the *Prins van Or-*
anje, then crossing the Javanese jungle, and, lastly, sitting at a table in a
garden with Delahaye.
   "When are you going off again?" Delahaye asks him.
   "As soon as possible," Rimbaud replies.
   Above them one sees the sailing ship tossing in the waves: "A little
storm—nothing to bother about." In fact it was terrifying, the ship lost its
mizzenmast, its topgallant masts, and all its tackle. According to Delahaye,
Rimbaud saw the crew kneel down and say their prayers during the assault of
the furious waves.
   Among the drawings not reproduced, one showed Rimbaud astonishing
the naked natives, carrying cooking utensils (no doubt with a view to cooking
him), another depicted the same Rimbaud at the townhall of Java, where
there is a bust of Thiers.
   The question now arises as to which ship Rimbaud took for the return
journey. It is something of a problem, for this ship has to fulfill three conditions: (1.) It must have been registered in Scotland, since Rimbaud, in his
letter of May 14, 1877, to the United States consul in Bremen, declares that
he has sailed "for four months on a Scotch bark from Java to Queenstown,
from August to December 76"; (2.) the ports of call must correspond to those
referred to in the letter from Delahaye to Millot quoted above, which were
given to Delahaye by Rimbaud himself; (3.) the ship must have left Semarang
around August 30, 1876, and Rimbaud must have arrived in Charleville on
December 9.
   Enid Starkie, rejecting the claim of *The Lartington, The City of Exeter,*
and *La Léonie*, discovered *The Wandering Chief*, but is surprised that Rimbaud's name does not appear on the Register General of Shipping and Sea-

men, which would have been the case if he had been taken on as a temporary seaman.[17] But the objection is not entirely well founded, for there can be little doubt that he would have avoided giving his real name, in order to avoid the Dutch police.

The Wandering Chief was a sailing ship registered at Banff in Scotland (under a Captain Brown), most of whose crew was Scottish, and it left Semarang with a cargo of sugar on August 30 bound for Falmouth (Cornwall). It put in for one day (October 23) at St. Helena—which undermines the legend of Rimbaud throwing himself into the sea to swim to the island because the captain had refused to put in, and having to be fished out by one of the sailors.[18]

They put in at Queenstown in Ireland on December 6. But as *The Wandering Chief* did not continue on its way to Liverpool (the stage indicated by Delahaye), Underwood has supposed, not unreasonably, that Rimbaud left the ship at Queenstown (which is confirmed by his letter of May 14 1877), and went on to Cork by ferry (a twenty-one-minute crossing). From there he may have taken a steamer to Liverpool, where he would have found a coaster to take him to Le Havre.[19] Then, having set foot in France, he could have caught a train to Paris, since he still had his booty.

In the capital he was seen, according to Delahaye, dressed as an English sailor—so Germain Nouveau called him "Rimbald-the-Sailor," an allusion to Sinbad-the-Sailor (or, to be more precise, Sindbad, a character in *The Thousand and One Nights*).[20]

The traveler must have spent the winter of 1876–77 at Charleville, absorbed in the study of modern languages.

With the coming of spring, he set off again. He had had an idea. Instead of being a recruit, why should he not become a recruiter of volunteers for some Dutch agent? Who better than he could sell the charms of Java—and drop hints as to how easy it was to desert? So, in May 1877, we find him in the bars of Cologne trying to tempt young Rhinelanders with a taste for heroism and exoticism to support the Dutch colonial cause. When he had caught a dozen victims, he could go off to Hamburg, the gate to the magical Orient, with the commission in his pocket. What he was looking for was some job in commerce overseas.

On his way, he stopped off at Bremen, from where, on May 14, 1877, he wrote a very curious letter in English—a far from faultless English[21]—inquiring about terms of enlistment in the American navy:

*The untersigned Arthur Rimbaud—Born in Charleville
(France)—Aged 23—5 ft 6 height—Good healthy—Late a
teacher of sciences and languages. Recently deserted from the
47ᵉ Regiment of the French army [the regiment in which his
father had served!],—Actually in Bremen without any means,
the French consul refusing any relief.*

*Would like to know on which conditions he could con-
clude an immediate engagement in the American navy.*

*Speaks and writes English, German, French, Italian,
and Spanish.*

*Has been four months as a sailor in a Scotch bark, from
August to December 76.*

Would be very honored and grateful to receive an answer.

John Arthur Rimbaud[22]

The consul probably replied that he was lacking in only one thing:
American nationality.

He then continued on his way. At Hamburg, with nothing better to do,
he went into a casino and lost all his savings (so he was not "without any
means" at Bremen).

But, this time, he did not go back to Charleville, as he had done when
his property was stolen in Vienna! The small ads were to be his providence.
A traveling circus needed a clerk to look after the cash and paperwork for a
tour of Scandinavia. Why shouldn't he reply? This was the Cirque Loisset,
which belonged to a certain François Loisset, a specialist in Haute Ecole,
who enjoyed a very high reputation at the time.[23]

We have only the evidence of Delahaye that he did join them: Isabelle,
incapable of admitting that her brother had joined a circus, spoke of a post
in a Swedish sawmill. However, when he left, he did not reveal where he was
going; that is why Delahaye, who came to Charleville in June and, no longer
finding them there, could only write to Verlaine: "Of the cracked traveler no
news. No doubt flown off far away, far, far away, for I haven't seen him since
my return here."[24]

In fact he was far away, for by the end of July he arrived in Copenhagen
from Stockholm. This we know from a letter from Delahaye to Ernest Millot,
discovered (in rather poor condition) and published in 1951: "He whom [I
have known since] my childhood and whom you see clinking glasses with a

[white bear] you will recognize easily enough. . . . I tell you that HE was recently seen in Stockholm, then in Copenhagen, and no news since. The most authoritative geographers suppose him to be around the 76th parallel, so I humbly make myself their interpreter . . ." (The rest is missing).[25]

On the back, we see a Rimbaud dressed in Eskimo furs, clinking glasses with a polar bear and saying: "O là! là! It's not Javanese men I need now!"

Verlaine was given the same information (but the letter has been lost) and the same drawing (it has survived) on August 9, 1877.

One imagines that if he left the Loisset circus, it was because of the military rigor of the discipline. Tradition has it that he was repatriated (or simply helped, for no trace of him has been found at the French consulate at Stockholm). The secretary of the Charleville town hall, Hémery, appears to have confirmed to Delahaye that he had received a letter from Stockholm concerning Rimbaud.[26]

We may suppose that when he was in Copenhagen, he was on his way home, but he may also have been going to Norway as Verlaine suggests in one of his "coppées."

He spent the late summer in Charleville. "Apart from HIS presence," Delahaye remarks to Verlaine, "nothing new. The sun still shines, the pavements fart from it, the streams stink from it."[27]

Meanwhile, Verlaine, who had returned definitively from England, was resting at Arras at his mother's. There, in September, he invited Germain Nouveau to spend a few days with him. Nouveau (almost certainly) handed over the manuscript of *Les Illuminations*. One can imagine how avidly, how enthusiastically Verlaine must have read his friend's dazzling poem in prose for the first time.

Moreover, his mother had brought back from Brussels after his trial the verses and songs of 1872, which Rimbaud had copied out at his request, for the original manuscripts had remained in Paris—they are hasty copies, unpunctuated, sometimes without titles, written from memory in Belgium and London in 1872.

So, naturally, Verlaine put all his friend's prose and verse into a single file. He was imprudent enough to lend this file shortly afterwards to Charles de Sivry, and Mathilde confiscated it for many years. Finally, when she remarried, she allowed Sivry to dispose of the manuscript as he thought fit, forbidding him, however, to give it back to Verlaine (1866). This explains how the prose and verse were published together in *La Vogue* by Gustave

Kahn, with the result that for a long time the public believed it to be a single work.

But to return to the Ardennes.

It is thought that it was in the autumn of 1877 that Mme Rimbaud moved to a house that belonged to her at Saint-Laurent, a village two kilometers from Mézières.

Rimbaud often went into Charleville, where, with old friends, especially Pierquin and Millot, he would drink a glass or two at the Café Duterme or in the small bar under the arcades of the Place Ducale. In his Memoirs, Louis Pierquin relates the following incident:

> After each great journey, he would come back to his native town. But contact with his friends had been broken. For him, they represented literature, the past. Long before his final departure, we were struck by his silence, his detachment. I imagine meeting him one day in the middle of the Sahara, Millot used to say, after several years of separation. We are alone and walking in opposite directions. He stops for a moment:
>
> "Hello, how are you?"
>
> "Well. Goodbye."
>
> And he continues on his way; not the least trace of emotion, not a word more.[28]

How he had changed! Isabelle, now eighteen, and very proud of her big brother, sketched him sitting, legs crossed, looking pleasant and serious; he could have been taken for what he wanted to be: a young engineer.

With the first signs of autumn he decided to leave the harsh Ardennais climate and try his luck in some hot country. He set out for Egypt.

Of this undertaking we know next to nothing. From now on Isabelle is our only source of information, but since she wrote a long time after the events, with very obvious afterthoughts, we lose as much in accuracy as in picturesqueness: there are no more entertaining anecdotes, drawings, "coppées"—Isabelle's notes have all the dryness of a medical file.

It would seem that Arthur went to Marseille, embarked for Alexandria, but, struck down with fever, did not return to ship when they put in at Civitavecchia. The ship's doctor seems to have diagnosed an inflammation of the walls of the abdomen, caused by excessive marching. After a few days' rest in a hospital Rimbaud seems to have visited Rome and returned home via Marseille.

He spent the winter in the warmth among his dictionaries and foreign grammars—and also scientific books, treatises on algebra, and various technical works.

I do not intend to recount the circumstances of the resurrection of the poet Rimbaud, as poems and works believed lost were discovered. However, I shall make an exception for the first sign of this resurrection, the publication in London, in January 1878, in the *Gentleman's Magazine*, of the poem *Les Effarés* under the title *Petits pauvres*—by Alfred Rimbaud. We do not know who supplied the review with the text of the poem. Did Verlaine, at some earlier time, give it to Camille Barrère, who was writing for the *Gentleman's Magazine*? Without investigating it further, we should perhaps see it as the symbol of that little flower, born from an unknown seed, that grew far away amid general indifference, a foreshadowing of a magnificent flowering.

In the spring of 1878, we lose trace of Rimbaud. He may have gone to Hamburg (according to J. M. Carré) or to Switzerland (according to Isabelle). We really know nothing. The only information we have—and it is slight—is this passage in a letter from Delahaye to Verlaine of September 28, 1878: "It is certainly true that Rimbe has been seen in Paris. One of my friends saw him in the Latin Quarter at Easter."[29]

On the basis of this "information" the hypothesis has been mooted that he was keen to visit the Exposition which took place in Paris in that year and which was opened on May 1. It is not entirely improbable.[30]

Delahaye was not kept informed of anything. In late July 1878, he was unable to say anything at all about Rimbaud's whereabouts: to Verlaine, who had just completed his first year at Rethel, he remarked: "*L'homme-aux-semelles-de-vent* (literally, "the man with the soles of wind") has certainly vanished. Not a trace."[31]

At this time Rimbaud was at Roche, where his mother had decided to settle because of the departure of her last farmer, who had not made a go of the farm and because Frédéric, who had served his time in the army, had now returned home. This time, Arthur lent a willing hand at harvest time.

"It was in August 1878," Louis Pierquin declared to Rimbaud's first biographers, "that we saw him for the last time. What we remembered of our meeting was the sarcasm that, for a whole afternoon, he poured on our budding literary enthusiasms."[32]

Later, Pierquin situated this meeting in 1879 (erroneously, it seems):

One day in the summer of 1879, Ernest Millot asked him to
spend the evening in a small café on the Place Ducale that
was later to become the usual venue of our meetings with Verlaine on his return visits to the Ardennes. "Rimbaud has just
bought a suit," Millot told me, "and instructed the tailer to
send the bill to his mother. That means he's off again." (Just
before going off on his travels, he did indeed always act in the
same way, without confiding in anyone.) Rimbaud arrived at
eight o'clock. He was fairly uncommunicative, and, when
Millot congratulated me on acquiring a number of books published by Lemerre, Rimbaud suddenly emerged from his silence and addressed me thus: "Buying books, especially books
like that, is completely idiotic. You've got a head on your
shoulders that should replace all books. All books are good for
is to stand on shelves and conceal the leprous condition of old
walls!" During the rest of the evening, he was in unusually
good spirits, even exuberant, and at eleven o'clock he left us
forever. [33]

Delahaye had lost all trace of his friends. At this time, late summer
1878, he sent Verlaine the five *coppées* that he had written, and asked him to
come and visit him at Charleville, without breathing a word about Rimbaud.
In October, he took up a post at Quesnoy, in the Nord.

Meanwhile, Rimbaud, still haunted by the sun, set off on his travels
once more on October 20, 1878. (He himself provides this date in a letter
written in December at Alexandria—in which he asks his mother to certify
that he worked on her farm.)

Concerning his journey to Genoa, we have a first-class document, the
long letter that he wrote to his family on Sunday November 17, 1878—the
very day that his father died at Dijon, though he was only to learn of it later.[34]
This is how it begins: "As to how I got here, the journey was eventful, and
freshened from time to time by the season. On the straight line from the
Ardennes to Switzerland, since I wanted to pick up the German connection
from Remiremont to Wesserling, I had to pass through the Vosges; first by
stagecoach, then on foot, since no coach could proceed through an average
depth of snow of twenty inches and with a blizzard forecast. But the expected
exploit was the crossing of the Gothard, which is no longer passed at this
season and which I could not pass by coach."

There follows an extraordinarily evocative account of the crossing of the famous massif from Altdorf, the precipices of the Devil's Bridge, and the ascent of Hospenthal:

> No more road, precipices, gorge or sky: nothing but white to think about, touch, see or not see, for it is impossible to raise your eyes from the stupid whiteness that one thinks is the middle of the path. Impossible to raise one's nose to such a cutting wind, one's eyelashes and moustache like stalactites, one's ears torn off, one's neck swollen. Without the shadow that one is oneself and without the telegraph poles that follow the presumed road, one would be as much at a loss as a sparrow in an oven.
>
> . . . But one loses the road. Which side of the road were the telegraph poles on? (There are only poles on one side.) One moves to the side, one plunges up to one's ribs, up to one's armpits. . . . A pale shadow behind a cutting: it's the hospice of the Gothard, a civil, hospitable establishment, an ugly building of wood and stone; a pinnacled turret. I ring, and a shady-looking young man receives you; one climbs up into a low, dirty room, where you are issued with the regulation bread and cheese, soup, and glass of wine. One sees the well-known fine big yellow dogs. The mountain stragglers arrive, half dead. By the evening there are about thirty of us, and, after the soup, we are given hard mattresses and inadequate blankets. Late in the night the monks could be heard breaking forth into sacred chants to celebrate their joy at having, once more, robbed the various governments that subsidize their hut.

Two days after his arrival at Genoa, he found a ship bound for Alexandria, which he finally reached at the end of the month. Good fortune smiled on him at once: he was offered a temporary job, replacing a French engineer in charge of works being carried out on the edge of the city. As far as the future was concerned, he hesitated between several possible jobs: on a large farm, in the Franco-Egyptian customs, or in a Cypriot firm as interpreter for a group of workers. In the end, he accepted the last proposition, and signed a work contract with the French firm of Ernest Jean et Thial fils, of Larnaca, the principal port of the island, and began work on December 16. We know the date, for, on February 15, 1879, Rimbaud was to write to his family: "Tomorrow, February 16, it will be just two months since I have been working here."

A parenthesis is perhaps in order here: an agent of the shipping line Messageries maritimes, Emile Deschamps, has stated that toward the end of 1878, a certain Rimbaud was in Aden, from where he was planning to set out with a small team to plunder a wrecked ship that had sunk off Cape Guardafui (the tip of Somalia). Now it cannot be our Rimbaud who, between late November and December 16, traveled the five hundred miles to Guardafui and back. The explanation is to be found in a few words appended by Rimbaud (the true one) to his letter home of September 22 1880: "Write the address clearly because there is another Rimbaud out here, who is an agent of the Messageries maritimes."[35]

So he was now working as foreman of a gang of men in a quarry on the coast, fifteen miles from Larnaca. Roger Milliex, formerly cultural attaché at the French embassy at Nicosia, has discovered the exact site, at a place known as "Potamos," near the village of Xylophagou.[36] He was in charge of about sixty workmen, Cypriots, Greeks, Syrians, Turks, and Arabs. He planned the day's work, gave out the material, made reports to the management, kept an account of the food and all expenses, and handed out the pay. He supervised not only the extraction of the stone but also its dispatch. But it was not an ideal situation, for the job was under threat, Cyprus having been ceded to the British. Furthermore, it was excessively hot (all the Europeans fell ill, and some died), and the fleas were a permanent torture. To this were added difficulties with his men, some of whom were violent and lazy. An undated note from him, in which he complains of not receiving the tent and dagger ordered, is quite definitely of this period, for, on April 24, 1879, he informs his family that he has quarreled with his workers, and has had to ask for weapons.

It was not a very quiet life. To Delahaye he gave an example of his difficulties: one day, the money chest containing the men's pay was rifled; the culprit was soon discovered. Instead of punishing him, Rimbaud explained to him what harm he was doing to his fellow workmen, and managed to persuade him to return the stolen money. "They took me very seriously," he concluded.

He liked this wild life, in the open air, far from all civilization, among simple, rough people, who taught him new languages—there was even an Orthodox priest among them. He slept in a cabin on the beach and lived out-of-doors, moving from one gang to another, and taking his siesta, half naked, in the sun. In the evening, he took part in the games of the workmen who made fire crackers with gunpowder.

Unfortunately, however, his health was undermined by a fever. In late May 1879 he was forced to return to Roche, where the doctor diagnosed typhoid and ordered complete rest. But, with country air and medical treatment, he soon recovered: in late July he was able to help in the harvest. A drawing by Isabelle on the cover of an accounts book shows him in his new transformation as agricultural worker, ill-dressed, ill-shaven, his hair unkempt, holding a farm implement (in the bottom left-hand corner is the outline of Mme Rimbaud, seen from behind (*Album Rimbaud*).

In September, Delahaye, having expressed a wish to see him again, was invited to spend a few days at Roche. It was the last time they saw one another.

Rimbaud, his friend relates, came to the door of the old farmhouse himself.

> *I didn't recognize him at first, except for his eyes, which were still extraordinarily beautiful!—with the pale blue iris surrounded by the deeper ring, the color of periwinkles. His cheeks, which had always been so round and full, were now hollowed out to reveal the hard, bony structure. The fresh complexion of an English child, which he had kept for so long, had given place in the two years that had elapsed, to the dark, tough skin of a Kabyl, and on that brown skin—a novelty that delighted me—was a light brown curly beard, which had been long in coming—he was nearly twenty-five—as, it is thought, sometimes happens with people of distinguished breeding. Another sign of his full physical virility was that his voice had lost the nervous, rather childish timbre that it had once had, and had become deep and grave, and imbued with calm energy.*[37]

He had just brought in the harvest as if he had done nothing but that all his life. After the first expressions of delight, he told Delahaye what he had been doing in Cyprus, and proudly exhibited (he had been told often enough that he was a good-for-nothing) the testimonial given him by his employers, dated May 27, 1879: "We hereby certify that M. Arthur Rimbaud has been employed by us as site foreman for six months. We have been very satisfied with his services and he is free of any commitment to the company."

Delahaye goes on:

> In the evening, after dinner, I made so bold as to ask him if he ever gave a thought to literature. He shook his head and gave a little half-amused, half-irritated laugh, as if I had asked him, "Do you still play with your hoop?" and replied simply: "I'm not concerned with that any more."
> In the tone that stressed the contemptuous monosyllable, and in the way that Rimbaud looked at me at that moment, there was a touch of ironic impatience that seemed to say: "I hope I don't have to say any more."[38]

They occasionally went out for a walk together. Rimbaud declared that he could now only live in a hot country, on the shores of the Mediterranean, in Africa, or in America! For the time being, he was planning to go back to Cyprus, via Alexandria.

On the road from Attigny to Chesne, Delahaye tells us, he suddenly left him: "The fever! . . . the fever is at my heels!" he said.

Meanwhile, Verlaine, after two years' teaching at Rethel, had left once again for England, with his favorite pupil, Lucien Létinois, and had found a post in a school at Lymington, opposite the Isle of Wight. It was while there that a letter from Delahaye told him that Rimbaud was leading a bucolic existence at Roche.

Shortly after Delahaye's visit, Rimbaud set out for Alexandria, but got no further than Marseille: apparently, he had not fully recovered from typhoid, and a violent attack of fever forced him to return home in great haste.

He was only happy, Isabelle tells us, in the heat of the stables, lying on the straw, leafing through science textbooks, increasingly uncommunicative and irritable, though sober to the point of asceticism. The time seemed so long to him that, two years later, he had not forgotten those bad days: "I wouldn't like to inflict on you," he wrote to his family on February 15, 1881, "a repetition of the winter of 1879–80, which I remember well enough to avoid forever undergoing another one like it."

In March 1880, being unable to wait for the return of the sun, he set off again—this time definitively—for Alexandria.

In the autumn of 1883, Delahaye, learning that Verlaine had settled at Coulommes, six kilometers from Roche, amused himself by illustrating a chance encounter of the two former friends, both dressed as peasants (clogs and cotton caps). Verlaine is digging in a field and calls out to Rimbaud, who is passing on the road: "Hey!" he yells, and Rimbaud replies with the traditional "Oh, shit!"[39] It is obviously a fantasy, for Verlaine himself would have mentioned such a meeting, whereas he wrote to Francis Viélé-Griffin on January 5, 1982: "My last meeting with Rimbaud was in February 1875."

In Alexandria, Rimbaud did not find a job that suited him, and returned to Cyprus. The firm of Ernest Jean et Thial fils no longer existed. The island had been ceded by the Turks to the British in June 1878, about the time he was leaving. It was thanks to this change of sovereignty that he was able to find a job as foreman. It again concerned stone. But instead of quarrying, it was now assembling. The British administration was building the governor's summer residence on the heights of Mount Troodos, at an altitude above 6,000 feet. Again he was in charge of a gang of about fifty men, and supplying them involved frequent trips on horseback. He earned only two hundred francs a month, but he would be getting a raise in May. "The rain, hail, and wind are enough to knock you over," he wrote to his family at this time, and his health (palpitations) were a cause of anxiety. A further complication was that the governor's palace had to be finished by September. In view of this new situation, he asked his family to send him two books, one in English, *The Album of Forest and Farm Sawmills*, the other in French, the *Livre de poche du charpentier*. Last, he asked for news of everything at home (Voncq), of *père* Michel, an agricultural laborer originally from Luxembourg employed by Mme Rimbaud, and of "Cotaiche" (the mare "Comtesse," thus called by *père* Michel).

With the return of good weather, things seemed to get better. Around June 20, he gave up his job for a better one in a firm dealing with ashlar and lime—with which he had no doubt been in daily contact. Shortly afterwards, he got into violent arguments with the firm's paymaster general and the engineer under whom he worked, and resigned. "If I had stayed, I would have reached a good position," he wrote on August 17, 1880. "But I can't go back there." This last sentence, provided that it is true, seems to support the memory of an Italian merchant, Ottorino Rosa, who claims that Rimbaud confided in him at Harar to the effect that, in a fit of anger, he had thrown a stone at the head of one of the workmen and killed him.[40] This would explain his sudden flight to Africa and the rather surprising statements that he made to his new employer at Aden, Pierre Bardey. But, in the absence of further confirmation, it must remain an open question.

When he embarked for the African continent, he had savings amounting to 400 francs, of which he was very proud. A new life, full of hope was opening up before him: Arabia, Abyssinia, the Sudan, Zanzibar . . . How beautiful those fabulous lands seemed on the map!

We shall soon see how, getting increasingly entangled in the spider's web that he himself was weaving between Aden and Djibuti, Zeila and Harar, he was to leave this hell only when death was upon him.

14

First Contacts with Africa

Rimbaud traveled the length of the Red Sea, putting in at Suakin (Egypt), Jidda (Arabia), Mesewa (Eritrea), and Hodeida (Yemen), but could find no work. At Hodeida, overcome with the heat, he fell ill and was nursed for a few days thanks to the kindness of M. Trébuchet, of the Maison Morand et Fabre of Marseille. Finally, he dragged himself as far as Aden. Surely, he thought, the great port would be able to offer him an interesting job, but, no sooner had he arrived than he succumbed to the torrid heat and fell ill again.

Armed with a letter of recommendation from M. Trébuchet, he turned up at the office of the agent for Africa and Arabia of the Lyon company of Mazeran, Viannay, Bardey et Cie, which had just set up a branch at Aden and already had warehouses at Berbera (Somalia) and at Zeila.

As a result, M. Dubar, a former colonel of the 5th legion of the Rhône, accepted his application in the absence of his boss, Alfred Bardey, who, at the time, was prospecting Menelik's kingdom, in Abyssinia. What struck him most was the already gray hair of this lively faced, twenty-six-year-old man. Since he did not appear to be stupid and was determined to work he was taken on at once.

The newcomer declared himself to be Arthur Rimbaud, born at Dole (Jura), just come from Cyprus, where he had been foreman of a gang of quarry workers. He had left the island because his firm had ceased all activity. (Is one to infer from these false, incomplete declarations that he did not have a quiet conscience, and wished, to some degree, to conceal his real identity? We cannot be sure. All the same it is curious that he should have lied on the matter of his place of birth.)

He struck M. Dubar and Pierre Bardey, Alfred's brother, as a serious young man, who, according to the latter, accompanied his brief explanation with short, sharp, uncoordinated gestures of the right hand.

All this is supported by Alfred Bardey, in his work *Bar Adjam (Terre des non-Arabes)*, which describes his time in Arabia and Africa.[1]

He was given the job of foreman of the "harim," workshops in which the coffee was weighed and selected by Indian women, most of whom were wives of soldiers in the Indian regiment stationed at Aden. His employers were completely satisfied with his work. He spoke enough Arabic to keep his job. He was liked by his staff, which did not prevent them referring to him as "Karani" (the harsh one), a name often given to foremen.

The Bardey premises, in which he lived, consisted of a large, rather handsome building, opposite the Court House, with six tall arcades and an upper floor containing rooms and offices.

Everything would have gone well for Rimbaud were it not for two things: the poor pay (3 shillings a day and his keep) and the stifling, unbearable heat. "Aden is a horrible rock, without a single blade of grass or a drop of good water: one drinks distilled seawater. The heat here is excessive, especially in June and September, which are the two canicular months. The constant temperature night and day, of a very cool and well-ventilated office, is 35 degrees (C). Everything is very expensive and so forth: I'm like a prisoner here, and I'll certainly have to stay here for three months before getting back on my legs and getting a better job."

He was to ask for another pound a month, bringing his salary up to £5.10s, or he would leave (for Zanzibar, or elsewhere), for he was not at all keen on staying at Aden which, he claimed, with his customary black humor, was "as everyone knows the most boring place in the world, after the one where you live."

What held him back was the hope of being promoted manager of a branch in Africa.

If, in his letter to Roche of September 22, 1880, he rejected the idea of getting married because he had not saved enough money, it was because Frédéric had taken it into his head, without any money, to marry a poor girl; he did not intend making the same mistake. The girl in question, it seems, was a certain Mlle Germain, whose family Mme Rimbaud detested. Indeed, Mme Rimbaud made her position so clear that the Germains had to leave the district. It would appear that Mme Rimbaud had even considered buying their house in order to have the pleasure, she said, of completely razing to the ground that lair of wild beasts![2]

Meanwhile, Alfred Bardey was examining the commercial possibilities of the upper plateaux of Abyssinia in the company of a young man, Lucereau (who died shortly afterwards, murdered by natives), a certain D. Pinchard, an adventurer of whom more later, and a young Abyssinian, Hej Afi—not to mention six Arab porters or servants.

He decided at once to set up a branch at Harar. The area was green, not at all unpleasant, and produced good mocca coffee (known as Berbera). There were lively markets, the climate was healthy, and the population welcoming.

Pierre Bardey and M. Dubar, who were kept informed of the good news, hinted to Rimbaud that he might be asked to manage the branch at Harar. But when Alfred Bardey came back to Aden with samples of Abyssinian produce, Rimbaud was disappointed: the job had already been promised to Pinchard, who had stayed out there with the task of setting everything up.

This Pinchard was a former infantry warrant officer, who had lived for a time in Algeria, and spoke Arabic fluently, something of a "tough guy" who had been part of a gang that had looted wrecks off Cape Guardafui.

Despite his disappointment, Rimbaud was delighted to be appointed to the branch at Harar: for him the important thing was to get out of the Aden furnace as quickly as possible. At once, on November 2, through his mother and sister, he ordered from bookshops in Paris a large number of technical books dealing with metallurgy, hydraulics, navigation, naval architecture, masonry, smelting, timber sawing, tanning, textiles,—even the handbook for the candle manufacturer! He already saw himself out there, as chief engineer, with unlimited finance at his disposal, a plentiful supply of manpower, with the authority to undertake whatever he decided to turn his hand to: improving the health and sanitation of the whole province, for example, or constructing arms factories, industrial complexes.

There, too, he was to be disillusioned. A single book would have served his purposes: the handyman's handbook. (J. M. Carré, his biographer, distinguished between the two sides of his personality, the adventurer of the ideal and the adventurer of the real, the poet and the explorer. In fact, all his life, he had been an adventurer of the dream.)

The work contract was signed with M. Dubar on November 10, 1880, to cover a period of three years to run from November 1. The salary specified was 150 rupees a month (about £14 at the time), plus his keep and a 1 percent commission on the net product of the branch. It was an appreciable improvement on what he had been earning in Aden.

About November 20 he set out westwards—first by dow to Zeila, then across the Somali desert. He was accompanied by a Greek clerk, Constantin Righas. Each was at the head of a caravan of camels driven by Arabs, loaded with cotton goods and manufactured articles.

So the great adventure began.

Harar, one of the sacred cities of Islam, was a rather mysterious town that had seldom seen white men. Lying along the crest of a plateau, at an altitude of over five and a half thousand feet, surrounded by a redocher wall ten feet thick, pierced by five gates, it then had a population of between 35,000 and 40,000 inhabitants. The Egyptians had occupied it since 1875, and kept a garrison of four to five thousand men there.

"The flaming red appearance of the city," wrote the Italian explorer Robecchi-Brichetti in 1888, "as it appears to the traveler who has just crossed rich, picturesque coffee plantations and banana groves, the reddish-brown color of its houses, with their long, horizontal, monotonous lines, interrupted by three minarets and a few scrawny sycamores, give the town a fantastic, extraordinarily magical character that fascinates the eye."[3]

It was a journey into the unfamiliar, through time and space: it was both Africa and the Middle Ages.

The Bardey branch had opened for business on the upper square of the town, near the main mosque, in the former "palace" (guebi) of the first Egyptian governor Rauf Pasha, one of the very few two-story buildings.

On the first floor was the "divan," the former reception room, supplied with cushioned seats, opening on to three or four rooms of various sizes, used for storing merchandise.

Rimbaud and Constantin Righas each occupied a room upstairs, overlooking the square. Behind the building was a small vegetable garden with one or two citron trees.[4]

The premises were far from luxurious. On the contrary, both inside and out, they were in a rather dilapidated state: the ceilings consisted of reeds rough cast with dry mud, which was peeling off; there were insects everywhere, gray flat-backed ants, earwigs, and other nightmares.[5]

At first, everything seemed to go very well. Rimbaud was content: "The climate here is cool, and not unhealthy," he wrote home on December 13, 1880, and, on January 15, 1881, he added: "The country is not unpleasant." He promised to send photographs, as soon as the camera he had ordered arrived. He was trying, he said, to make his work interesting and lucrative. He continued to order specialized catalogues (astronomy, optics, electricity, meteorology, mechanics, etc.)

Then, suddenly, he fell into a black depression. His letters reflect the darkest pessimism: "I have not found what I expected, and my life here is very boring and unprofitable. As soon as I've saved 1,500 or 2,000 francs, I shall get out, and I shall be very pleased to do so. . . . I'd even be quite happy to leave now."

What had happened?

To begin with, he found it difficult to adapt to the environment: Harar, a dirty, stinking town, its alleyways swarming with beggars, cripples, and the sick, was no paradise. In the evening, the curfew forbade one to go out, the city gates were locked, and wild dogs and hyenas fought over the rotting meat and other refuse that was left lying about everywhere.

Besides, working conditions were hardly more pleasant: most of the time was spent writting up extremely complicated accounts, for the finicky and spiteful customs men—"a pack of dogs and bandits," in his words—turned out to be impossible to deal with, not to mention questions of currency exchange, tariffs, and transit.

As for the natives, they thought only of deceiving and robbing the whites during their interminable palavas. One also had to distrust Greek or Armenian competitors, who were always out to grab the best merchandise from the suppliers.

But the worst thing was loneliness: there was no one with whom he could have an interesting conversation.

Lastly, to crown it all, he had to admit to his family that he had "picked up a disease, that, in itself, is not very dangerous," but, he added, "this climate is treacherous for any kind of disease." In fact, he had contracted syphilis, which was very widespread in those unhygienic countries, and this irritated him immensely.

In short, everything was going from bad to worse.

"Well, see you soon!" he wrote to his family on February 15, 1881. "Let's hope we'll have better weather and a less stupid kind of work. You may think I live like a prince, but I'm sure I live in a very stupid and stupifying way." More than ever he wanted to leave: "I've had to put up with absurd difficulties at Harar, and we can't do there for the moment what we thought we could." He was haunted by Zanzibar; he was willing to go anywhere, "to traffic in the unknown" (letter of May 4).

Faced with this worsening situation—Pinchard was ill, too—Alfred Bardey decided to go out himself, with his partner's brother, Pierre Mazeran, try to sort things out and get the branch going again.

The day before he was due to leave, Mgr. Taurin-Cahagne, bishop of Adramynthos and vicar apostolic of the Gallas, then fifty-five years old, suggested joining him, together with five Capuchin friars, Father Louis de Gonzague, Fathers Ernest and Julien, and two brothers. (Rimbaud knew that they were coming: "We are going to have in this town," he wrote to his family on January 15, 1881, "a Catholic bishop, who will probably be the only Catholic in the country.")

The small company set out on March 15. On the coast they met up with young Hej Afi, who had hired camels and mules for the desert crossing, and Pinchard, who had come from Harar, ill with malaria. One presumes that he then gave notice: it is said that he set out for Egypt; in any case, there is no further mention of him.[6]

At Harar, Alfred Bardey was pleased to see his new branch for the first time. He was not displeased with Rimbaud either: this excellent employee was hard working and kept his books in exemplary fashion. "He stored the produce he bought for us," he was to write to Paterne Berrichon on July 16, 1897, "including animal skins that had been dried in the round common houses in the Harar countryside. He slept in the middle of this unhealthy merchandise. I have to say that he contracted syphilis, and had unquestionable signs of that disease in his mouth. He took the greatest possible precautions not to pass on his disease through contact with utensils used for eating and drinking. I certainly treated Rimbaud, perhaps not always very willingly, for he was excessively irritible during his illness, but it was not I who cured him, for in 1881, we had doctors of the Egyptian army of occupation in Harar, and we had a fairly complete pharmacy."[7]

Indeed his illness made him very depressed. In a letter to his mother and sister, he declared on May 25: "Unfortunately, I don't care a bit about life. Nevertheless, I'm forced to go on, as now, wearing myself out, living on nothing but absurd, terrible worries, in these awful climates. I greatly fear that my life will be shortened. . . . Well! Let's hope that we may enjoy a few years of real rest in this life. It's fortunate that this life is the only one, and this is quite certain, since one cannot imagine a more boring life than this one."

Alfred Bardey and Pierre Mazeran took over the management of the branch, the staff of which consisted of Rimbaud, Sotiro (a Greek), Constantin Righas, and Hej Afi.

In June, Rimbaud was able to get a little rest, and soon he was on his feet again.

To make amends for his ill-humor, he suggested to his employers that he should go to Bubassa, about thirty miles from Harar, where there were large stocks of goat and ox skins, which the natives did not dare to bring because the tracks were too dangerous. Apparently, the Egyptian army never left their barracks.

"In a few days," he wrote to his family on July 2, "I am going into country that has never been explored by Europeans, and if I finally manage to get myself on the road, it will be a six-week journey, difficult and dangerous, but it could be highly profitable." A caravan of camels was packed with cotton goods and various articles intended for the natives.

"Just as he was about to leave," Alfred Bardey recounts, "Rimbaud wrapped his head in a towel by way of a turban and draped a red blanket over his usual clothes. His intention was to pass himself off as a Muslim. This costume, which made us laugh, must have seemed less ridiculous in the eyes of the natives, who wore nothing but red goatskins or short robes, as dirty as our trousers and jackets. Rimbaud, who was amused as we were by his outfit, agreed that the red blanket that orientalized his European dress might act as a bait for looters, but he was anxious to maintain the prestige of the firm and to be regarded as a rich Muslim merchant."[8]

The village of Bubassa, made up of about sixty round huts, was a very active market in durra seed and dried skins.

Rimbaud bought a large quantity of skins—far more than he could take back with him—and stored the surplus in shelters along the return journey, where he would later go and fetch them.

We have very little information about this journey, though it must have been extremely tiring for him: the natives received them in friendly fashion, Alfred Bardey tells us, but the lions were less friendly—Sotiro had to come back on a mule, for one of them had eaten his horse.

Rimbaud was forced to cut his expedition short following an attack of fever that forced him, as soon as he got back, to take to his bed. "And what shall I tell you about my work here," he writes ill-humoredly to his family on July 22, "which I am already so sick of, and of the country, which I detest and so forth. When I tell you of the efforts I have made, and of the extraordinary exhaustion which it has cost me, and which has brought me nothing but a fever that has had me in its grip for the last fortnight, just as it did when I had it at Roche two years ago? But, what is to be done? I've got used to everything now. I'm afraid of nothing."

Shortly afterwards, Alfred Bardey, accompanied by Sotiro and Hej Afi, all three armed, set out for Bubassa, to try to exploit the openings made by Rimbaud and to pick up the skins that he had put in store. The journey took place without serious incident, but turned out to be useless: no lasting link could be made, since there were so many gangs of looters roaming around Harar.

After these expeditions, the branch resumed its normal working routine: buying raw materials and delivering them to the coast, collecting and selling stuffs and manufactured articles—all at an Oriental pace. This monotony was sometimes broken by festivals and celebrations, for example, the departure accompanied by fanfares of the tax inspectors to collect taxes in kind (oxen, sheep, goats), or the playing of tamtams to disperse threatening clouds of grasshoppers.

However, the general situation was depressing: many undernourished natives had to be helped, and plague, typhus, and cholera were endemic to the area. Every morning, Alfred Bardey recounts, twenty corpses were collected from the square in front of the premises.

When September came round, Alfred Bardey considered going back to Aden, and there was some question of his brother Pierre, who was managing the branch at Zeila, coming to run the one at Harar.

Here we might insert a digression: shortly after his departure, a certain Pierre Labatut, who was living at Ankober, the royal city, proposed a "wonderful" deal to Alfred Bardey, which consisted of importing guns and selling them to king Menelik, who had a permanent need of them. Despite the large profits likely to accrue from the operation, Alfred Bardey refused categorically: it was too dangerous a game. Inevitably, those rifles would end up in the hands of robbers, and then the whites would have no alternative but to get out (later, as we shall see, Rimbaud was to fall fearlessly into the trap).

As one can imagine, Rimbaud was angered and hurt at not being promoted branch manager. He could not bear the thought of spending the rest of his life as a mere clerk, like Sotiro or Constantin Righas. So, after "unpleasant arguments with the management, etc.," he resigned his post, as he confesses in his letter home of September 2, 1881. This did not at all suit Alfred Bardey, who was already worried about M. Dubar's health. He begged Rimbaud to take over temporarily, until his brother Pierre, who had been summoned urgently, arrived.

On December 3 1881, Pierre Bardey made a triumphal entry into Harar. "This is paradise!" he exclaimed.

Rimbaud could now leave.

However, he had second thoughts, and decided not to leave the Bardey firm; it was agreed that he would resume work at Aden.

How very different he was now, on his return, to what he had been on arrival: he was now disappointed, embittered, prematurely aged. His (already low) reserves of patience had long been exhausted in interminable waiting: waiting for caravans that moved at a snail's pace, waiting for books ordered from Roche (his father's Arabic notebook, technical handbooks, the Bottin directory of streets and trades, catalogues), waiting for medicine from Aden or various instruments that he needed. Nothing ever came, he was everlastingly repeating the same request, begging—in the void.

Besides, at the end of the year, a new catastrophe struck him: he learned that he had been summoned to perform a twenty-eight-day period of military instruction, beginning on January 16, 1882. This was the last straw! Of course, there was no risk of the French police turning up to take him away, but it meant more letters, more forms to be filled up: he would have to write to the consulate at Aden, get a certificate from M. Bardey, apply for a deferment from the military authorities in Mézières. Last, to crown it all, he had lost his service record!

It was disappointment and failure all along the line.

On December 15, he left for Aden, hoping to find other work there or to move on. In any case, he had made up his mind that he would never set foot again in that accursed Harar.

The Bardey brothers had also made up their minds about him: he was a conscientious lad, but of an impossible character.

As for Rimbaud himself, this is what he thought of them: "Those people are swindlers and thieves, good only to exploit the labors of their employees."

15

Rimbaud at Aden,

Branch Manager at Harar

The same troubles pursued him to Aden. Thus, in August 1881, he had decided to invest his savings in France, since he spent nothing and it was dangerous to carry gold around with him. Of course, he could have opened a bank account in Aden, but he was suspicious of everything and everybody. He preferred to send his money to Roche by postal orders, a total of 1,165 rupees, 14 anas (2,478 gold francs), his salary and commissions from December 1, 1881, to July 30, 1881. His mother could have invested this sum to some advantage with a bank or a notary. But, three months later, the money had not yet reached Roche! When it finally did arrive, Mme Rimbaud received only 2,250 F as a result of a mistake in the exchange. This "swindling" threw him into a violent temper, and he wrote angry letters to the head office at Lyon and to the French consulate at Aden.

But he was even more disappointed to learn that his mother, cunning peasant woman that she was, had bought land with the money! Colonel Godchot has found in the cadastral survey of Chuffilly-Roche the following item: the purchase in 1882, from a M. de Lapisse of Paris, of a plot of 37 acres 70 centiares, of which the transfer of ownership was made in the name of "Jean Nicolas Arthur Rimbaud, teacher of Hazar [sic] (Arabia)." By the same token, his name was placed on the electoral registers of the commune.[1]

"What the devil do you think I'm going to do with that real estate?" he asked his mother on November 7, 1881, as soon as he heard of the purchase.

One has to admit that, although he was impatient, and easily angered, he meant well. After giving vent to his anger, he adds: "If you need anything, take what is mine: it's yours. As for me, I've no one to think about, except my own person, which asks for nothing."

In the future, he avoided sending any more money home, and invested his savings in a savings-bank in Aden, at an interest of 4.5%.

Alfred Bardey did not put him back in his coffee-sorting warehouse: he deserved more than that. He was promoted, one might say, to assistant manager. (Alfred Bardey says that he himself was manager of the main branch at Aden, "assisted by Rimbaud.")

For his part, Rimbaud now had time to reflect and to convince himself that he did not have the soul of a tradesman, and that his true vocation was to be an explorer-writer.

At this point, we should go back in time: in late 1881, Verlaine, who was still a "farmer" at Juniville, had begun, with a view to preparing his return to the literary world, to collect Rimbaud's poems. These were still in the hands of former friends in Paris, for he himself no longer had any of Rimbaud's manuscripts in his possession. His thoughts returned to the author of whom he had had no news for two and a half years. Where was he? What had become of him? Verlaine then entrusted the faithful Delahaye with a little investigation. Delahaye, unaware that Rimbaud was in Africa, wrote to him at Roche. This is how he describes what followed:

"Mme Rimbe opened the epistle and replied with a charming idem, served with watercress, in which she informs me that 'poor Arthur' is at present in Arabia, at Harat or Harar, I couldn't make out the name. I'm replying today to Mme Rimbaud asking her to send me my chicken, if she knows the exact address of *l'homme-aux-semelles-de-vent*."[2]

Rimbaud replied to his friend's letter on January 18 1882:

> *My dear Delahaye,*
> *It was good to hear from you.*
> *Without further preambles, I shall explain to you how, if you are staying in Paris, you can do something for me.*
> *I want to write a book on Harar and the Gallas, whose territory I have explored, and submit it to the Geographical Society.*

What he had in mind was a complete, illustrated scientific work, so he needed precision instruments: a traveling theodolite, or a good sextant, a compass, plus a collection of minerals consisting of three hundred samples, a pocket aneroid barometer, a surveyor's measuring tape, a "mathematics case" containing ruler, set square, reducing compass, in addition to books on topography, geodesy, hydrography, industrial chemistry—and, last, the *Manuel du Voyageur, le Ciel*, the yearbook of the Bureau des Longitudes for 1882, etc. The excellent friend was to obtain all this and be reimbursed at Roche, where there was money. The end is as curt as the beginning: "Pack everything carefully. By the next post, which leaves in three days, details. Meanwhile, hurry. Cordial greetings. Rimbaud." This letter was discovered among the papers of the Rimbaud family: one can only suppose that it was never sent on to Delahaye.

So Rimbaud's hopes were now pinned on a new obsession: the Geographical Society would pay him to go on magnificent journeys. A further list of things to be ordered arrived in Roche, including a telescope and a special weapon for elephant hunting! He was living in a dream: his exploits would take place in Abyssinia or Zanzibar. He had learned that M. Dubar was on very good terms with M. Ledoulx, the French consul in Zanzibar, and therefore asked him to put in a good word for him. This he did on March 6, 1882—it is clear that his "friend and colleague" Rimbaud had risen in his employers' estimation.

However, on November 3, 1882, he announced to his family that he would be leaving in January 1882 for Harar, as branch manager. At this time the firm employing him was going through a difficult period: in order to keep afloat, an internal reorganization was required. M. Dubar would retire and return to France. He would be replaced by Pierre Bardey, which would leave the job of manager at Harar vacant. Rimbaud was very attentive to all these rumors and, for a time, indulged a hope of being appointed M. Dubar's successor, as general manager for Africa and Arabia, which would have brought him in an annual salary of 10,000 F. But this illusion did not last long. There was also some question of setting up a branch in the province of Shoa, where king Menelik resided.

His imagination became wilder: he saw himself traveling on horseback through immense virgin territory, where no white man had ever been, heavily subsidized by the Geographical Society, accompanied by a troop of mules carrying new precision instruments.

Since M. Dubar was going to Lyon, he asked him to buy a good camera for him (for the one that he had already ordered had never arrived), convinced that in a short space of time it would bring him in a "small fortune." So it was a matter of no importance whatsoever that such an instrument was very expensive (1,850 F with all the accessories), his mother had money; she would settle the expenses incurred out of the 1,000 F that she must have received from the head office in payment of a check, and the balance could be paid out of his account at Roche.

He was imprudent enough to add, on November 3, 1882: "When I have settled this business I shall send you a list of new things to buy, if there is any money left."

This was too much! Mme Rimbaud was losing all patience with her son's whims, orders, and countermanded orders: the sun of the Red Sea must have gone to his head! She had something better to do than get involved with long correspondence with booksellers in Paris, or with dealers in scientific instruments, or going every day to the post office to pay, receive, or claim money! Anyway, these expenses were quite extravagant: one must be off one's head to pay 1,850 F for a camera when one could get one for 200 or 300 F! So she made it quite clear to "poor Arthur," that she refused to have anything more to do with his purchases.

This decision dismayed him: "This is no way to help a man a thousand leagues from home," he replied to his mother on December 8, "traveling among savage peoples, with only one person to write to in his own country! I sincerely hope that you will alter this somewhat uncharitable decision. If I can no longer even ask my family to do a few things for me, who the devil can I ask?"

Without the books and instruments he needed, he would be like a blind man. He took advantage of this letter to order a few new books: a complete treatise on railways and the *Traité de mécanique de l'Ecole de Châlons*.

The sudden, unexpected defection of his family put him into a very bad mood indeed.

On January 28, 1883, he struck one of the storekeepers, Ali Shemmak, for being insolent. The Arabs present at the time, porters and packers, rushed at him and pinned him down, while Ali Shemmak struck him in the face, tore his clothes, and threatened him with a stick. The incident must have come to him as quite a shock, but it did not end there. Ali laid a charge for assault and battery with the municipal police, supported by false witnesses claiming to have seen Rimbaud draw a dagger.

The French consulate at Aden was informed of the incident by Rimbaud himself, who, before the police tribunal, asked for the protection of the consular authorities. The affair might have gone badly for him, and he ran the risk of a severe sentence, perhaps even expulsion.

Alfred Bardey saved the day by acting as a guarantor of his colleague's future actions. But, "out of solidarity," he had to sack Ali Shemmak, rather regretfully, for he was one of his longest-serving storekeepers.[3]

It is quite possible that this incident hastened Rimbaud's departure.

After his mother's bombshell, better relations were established with Roche: he received chests of books—and, from Lyon, his camera. If he were not careful, he would be visited by Isabelle! His younger sister, now twenty-two years old, was dreaming of Africa.

"Whatever you do, get that crazy idea out of your head," Arthur replied to her on January 15, 1883. "You are quite wrong to want to see me in this country, which is like being at the bottom of a volcano without a blade of grass! At present it's only 30° (C) in the shade, though personally I'm very fond of this climate."

"For me, the most important and urgent thing," he had admitted to his friend on November 16, 1882, "is to be independent—wherever I am."

His wish was soon to be fulfilled. Around March 20, 1883, he signed a new contract with the management, to run to the end of December 1885, at a salary of 160 rupees a month, plus a cut of the profits of the branch—amounting in all to 5,000 F a year, plus his keep.

He set out on March 22, 1883, with a long-term program in his head: "Over the next four or five years, I'd like to make about fifty thousand francs, then I'll get married," he wrote to his mother three days before leaving.

The situation at Harar had considerably worsened over the past sixteen months. Led by a Muslim fanatic, Mohammed Acmet, known as the Mahdi (Messiah), a revolt had spread through the Egyptian Sudan (1881), and was now threatening Abysinnia. This led to a weakening of the central government, permanent agitation, and an aggravation of the natives' zenophobia—conditions that did little to encourage expeditions and explorations. Against this gloomy background there were also political dissensions and international complications. The province of Harar was coveted both by the king of Shoa, Menelik, and by the king of Tigré, Atié Yohannes IV, theoric emperor of Ethiopia, his suzerain and rival. On the borders of the empire, the British, who supported Yohannes, stood by passively, observing the upheavals, lootings, and disorders, so that the interior of the country soon became an untenable hornet's nest. In the midst of this agitation, like a child playing with a new toy, Rimbaud carried on with photography. On May 6 1883 he wrote home: "Here everyone wants to be photographed. I'm even offered a guinea a photograph. . . . Enclosed are two [in fact there were three] of me that I took myself. . . . They show me standing on a terrace of the house, standing in a coffee grove, and arms folded in a banana grove. They have all bleached because of the bad water I used to wash them in. But I'll make a better job of it in the future. These are just to remind you of my face, and to give you some idea of the landscape here."

These three self-portraits have been published.[4] They come as a surprise to us, as they must also have done to his mother and sister, on account of the sad, resigned expression of the face. Paul Claudel spoke with feeling of the portrait (the second) showing "a very dark creature, with bare head, bare feet, wearing the convict's clothes that he once admired."[5] Augustin Bernard, who knew him at Harar, must have been right when he said that he looked more like some poor Armenian or Greek than a Frenchman.[6]

A number of photographs taken by him with his expensive camera have also been found—almost all of them are in the Musée Rimbaud at Charleville-Mézières. They are of the branch office at Harar, an Abyssinian hut, the "weighing house," views of Harar market, an elephant hunt scene (in which he himself does not appear), and a few portraits, that of his Greek clerk, Constantin Sotiro, looking very proud and brimming with health, and that of the army chief of staff at Harar, Ahmed Waddy Bey.

Proud of his successes, he sent a few examples of his work to his immediate boss, Pierre Bardey, in Aden, who sent them on to his brother Alfred, who was taking the waters at Vichy. From there, on July 24, he wrote to thank Rimbaud:

> *My dear M. Rimbaud,*
> *My brother has sent me the photographs that you were kind enough to send him for me.*
> *Several of your photographs are rather blurred, but you have obviously improved, since the others are perfect.*
> *I would like to be able to express my thanks for your kindness, but you are rather strange, and I don't know what to send you to please you.[7]*

Unfortunately, photography was not enough to dispel his deep, incurable boredom:

> *Isabelle is wrong not to get married if some serious, educated fellow asks her, someone with a future. Life is like that, and*

solitude is a bad thing in this world. Personally I regret not being married and having a family. But I am now condemned to wander about, associated with a business in a distant land, and, with each day that passes, I feel less and less drawn to the climate, way of life, and even the language of Europe. Alas, what is the point of these trips back and forth, the exhaustion and the adventures with unfamiliar races, and the languages with which I fill my head, and my endless discomforts, if I cannot one day, after a few years, settle down in some fairly pleasant place and have a family of my own, or at least a son whom I will spend the rest of my life raising in accordance with my views, forming and strengthening with the most complete education that can be obtained today, and whom I'll see grow into a famous engineer, a man made rich and powerful through science? But who knows how long I may last in these mountains? I could disappear among these tribes, without news of me ever getting out.

As we can see, resentment seems to be giving way to regret, then to an acceptance of fate and daydreaming about distant, inaccessible states. It is about this time that he begins to be drawn to Islam: on October 7, 1883, he ordered from Hachette an edition of the Koran, in Arabic and French. "Like the Muslims," he says again, "I know that what will be will be, and that's all."

However, his resignation was not to make relations with his employers any easier. In his letter of August 25, 1883, after describing the sluggishness of the Harar market, he gives free vent to his indignation: "We are now weary of protesting against the situation that is inflicted on us. We simply declare that we are not responsible in any way for the losses incurred. However, we are recommending once again, for the last time, that all our orders for goods be produced in the quantities and qualities ordered. We recommend them all, one by one, and insist on their being carried out. But if nobody wants to do anything about it, they won't get done."

The style is restrained; sometimes he goes so far as to be insolent. On August 26, after receiving a message from Pierre Mazeran (who had accompanied Alfred Bardey on his visit of inspection in the summer of 1881), informing him of his intention of returning to Harar in October, he dared to write the following to Alfred Bardey: "I hope nobody will blame us for the new expenses, and that one will refrain from worsening our situation by send-

ing an individual incapable of anything but dissipating our capital and contradicting, ridiculing, and ruining us here in every possible way. Personally I
can bear every privation without fear, and every irritation without impatience,
but I cannot bear the society of a [the word is difficult to read: it could be
aliéne, 'madman']."

In August 1883 Rimbaud sent his clerk Sotiro with a caravan heavily
laden with goods and presents on a reconnaissance mission into the province
of Ogaden, a vast region situated between the region of Harar and Somali-
land. Little was known of it, but the German Haggenmacher was not able to
reach it until 1875.

It is likely that this expedition was ordered by Pierre Bardey, for he
thought highly of Sotiro (at the time when he was running the Harar branch
he had written to his brother Alfred: "The surrounding markets may be held
by Sotiro, a rich employee by the way"). Pierre Bardey believed that Sotiro
should play the role of prospector and commercial traveler, since the place of
the branch manager was at Harar. This did not at all suit Rimbaud, who was
bored to death in his trading post, and could not wait to put on his explorer's
boots. He protested: "We regret having to send our employees out on these
unproductive journeys when we need them so much here for the outside
work" (August 25). But orders are orders.

Furthermore, such an expedition was not without its dangers: the tribes
of the Ogaden did not care for the whites, and lived very largely from looting.
The Italian explorer Piero Sacconi was murdered on August 11 with three
servants, over some stupid arguments about guides at Carnagott (about a hundred and fifty miles from Harar), not far from the place where Sotiro now
was.[8] But this was his own fault, Rimbaud explained. His caravan was badly
organized, the route he had taken was particularly dangerous, and, above all,
he had upset the natives: "M. Sacconi walked around in European dress, even
dressed his Sebians as hostranis [Christians], ate ham, drank alcohol during
the councils of the sheiks, fed himself, and carried out his suspicious geodesic
sessions and twiddled his sextants, etc., all along the route" (letter to Aden of
August 25).

Though dressed as a Muslim and calling himself Aji-Abdallah, Sotiro
nearly suffered the same fate. Held prisoner at Galdda at Amaden by a tribe
of the ughaz (chief) Omar Hussein, he was released only after a personal
appeal from Rimbaud to the ughaz.

Sotiro was able to reach a point nearly ninety miles from Harar. His
journey was a success on the level of discovery and commerce. He had turned

out to be very skilfull (Rimbaud was to praise his wisdom and diplomacy); he knew how to speak with firmness, and was generous when giving gifts.

This great "sortie" aroused great hopes in Rimbaud. On Sotiro's return, he organized three new incursions, one to the Itu Jardars, in the vicinity of the Hawash River, the other two in the valley of the Wabi in Ogaden. He took part in one of the latter, summoned and assisted by Omar Hussein, which enabled him to check on the spot the information collected by Sotiro.

On his return, he wrote an overall report on the Ogaden for M. Bardey. It is a clear, well constructed piece of writing, dealing with geography and, above all, ethnography, listing the resources of the regions visited.

Here is an example of his pleasantly smooth style:

> The Ogadins, at least those whom we have seen, are tall, and more usually red than black; they keep their heads bare and their hair short, wear fairly clean robes, carry a sigada slung across one shoulder, a saber and washing gourd on their hips, a cane and a large and small spear in their hands, and wear sandals on their feet.
>
> Most of their day is spent squatting in groups under the trees, at some distance from the camp, and, weapons in hand, deliberating endlessly on their various pastoral concerns. Apart from these sessions and the patrols on horseback for watering and raids on their neighbors, they are completely in-active. The care of the animals, the making of household utensils, the repairing of the huts, the loading and prepara-tion of the caravans are all left to the women and children. The utensils referred to are the well-known milk jugs of the Somali. Mats of camel hair, raised on poles, form temporary dwellings in the gacias (villages).
>
> A few blacksmiths wander from tribe to tribe making spear heads and daggers.
>
> The Ogadis know of no mineral ore on their territory.

Alfred Bardey found this report so interesting that he sent it on to the Geographical Society, of which he was a member. It was examined in the session of February 1, 1884, and put into the Society's bulletin, where it did not pass unnoticed: the celebrated Austrian geographer-explorer, Philipp

Paulitschke, for instance, said that it was "very important and of great value despite its dryness of style."

Better still, the Geographical Society asked Rimbaud to write a short biographical note about himself, and to send it, with a photograph, for inclusion in a book that was being prepared on individuals "who have made a name for themselves in the geographical sciences and travel."

In all decency, Rimbaud could not accept the honor for work that had really been done by Sotiro: he had merely checked his subordinate's observations and written them up. So he did not reply. But it gave him pleasure for he had found his way at last: he would be the pioneer of East Africa, would become a member of the Geographical Society, and figure in their publications. His desire in this regard was as strong as the one that, in 1870, had driven him toward *Le Parnasse contemporain.*

Unfortunately, bad luck barred his way once again. The political events were fast turning into a catastrophe. The Egyptian army, beaten in November 1883 by the Dervish supporters of the Mahdi, were thinking of evacuating the province of Harar: they would have to leave. Furthermore, the company of Mazeran, Viannay, and Bardey, as a result of poor business in Marseille, the Indies, Greece, and Algeria, had gone into liquidation with liabilities of close on a million francs. The branches at Aden, Zeila, and Harar, though in themselves profitable, were to disappear in the upheaval.

In January 1884, Alfred Bardey, who had returned from Marseille with but little hope for the future, ordered Rimbaud to send a last caravan to Zeila, after which the branch in that town, run by Charles Cotton, would be closed down.

At Harar there was a turmoil: Egyptian troops were evacuating the town and being replaced by a local militia, until such time as the British arrived.

It was time for Rimbaud to be off.

He set out in March, and after six weeks' traveling through the desert reached Aden about April 23. Though now without work, his salary was paid to him until the end of July.

He had the satisfaction of receiving the following highly laudatory testimonial:

> *Dear Monsieur Rimbaud,*
> *The events that have forced us into liquidation give us no alternative but to deprive ourselves of your excellent services.*
> *We would like to express our gratitude for the hard work,*

intelligence, probity, and devotion that you have always
shown in defense of our interests, in the various posts that you
have occupied in our firm over the last four years and, in par-
ticular, as manager of our branch at Harar.
    Please accept our thanks and every good wish for the fu-
ture.

                    Mazeran, Viannay, Bardey
                    Aden, April 23, 1884

Let us now move on to a quite different subject, concerning not commerce, but literature.

In the summer of 1883, war broke out at Tonkin. One of the correspondents of the newspaper *Le Temps* was called Paul Bourde. He was also a
literary critic who was well informed about the avant-garde literature then
fashionable among the young decadents. For them Rimbaud was an idol: his
sonnet *Voyelles* was their multicolored standard.

In July or August, on his way to Tonkin, Bourde met on board Alfred
Bardey, who, after taking the waters at Vichy, was returning to Aden. The two
men got into conversation. Bardey must have talked about his firm, which
was doing badly as a whole, even though his own side of the business was
doing very well. For example, there was the branch at Harar, which was
extremely well run by a manager called Rimbaud.

"Rimbaud?" Bourde started. "I knew a Rimbaud at school in Charleville, around 1870 or so. What does your Rimbaud look like?

Everything coincided, the Christian name, the age, the general appearance. So this secretive, strange, but methodical young man had been a poet,
and was still remembered in Paris. When Bardey saw him again at Aden, he
told him of the astonishing meeting and gave him Paul Bourde's card.

Rimbaud looked embarassed, blushed, and muttered: "Absurd . . . Ridiculous . . . Disgusting!" (M. Bardey's letter to Paterne Berrichon, July 16
1897).

That was probably not all. In the autumn of 1883, Verlaine had managed to collect enough of Rimbaud's poems to fill out a study he was hoping
to publish on him and a few of the "poètes maudits" in a minor Latin Quarter
review, *Lutèce*, to be followed later by publication in book form,

Now, it is improbable that he did not ask Rimbaud's permission to publish his verse. To begin with, out of prudence: one did not have the right to
publish the works of a third person without his consent. Anyway, it was not

something Verlaine would do: after all, it was he who had first put him on the road to fame!

It was therefore logical that Verlaine should contact Rimbaud. Alfred Bardey told the Ardennais writer Jean-Paul Vaillant that, on a single occasion, Rimbaud had written to "Monsieur Verlaine." His letter was firm and laconic, amounting, more or less, to: "Leave me in peace!" (Bardey places the episode in 1885).

Verlaine must have had Rimbaud's address; how else would he have come by it except through Delahaye? Now, it is quite likely that Delahaye never received the letter that Rimbaud sent to him on January 18, 1882, via Roche. There is something of a mystery here which, given the present state of our evidence, cannot be cleared up. Nevertheless, Verlaine's words in *Les Poètes maudits* ring false: "Had we consulted M. Rimbaud (whose address is quite unknown to us), he would probably have advised against undertaking this work in so far as it concerns him." Verlaine was quite capable of dissimulation and of converting a past tense into a conditional.

To return to Aden, where Rimbaud was vegetating, quite wretched at having nothing to do.

It is likely that he fell into a new depression at this time, some echo of which is to be found in his letters to his family: "What a desolate existence I am spinning out in these absurd climates and in these senseless conditions! . . . My life here is a real nightmare. Don't imagine that I'm having a good time. Far from it: I have long since realized that it is impossible to live more wretchedly than I."

He was aware that at thirty he had achieved nothing, and that in France, where he would now feel a stranger, he would not find work (letter of May 5, 1884).

Soon he received a telegram from Bardey asking him to stay put. Was the good news that was doing the rounds, and in which he dared not believe, about to be confirmed? But time was passing and his impatience growing: if he delayed his return home much longer, he wrote to his family on May 29, people would think of him "only as an old man," and only a widow would agree to marry him.

Finally, in June, Alfred Bardey came back to Aden. With capital provided by the Société Ulysse Pila et Cie of Lyon and Marseille, he was able to set up a new company (Bardey et Cie) with his brother.

A new contract was signed with Rimbaud for six months, to run from July 1 to December 31, 1884, on the same conditions as before. Business was picking up, it was said; but it was difficult to see how, when, thanks to the combined efforts of religious and nationalist movements in Abyssinia and the anti-Egyptian policy of the British, any trade had become impossible in the interior.

Rimbaud was not slow to see that he had been duped: "Business is bad," he wrote home on September 10. He was leaving. "I am aging very quickly in these stupid jobs, and in the company of savages or fools. . . . Now, it is more than likely that I shall never have enough to live quietly. Anyway, as the Muslims say, 'It is written!—That's life: it's no joke!'"

It was at this time that an incident in his family sent him into a tantrum. Frédéric, constantly at war with his mother, had decided to get married, and had broken with his family. He did not know that his brother Arthur had taken his mother's side: one does not marry when one hasn't got a penny.

"Arthur's preaching morality," he repeated to whoever would listen to him. "To think that, when he was twenty, he never earned a penny, and was being kept by Verlaine and others!"

From whom had he learned that? Certainly not from his mother or Isabelle, and Arthur had never boasted of his past. Now it is curious to note that at this time Verlaine was living at Coulommes, six kilometers from Roche, and that Frédéric, a van driver for a hotel at Attigny, saw a great many people. It is not improbable, therefore, that Verlaine should have met Frédéric in the hotel bar.

This information came to Mme Rimbaud's ears, and she lost no time in passing it on to Arthur, who replied in furious vein on October 7:

> *My dear friends,*
> *I have received your letter of September 23. I am saddened by what you tell me of Frédéric. It is extremely annoying, and may reflect badly on us. I would be quite embarrassed, for example, if anyone knew that I had such a fool for a brother. But it comes as no surprise: that Frédéric is a complete idiot, we've always known that, and we always wondered at the hardness of his head.*
> *You don't need me to tell you not to engage in correspondence with him. As for giving him anything, what I've earned here has taken me too much trouble to amass for me to make a present of it to a Bedouin like him, who is considerably less*

tired than I am. Lastly, I hope all the same, for you and for me, that he'll soon put an end to this farce.

As for wagging his tongue on my account, my conduct is well known here as elsewhere. I can send you evidence of the exceptional satisfaction that the liquidated Mazeran Company has given me for my four years of service, from 1880 to 1884, and I have a very good reputation here that will enable me to earn a decent living. I have had unhappy times in the past, but I have never tried to live at someone else's expense or by doing ill.

The incident was not to go any further: nothing more was said about Frédéric. He was to marry the following year (August 11, 1885), when he was already the father of a one-month-old girl.

Rimbaud had not come back from Harar alone: a young native woman accompanied him. "It was at Aden that the affair with the Abyssinian woman took place from 1884 to 1886," wrote Alfred Bardey to Berrichon on July 10 1897. "The union was an intimate one, and Rimbaud, who lived and ate at first in my home, rented a special house to live with his companion, outside the hours that he spent on our premises."[9]

Indeed, as from May 5, 1884, he sometimes gave his address at Aden camp, about three miles from the town.

We shall see later, how, according to Rimbaud himself, he had brought this woman from Shoa—a region that he had never seen. Did he mean, perhaps, that she was a native of that region? Moreover, if he had brought her to Aden, he must have already been living with her at Harar. This would confirm a statement made by the bishop of that town—to Evelyn Waugh around 1930—to the effect that Rimbaud had lived with a native woman who was not from Harar, and with whom he did not have a child.[10]

We need not dwell on the legends according to which this affair served as a screen for homosexual practices.[11] On this practice, Alfred Bardey is categorical: "I never believed in the accusation of sodomy," he declared to Berrichon.[12]

Furthermore, a French civil servant, who did research on Rimbaud at Obok and Djibuti between 1906 and 1925, wrote: "Where women were concerned, Rimbaud made use of the native element. In 1884, at Aden, he had an Abysinnian wife. He is also known to have had an Argoba wife, from whom he had several children, but all have disappeared without trace."[13] The Argobas (or Argobbas) are an Islamicized Amhara tribe living some twelve miles south of Harar. They are a fine race, who claimed descent from early Portuguese settlers who had sided with the kings of Ethiopia against Islam.

The existence of an Argoba wife is again confirmed by Ottorino Rosa, Rimbaud's Italian friend mentioned above, but his evidence is not reliable (he situated the affair at Aden in 1882), and there is nothing to prove that the photograph of the "Donna Abissina" in his book *L'Impero di Leone di Giuda* (The Empire of the Lion of Juda, [Brescia: Lenghi, 1913] is that of Rimbaud's mistress).[14]

None of this is very conclusive, but it is not impossible that an Argoba woman should have been living in Shoa, come into contact with the Europeans frequenting the royal palace, and that Rimbaud should have met her through some friend in Ankober, the royal city. The portrait that follows will support this hypothesis.

So, in 1897, Berrichon, intrigued by Alfred Bardey's revelations, got from him the address of his former maid, Françoise Grisard, who was in his service for eight years (and occasionally in Rimbaud's). She had become a laundress and the wife of a stoker-mechanic on the shipping line *Messageries maritimes*. She knew the Abyssinian woman well, and had given her sewing lessons. Her evidence has all the guarantee of authenticity, for it is that of a woman who had nothing to prove and nothing to hide:

> *Marseille, July 22 1897,*
> *Monsieur,*
>   *It gives me great pleasure to reply to your letter. It is true that I went almost every Sunday after dinner to M. Rimbaud's; I was even surprised that he allowed me to do so. I think I was the only person he ever received in his house. He spoke very little; he seemed to behave kindly toward that woman. He wanted to educate her; he told me that he wanted to send her for a time to the nuns, at the Mission run by Father François, and that he wanted to marry her because he wanted to go into Abyssinia, and that he would not be returning to France until he had amassed a large fortune, otherwise he would never come back.*
>   . . . *As for that woman, she was very gentle, but she spoke so little French that it was difficult for us to keep up a*

*conversation. She was tall and very slim; she had a fairly
pretty face, fairly regular features, and was not too dark. I
don't know the Abyssinian race: she seemed to me to look very
like a European woman. She was a Catholic. I can't remember her name. For some time she had her sister with her. She
went out only in the evening, with M. Rimbaud; she wore
European clothes, and their home was just like those of the
local people. She was very fond of smoking cigarettes.*

*I don't really know what else I can tell you, for all this
was fourteen years ago, and above all I was very discreet as far
as they were concerned. I regret, Monsieur, that I am unable
to give you more detailed information.*[15]

As we can see, the woman whom Rimbaud had chosen was no savage.

Meanwhile, politically, things were going from bad to worse. In September 1884, it appeared that Egypt would be evacuating Harar: the town was
administered by a local militia led by Raduan Pasha—assisted by a British
officer without powers, Peyton, who had set himself up in Bardey's office.
Mgr. Taurin-Cahagne felt that the Christians were about to be thrown to the
wild beasts, given the rise of blind, fanatical intolerance among the masses.
He said as much in diplomatic terms—and unsuccessfully—to Major
Hunter, who could do nothing, and, anyway, did not approve of his country's
policy. In the end, the emir Abdellahi was appointed governor of the province
of Harar. His dream was to isolate the town from the coast and to murder all
the Christians, whether white or black.

Since the situation was becoming untenable, Mr. Taurin-Cahagne resigned himself to leaving—with the last detachment of the Egyptian army.

The passivity of Great Britain in the face of the Islamic revolution and
the activities on the coast of the French (at Obok and Djibouti), and Italians
(at Assab and Messewa) enraged everybody. Worse, the British government
had sent General Gordon to prepare for the withdrawal of all soldiers, civil
servants, and civilians from the Sudan.

Rimbaud was in a constant state of anger. On December 30, 1884, he
wrote home:

*It is the British with their absurd policy who are now
ruining trade on all these coasts. They wanted to turn everything upside down, and they have succeeded in making a*

*worse job of it than the Egyptians and Turks whom they have
ruined. Their Gordon is an idiot, their Wolseley, an ass, and
everything they do a senseless string of absurdities and degra-
dations. As for news of the Sudan, we know no more than you
do in France, no one comes from Africa any more, everything
is disorganized, and the British administration of Aden is interested in nothing but issuing lies.*

*. . . I don't believe any nation has a colonial policy as
inept as France. England may make mistakes and try to
please everybody, but she has at least serious interests and
considerable prospects. But no country would waste her
money in impossible places as France is doing.*

It is clear that it would have been in France's interests to have negotiated
with the Abyssinian authorities: in exchange for her presence, as a guarantee
of security, she would have won outlets on the Red Sea (Menelik was not
opposed to this). But, since no one listened to common sense it was better to
resign oneself to the inevitable, and wait for better days.

Without the slightest enthusiasm, Rimbaud had to extend his contract
for a further year, from January 1 to December 31, 1885—on the same conditions as before—150 rupees a month, plus keep. It was stated in the contract that if M. Bardey dismissed him, he would owe him three months'
salary; but it Rimbaud himself wished to leave, he would be held to three
months' notice.

Never in his life had inactivity weighed so heavily upon him. On January 15, he wrote home: "If I was able to travel without being forced to settle
down in order to work and earn my living, I wouldn't be seen for two months
in the same place. The world is very big and full of magnificent places that it
would take more than a thousand lives to visit, but, on the other hand, I have
no wish to wander about in poverty, I'd like to have a few thousand francs'
income and be able to spend the year in two or three different places, living
modestly and doing a little dealing to pay for my expenses. But living always
in the same place, I will always find wretched."

Unfortunately, he was still only a little clerk with a stomach complaint—
brought on by eating too much highly spiced food, living very frugally (40 F
rent a month!), with no intellectual activity whatever: "We get no newspapers
here, and there are no libraries; the only Europeans are a few idiotic commercial clerks, who splurge their salaries in the billiard-saloons, and then

leave the place cursing it" (April 18, 1885). As a matter of fact, Bardey protested to Paterne Berrichon about this passage (letter of January 20, 1888): "We always took the greatest care to raise the morale of those in our employment. Apart from the serious newspapers, they also had the satirical and illustrated magazines."[16] (Another eyewitness has declared that they read *Le Rappel* and *La Lanterne*.)[17]

Rimbaud's letters at this period suggest the infernal circles of Dante: "We are in our spring bathhouse; sweat pours off our skins, our stomachs turn sour, our brains grow dim, business is awful, the news bad" (May 26, 1885), or again: "One really must be forced to work for one's living, to accept a job in such a hell! There is no company but the local Bedouins, and so one becomes a complete imbecile in a few years" (September 28).

He was ready to do anything to get out of it—however stupid.

16

A Crazy Escapade into Shoa

In September 1885 Rimbaud met a Frenchman of Gascon origin called Pierre Labatut, who offered him what seemed like a wonderful deal importing arms into Shoa, the Abyssinian province in which King Menelik resided. He had, he said, received from the king and from a number of dignitaries, such as the Ras Govana, a large order for arms to be used in the military operations that were being planned there.

This Labutut, who had been the Bardeys' agent in Shoa, was very well known in European circles. Paul Soleillet, a merchant and explorer, has provided the following description of him: "M. Pierre Labutut, after working as a salesman in France and Italy, and as a contractor in Egypt, came to Shoa some ten years ago and was able, through charm, honesty and loyalty, to gain the confidence of the king, the respect of the great, and the affection of the small. M. Labatut is the only European merchant to have settled in southern Ethiopia. He does a great deal of trade between Shoa and Aden" (*Voyage en Ethiopie*, Rouen, 1884). He was married to an Abyssinian woman and lived as a native among his horses, mules, farmyard animals, and servants. He was a serious potential partner, since he had gained the friendship of the king.

Rimbaud was won over by the plan that was outlined to him. It consisted of buying, in Liège and in France, outdated old piston guns at seven or eight francs a piece, and delivering them to Menelik, who had urgent need of them. He would pay in kind (ivory, musk, gold) on the basis of forty francs a piece, and the resale of this merchandise at Aden would bring in an additional profit. Of course, there were expenses and dangers, but, on paper, the deal seemed very lucrative: with two thousand guns—a capital of between fifty and twenty thousand francs, one could make a gross profit of sixty thousand francs, without counting the profit to be made on the merchandise given as payment. The game was worth the candle. And, anyway, it was something to do at last.

Immediately (October 5) Labatut agreed in writing to pay Rimbaud five thousand "Maria-Theresa dollars" (old Austrian silver coins accepted as currency in Aden), that is, 21,500 F, within a year and to bear all the costs of the operation himself. (A little later, on November 23, Labatut borrowed eight hundred M.T. dollars [3,440 F] from him for a year.

The guns were ordered.

At last, luck was smiling on Rimbaud.

To pull off the undertaking he had to have his hands free—and for that, he first got rid of the Abyssinian woman. That did not take very long.

It seems that the Italian journalist-explorer Augusto Franzoj, a correspondent on the *Gazetta di Torino*, who was at Tajura, waiting for permission to set off for Shoa with a scientific expedition, asked Rimbaud if he would be taking his companion with him. We have Rimbaud's reply:

> *Dear Monsieur Franzoj,*
>
> *Excuse me, but I have dismissed that woman permanently.*
>
> *I shall give her a few thalers and she will take the dow now at Rasali for Obok, where she will go wherever she wishes.*
>
> *I have had that masquerade in front of me for long enough.*
>
> *I would not have been so stupid as to bring her out of Shoa, and I shall not be so stupid as to take it upon myself to take her back there. Yours,*
>
> > *Rimbaud*

Secondly, he had to free himself from the servitude of the Bardeys.

No sooner had Rimbaud begun to make his intentions plain, than Alfred Bardey interrupted his employee: "It isn't very fair to leave us like this. Before making up your mind you should have consulted us. Everyone knows everything here. We knew about your plans. You are free—or rather you will be in three months, according to your contract."

Rimbaud, annoyed at having been anticipated, lost his temper: he had had enough of being exploited, they had done nothing but make promises to him, none of which had been kept; for four years he had been kept in a subordinate position. Did they imagine that he could be kept forever in such servitude? As for the contract, had they not unilaterally broken his in 1884? He demanded to leave at once.

But what exasperated him most of all was Alfred Bardey's reply: "You wish to leave? Very well. We won't stand in your way. But be careful. Your plan to import arms into Shoa may well turn out badly. I myself refused such a proposition from Labatut three years ago, and what he offered seemed very profitable. Believe me when I tell you that you are throwing yourself into a hornet's nest. You will lose everything you have!"

Rimbaud may have replied that he preferred ruin to slavery, but his fine confidence had been shaken, for Alfred Bardey knew what he was talking about.

On October 22, he announced the news to his family: "I have given up my job in Aden after a violent argument with those wretched skinflints who were trying to enslave me forever. I've done a lot for those people; and they imagined that I would spend the rest of my life with them just to please them. They have done all they could to keep me, but I've sent them to the devil, with all their advantages, their business, their frightful house, and their dirty town!"

He had in his pocket a certificate dated October 14, 1885: "I, Alfred Bardey, declare that I have employed M. Arthur Rimbaud as manager and buyer from April 30, 1884, to November 1885. I have always been pleased with his services and his honesty. He is free of all commitments to me."

The fact that he had asked his family for moral support shows that his previous optimism had given way to apprehension: "I hope that it will all turn out well. Keep your fingers crossed for me, too; I need it."

He was well aware that the guns that he was going to collect on the coast had to be transported across frightful deserts overrun with gangs of greedy bandits. But, after all, if the risks were great, the reward was greater.

Before leaving, he wisely came to a reconciliation with the Bardeys, promised them M. d'Abbadie's *Dictionnaire Amhara* (which took six months to reach them), and ordered camping material from them for the king's troops (cups and steel sheets to cook durra pancakes on).

He now waited for Labatut's promises to be fulfilled, having sunk almost all his savings to buy the weapons.

He was hoping to go at once to the port of debarkation, Tajura, on the Danakil coast next to the French colony of Obok, but he was held up by complications. He then took up residence in Aden Camp at the Grand Hôtel de L'Univers, a magnificent establishment (the sign was ten feet high), run by Jules Suel, M. Dubar's brother-in-law, a tall, alert man of about fifty, who had long since been connected with the Bardeys, who had once considered making him manager of the Aden branch.

Finally, in early December, he was ready to set out. "Tajura," he wrote on December 3, "is a small Danakil village with a few mosques and a few palm trees. There is a fortress built long ago by the Egyptians, where six French soldiers sleep at present under the orders of a sergeant, who is in command of the post." It was a hostile environment. These Bedouins traded mainly in slaves ("Don't imagine that I've become a slave dealer," he wrote to Roche).

Early in 1886, he was still there, completely inactive: "Things are moving very slowly, but I hope it will work out all the same. One must have superhuman patience in these countries." If his plans were postponed much longer, he would not be able to return to France until the spring of 1887.

The Italian explorer Ugo Ferrandi met him about this time: "The Soleillet caravan and that of M. Franzoj were camping in the palm grove just outside the Danakil village. Rimbaud was living in a cabin in the village. Tall, skinny, hair graying at the temples, he was wearing European dress, but of a very rough and ready kind, with rather wide trousers, a jersey, a loose-fitting gray khaki jacket. On his head he wore only a small skullcap, which was also gray and braved the torrid sun of the Danakils like a native."[1]

A researcher obtained these rather unflattering comments from the hoteliers and traders of Obok: "Physically Rimbaud was of above average height, rather thin, with a rather unpleasant, not to say ugly face, that seemed to be saying to his hotelier: 'Abysinnia won't be getting a particularly brilliant sample of the French race with this one.'" It was also said that, in his struggle against depression, he drugged himself with alcohol, tobacco, hashish, even opium, and that he emerged from these excesses "drawn, haggard, surly, hardly eating, but still drinking quite a lot."[2] (If that is true, then he had changed: on April 14, 1885, he wrote that he drank "absolutely" nothing but water, and never smoked.)

Disturbing news was circulating: one could find neither camels nor caraveneers for the interior, as the result of a protest strike against the shackles placed by the great powers of the slave trade.

Was the whole thing going to fall through?

"Everything is going very badly," Rimbaud wrote home on January 6, 1886. His pessimism had resurfaced: "In the end, man expects to spend three-quarters of his life suffering in order to rest during the last quarter; and as often as not he dies in misery without knowing where he has got with his plans!"

The supply of weapons finally arrived: 2,040 guns, 60,000 Remington cartridges, and various other merchandise. Rimbaud stored everything away in his own well-guarded hut.

At Tajura other caravans—belonging to Soleillet, Savouré, and Franzoj—were preparing to go into Shoa, in spite of the difficulties. They were all awaiting official permission from the governor of Obok and the sultan of Tajura—usually this was a mere formality.

In February, following a request from Soleillet, whose weapons were in transit in Aden and on the Somali coast, the British governor of Aden reminded the French consul in that city that, according to the terms of an Anglo-French convention of 1884, it was forbidden to import weapons into the interior. There were several reasons for this. To begin with there was the danger that these weapons might fall into the hands of the marauding tribes, and be turned against the whites. Furthermore, it was said (though Rimbaud denies this) that the slave trade flourished under cover of gunrunning. Finally—and this was a secret reason—Great Britain, who was no friend of Menelik, feared that it would enlarge his kingdom and increase his power. However, an exception—the last—was made in Soleillet's favor.

So, on April 12, 1886, Rimbaud learned that the governor of Obok and the sultan of Tajura were opposed to his departure!

All he could now do was to bury his weapons in the sand to avoid their being seized, and to protest, in conjunction with Labatut, to the French minister of foreign affairs in Paris (April 15): "We have committed to this single undertaking all our capital, all our equipment, and all our personnel, all our time and even our lives." If the French government maintains its veto, it would be in debt to the two partners to the sum of 258,000 F.

In fact, the arguments advanced to justify the cessation of arms trafficking were fallacious, for it was well known that the tribes did not like firearms. For them, the spear was enough, as they proved in massacring the caravan of the Frenchman Barral on its way back from Ankober. As soon as they heard the news, the Europeans in Tajura became very worried: "There have been certain unpleasant incidents here," Rimbaud wrote to his family on July 9, "but no massacres on the coast, a caravan has been attacked on the road, but that was because it was badly guarded."

The protest from Rimbaud and Labatut was conveyed with a note to the minister of the navy and of the colonies (May 24): the note requested an investigation of the alleged fact and a comment on the need to define a clear, coherent doctrine on the matter of arms dealing, since the present uncertainty could only favor the British and Italians, to the detriment of the French.

In the end, everybody had had enough of the matter and Franzoj declared that he intended setting out at his own risk with a French caravan. The minister of the navy, informed of this decision on June 10, 1886, by the governor of Obok, a certain Lagarde, replied that he was unable to give his good offices to the Italian mission and to the French caravan.[3]

Rimbaud did not ask for more. He could leave at last. Everything was ready: in May, by way of precaution, he had left his contract with Labatut at the French consulate at Aden (it has not been found).

Unfortunately, Labatut was now suffering from cancer of the throat and was unable to leave. Shortly afterwards he returned in haste to France to consult a specialist.

By summer, Franzoj had left and Rimbaud was still waiting. Around September 15, the news of Labatut was so disturbing that he was soon given up for lost.

Rimbaud did not know what to do: he considered combining his caravan with that of Soleillet, who was still at Tajura. It was a good idea, for Soleillet knew the road to Shoa well and would be a good guide.

Catastrophe struck again! Paul Soleillet died on September 9, after suffering a stroke in a street in Aden.

Before these blows of fate, Rimbaud gritted his teeth, and decided to set out alone. On September 15, he announced the news to his family: he would be setting off at the end of the month.

"My journey will last for at least a year. I'll write to you at the last moment. My health is very good. Keep well."

Labatut's death must have been just one more incident on the way. "You'll have time to sell off everything without being worried about his heirs, who have probably not yet been informed of his death," Jules Suel wrote to him from Aden on September 16. So he had no worries on that score.

His carvan consisted of about fifty camels and an escort of thirty-four Abyssinians. Just as he was leaving he learned of Labatut's death. The great departure, so long awaited, had nothing triumphal about it. It was more like a flight.

He left with no illusions, expecting "many dangers, and, above all, indescribable unpleasantness." He was still erring on the side of optimism. The Shoa, or Gobad road, as it was called, was one of the most frightful on earth. It crossed arid plateaus, "strewn with ferruginous stone that gave off a fiery heat."[4] (Quite often the thermometer exceeded 72°C.) One can imagine what he must have endured, for he traveled most of the journey on foot, beside his mule.

First they descended to Lake Assal, whose edges were fringed by a thick layer of blue salt crystals. But Rimbaud saw things more as an economist than as a tourist: he decided that it would not be profitable to transport the salt to the coast by narrow-gauge railroad (letter to Alfred Bardey, August 26, 1887). The route from Assal, through Gobad, to Herer (twenty-three stages) crossed a volcanic desert suggestive of "the presumed horror of the lunar landscapes," made dangerous by the incursions of the Debne tribes, who were permanently at war with their neighbors. To reach the river Hawash from Herer took a further eight or nine days. Rimbaud was able to realize the stupidity of the projects to pipe water from this river, which flowed from the southwest to the northwest. "Poor Soleillet," he wrote to M. Bardey on August 26, 1887, "had a special embarkation of construction materials sent from Nantes for this purpose!" The Hawash is "a tortuous ditch, obstructed at every turn by trees and rocks."

He finally reached Farré, on the Shoa frontier. Just as he was entering the town square with his camels, there appeared the sorry-looking caravan of the hazage (Rimbaud writes "Azzaze"), the king's minister-commander, who had come to meet him. After the usual greetings, the hazage insinuated that the "Frangui" in whose name he had come (Labatut) owed him an enormous amount of money. "He seemed to be asking for the entire caravan as security," Rimbaud wrote. "I cooled his ardor, temporarily, with the offer of one of my field glasses and a few bottles of Morton [laxative] pills. And I later sent him what really did seem to me to be his due. He was bitterly disappointed, and always acted in a hostile manner toward me; among other things, he prevented the other sycophant, the abuna [a dignitary of the Coptic orthodox clergy] from paying me for a delivery of raisins that I had brought him for making communion wine."

Things were beginning well!

Rimbaud continued on his way through greener, pleasanter country and, on February 7, 1887, reached Ankober, the capital of Shoa, a township made up of huts built with branches. There was a further complication: Menelik was not there.

Poor Rimbaud! He arrived at a historic time. There was a war being waged with the emir of Harar, Abdellahi. The king had grown tired of his constant attacks on the frontiers and had decided to go over to the offensive and liquidate him. At the head of his army, he had defeated the emir at Chalanko, on January 6, 1887, and captured a large quantity of weapons. He then entered Harar in triumph some days later and set up the new governor,

Ali Abu Bekr, the uncle of the conquered emir (whom, shortly afterwards, Makonnen removed from office and sent in chains to Menelik).

In his diary the explorer Jules Borelli wrote on Wednesday February 9, 1887: "ANKOBER. Left at six o'clock. M. Rimbaud, a French merchant, arrived from Tajura with his caravan. His journey was far from untroubled. Always the same program: bad drivers, the greed and treachery of the men, the harassments and ambushes of the Adals, lack of water, exploitation by the camel drivers. Our compatriot has lived in Harar. He knows Arabic, and speaks Amarigna and Oromo. He is indefatigable. His aptitude for languages, great will power, and patience under every trial place him among the most accomplished travelers."[5]

For his part Rimbaud was delighted to make Borelli's acquaintance. At last there was someone intelligent to talk to!

As soon as he arrived at Ankober, he wrote to Menelik, who replied as follows: "Sent by King Menelik. May this be sent to M. Rambaud. How are you? I, by the grace of God, am well. Your letter has reached me. I have arrived at Fel Uha. Five days will suffice me to see the merchandise. You will then be able to leave. Written 3 myarzya [February 1887]."[6]

Rimbaud's stay at Ankober was not entirely restful. To begin with, he fell into dispute with his camel drivers: he had agreed to pay each of them 15 thalaris (the plural of thaler in Abyssinian), plus two months' pay due. But, enraged by their insolent demands, he tore up the contract, which resulted in his being brought to trial before the hazage. A second case was brought against him by Labatut's widow, who was being advised by a Frenchman called Hénon, a former cavalry officer, a scheming character, who seemed to regard himself as the ambassador of the French republic at Menelik's court. "After odious arguments, in which I sometimes had the upper hand and sometimes not," Rimbaud writes, "the hazage granted me an order to seize the dead man's property. But the widow had already hidden at some distance away the few hundred thalaris' worth of merchandise, effects, and curiosities left by him and, when I carried out the seizure, without resistance, I found only a few old pairs of underpants, which were seized by the widow, with tears in her eyes, a few bullet molds, and a dozen pregnant female slaves, which I left" (Letter to M. de Gaspary, French vice-consul at Aden, November 9, 1887). However he did seize Labatut's accounts, which filled thirty-four ledgers. Having found in one of them a receipt from the hazage for a delivery of ivory worth three hundred thalers he agreed to pay this debt, but would not go further, and threw the ledgers into the fire, despite the widow's "imprecations": they contained, it seems, title deeds to property and other irreplaceable documents.

Labatut's widow appealed, and the bewildered hazage "abandoned the thing to the judgment of the Franguis then present at Ankober."

The "court" presided over by M. Brémond, the doyen of the French nationals, made a judgment ordering the annulment of the seizure and the return to Mme Labatut of her lands, gardens, and animals. It was also decided that the Europeans present at Ankober should club together to raise 100 thalaris for the widow of their late lamented colleague (this never took place).

When the hearing was over, Rimbaud learned that Menelik had stopped on his return journey at Entoto, which was seventy-five miles away. So Rimbaud set off with his cargo for that town, another group of primitive huts.

On arrival, Rimbaud had yet another disappointment: he learned that the king had not yet arrived, but was pursuing rebellious tribes. This new wait enabled Rimbaud to make the acquaintance of the Swiss engineer Alfred Ilg, the king's counsellor. Born in 1854, he had settled in Shoa since 1879. He was a tall, well-built, sometimes surly, but generally friendly and open man. He was the simple, direct kind of person that Rimbaud liked.

Finally, on March 6, 1887, the king entered Entoto. Rimbaud was there and recounts the occasion: "He entered Entoto preceded by musicians emitting ear-splitting noises from Egyptian trumpets found at Harar, and followed by his troops and loot, which included two Krupp canons, each drawn by eighty men" (letter to the editor of Le Bosphore égyptien of August 20, 1887).

A few days later, Rimbaud was at last summoned to the royal "guebi," accompanied by Ilg. This was a large round hut divided up into three rooms, the walls of which were covered with trellis work on which were hung weapons of all kinds.

The "negus" was a fine man in the prime of life, whose face was pitted with smallpox. "His eyes were bright and intelligent," Enid Starkie writes, "though at times their expression could be crafty. His general appearance was of undisguised and unashamed good-humoured knavery. He received Rimbaud dressed in his usual manner, in a black silk embroidered cloak over a profusion of muddled, shapeless, white linen garments; with this he wore incongruously a black, wide-brimmed, quaker's hat over a white silk handkerchief that tightly bound his head."[7]

He did not seem impressed with the guns on offer. He had just recovered a large quantity of weapons at Harar, and was awaiting others from Assab. In any case, he had been sold much better Remingtons than these old, out-of-date models. However, dreaming of new conquests in the south, he finally agreed to take the stock, and offered 14,000 thalaris for the lot. When Rimbaud expostulated, he replied that it was take it or leave it, and if he were not satisfied he had only to take the guns back with him to the coast. History— or legend—adds that Queen Weizeno Taitu had some part in this cruel decision, but that he might have got a better deal if he had indulged in flattery and showered the king with personal presents. But this was too much to ask of Rimbaud!

The French vice-consul at Aden was later to reply to Rimbaud's complaint (November 8, 1887): "Your losses might have been appreciably mitigated if, like other traders called upon to traffic with the Abyssinian authorities, you had been willing or able to adapt yourself to the particular requirements of these countries and their leaders."

"By the way," Menelik continued, "Labatut owes me a great deal of money."

"It was a Saturday," Rimbaud relates in a letter to M. de Gaspary, dated November 9, 1887, "and the king withdrew to consult the accounts. On the Monday, the king declared that having unrolled the scrolls that served as archives he had found a sum of about 3,500 thalaris, and that he was subtracting this sum from my accounts, and that, anyway, all Labatut's property ought really to go to him, all this being stated in a tone that admitted of no challenge. I pleaded that I had European creditors, producing my accounts as a final resort, and, under M. Ilg's remonstrances, the king consented hypocritically to give up three-eighths of his claim."

But he at once made up for this generosity by new deductions: to begin with, 2,500 thalaris for the expenses of maintaining the caravan which were due to the Hazage, then 3,000 more as pledges of Labatut's various accounts, etc.

In the end, Rimbaud was forced to accept what was rapidly becoming the obvious: Menelik had no money—or at least, was unwilling to spend any. Would he consider a payment in ivory, then? No, this was unacceptable at the rate offered, which was quite excessive.

A compromise, which he had no alternative but to accept, was found: Rimbaud would be given an I.O.U. for 9,866 thalaris (to which would be added interest, though this was reduced at the last minute). This I.O.U. would be redeemed at Harar by the king's cousin, the Ras Makonnen.

Did Rimbaud remember Alfred Bardey's gloomy predictions? In any case his correspondence with his mother and sister becomes sparse and laconic at this time: "I hope to be back in Aden around October, but everything takes so long in these filthy parts" (April 7, 1887).

It was not over yet. When he came back next day to collect the I.O.U., payable at Harar, accompanied by Ilg, he saw to his horror the helmet of M. Hénon and, behind it, "the burnous of the frenetic widow winding their way along the precipices." As he waited in the antechamber, his adversaries, who had got there first, were trying to persuade Menelik to add to his debt the 100 thalaris promised to Mme Labatut, for, of course, the collection for her had never been made. The king declared that he did not intend to transfer to his heirs the friendship that he had shown to Pierre Labatut, and, by way of proof, he immediately took back from the tearful widow the right to use the lands previously given to her husband.

In no time at all the news spread that the "Frangui" was paying all Labatut's debts. A horde of so-called creditors appeared as from nowhere, begging or threatening, "enough to make one pale with fright," Rimbaud remarks, widows of servants who had died in Labatut's service, to whom he had promised a gun or a piece of material—or who claimed repayments of loans. "These poor folk are always in good faith, so I let myself be moved and paid up," Rimbaud confesses. "Thus a sum of twenty thalaris was demanded by a certain M. Dubois, I saw that he had a right to it, and I paid up, adding by way of interest, a pair of shoes, since the poor devil complained of going about barefoot."

He had a curious mixture of charity and impatience: he could not stand long drawn-out negotiations, and he paid up as much to have done with the matter as out of pity. So he took refuge in his hut, but this offered no protection: "For example, a Dejach turned up at my hut, and sat down to drink my tej, praising the noble qualities of the *friend* (the late Labatut), and expressing the hope of finding the same virtues in me. Seeing a mule grazing on the grass outside, he exclaimed: 'That's the mule I gave Labatut!' (He did not say that the burnous on his back had been given him by Labatut.) Anyway, they would add, he owed me 70 thalers—or 50 or 60, etc.! And they would insist on these claims until I got rid of them with a 'Go to the King!' (Which is as much as to say: 'Go to the devil!')"

In the balance sheet of his disaster one reads:

"Various debts to the natives paid by me, for Labatut (and to Europeans) about Th. 120."

Had he extended his stay in Entoto he would have ended up with nothing; so he hastily requested a safe conduct from the king to reach Harar by the shortest possible route. When he had obtained it, Jules Borelli, who was very interested in the proposed itinerary, asked permission to accompany him, and this was granted.

They set out on May 1, 1887. "I remember how on the morning of my departure," Rimbaud noted. "while already moving N.N.E., I saw emerge from a bush a delegate from the wife of one of Labatut's friends, asking me in the name of the Virgin Mary for a sum of 19 thalers and, further off, a creature leapt off the top of a promontory wearing a sheepskin cape, asking me if I had paid 12 thalers to his brother, which had been borrowed by Labatut, etc. I yelled out to both these two that it was too late!" (letter to M. de Gaspary, November 9, 1887).

The track from Entoto to Harar (over 300 miles), known as the King's Road, was practically unknown; only one European had traveled on it during the previous year, the Italian doctor, Vincenzo Ragazzi, who traveled with Menelik's army. Rimbaud had tried to venture on this route when he had left Harar, but had been unable to get very far. The whole of the plain of Minjar, all the countries beyond Careyu and Itu, were completely unexplored. So, for Rimbaud, it was an exceptional opportunity, a deserved compensation after so many disappointments, and, for Borelli, a seasoned traveler, a pleasant bonus, for he liked Rimbaud's company ("Our pleasant and intelligent compatriot," he said of him).

This route was made up of eight stages of between 15 and 20 miles to the river Hawash and ten more to Harar. We have this information from an itinerary drawn up by Rimbaud that he obtained from Alfred Bardey. In this dry, brief document, there are no descriptions, only laconic details, such as: cultivated plateau, numerous cotton fields, scrub and mimosa woods, large forests and fine mountains opening out into panoramas, coffee plantations, etc.

If we want a vivid, picturesque account, we must turn to Borelli's Journal.[8] He is the poet, Rimbaud the scientist. Here, for example, is an abstract from the Journal: "But what an earthly paradise it is sometimes! Jasmine, eglantine, sycamore. The lianas interlace to form garlands of greenery that sway from the branches of magnificent zygbas, centuries-old olive trees, mulberries, and euphorbias of colossal size."

We are spared no incident: desertions of muleteers or guides, receptions laid on for them by notables, quarrels between natives who were hardly pleased at the arrival of these foreigners. On May 20, they crossed the battlefield of Chalanko, the scene of Menelik's victory, still strewn with the skeletons of those abandoned to the hyenas. A little further on, at Warra-Bellé, they were shown the tree trunk to which the Frenchman Lucereau had been tied when he was murdered.

Rimbaud was anxious to get to his destination as soon as possible. Borelli's diary entry for Saturday May 21 reads: "ARRO By midmorning we were on our way. M. Rimbaud went ahead. He wants to arrive this evening."

Harar gave great concern to both of them: the town had become a "cess-pit," ridden with famine, plague, looting, and crime: a silent, stinking town in which a few terrorized Greeks and Armenians lived behind barricades. Rimbaud was met by an additional scourge: Labatut's creditors had pursued him even that far!

Jules Borelli did not stay for long, and went back to Entoto, where he was able to get the king's permission to explore the southern provinces. Poor Rimbaud, however, had to wait—he was always waiting—for a good month to get his credit note paid.

He liked the Ras Makonnen's refinement and politeness: beside his thirty-five-year-old cousin, Menelik was a bumpkin.

As soon as he had his money, Rimbaud got out. He did not, of course, return by the northern road. He took the Zeila road, which he knew very well, and, after a fortnight's crossing of the desert, arrived in Aden on July 25, 1887.

One of his first tasks was to give an account of his operation to the French vice-consul at Aden. Indeed it was indispensable that his account should be clear and incontrovertible, for he had agreed to make certain payments in Shoa at the request of various people. He concludes a letter of July 30: "I have emerged from the operation with a 60 percent loss on my capital, not to mention twenty-one months of appalling exhaustion expended on this wretched affair."

The heat was getting intolerable: it was permanently between 50° and 60°C. It is understandable that Rimbaud, weakened by seven years of exhaustion and "the most abominable privations," as he puts it, should have felt the need for a change of air.

In early August 1887, disdaining old Europe, he left Aden for a few months rest in Egypt. At Obok, he embarked on a ship of the Compagnie nationale, with his servant Jami Wadai, who was then sixteen or seventeen, whom he had brought from Harar to save him from famine. At Messewa, which had been an Italian possession since 1884, and where he put into port, the *carabinieri* asked him for his identity papers. He had only letters of procuratory signed at the French consulate by himself and a certain Labatut, and two bills together worth 7,500 thalaris drawn on Italian and Indian traders. He was brought before the French vice-consul, Alexandre Merciniez, who asked for information about him from his colleague at Aden (August 5):

"A Monsieur Rimbaud, who claims to be a merchant at Harar and Aden, has arrived at Messewa on board the weekly packet from Aden. This Frenchman, who is tall, thin, with gray eyes, almost blond, but small moustaches, has been brought to me by the *carabinieri*. . . . I would be obliged to you, Monsieur le Consul, if you would give me information concerning this individual, who at first sight seems rather suspicious."

M. de Gaspary quickly reassured his colleague and Rimbaud, given a regular passport by the consulate at Messewa, continued on his way.

To make up for his blunder, Alexandre Merciniez recommended him to the Marquis Grimaldi-Régusse, a barrister at the court of appeal in Cairo: "It gives me great pleasure to recommend to you particularly M. Rimbaud, Arthur, a very honorable Frenchman, a merchant-explorer in Shoa and Harar, regions that he knows extremely well, where he has been living for over nine years. M. Rimbaud has gone to Egypt to rest a little after his long exertions: he will give you news of M. Borelli Bey's brother, whom he met in Shoa."

After stopping off at Suakin and Suez, where he met Lucien Labosse, the French vice-consul, he reached Cairo about August 20.

Jules Borelli had given him the address of his brother, Octave (Borelli Bey), a rich barrister in Cairo and contributor to *Le Bosphore égyptien*, a daily newspaper run by Barrière Bey.

Rimbaud, gripped once again by the journalistic passion of his youth, made contact at once with *Le Bosphore*, which, on August 22, announced: "M. Rimbaud, a French traveler and merchant in Shoa, arrived in Egypt a few days ago. We understand that M. Rimbaud will not be extending his stay here, and is arranging to go to the Sudan."

We know very little about his time in Cairo, except that he stayed at the Hôtel de l'Europe—and wrote a great deal.

First he recounted his misadventure in Shoa to his mother and sister: "If my partner had not died, I would have earned some thirty thousand francs, as it is I've ended up with the 15,000 F that I started with, after exhausting myself in the most horrible way for nearly two years. I really am very unlucky!"

He gives news of his health, which is not very good. He feels very weak and suffers from rheumatism in the left knee, in the back, and in the right shoulder. "My hair has turned absolutely gray," he says. "I sometimes think my very life is in danger." His resumption of contact with civilized life soon convinced him that he would never be able to adapt to it, and would be condemned forever to his savage hell: "So I must spend the rest of my days wandering, in exhaustion and privation, with no other prospect than that of dying in harness" (August 23). "Life here bores me and is too expensive" (August 25).

Since he always carried around with him on his belt 8 kilos of gold coin worth almost 16,000 F, he considered that it would be more practical to invest his money for six months in the Crédit Lyonnais at an interest of 4 percent. The bank receipt for the transaction has been found.[9]

His future seemed precarious and uncertain: "I cannot go to Europe for many reasons; to begin with, the winter would kill me." Where should he go? Arabia? Abyssinia? Zanzibar, where he had recommendations? China, perhaps, or Japan? It is likely that he would have caught the steamer for Zanzibar that was passing between September 15 and 18, had his mother sent him in time the 500 francs he needed if he were not to draw money out of his account. But the money arrived too late—or did not arrive at all.

He was gratified to see his letter to the editor of *Le Bosphore égyptien* relating his journey in Shoa appear in the numbers for August 5 and 27, 1887. This highly interesting letter is a general summary of the political, geographical, and economic situation of Shoa. The author is discreet about his disappointments, but he provides authoritative advice concerning the possibilities of penetrating into Shoa, stressing that, thanks to the route he discovered in the company of Jules Borelli, "notre aimable et courageux compatriote," huge fertile territories, "well adapted to European colonization" could be linked to the coast in a little over a month by caravan.

Behind this report one senses a clear-sighted, confident man, well versed in things African (he was one of the first to see the expansion that Djibouti would undergo if a railroad were built into Shoa). The plain style is perfectly adapted to the subject; it is that of a man of action, not a theoretician or a poet.

Le Bosphore égyptien was satisfactory, but Rimbaud was aiming higher: on August 26, he wrote to the Geographical Society proposing to submit a detailed memorandum of the road from Entoto to Harar, for a fee that he himself fixed. The same day he sent Alfred Bardey a summary of the eighteen stages of the itinerary. His very pleasant accompanying letter is laconic about his own bad luck: "My undertaking turned out very badly, because I had as my partner that idiot Labatut, who, to crown it all, has died, which has landed me with his family in Shoa and all his creditors." The end of the letter is rather surprising: "I shall be at your service whenever you have any undertaking in which I might be of use. I cannot stay here because I am used to a free life. Be kind enough to think of me."

Alfred Bardey found the itinerary from Entoto to Harar so interesting that, on September 22, he sent a copy to the Geographical Society, of which he was a corresponding member. Rimbaud's account was examined at the session of November 4, 1887, and published in the record of the society's proceedings.

It was then that the general secretary, Charles Maunoir, remembered the letter from Rimbaud, and replied to him on October 4, expressing regret that he could not accept Rimbaud's offer "on account of the strict economies that have been imposed on the ministry for some months." The suggestion that he made to Rimbaud that he apply for an official mission from the Ministry of Education might have been of interest to him were it not for those "strict economies." So Rimbaud did not pursue this idea.

The fact is that the Geographical Society had obtained from Alfred Bardey, for no fee, a valuable report for which the author was asking a fee that was considered too high.

It is even possible that Bardey may have taken credit himself for discovering the itinerary from Entoto to Harar. Indeed in 1898 he writes in his "Notes on Harar": "This route was taken by M. Arthur Rimbaud, who was my employee in Harar."[10] And he adds that the Rimbaud in question is "the well-known decadent poet."

At the time, Rimbaud's article made quite a stir among the specialists: geographers quoted it in Germany (Peterman's *Geographische Mitteilungen*, 1887), in Austria (*Das Ausland*, 1888), in England (*Proceedings of the Royal Geographical Society*, 1888), in Italy (*Bolletino della Società Geografica Italiana*, 1888), but it is probable that he was unaware of his reputation; his destiny was to pass glory by without recognizing it.

At the end of September 1887 he finally made up his mind: he would go to Syria, on Menelik's behalf. He was to buy four strong stallion asses and bring them back to Shoa, where the mules were of a small breed. With this in view, he obtained a passport for Syria from the French consulate at Beyrut. This document has been found.[11] It is interesting for the information it gives of Rimbaud (height: 1.80m), and confirms the presence in Cairo of young Jami.

Although the consul's response to the undertaking was favorable, as soon as he had received his passport, Rimbaud changed direction: he went not to Beyrut, but to Aden.

17

Rimbaud, Independent Merchant

at Harar

Why Aden?

Because, to begin with, the Syrian deal was not ready, and he could not see himself going back to Shoa, crossing deserts, and risking his life in order to bring four he-asses to Menelik. Secondly, it was not out of the question that he might return into the Bardey fold.

On his arrival, a surprise awaited him: a certain A. Deschamps of Aden had lodged a complaint against him at the French consulate at Aden (October 28, 1887). Again it concerned the Labatut affair. This Deschamps, it seemed, had entrusted Labatut with the task of paying 1,810 thalaris to his correspondent in Shoa, a certain Audon. Now, Rimbaud had done nothing about it. So the vice-consul, M. de Gaspary, asked him to explain his conduct and to give him a detailed account of his operation, with documentary evidence. On November 3, Rimbaud handed him a brief account, without records of payments, in which we find the following mention: "Paid to M. Audon for Labatut's debt: Th. 1,088." But this was not convincing proof, since M. Audon persisted in affirming that he had received nothing. On November 4, Rimbaud informed Mgr. Taurin-Cahagne of the incident and asked him to arbitrate. This is what had happened. Since his credits had been reduced by Menelik, who had shamefully robbed him, Rimbaud, who had very little money remaining when he left Shoa, decided to reduce the debts of third parties that he had inherited in the same proportion, applying a sort of bankruptcy settlement. Since this M. Audon had protested, Rimbaud asked Makonnen, with whom he had an account, to pay 866 thalaris (47 percent of

M. Deschamps' debt) to M. Audon. Makonnen sent him a receipt for 866 thalaris "for M. Audon," who in fact never received anything.

From then on, Rimbaud suspected Makonnen of having robbed both himself and M. Audon by keeping the money.

Rimbaud now complained to the Aden consul that he had had to give up two-thirds of what was due to him to various creditors.

"That is because you handled it badly," the consul replied (November 8 1887). "So you have only yourself to blame."

Thereupon Rimbaud picked up his pen again and gave a vivid account of his dealings with Labatut's creditors (or so-called creditors): this was the purpose of his letter of November 9 to which I have already referred.

It was very amusing, but it did not clear the matter up.

Rimbaud may have believed that it had. But, in 1890, when he went back to Harar, he was met with fresh troubles, again concerning Labatut's debts.

On January 8, 1891, Menelik seized the merchandise that he had stored with Ilg at Entoto, because, it seems, he owed 100 thalaris to Labatut's child! Deschamps immediately sent an emissary, Chefneux, to Harar, with the mission of joining in the seizure. Rimbaud showed him Makonnen's receipt, and proved that in all he had paid M. Audon 80 percent of M. Deschamps' debt. The investigation proved that Makonnen had used the funds to pay off another of Labatut's debts, this time to the Ras Govana—for he did not know who to give this money to! Since no conclusion emerged from all these investigations, Deschamps returned to the attack some time later and sent Chefneux's brother-in-law, a certain Teillard, to settle the matter, which had been dragging on for five years, once and for all. Rimbaud was forced to give in, but limited the damage to 600 thalaris (plus the 100 thalaris for Labatut's child, which he could not escape). Deschamps freed him of his debt on February 19, 1891.

Let us return to Autumn 1887.

Since the only possible deals were arms deals (Menelik had told the Europeans, "If you do not bring me weapons, I shall forbid your trading"), Rimbaud had the idea of importing into Shoa material required in the manufacture of weapons and cartridges. Why should he not set up as an industrialist at Ankober? If he managed to interest a few capitalists in the affair, he would be able to manage the factory. But such a project was subject to permission to import weapons. Now, since Soleillet's rifles, which had long remained in abeyance at Tajura, had finally been taken into Shoa, was not this proof of a more flexible attitude toward the arms trade? In reality, nothing had changed: the Anglo-French convention of November 16, 1886, forbidding the conveyance of any military equipment, was still in force, except in a few very specific cases. However, France seemed to be less strict in the application of the principle.

To test the water, Rimbaud put in an official request to the minister of the navy and colonies, Félix Faure, supported by the deputy for Vouziers, M. Fagot. The request was, he said, to deliver to Shoa, "a Christian country well-disposed to the Europeans," materials for the manufacture of arms ammunitions, without the factory ever leaving French hands.

The reply (January 18 1888) was brief and negative: it would be against the treaties.

Rimbaud was not particularly surprised: he had never expected much success in that quarter. The attempt, he said, had only cost him paper.

The extent to which the official doctrine was flexible was to be shown later: on May 2, 1888, Rimbaud received from the ministry a counterorder—therefore an authorization—which was annulled a few days later, on May 15.

But this game was no longer of any interest to Rimbaud, who was required elsewhere. His idea was to be exploited by Ilg, who, not without difficulty, set up a cartridge-factory at Ankober.

At the end of 1887, then, Rimbaud was still in Aden, with no commitments, undecided, and dissatisfied. In his idleness, he was seized again by the demon of the pen. "I have written up an account of my journey in Abyssinia, for the Geographical Society," he admitted to his family on December 15. "I have sent articles to *Le Temps*, *Le Figaro*, etc. I am also going to send to *Le Courrier des Ardennes* a few interesting accounts of my travels in East Africa. I don't think that can do any harm." But nothing appeared. The Europeans were quietly making fun of him: "Rimbaud is amusing himself writing cock-and-bull stories for the press," Soleillet wrote to Ilg, on February 13, 1888.

On the matter of *Le Temps*, Berrichon says that Rimbaud offered his services to the paper, using a recommendation from Paul Bourde, a former fellow pupil at the Collège de Charleville. But the terms suggested seemed to have been regarded as too high, and nothing came of it. Berrichon quotes a letter (undated) from Bourde to Rimbaud telling him—by way of consolation—that in Paris he was already famous. "This small group that recognizes you as its master, without knowing what has become of you, hopes that you will reappear one day and drag them out of their obscurity."[1]

The authenticity of this letter is debatable (since former fellow pupils would use the "*tu*" form, and Bourde addresses Rimbaud as "*vous*").

The economic slump—one can even speak of paralysis—consequent on the political anarchy, the policy of each one for himself practiced by the great powers, persisted. Everywhere there were shortages, if not famine, insecurity, if not war (the Italian-Ethiopian conflict was brewing). "It's the invasion of the Europeans, from every quarter, that has caused this," Rimbaud wrote home on January 25, 1888. "The British in Egypt, the Italians at Messewa, the French at Obok, the British at Berbera, etc. And it is said that the Spanish, too, are about to occupy one of the ports around the straits! Every government has sunk millions (in all a few billions) along these accursed, desolate coasts, where the natives wander for months on end without food and water, in the most terrible climate on the face of the earth."

There then appeared on the horizon a possible undertaking that consisted of conveying a large caravan (of over two hundred camels) of merchandise and weapons, on behalf of a colleague, Armand Savouré, from the coast to Harar (from there, no doubt, someone else would continue the journey into Shoa). For this routine job, a commission of 2,000 F was agreed, plus a percentage on the resale of the Remington rifles.

Rimbaud set off around February 14, 1888—and not in late March, as Miss Starkie says on the evidence of a letter from Savouré dated January 27 informing Rimbaud that a dow would be waiting for him between Doralé and Ambadu from March 15 onwards. The program was quite simply postponed by a month. The route followed, under the direction of Savouré's servant, Ali Fara, was a "slave route," and therefore a secret one.

Rimbaud was back in Aden on March 14. In a letter to Ilg, written on March 29, he provides all the necessary details about this trip, which, apparently, went off without incident: "Got back to Aden two weeks ago, and found your friendly letter. Thanks. In fact I have already made the journey to Harar, six days there and five back, eight staying there, and about ten days in the dows and steamers (for this is the longest and most boring part). The whole campaign took a month."

It was a lightning campaign, conducted at top speed, and Savouré was very pleased with the outcome. "With you everything works at full steam ahead," Ilg wrote to Rimbaud, "an excessively rare thing this side of Africa" (April 27, 1888). What was he to do now? He was not going to bore himself at Aden or spend his time journeying through hell on horseback or mule, wearing himself out for a handful of thalers. He did not remain inactive; patiently he was building the future to which he was condemned: he would go back and live at Harar—this time independently—where he would be the recognized agent of a respected merchant, César Tian.

At this time, Savouré was counting on Rimbaud for a new mission. This time it was simply a matter of recruiting camels on the coast, to join up with a certain Maconel, with a view to forming a large arms caravan (3,000 rifles, 50,000 cartridges) that was to be delivered to Mohammed Abu Bekr. There were strict instructions: above all do not accompany the caravan—because of the Italians, it was said officially, in fact because the dealings and itineraries of the Abu Bekrs, who were active slave traders, had to be kept secret.

This mission no longer held any interest at all for Rimbaud, who, though he had received 2,000 F on account, did absolutely nothing. So the criticisms addressed to him by Savouré (April 26, 1888) were justified: "I consider that your mission has not been carried out, especially because you have not been affirmative enough, and not trusted my instructions."

Quite rightly, Rimbaud did not wish to become compromised in a shady deal. In any case, when Savouré wrote this letter to him, he was already in sight of Harar.

At the same time, in the opposite direction, another caravan of ivory and slaves, led by Ibrahim Abu Bekr, Mohammed's brother, arrived on the coast from Shoa and Harar.

A secret report of May 22, 1888, from the Italian consul general in Aden, Cecchi, addressed to the minister of foreign affairs, Crispi, stated: "From confidential information given me by the governor of this place [Aden], and other information obtained directly at Zeila, I have learned of a large caravan led by Ibrahim Abu Bekr (one of the many sons of the well-known late Abu Bekr, first emir, then pasha of Leila). The caravan was accompanied by a French merchant, M. Rembau, one of the most intelligent and active agents of the French government in this area."[2]

Naturally enough, the British governor in Aden sent the Foreign Office (June 16 1888) a similar report (from which the date May 10 is absent, and in which the Frenchman referred to emerges as "Remban," rather than "Rem-

bau"). Miss Starkie discovered this report and concluded from it, in her book
Rimbaud in Abyssinia that Rimbaud, in partnership with the worst "bucca-
neers" of the Red Sea, had taken to slave trading and other undesirable practices. The information was false, but this "discovery" caused a sensation—
until Mario Matucci reestablished the truth.[3]

The fact that Rimbaud's name was cited in so uncomplimentary a manner in a British report should come as no surprise, for, as we have seen, he
did not have a very high opinion of British policy; any bit of gossip likely to
discredit him would have served as a weapon in the petty war of influence
between the British and the French in that part of the world.

One does wonder what sudden madness could have taken root in Rimbaud's head to make him fall into such a hornet's nest, for it would have
placed him beyond the pale among the traders who gravitated around Menelik. Indeed no Europeans had ever had anything whatsoever to do with the
slave trade, which was a monopoly of the Abu Bekrs (old Abu Bekr had died
in 1885, leaving eleven sons!), who, in any case, would not have tolerated
any competition in their secret dealings.

If we return to chronology, we can demonstrate the falseness of the British accusation.

We have at our disposal an irrefutable document concerning Rimbaud's
journey from Aden to Harar, namely, the diary of Ugo Ferrandi, who accompanied him:

> *Friday April 13. Today we set sail on a steamer built in
> England, which is not quite, I think, a 200-tonner. . . .
> Among the passengers for Zeila are M. Rimbaud, the two
> Righas [Dimitri and Athanasius, who may have been relatives
> of Constantin Righas, whom Rimbaud had known at Harar
> in 1881], myself and a young man with a black beard, Cristos
> Mussaia, a Greek.*
>
> *Saturday April 14. We are at Berbera.*
>
> *Rimbaud, Dimitri Righas, and I went ashore and into
> the native city where, in a large hut, we drank very good tea,
> made by a Turkish planter.*
>
> *Tuesday, April 17 (at Beila). In the evening I am seeing
> MM. Sotiros [sic] and Rimbaud.*
>
> *Tuesday April 24. A Somali brings a letter from M. Rim-
> baud, from Ensa, all is well.*[4]

As soon as he reached Harar, Rimbaud informed Alfred Bardey, who sent the following note to the Geographical Society (June 4): "I have just received from Harar a letter dated May 3 from Arthur Rimbeaud, who tells me: 'I have just arrived at Harar. The rain is extraordinarily heavy this year, and my journey was accompanied by a succession of cyclones, but the rain in the lowlands will cease in two months. The Dejash Makonnen has just returned from an expedition to the Guerris, where he has learned very little. And he is extremely angry.' "

Rimbaud's letter to his family, written some days later, on May 15 ("I am back here again and expect to stay here for a long time") clearly proves that, five days later, he could not have been on the coast with Ibrahim Abu Bekr's slave caravan.

So Rimbaud is now "back" at Harar, living in a small rented house (which disappeared long ago, but of which we have a photograph,[5] in which he lived so to speak alone—Sotiro had settled at Zeila, the Righas brothers, Dimitri and Athanasius, were engaged in their own affairs—alone, that is, with his servant, Jami Wadai, who was later to marry. He never seems to have had a permanent staff: he took on laborers when he needed them. He preferred to be alone, dependent on no one. His relations with César Tian, his colleague in Aden, were limited to the strict minimum. He was just the sort of man Rimbaud needed: placid, a little slow perhaps, but dependable. He always had excellent relations with him: he did not keep an eye on him or issue orders. Moreover Tian did not travel, which was no bad thing. How different he was from the Bardeys—they were honest enough, of course, but they could never take criticism, and were rather too fond of making it clear that they were the bosses. This is proof that, providing things ran along correct lines, it was still possible to get on with Rimbaud. In any case, he never bore a grudge for long: despite past disagreements, he corresponded and had dealings with the Bardey brothers—when it pleased him to do so.

For three years, he was to occupy at Harar, the pivot between the coast and Shoa, a situation of vital importance. He was the only Frenchman—apart from one of the fathers of the Catholic mission. He was constantly in business contact with the twenty or so Europeans living in the region and the travelers who came to prospect it for economic, geographical, or political ends. He bought in Aden and sold in the capital, or the reverse, acting in turn as agent, banker, or warehouseman. "We import silks, cotton goods, thalaris, and certain other objects," he writes on August 4, 1888. "We export coffee, gums, perfumes, ivory, and gold, which comes from a great distance."

The list is incomplete: the "certain other objects" consisted of a whole range of things: Hardware (saucepans, goblets, various utensils), glassware (pearls, ornaments, imitation jewelry), and small instruments (weighing scales). Among the exports one should add leathers, and the skins of goats and monkeys. The main perfume was musk of civet.

He received and recorded merchandise coming from Aden or Zeila, and concerned himself with their resale—very little on the spot, usually at Ankober, where the king was a big customer. Almost all his cheap goods were bought by Ilg. At Harar and the surrounding district he bought coffee and ivory, loaded the caravans bound for the coast, but did not accompany them: for that he used "abbans" (native drivers).

He constantly complained of loneliness, as if he lived as a hermit: "deserts populated with stupid negroes, without roads, without mail, without travelers: what can I write about all that? That one is bored, that one is getting more and more stupid; that one has had enough of it, but that one cannot give it up, etc., etc.! That's all, all that can be said about it then; and since that is of no interest whatsoever to anyone else, one must remain silent."

Far from being isolated, he received messages or visits every day. All the merchants who were going to the coast, or who were on their way back from it, called on him. He also received visits from French or foreign travelers. For several days or even weeks, he would put up Borelli, Savouré, Ilg (late 1888), and a few Italians.

He belonged to a very active European community, which was also very closely knit, as one had to be in face of the arbitrary caprices of Menelik and his functionaries.

He was at the center of a network of information that functioned almost as rapidly as if there had been telephone and telegraph.

His best friend was Alfred Ilg, the Swiss engineer, who was to become Menelik's prime minister. Rimbaud liked his overwhelming, open friendliness, which made a great change from the devious Abyssinians or reticent Europeans whom he dealt with throughout the day.

Thus, one day, after receiving a cargo of miscellaneous objects to be sold, Ilg replied to Rimbaud:

> *I have just looked over the marvelous bazaar you've just sent me. Are you trying to ruin me? It's common enough nowadays. Propagandizing with rosaries, crosses, religious statues, etc., just when His Majesty has given the Rev. Father Joa-*

chim strict orders to return to Harar, is more dangerous than a journey into the desert. For the time being, I wouldn't even dare to give your objects away, lest the Abyssinians took me for a Capuchin in disguise. . . . Selling notebooks at 2½ per thaler to people who can't write, and don't even know the secret uses of such instruments, is really asking too much. It's a great pity you haven't got a few hundred bits of carved mother of pearl and boot jacks to send me. . . . Lastly, my dear Monsieur Rimbaud, be so kind as to send me things I can sell, otherwise I shall send your bric-à-brac back, at your own risk, together with some of God's thunder (September 19 1889).

Another day he is berating Rimbaud for his gloomy pessimism:

We have absolutely no news here of the grrreat embassy [Makonnen was in Italy negotiating a loan and buying weapons—since the Italians were hoping to get a protectorate over the whole of Abyssinia]. I'm waiting for interesting details from you, since you're such a good storyteller when you want to be, but it seems that your wonderful deals have completely deprived you of what good humor was left to you. Come now, my dear Monsieur Rimbaud, we only live once, so take advantage of it and send your heirs to the devil. If nothing's doing any more, we'll form a partnership to bother the others, but not each other, understood. Today, with a mechanical steam plow one could soon get rich here—one no longer knows what to eat. Think about it and come here and plant your cabbages—with the help of modern mechanics.

It will be noticed that the style of Rimbaud's letters to Ilg is more fanciful, more caustic, too, than the one he employs for other correspondents; only with him does he make an effort.[6]

On the other hand, his epistolary relations with Armand Savouré were polite, but little more: there is never an amusing or personal word. Once he quarreled with him over some business involving coffee that he had had to buy with great difficulty in order to give it to him in payment for merchandise. But Savouré had refused the coffee, demanding to be paid in thalaris, imported from Aden. We have found the draft upon pink copying paper of the letter that Rimbaud sent him—or did not send. It amounts to a page of violent abuse ("I don't need your filthy coffee"). This diatribe did not impress Savouré, who, on May 4, 1890, replied: "As for your letter, thank you for your advice, I realize that, making allowances for your usual exaggeration, there is some truth in what you say, but you would change your opinion if you knew what I am hoping to do, if those bandits don't force me to leave here before getting much further with it."

Among Rimbaud's other correspondents and colleagues, apart from Jules Borelli, one should mention: Antoine Brémond, the doyen of the French in Abyssinia, a lovable individual, widely regarded as a sage; Eloy Pino, a former deep-sea captain, a representative of the firm Tramier-Lafarge of Marseille, who had settled in Ankober, and acted as an adviser to the Ras Govana; Léon Chefneux, who was Soleillet's representative before working for Deschamps of Aden; E. Laffineur, who went to Abyssinia from Fécamp to buy collectors' weapons and who, seized by the fever for trade of all kinds, stayed there; Bidault, whom Rimbaud made fun of, in the friendliest way ("He's always lost in contemplation," Rimbaud said of him to Borelli on February 25, 1889), and who had to leave the stage in June 1889, as a result of serious trouble; Ernest Zimmerman and Appenzeller, compatriots of Alfred Ilg, the first a joiner, the second a mechanic, both attached to the royal court.

Last, among the many Italians who traveled up and down the country as merchants, political agents in disguise, engineers, or geographers, we should mention Ugo Ferrandi, Cesare Nezarini, Luigi Robecchi-Brichetti, Ottorino Rosa, Armando Rondali, Naufragio, Traversi.

As we can see, Rimbaud could hardly complain of loneliness.

At first, business went well. "The commercial situation in Shoa isn't bad," Rimbaud wrote to Ilg on June 25, 1888. "The obsession with guns is more frenetic than ever. Relations with Shoa from here are fairly active, and the road from here to Zeila is a good one." It was not always to be so. On December 23, 1889, a caravan transporting merchandise and 25,000 thalaris (10,000 of which were intended for Rimbaud) was attacked near Ensa, between Zeila and Harar. Two French Capuchins (Father Ambroise de Cirières and Brother Etienne d'Etoile) were murdered, as they were resting in their tent, together with two Greeks and several men of the escort. César Tian, fearing that Mme Rimbaud might learn of the incident in the newspaper, was thoughtful enough to reassure her by letter on January 8, 1890.

The sky soon clouded over.

First the political events.

In January 1887 the Italians had declared war on John, emperor of Ethiopia: this was the signal that was to trigger off a sequence of events and put an end to the rivalry between the emperor and King Menelik. The latter greedily accepted the Italians' gifts and weapons, but did not give them his alliance in exchange. Their scheming attitude irritated the emperor, who wanted to lead a national resistance against Italian intentions. Furthermore, he accused Menelik of getting the king of Gojam to rise up against him. Despite the protestations of friendship on both sides, a confrontation of the two armies was expected. Then, at a highly opportune time for Menelik, the Muslim integrists (Mahdists) revolted. The emperor set out to quell them, but, though victorious, he was seriously wounded at Metemma and died the next day, May 10, 1889.

Here is Rimbaud's version of events, as recounted in a letter to his family dated May 18: "You must have read in the newspaper that the emperor (what an emperor!) John is dead, killed by the Mahdists. We here also depended indirectly on this emperor. However, we depend directly on King Menelik of Shoa, who himself paid tribute to the Emperor John. Last year, our Menelik revolted against this frightful John and they got ready to bite off each other's noses, when the said emperor took it into his head to go first and give a sound thrashing to the Mahdists, near Metemma. He stayed there: let him go to the devil!"

Although John had appointed the Ras Mangash to succeed him, Menelik managed to impose his will and was crowned negus (emperor), King of Kings, Lion of Judah, on November 3, 1889, in the church of Entoto.

Subsequently, he needed all his tortuous Machiavellianism to stem the greedy activities of the Italians—especially in the northern province of Eritrea. On May 2, 1889, he signed with Count Antonelli the treaty of Ucciali, a masterpiece of hypocrisy that committed him without committing him. However, each side remained convinced that sooner or later war would break out (as it did in 1896).

These events did not leave local commerce unaffected. Pride made Menelik authoritarian, distrustful, and impossible in his dealings with the Europeans, whom he detested beneath his paternalistic exterior. He preferred the Italians, who lavished presents and advantages on him. The other Europeans were there simply to fill his coffers through ever more exorbitant taxes.

To this were added the exactions of the Harar functionaries, who, in the absence of Makonnen, who had left for Italy, had set up new customs duties on the entry and departure of merchandise.

Last, in September 1889 Menelik took it into his head to levy an exceptional contribution on all foreigners and force them to agree to an obligatory loan.

A "horrible tyranny" was how Rimbaud described this to Ilg in a letter of September 7, 1889: "For a month now they have been sequestering, cudgeling, dispossessing, imprisoning the people of the town, in order to extort from them as much as possible of the sum demanded. Meanwhile, every inhabitant has already paid three or four times over. All the Europeans are treated the same as the Muslims and are covered by this tax. Two hundred thalaris have been demanded from me, and I've already paid half of it and I'm afraid I'll be forced to lend them money, 4,000 thalaris, in the most arbitrary, most piratical manner—an incident that is the subject of the enclosed demand, and I shall be infinitely obliged to you if you would present it to the king on my behalf."

The protest fell on deaf ears.

Indeed the situation was "abominable," for the king's functionaries took money with menaces, without issuing a receipt, without giving the slightest guarantee, without fixing a time by which repayment of the loan would be made. "I find all this highly discouraging," Rimbaud concluded, "and, if it continues, I shall find it impossible to stay on."

In the midst of these storms and difficulties, which were as unexpected as they were disagreeable, he tried to keep a cool head.

Everyone regarded him as an honest, scrupulous, methodical man, who was as demanding of himself as he was of others. His accounts were impeccably kept—and God knows they were complicated enough, as a result of the endless variations in the exchange rate at Aden, Harar, or Obok, and the mobility of the customs duties.

Mgr. Jarosseau, an accountant and an ascetic combined, told the Tharaud brothers: "He led the simplest of lives. How many times have I seen him walking behind his mules and asses, carrying in his pocket no other food than a little grilled millet!"[7] "He lived a chaste and sober life, to be more precise, if I may employ this comparison, he lived like a Benedictine."[8]

He was a methodical businessman. Through the rectitude of his character, Jules Borelli wrote to Paterne Berrichon, he was able to gain the respect of the Abyssinian chiefs.[9]

But then, in a letter sent from him to Ilg on December 20, 1889, in the midst of the usual details of orders or acknowledgement of receipts, one reads the following sentence, which has been much commented upon: "I would confirm very seriously my request for a very good mule and two slave boys." Ilg replied on August 23, 1890 with a blank refusal: "I've looked for a good mule for you. . . . As for the slaves, forgive me, but I cannot concern myself with that. I have never bought slaves and I am not going to start now. I fully recognize your good intentions, but I will never do it, even for myself."

So, Rimbaud is accused once again of trafficking in human flesh— caught in the act as it were. He bought and sold slaves to whoever wanted them, it has been said, not without some bad faith and a great deal of ignorance, for we know that the private trade in slaves was extremely small in Abyssinia. Europeans reacted almost unanimously as Ilg had done: there were very few indeed who, trying to get servants at the best possible price, asked for slaves. Signor E. Emanuelli, for example, has shown that Augusto Franzoj had three slaves whom he treated and paid like ordinary native servants.[10]

It should be added that in Shoa slavery was nothing like it was in ancient Rome: no one knew who was really free and who was not. Corporal punishment was unknown. "The slave is free," Jules Borelli wrote to André Tian, César's son, on March 28, 1939, "works very little, and always has plenty to eat, for his master doesn't have the right to dismiss him."[11]

Rimbaud's request for slaves for domestic service must, then, be seen in its right perspective, as that of a venial sin.

Another reproach made about him in his lifetime by Ilg (October 8, 1889) concerned the deplorable state of his caravans, the animals of which arrived hungry and wounded. Rimbaud protested, referring to his well known "generosity." But it was probably not his fault in any case; his drivers, out of greed, must have neglected the animals in their care. This seems much more likely than a petty, stupid, meanness unworthy of a man like Rimbaud.

He had all the qualities required of a boss: a sense of order, methodicalness, foresight, humanity. However, he did lack one quality, and that was consistency: he could be moody and unpredictable.

His good humor generally took the form of making fun of people: "I think I may add," Alfred Bardey wrote to Berrichon, "that his caustic, biting wit made him many enemies. He was never able to rid himself of that poor, wicked, satirical mask behind which he concealed his very real kindness. He scratched a great deal, but never did much harm, except to himself, as a repercussion of his cruel mockery, which certain travelers in Shoa and Harar still remember to this day" (July 7, 1897).[12]

People liked having him as their guest because his brilliance amused at others' expense. "With your details concerning M. Bidault, you have amused divinely," Ilg wrote to him on June 16, 1889, "and I regret not being able to portray him as you do. If I had, I would certainly have had great success."

Armand Savouré has spoken of his letters "written in a really hilarious style." "We would gather round to read his letters and he never failed to amuse us. A man of dry humor, I have seldom seen him very gay, but he had a talent for delighting his audience with stories and anecdotes told in words so funny that one wondered where he found them."[13]

The explorer Luigi Robecchi-Brichetti, in a work published in 1896 (*Nell'Harar*, Milan), has an agreeable description of Rimbaud, who, after abandoning his pen, went to seek his ideal in Africa, without losing his wit, his brilliance, his "skill in the truly French art of conversation."

He retained, deep-down, certain childlike qualities, like his way of dismissing a Bedouin, looking at him critically, or sticking his tongue out at him when his back was turned.[14]

One could quote innumerable incidents described by Luigi Robecchi-Brichetti. I shall confine myself to this passage from one of his letters to a friend (December 31 1888): "We spent Christmas in very good, very merry company. We celebrated it in my house, with the engineer Ilg, who had arrived here the day before. Father Joachim of the Missions, M. Rimbaud an experienced merchant, as well as a traveler and very distinguished writer, M. Bidault, a photographer, and two other Italian friends, a certain Rosa representing the firm of Bienenfeld of Aden, and the eccentric, delightful Ferrandi, who has been here for some time, trying to arrange a few small commercial speculations."[15]

Similar celebrations must have taken place at Easter 1889, since Rimbaud wrote to Ugo Ferrandi on April 30: "Nothing new here: the orgies of Easter week are over."

But good moods were followed by bad, and in his periods of depression Rimbaud proved irritable, bad-tempered, unpleasant, forever complaining of his lot, finding everything around him sordid and disgusting, as Alfred Bardey wrote to Berrichon on December 9, 1897.[16]

The same Bardey, whom Berrichon had asked to write the preface to Rimbaud's letters from Africa, declined this honor with the following excuse: "I don't want Rimbaud to come and haunt me at night. He was irritating [the word *"désagréable"* has been scratched out] when he was alive" (same letter of December 9).

Armand Savouré, who knew him well, wrote to him one day (December 10, 1889): "I have something of the opposite fault from you: instead of believing that all men are knaves, I tend all too easily to think that they are all honest." This is the same reproach that Verlaine made of his "disgust with everything and everybody." And his "perpetual anger with everything" (letter of December 12, 1875).

Then, again, there are innumerable examples of his unsociability.

One day he agreed to join a hunting party organized by a group of Europeans, but, in the evening, when they all met, he was no longer to be found; he had gone home alone, without warning anybody (statement by G. L. Guigniony, one of Savouré's young representatives, quoted by Pierre Ripert).[17]

Once Jules Borelli had been staying with Rimbaud at his invitation, and just as he was leaving and his mules were packed, Rimbaud tried to get him to sweep the house! Borelli did not take kindly to this order, which was not a joke, and addressed his host in "unseemly language," for which he later apologized (letter of July 26, 1888).

But the incident that caused most stir was that of the poisoned dogs.

Since dogs soiled with their excrement the skins that he was drying outside his warehouses, Rimbaud poisoned a great many of them. It is also said that sheep died from this poison, in addition to those who ate them, "hyenas or Greeks" (G. L. Guigniony).

It is all no doubt exaggerated. Nevertheless he nearly went—or did go—to prison.

The story caused a great deal of amusement, and since gossip traveled fast from Harar to Shoa, echoes of it came back to Rimbaud himself: "We'll chat a great deal when I see you," Brémond wrote to him on February 10, 1889, "and decide if there is anything we can do together, providing you don't go on poisoning all the dogs in Harar, beginning with the hyenas, the sheep, and even the Greeks. The last seem to have satisfied your vendetta, and, by ricochet, mine (take, of course, only what is there to be taken)."

Savouré is more brutal (April 11, 1889): "And what is all this about your being locked up in jail. It seems that one now speaks of Rimbaud or the terror of the dogs."

Such actions should be attributed to a certain impetuosity of character, rather than to cruelty. We should, in any case, temper our judgment by recognizing that he was much given to helping those around him. This has to be said, because it is true—though, of course, we must avoid the opposite excess, that of portraying him as some kind of angel of charity or saint.

Alfred Bardey wrote to Berrichon: "He was helpful and charitable especially to those poor ex-patriots who had gone off to seek a quick fortune, and who, completely disillusioned or broken, wanted simply to get back home as quickly as possible. His charity, which was considerable and very discreet, was probably one of the few things he did without sneering or claiming to be disgusted" (July 10, 1897).[18]

He was just a good, kindly man, easily moved to pity. As he wrote to his family on February 25, 1890, "In the country and on the road I enjoy a certain consideration on account of the way I treat people. I've never done any harm to anyone. On the contrary, I have done some good when the opportunity has arisen and it's the only thing that gives me pleasure."

He was surrounded by the most frightful poverty, more unbearable than any he had encountered in Europe. So he had plenty of opportunity of indulging this pleasure: to one he would give a few rupees, to another a little grilled millet, to a third a shirt.

His friendship with the members of the Catholic Mission—the example of their devotion, rather than any indoctrination, to which he was resistant—may have strengthened him in this course.

The Mission, set up in April 1881, occupied a two-story, clay-and-wattle house[19], comprising a chapel, a meeting hall, a school, a dispensary, together with a number of outhouses, and a small farm. It was not a very large community, consisting of half-a-dozen priests and brothers, Italian, Spanish, or French—Joachim, Césaire, Ferdinand, Julien, Ernest, Louis de Gonzague, the future Mgr. Lasserre, and a few nuns.

The most noteworthy figure in this community was Father André (Jarosseau), who, in 1900, was to succeed Mgr. Taurin-Cahagne as bishop of the Gallas.[20]

The activities consisted in giving religious instruction to about twenty children—especially those who had come from other (Coptic) provinces, for, at Harar, the dominant religion was Muslim, caring for the sick, making themselves useful whenever possible.

Rimbaud had good neighborly relations with the Mission. "He would come over to the Mission from time to time," Mgr. Jarosseau told Henriette Célarié. "Knowing how poor we were, he would bring samples that he got from France. Our sisters would turn them into ornaments for the altar. We used to say that he had missed his vocation, and that he should have been a Trappist or Carthusian."[21]

Both sides were careful to avoid any theological discussion. Their conversations were about more immediate concerns: the Europeans had to display their solidarity and defend themselves against the whims of Menelik and his functionaries.

All this represented the "Gospel" side. There was also a "Koran" side.

I have already remarked that he had acquired, or tried to acquire, the serenity and fatalism of the Muslims. He had read and assimilated the Koran that he had ordered from Hachette in October 1883. He went further, and became a propagandist for the cause. It has been said that he did so in order to win the goodwill of his clientèle—Muslim coffee sellers—and this may well be true. When he went to Bubassa, he disguised himself as a Muslim. Indeed he assumed not only Muslim costume but also Muslim customs, like squatting to urinate, for instance. "He advised me to do the same," Ugo Ferrandi wrote.[22]

M. Lagarde, who was governor at Obok, tells us that he tried to make the Muslims that he met share his koranic convictions. "These attempts might have ended badly for him," Henri d'Acrement adds. "His personal interpretations seem to have angered many Muslims, and, one fine day, somewhere on the outskirts of Harar, a group of fanatics attacked him and beat him with sticks. He might have been killed were it not that Muslims do not kill madmen. When he finally escaped, it took him some time to recover."[23] Isabelle Rimbaud confirms this (*Reliques*, p. 89) as also does Ugo Ferrandi[24] and a researcher at Obok.[25]

A further proof of his Islamicization is the celebrated seal that once belonged to him, and which Mme Rimbaud used on March 30, 1897, to seal a letter asking Ernest Delahaye for information about Pierre Dufour (Paterne Berrichon), who wanted to marry her daughter Isabelle. This seal bears a few Arabic words:

..............................(?)

NAQQUAL LUBA   (?)

(A)BDOH RINB(O)

TRANSPORTEUR D'ENCENS   (?)[26]

Abdoh is the abbreviation of Abdallah, servant of God, a koranic formula.

It would seem to be a password, rather than a personal conviction. Already Sotiro, a Greek Orthodox, called himself Aj Abdallah when he traveled in Ogaden. In these regions trade went hand in hand with religion.

Is it because he had really become converted to Islam that he felt he was different from the other Europeans, that he had nothing to say to them? His new convictions may have accentuated his silence, but the causes of this silence went deeper. His life, which had been consumed in action, had made him miserly of words.

When one speaks of Rimbaud's silence, one thinks above all of the poet and his literary life—but, in Africa, his silence covered the whole of his earlier life. He was no more communicative about his country, his background, his family, than he was about Verlaine or the Parnassians.

Indeed what could he have said about his passage through the world of Letters? That at first he had had some success in Paris, then that he had been treated like a leper, that the only work that he had had printed had not been distributed, that the edition had been pulped, that that period of his life had taken place in a sordid atmosphere of poverty, vice, and lies. It is understandable that he kept silent: one does not boast of one's failures.

All those who knew him in Africa have described him as taciturn, withdrawn, unsociable. People felt no desire to question him, immured as he was in his secret; he always seemed to be "far away from everything" (Mgr. Jarosseau).

That is why evidence to the contrary, coming from individuals who were probably aware of his celebrity, seem a priori suspect. For example there is this belated revelation from a researcher in Obok: "To amuse his companions, perhaps, or to enable them to know him better, he took it into his head one day at Obok to converse with a highly educated Greek priest, who had great difficulty standing up to him. The conversation was carried out in ancient Greek, and subsequently, the priest always referred to Rimbaud as 'the superior man.' "27

To this may be added the rumor, deliberately put about to create a sensation, that, while in Africa, Rimbaud had written thousands of lines of poetry and a new *Illuminations*.

It is certainly true that he did write a great deal. There are a great many witnesses to this fact: "I said that, out there, we did not know that he was a talented poet. Whenever we saw him he was always writing, day and night, but we did not know what he was writing" (letter from A. Savouré to G. Maurevert, April 23, 1930),28 or again: "He wrote a great deal. He used to tell me that he was planning to write some magnificent book or other. I don't know from whom, but I learned that all his books and papers had been deposited with Father François, but, I must admit that my memory has not been too good over the last few years" (letter from Françoise Grisard to Berrichon, July 22, 1897).[29] (Father François, who was of Spanish nationality, replied on August 10, 1897, to the questionnaire that Berrichon had sent him: Rimbaud never entrusted any books or papers to him).[30]

He spent a great deal of time at his correspondence and accounts. But there may have been something else: Alfred Bardey told J.-P. Vaillant that, one day, the conversation turned in Rimbaud's presence to the book on the Gallas that Mgr. Taurin-Cahagne was writing. Suddenly Rimbaud announced proudly: "I, too, am writing one and it will cut the ground from under the Monseigneur's feet."[31]

So it seemed that an impenetrable wall separated Rimbaud's two lives, the European and the African. I have shown how Paul Bourde twice made a link (or tried to) between them.

Were there any other examples?

Alfred Bardey confided to J.-P. Vaillant a few of Rimbaud's remarks on the Latin Quarter—where, he said, he had met writers, painters, and artists, "but not musicians" (he had forgotten Cabaner). He did not dwell long on the subject and broke off the conversation, saying something to the effect that he had known quite enough of those types—which was just like him.[32]

Rimbaud also mentioned to him, in veiled terms, a period living in London, which he seemed to remember only as a time of constant drunkenness.[33]

There is another clue. On December 10, 1889, Savouré wrote to Rimbaud: "A charming young man, M. Georges Richard, will soon be calling on you with this letter. He knows much more about the Exposition than I do— I was able to see only very little of it. He will recount marvels to you. He has friends, I think, who were once yours." Which friends? Mystery.

Then there is the more credible evidence of Maurice Riès, who was César Tian's manager from September 1889, and, as such, often had occasion to correspond with Rimbaud. One day, Rimbaud admitted to him that in his youth, he had written poetry, adding: *"Des rinçures! Tout cela n'était que des rinçures"* [Hogwash! Pure hogwash!].

The words, related by Henri Tian, César's son, have the ring of authenticity.[34]

But, more curiously, a letter was found in Rimbaud's papers from a literary, scientific, and artistic journal published in Marseille—*La France mo-derne*, editor Jean Lombard—dated July 17, 1890, and addressed to the French consulate at Aden: "Monsieur et cher poète, I have read your fine verse: this is to say how proud I would be to see the leader of the Decadent and Symbolist school[35] write for *La France moderne*, of which I am the man-ager. I hope you will become one of us. Many thanks and my deepest admi-ration. Laurent de Gavoty."

Did he reply? He may have done so, since, in the number for February 19-March 4 1891, one reads: "This time, we have him! We know where Arthur Rimbaud, the real Rimbaud, the Rimbaud of *Les Illuminations*, is to be found. This is no decadent practical joke. We declare that we know where the famous poet is hiding himself."

But it may also be that the French consul at Aden, when questioned, declared that this letter had been sent on to Harar, where the addressee was to be found.

This letter from *La France moderne* is astonishing, but even more aston-ishing is the fact that Rimbaud did not destroy it.

In the early part of 1891, Rimbaud was more tired, more discouraged than ever. In Shoa trade was sluggish. To Ilg, who could no longer sell any-thing, Rimbaud complained that he had got him into a mess. A "horrible stagnation" reigned at Aden. The exchanges were constantly going up and down, and the thaler was continually falling. The future seemed tragic. "In a few months we'll have a terrible famine," Rimbaud wrote to Ilg on February 5, 1891 (and indeed it did take place.) The political news was no better: the breakoff of relations between Menelik and the Italians meant imminent war. Everything suggested that they had reached the end of an epoch of peace and prosperity. Rimbaud felt this, he saw the catastrophe coming, and was con-sidering how to "alter his situation," in other words, to sell up and get out. The idea of going back to France and finding a wife crossed his mind again; but he knew that it was unrealizable. He needed a woman who would be willing to follow him on his travels. And, anyway, he was getting old. As early as April 21, 1890, he was writing to his mother and sister, "one of my hairs turns white every minute."

On the edge of ruin, faced with a rising mass of perils, he was aware that he was moving toward the edge of the abyss.

18

Amputation: The Calvary
at Roche

*I*t was on February 20, 1891, that Rimbaud revealed to his family the extent of the illness that, slowly, inexorably, was laying siege to him: "I'm not well at the moment. At least, I have varicose veins in my right leg that are very painful. That's what you get for slaving away in these miserable parts! And these varicose veins are complicated by rheumatism. Not that it's cold here, but it is the climate that causes it. For two weeks now I haven't slept a wink because of the pain in this wretched leg."

He was already considering leaving Aden where, without much conviction, he had ordered a special stocking for varicose veins, but he hesitated because he was owed a great deal of money.

One of the few replies from Mme Rimbaud that has survived is her response to this letter of February 20. Dated March 27, 1891, it enclosed an ointment "to grease the varicose veins" and two elastic stockings ordered from Paris. Her advice is much the same as any mother would have given her son in such circumstances:

> *I enclose with this letter the doctor's prescription and instructions. Read them attentively and do exactly what he tells you. Above all you need rest, and rest not sitting down, but lying, because, as he says, and as he can tell from your letter, your illness has reached a point that is very worrying for the future.*
>
> *. . . Isabelle is better; but not quite well again. It's still*

winter here, the weather is very cold, the cereals are com-
pletely lost, nothing is left. General desolation everywhere—
no one knows what will become of us.
   Goodbye, Arthur,
   And above all look after yourself, and write to me as soon
as you receive this parcel.

In another letter addressed to Isabelle on July 15, 1891, the unfortunate man gives further details concerning the origin and rapid extension of his illness, which he blames on the climate, overwork, and lack of proper medical treatment: "I've been in the habit of wearing hardly any clothes: just linen trousers and a cotton shirt. Dressed in this way I've had to walk between 15 and 40 kilometers a day on senseless cavalcades through the steep mountains in this country."

Others have spoken of a fall from a horse, of a prick from a thorn from an umbrella mimosa, of an accident during a hunting party with the Righas brothers.[1] None of these pieces of evidence is verifiable, but it is not surprising that attempts have been made to explain the suddenness of the attack by some traumatism.

The medical description of the pain in his knee, in that letter of July 15, is very moving:

I was still walking and working a great deal, more than ever,
thinking that it was just a chill. Then the pain inside the knee
got worse. With each step I took, it was like a nail driven into
the side. I went on walking, though with a lot of pain; I
tended to ride more, but when I dismounted I felt more
crippled each time. Then the leg began to swell just above the
knee, the kneecap also swelled up, and the ham was also af-
fected. The circulation became difficult and pain racked the
nerves right down to the ankle and up to the small of the
back. I could now only walk with a limp and I seemed to be
getting worse all the time, but I had to go on working, there
was no alternative.—I then began to keep my leg bandaged
from top to bottom, rubbed it, bathed it, etc., but to no ef-
fect. Meanwhile, I began to lose my appetite. I couldn't sleep
for days on end. I grew weaker and much thinner—around

March 15, I decided to take to my bed, at least to remain in a horizontal position. I arranged a bed between my chest, my papers, and a window, from which I could keep an eye on my weighing scales at the end of the courtyard, etc.

Then the swelling increased, especially inside the knee, and the joint stiffened. The leg and the upper part of the thigh continued to grow thinner and desiccated. A hard ball, like a stone, appeared at the level of the knee. But, of course, he grew rapidly weaker and more demoralized: such a tumor would never subside of its own accord.

Then, at the end of March, he courageously decided to leave. Everything he had was sold off, at a loss.

What was the nature of this sudden illness?

All the Rimbaud children inherited hydrarthrosis, a disease resulting from the accumulation of serous or synovial liquid in a joint. Vitalie died from synovitis complicated by tuberculosis. Isabelle was to die of a similar illness. In Arthur's case, it is thought, the old forgotten syphilis may have returned and seized upon the illness and further aggravated it. Very soon the rheumatism degenerated into synovitis then into a tumor (sarcoma), and the tumor became cancerous (carcinoma).

It is probable that by the time he left Harar, Rimbaud was already beyond cure: the disease met no resistance in that undernourished, overworked, exhausted organism.

He had a litter made, covered with a skin, from a sketch that he himself drew and which has been discovered, and hired sixteen porters at 15 thalaris each to take him to the coast.

The Diary that he kept in a notebook of this painful journey, made even more difficult by the rainy season, is an extraordinary document. It is the first and only time in his life that he kept a diary. Between the lines one can sense the implacable presence of pain and anxiety.

Here are two passages describing this two-hundred-mile way of the cross, complemented by two extracts from letters to his mother and Isabelle: "Tuesday April 7. Left Harar at 6 AM. Arrived at Degadallal at 9.30 in the morning. Swamp at Egon. Upper Egon, noon. Egon to Fort Ballawa, three hours. Descent from Egon to Ballawa very difficult for the porters, who stumbled at each stone, and for me—I'm nearly overturned every minute. The litter is already half dislocated and the people completely done in. I try to mount a mule, with my sick leg tied to the neck; I have to get off after a few minutes

and return to the litter, which is already a kilometer behind. Arrived at Ballawa. It's raining. Furious wind all night."

During the next few, more monotonous days, the caravan meets storms
and much cooler weather. On Thursday the ninth, Rimbaud camps at Bussa
with an English traveler, a Mr. Donald, his wife, and two children. Next day,
he has to wait for sixteen hours for the arrival of the camels that have failed
to follow. They do not appear until Saturday the eleventh, with their supplies,
after thirty hours entirely without food, during sixteen of which they were
exposed to constant rain. "Tuesday 14th. Rose at 5.30. The porters walk very
badly. At 9.30 halt at Arrowina. They throw me to the ground on arrival. I
impose a fine of 4 th: Muned-Suyn, 1 th ; Abdullahi, 1 th ; Abdullah, 1 th ;
Baker, 1 th . Rose at 2. Arrived at Samado at 5.30."

The following stages were Lasman, Kombavorena, Ensa, Duduhassa,
Dadap. The diary ends with the following words: "Rose Dadap, 9.30. Arrived
at Warambot, at 4.30" (Warambot is just over six miles from Zeila).

> *Useless to tell you what horrible suffering I have endured
> en route. I could never take a single step outside my litter; I
> could see my knee swelling, and the pain increased contin-
> ually [to his mother April 30, 1891].*
>
> *En route, I could never leave my litter, they erected the
> tent over me wherever they laid me down and, digging a hole
> with my hands near the edge of the litter, I managed with
> great difficulty to position myself a little on the side to go to
> stool over the hole, which I then filled with earth. In the
> morning, they took down the tent over me and hoisted me up.
> I arrived at Zeila quite exhausted, paralyzed. I rested there
> only for four hours—a steamer was leaving for Aden. Thrown
> on to the deck on my mattress (I had to be hoisted on board in
> my litter!), I had to endure three days of sea without eating
> [to his sister, July 15 1891].*

On April 24 he reached Aden. First he had himself taken to the home
of M. Tian, where he remained for a few days working at the accounts, before
being taken off to the European Hospital. There, an English physician, Dr.
Nouks, diagnosed synovitis, and declared that it had reached a very dangerous
point. First he considered amputation, then decided to put the patient under

observation. If no improvement was made, he would have to return to France. However, he was not to lose all hope; at best, three months of care and rest would be necessary.

Rimbaud himself remained lucid throughout. "And I am stretched out, with my leg bandaged, tied, retied, changed, in such a way that I cannot move it. I've become a skeleton: I'm an object of fear. My back is all sore from the bed; I can't sleep a minute and it has got terribly hot here."

It was little use his adding, "Don't be too worried about all this, however. Better days will come." He could not restrain a sigh of bitterness: "But it's a pitiful reward for so much work, privation, and struggle! Alas! How wretched our life is!" (to his mother April 30, 1891).

As the pain began to subside, he was able to see César Tian several times and sign an agreement with him about the accounts, which were somewhat complicated by the fact that certain deals had been made in partnership and others separately. Tian was surprised to see that he was perfectly aware of the difficulties existing between himself and Maurice Riès, his manager. Everything was ready by May 6, except for the accounts from Harar, which were also very complicated, and in the end Rimbaud accepted a draft at sight, with a delay of ten days, on the Comptoir national d'Escompte de Paris—the Marseille branch, payable in Paris—for 37, 450 F.

It was a pitiful end! What exhaustion, what struggles, what privations were represented by this draft, which he was actually unable to cash! It was for this piece of paper that he had burned up his life!

After two weeks, Dr. Nouks advised Rimbaud to return to France, which was tantamount to saying: this man should go home, he will find it easier to die there.

A ship coming from the East, the *Amazone*, of the Messageries maritimes, put in at Aden, en route for Marseille. Rimbaud had himself hoisted on board on May 9. His voyage, lasting about ten days in all too imaginable conditions, helped to weaken him still further. On May 20, exhausted, broken, and shivering with fever, he entered the Hôpital de la Conception at Marseille.

His admission form, his so-called Billet de salle, has been discovered:

Salle Officiers[2]—*May 20, a man in the name of Raimbaud, Arthur, aged 36—Profession: merchant—Born at Charleville, department of the Ardennes, passing through.*
Illness: Neoplasm of the thigh.

Physician: P. Ullier (?)
Number in the entry register: 1427.

The letter that he wrote home on the following day, Thursday May 21 (and not, as he writes, Friday 23), describes his sad situation:

> *I arrived yesterday, after thirteen days of pain. Feeling too weak on arrival here, and overcome with the cold, I had to enter the* Hôpital de la Conception, *where I pay ten francs a day, doctor included.*
> *I am very poorly, very poorly. I've shrunk to the state of a skeleton through this disease in my left leg.[3] which has now become huge and looks like a huge pumpkin. It's synovitis, hydrarthrosis, etc., a disease of the joints and bones.*
> *It will last a very long time, unless complications force them to cut off the leg. In any case, I shall be crippled. But I doubt if I shall wait. Life has become quite impossible for me. How wretched I am! How wretched I've become!*

"I doubt if I shall wait . . ." The idea of suicide crossed his mind—and it was to remain with him to the end.

His inability to cash his draft at the Comptoir national d'Escompte added to his torment. He was alone, powerless, and, he thought, ruined to boot. He was handed a letter from Harar, dated May 13, from the manager of the Maison V. Bienenfeld and Cie of Aden, a certain Felter, containing good wishes that could not but sound hollow: "I hope you have a good voyage and my best wishes for a speedy recovery. Hoping to see you here soon, I affectionately shake your hand."

Next day, Friday May 22, during the visit of the physician-in-charge, Dr. Trastour, he learnt of the tragic decision: immediate amputation of the diseased leg, at the top of the thigh.

Early in the afternoon, Rimbaud sent the following message to his mother at Roche: "Today, you or Isabelle come to Marseille by express train. Monday morning, they are amputating my leg! Danger of death. Serious matters to settle. Hôpital Conception. Reply."

Mme. Rimbaud received the telegram in the late afternoon and had time to be taken to Attigny before the post office closed where, at 6.35, she sent the following message: "I'm leaving. Will arrive tomorrow evening. Courage and patience. V. Rimbaud."

She arrived at Marseille on Saturday May 23, and rushed to the hospital. One can imagine her shock on seeing her beloved son, after twelve years, in such a pitiful state. Through her presence, her unshakable trust in God, her steady attitude before adversity, she managed to prevent him from sinking into the worst despair and prepared him to face with courage the most terrible trial of his life.

The amputation took place on Monday May 25 as arranged. It was carried out by the surgeon E. Pluyette, assisted by his intern, Beltrami, and a kindly extern Louis Terras. M. Pierre Ripert of Marseille, to whom we owe this information, obtained them from Dr. Paul Sepet, who did research into the subject.[4] He adds that Mme Rimbaud and Maurice Riès took turns at the patient's bedside, but, since the archives of the Hôpital de la Conception have been destroyed, we have no proof of this. However, Paterne Berrichon declared that the surgeon who operated on Rimbaud was Dr. Henri Nicolas[5] and, indeed, the Matarasso collection does contain a letter from Nicolas to this effect dated October 1, 1897, addressed to Berrichon. It may be that Dr. Henri Nicolas—an intern or extern at the time?—attended the operation.

"However, the wound healed extraordinarily quickly," Isabelle notes, "which surprised the surgeons and physicians, so much so that they said that they had never dealt with so healthy and vigorous a constitution."[6]

Indeed the doctors were optimistic. On May 30 Rimbaud, thinking he was on the mend, sent the following note to the Ras Makonnen: "I am writing to you from Marseille, in France. I am in hospital. I had a leg amputated six days ago. I am well at present and in three weeks or so I shall be cured. In a few months, I expect to come back to Harar to trade as before, and I thought to send you my greetings."

After ten days spent beside the patient, Mme Rimbaud was thinking of getting home: Isabelle was ill, and there was work to be done. Her presence had become less indispensable, since Arthur's state was satisfactory. His physical state, that is—for from the point of view of morale he was not well at all.

On June 8 she wrote to Isabelle: "My parcels are ready. I expect to leave tomorrow, Tuesday, at 2 o'clock in the afternoon, I shan't be at Roche until Thursday evening via Voncq station. I don't want anyone to bother meeting me: I'd prefer to arrive alone. I wanted to leave today, but Arthur's tears upset me, and, anyway, if I were to stay, it would be for another month, which is not possible. What I am doing is for the best, may God's will be done! Don't write to me here any more."

Her departure plunged the wretched patient into the depths of despair. Alone he felt unable to control himself, and could not understand how his family could abandon him like a wrecked ship. He had begged his mother to stay, but to no avail: she had done her duty, it was pointless to ask her to do more. She left him in tears, choking with bitter resentment.

At Roche, Isabelle, overcome by her mother's account of her brother's suffering, realized that a mission had been assigned to her: to devote herself to her big brother, whom she admired so much and of whom she was so proud (unlike that good-for-nothing Frédéric, he had managed to make a position for himself), but whom she knew only from the letters, lacking in any human warmth, that had come from Arabia or Africa. He had always been away, and at the time that he had decided to seek his fortune abroad, he was nineteen. She was now thirty-one. Since there was now no question of her marrying, and since she loved nobody, her capacity for tenderness and devotion was intact. He too—she guessed—needed someone to love and to confide in. So she would be his confidant, his attentive friend, his spiritual guide, for part of her mission was also to bring him back to religion. In short, it was a love that had come at the right moment, and which could measure up to her hunger for sacrifice.

From mid-June her correspondence with her brother was to become very active. His letters, like waves of the sea, had their crests and their depths, alternating recovery and despair, very soon to be dominated by pessimism.

On June 17, he apologized for being "very angry" at his mother's departure, for he did not know that Isabelle was ill. Forgetting himself, he tried to reassure her: "All illnesses are curable with time and care. In any case, one must resign oneself to one's fate and not despair." He clung to something that a doctor had told him, that, in a month, he would be able to walk again—if very slowly at first.

And then, some days later, on June 23, his fears resurfaced: "All I do is weep night and day, I'm as good as dead, I'm crippled for life. . . . I've no idea what to do. All these worries are driving me mad: I can't sleep for a minute. Yes, our life is a misery, an endless misery! So why do we exist?"

On top of all this, there was a new catastrophe. Isabelle told him that the police had turned up at Roche asking questions about his military situation: they talked of insubordination, prosecution, court martial.

This was the last straw! "Prison after all I've gone through. I would rather be dead!"

It has to be said that Isabelle and his mother behaved rather clumsily: instead of telling the truth, and asking for a permanent discharge, supported by medical certificates, they had concealed from the authorities that Arthur had returned to France and undergone amputation. They employed a lawyer to consult his file at the military headquarters at Châlons-sur-Marne, but found nothing.

The worst thing about it was the uncertainty: "We cannot find out anything," Isabelle wrote to him, "without betraying you." He felt that he was being pursued like a criminal. No, no! He would not go back to Roche only to fall into the wolf's jaws! At the first alert, he would get on a ship for Africa.

"Don't go and betray me," he begged. "Don't let my name be noticed at the post offices at Roche and Attigny. Write to me less often. Don't put Arthur, just put R."

Steps were then taken at the recruitment office at Mezières. A certificate declaring his military situation was issued, and, on July 8, 1891, Isabelle sent it on to her brother, believing that the whole matter was now settled. The certificate reads as follows: "Rimbaud, J.-N. A, has been in Arabia since January 16, 1882; his military situation is therefore legal he does not therefore have to perform his period of instruction and is under renewable deferment until his return to France."

But nothing in fact had been settled, since he was in France!

It was becoming an obsession. The poor man believed that he was constantly being spied upon: "There was a sick police inspector at my table who was constantly bothering me with his stories about army service and was planning to play some trick on me."

In the end Rimbaud did what should have been done at the beginning: he copied out a statement prepared for him by Isabelle and sent it to the recruitment center at Marseille. All the relevant information was included, the stay abroad, the deferment obtained, the return to France, and the amputation that justified a permanent discharge. But he was still only half convinced: "The military authorities are quite capable of locking up a cripple, even if it is only in a hospital" (July 15).

From June and July 1891 date the most pathetic letters that Rimbaud ever wrote: they are simply a cry of pain and fear.

Two themes dominate, apart from that of fear of military punishment:

regret that he had allowed his leg to be amputated and the uselessness of crutches or any artificial leg.

"Never allow yourself to be amputated. Have yourself cut up, torn apart, taken to pieces, but don't let them amputate you. If death comes as a result it would be always preferable than life with a limb missing. . . . Rather suffer the torments of hell than be amputated" (July 15). Indeed as is very well known, doctors know little more than how to wield the knife; for them patients are just subjects for experiments, as was proved by the fact that they no longer showed any interest in him. "I would have been better dead long ago," he concluded.

Crutches, wooden legs, artificial legs were all so much useless eyewash. He had just tried them out: he had not been able to adjust the wooden leg, "Very light, varnished, and padded, very well made," which he had ordered for 50 francs, to his swollen, inflamed stump.

He was left with the crutches. But they were not much use: one could neither go up nor down a slope, and that "frightful gymnastics" was a "terrible business." "Here is what happens! I'm sitting down, and from time to time I get up, hop a hundred or so steps on my crutches, and sit down again. I can't hold anything in my hands. As I walk, I can't take my eyes off my only foot and the tips of the crutches. Your head and shoulders are bent forward, and your back is bowed like a hunchback. You're terrified at the sight of objects and people moving around you, lest they knock you over and break your other leg. People only grin at the sight of you hopping about like that. When you sit down, your hands twitch and the expression on your face is idiotic."

He greets with a shrug of the shoulders Isabelle's attempts to be soothing and encouraging—one can perfectly well lead a normal life with one leg, she has known people with one leg who were amazingly agile, etc.—or her sermons—one must never give in to despair, "Serenity and peace will come back to you just when you are most desperate" (July 13). It was all lies. The truth was that he did not feel well, which was proof that he was not cured inside: his remaining leg was weak and congested, which was not a good sign: "What if I have some disease of the bone and will have to lose the other leg?" he asked (July 2). He was afraid of some sudden accident, and was expecting "some explosion." What would he do if he were crippled and incurable? Go back to Africa? There he would be having to move all the time: he could not see himself as a shopkeeper working behind a counter for the rest of his days. Go back to Roche, as Isabelle was constantly urging him to? "Come," she said, "travel in a *coupé* [a private half-compartment with a seat or bed, placed at the end of a carriage], we'll meet you at Voncq station, you can have a room on the first floor or upstairs if you like, but come, the change of air will do you good."

This appeal aroused his caustic irony: "To think I was planning to come home to France this summer, to get married! Farewell, marriage! Farewell, family! I'm nothing more than a dead tree trunk!" (July 10).

Fortunately, messages of encouragement and friendship reached him from Aden, Zeila, and Harar.

A letter from Sotiro did much to mitigate his regret at not being at Harar, which had been struck by a terrible famine ("Makonnen has shot many Itu Gallas, who were eating their brothers and children"). Sotiro was still the same good friend, sensitive and thoughtful: "I have received your very friendly letter of June 26 and my heart is filled with sorrow at what you say; nevertheless one must always thank God. I wrote to you while I was at Aden; God is great and, with the help of friends, we hope to be able to find you some position at Zeila or Aden. M. Tian thinks highly of you. Have no fear, you may have no family, but you have good friends" (July 10). Indeed, César Tian had hinted at some possible collaboration in the future.

Felter, branch manager of the firm of Bienenfeld at Aden, wrote: "I have learned the sad news, and I assure you that it has upset me deeply. Fortunately, however, I know you are strong-willed and philosophical enough to be convinced that, once the illness is over, having one leg more or less will not stop you on your road through life. . . . Your servant Jami is now in my service" (July 13).

Even the Ras Makonnen deigned to write this friendly note: "How are you? I, thank God, am well. I have learned with surprise and sorrow that you have had to lose a leg. From what you tell me, the operation was successful. May God be praised! It is with pleasure that I learn that you are proposing to come back to Harar to continue with your trading: I'm very glad. Yes, come back quickly and in good health. I am always your friend" (July 12).

In very approximate French, Dimitri Righas wrote: "It was only today that I received your letter of May 30 and June 17 in which you tell me that you have undergone the operation, that is to say, that you have had your leg cut off, and that made a deep impression on me, as it has done on all your friends in Harar. I would have preferred them to have cut off mine rather than yours. Anyway I wish you a good recovery."

So good people were to be found in this world. But instead of comforting Rimbaud, this realization made him all the more sad.

Suddenly, on July 23, in order to get out of the hospital, where every day he ran the risk of catching "smallpox, typhus, and other plagues that thrive here," he asked to leave. When the physician-in-charge made no objection, he dragged himself as best he could (he had to change trains at Paris and Amagne) to Voncq station, where a carriage awaited him. We have no details about this journey, which must have been extremely painful for him.

At his request a room had been prepared for him on the second floor. On entering the room, which Isabelle had decorated with vases of flowers, he murmured: "It's Versailles here!"

He attributed the fever and insomnia of the first few days to the exhaustion of the journey, but he continued to suffer from both. Isabelle cared for him as for a child, fed him, and guided his tottering steps, seldom leaving his side. Her thirst for devotion was satisfied; she sat at his bedside, chatting to him, or reading the newspapers and reviews to him, or simply watching over him, her hands occupied with some tapestry work or embroidery. They went out in an open barouche, despite the dull weather and the bad state of the roads, each bump bringing a grimace of pain to his face. He loved to see the crowds at the fairs, markets, or festivals, silently, hungrily observing the healthy people around him.

Did they go into Charleville? Isabelle does not say, but a physician in the town, Dr Emile Baudoin is convinced that he met him there, when he himself was seventeen.

"He was a tall, slim, thin man, still young, with a rather small head and short hair," he writes. "He was wearing a pearl gray suit and a black bowler hat. Leaning on a stick, he moved slowly, cautiously, dragging his leg somewhat. He often stopped to rest and looked around him attentively, examining in turn all the neighboring houses." The scene took place on July 31, 1891, in the Rue du Petit-Bois, not far from the Place Ducale, about 2 o'clock in the afternoon, some hours after the prize-giving at the Collège. Our narrator continues:

> It was then that M.L.M. . . . saw him:
> "Well, well!" he cried. "There's the famous Rimbaud!"
> "And what's this Rimbaud?!" my father asked him.
> "It's Père Cuif's grandson, a ragamuffin, a Communard, a good-for-nothing who painted the town red. . . ."
> The gentleman, who had stopped, resumed his walk to-

*ward the Place Ducale, and disappeared at the corner of the
Joly-Mailfait bookshop.*
*I wonder if Rimbaud did not take it into his head, on
July 31, to go and attend incognito the prize-giving at his old
school, and in this way to see his native town again.*[7]

There are two objections to this piece of evidence: to begin with, it seems
unlikely that Rimbaud would have been capable of walking with a stick,
"dragging one leg slightly" (there were no sticks with elbow rests at that time).
Secondly, and above all, it is unlikely that Isabelle would have left him to
walk on his own. It may be, then, that the passerby was victim of the same
illusion as Mme Rimbaud, who, having caught a glimpse in a church of a
young cripple with short moustaches, eight years after her younger son's
death, began to think: "My God, has my poor Arthur come back to fetch me
then?" (letter to Isabelle, June 9, 1899).

He often spoke of his past life, his life in Africa, which he was anxious
to resume. But could he still go about on horseback? There could no longer
be any question of marriage, except, as he said, smiling bitterly, with an
orphan or Abyssinian girl. He often joked, Isabelle recounts, making fun of
everything, especially people they used to know in Roche or in Charleville,
including himself. But these moments of gaiety were not to last; he soon fell
back into semiprostration, a state that became more and more habitual
to him.

He had an articulated artificial limb made, but because of his stump
which was still very painful, he could bear it no more than the first. He
preferred to sit for hours on end in the yard, under the shade of the hazel
trees. An inhabitant of Roche, Mme Lefevre, relates that when he was in too
much pain he was taken up into his room on the second floor. The neighbors
said among themselves that he had become an "innocent." Another inhabitant of Roche, Père Bertrand, confided, at the age of eighty, to Robert Goffin
that he had often helped Arthur unbandage his leg in the farmyard: "He
would swear like a trooper," he added, "and made fun of me because I went
to mass."[8]

It rained, it was cold. Never had Roche, which he nicknamed the
"wolves' lair,"[9] filled him with so much horror. He was convinced that the
climate was killing him. Slowly but surely his state worsened, his stump became more inflamed, his right leg and shoulder were getting stiff, his left leg

in turn was getting congested. Would they end up having to cut off all his limbs, one by one?

The physician at Attigny, Dr. Henri Beaudier, believed it to be a case of tuberculosis of the bone, and did little more than prescribe anaesthetics. "I can still see him," he confided to Robert Goffin, "sitting in the kitchen, with his good leg on a chair. He would look at me with those steely, penetrating, interrogating eyes. He emerged from his stubborn silence only to swear like a trooper when I lavished my attentions on him."

When Dr. Beaudier mentioned the possibility of more surgery, Rimbaud replied, categorically, that he was beyond caring.

"Several times," the doctor continues, "as I was talking to him, his mother poked her head around the half-opened door. Immediately Rimbaud's features hardened and I remember that once he simply told her to get out."[10]

This is all very probable. What is less so is that Dr. Baudier (then thirty-nine years old) asked his patient, as he says, if he still had anything to do with literature (he says that Rimbaud replied: "Shit to poetry"). Indeed, the celebrity of the poet at this time hardly went beyond the frontiers of the Latin Quarter. Neither at Roche, nor at Charleville—apart from a few individuals—did anyone know that he was the author of poetry worthy to survive. In this respect Isabelle was in complete ignorance. One must distrust evidence that is necessarily a posteriori, altered by everything the narrator has learned since the facts he is recounting.

The only remedy the wretched man took was sedatives, infusions of poppies, which Isabelle picked herself, but these analgesics plunged him into a deep torpor from which he emerged congested, bathed in sweat, and shivering. Once, during a nightmare, he fell out of bed, to everyone's horror. The doctor got him to give up tranquilizers.

Then, with the pain, returned the despair. He cried a great deal, considered himself doomed, became irritable, whenever he did not get his own way, but, immediately regretting his behavior, became lively again, had a kind word for the gentle Isabelle, and a faint smile. Then she, overcome with gratitude, began to weep in turn. That was how it was every day.

Now he no longer went out. In his room, with the shutters closed, his mind began to wander, as he listened to the sound of an old barrel organ. He was obsessed by the sun, by Marseille: there he would have a surgeon, and, at the first sign of improvement, he would board a boat for Aden. Letters continued to reach him from out there, anxious or reassuring, all filled with friendship.

César Tian wrote: "M. Helder has sent me the receipt for the 504 tha-laris. This gentleman asks me to tell him exactly when you'll be returning to Harar. I shall write to tell him that it will probably be late September or early October, but that you will inform him in due course. . . . As you say, we will be able to talk about business when you are here." (July 23).

Sotiro, too, continued to write: "And always remember that in our coun-try there is someone who has a good word to say about you, and who knows you, and that fortune may come to us if God gives you health" (July 25). And again: "Very dear friend, A. Rimbaud in the Ardennes—I have received your agreeable letter of July 30. I learned with great pleasure that you are at your mother's in your own country. You are fortunate, it seems to me, to see it again. . . . Try to do as your mother tells you: no one loves one more than a mother! Her blessings will bring you happiness. Something tells me that you are not used to them, but that does not matter: one must follow reason and respect for one's mother, who wishes nothing but good for you" (August 14).

"I hope that you will soon be better and be out here again," Savouré wrote. "The Ras in particular talks of nothing but you, he was very affected to hear of the operation that you have had to bear. He has told us about it twenty times, adding that you were his *true friend*. . . . Better luck, good health, and speedy return, in the hope of seeing you here within two months, or three at the most, I shake your hand very affectionately." And he added as a postscript: "Everyone brings his wife, only you and I are left who are not married" (August 15).

On August 10 a sudden, violent storm burst that stripped the trees and covered them with frost. This event helped him to make up his mind: winter was coming, he would have to leave. It was a question of life or death. On August 23, a month after he had left hospital, he set out again for Marseille, guided and supported by Isabelle.

19

Return to Marseille and Death

Our only evidence about this journey comes from the pathetic account of his sister, who, through her veracity and the accumulation of detail, enables us to accompany the wretched invalid in his hopeless flight.[1] There is no striving after literary effects; what we are given is reality in its tragic dimension.

So, on August 23, at three o'clock in the morning, Arthur asked to be dressed: he must not miss the 6:30 A.M. train from Voncq. But the farmhand had left the harnessing of the horse to the last minute, and seemed reluctant to make up for lost time. So, despite a mad cross-country race (Arthur, swearing the whole time, even took off his belt to whip the horse), the carriage reached the station two minutes after the train had left. What was to be done? He took it into his head to wait until 12.40 for the next train, but the cold, foggy weather and Isabelle's supplications persuaded him to change his mind. Back in his room, he lay fully dressed on his bed, dozed off, and woke at 9 o'clock demanding to leave at once. Three hours and a half to cover three kilometers did not strike him as excessive.

What could be done with an obstinate individual in the grip of an obsession? The more time went by, the more his impatience grew. At the last moment, however, he could not hold back his tears. He knew that this would be a final farewell, that he would never see again either his mother or that accursed Roche, where he was leaving part of himself.

"Stay here. We will look after you," his mother said.

"No. I must try to get myself cured."

His only chance, he thought, was a dry climate, in the south of France or in Africa: Roche was tantamount to a death sentence. At the station, a flicker of gaiety lit up his eyes when he noticed the two farmhands glancing greedily at the bottle of bromide elixir from which he drank a mouthful: those bumpkins were waiting for their traditional nip of brandy! Similarly, the stationmaster's mean little garden excited his scorn.

After a very long wait the puffing, squeaking train arrived in a cloud of smoke. Isabelle helped him into the compartment and wedged him on the cushions and pillows that she had brought, but the vibration of the train seemed to arouse the pain in every part of his body—back, hips, shoulders, legs. It soon became unbearable.

"Oh, the pain! The pain!" he moaned, almost unceasingly.

At Amagne, where they had to change, the station staff helped Isabelle carry him in a chair to the waiting room. When he had had to stop there on his journey to Roche, he had been able to walk, more or less, with the help of his crutches; now he was just a dislocated, pain-ridden body, incapable of any movement. He could hardly speak for the lump in his throat, but he managed to summon up enough courage to smile at his sister. He told her that she should not deprive herself of anything, she should think of herself a little.

The stationmaster and several members of the staff managed, with some difficulty, to get him into the Paris express:

"They're bound to cut off the whole leg," he said, "something diseased, some seed, is still there that will have to be taken out."

Some passengers got in at Rethel, others at Reims—a young married couple, then a family with children. He observed the animation around him with strangely excited eyes, but soon his curiosity gave way to tiredness and indifference.

Everything seemed like an invitation to pleasure: it was Sunday, it was a beautiful day, young women in their summer dresses were canoeing on the Marne. As the train passed, one could hear music from the open-air cafés. He lay there motionless, eyes half-closed, already outside the world.

They reached Paris at 6:30 P.M., and new tribulations awaited him: getting off the train, getting out of the station, getting into a cab. A good night in a hôtel in some quiet quarter, Isabelle thought, would give him the strength to bear the next, more fearful stage.

Suddenly a storm emptied the streets of passersby. The rain beat down on the cab windows. The deserted streets, with their shiny paving stones, streaming with rain, the sudden coolness of the air was more than he could bear. Then, suddenly, he ordered the driver to go straight to the Gare de Lyon. In vain Isabelle begged him not to leave that same evening.

Isabelle writes:

He collapsed pitifully into the velvet seats, impatiently await-ing the departure of the express for Marseille. He had eaten nothing since morning, and tried to take a little food, but he could not face anything. The fever so excited his brain that he was almost delirious. He had one moment of extraordinary and irritating gaiety when he caught sight of an officer in uni-form. He ordered a soporific potion. Since moments of nervous excitement were followed by extreme exhaustion, it was an al-most inert body that the railway staff, when the time came to leave, about eleven in the evening, carried as gently as pos-sible to the reserved coupé-lit, *where the unfortunate traveler was stretched out.*[2]

It was an appalling journey, for him, burning with fever, unable to find a comfortable position, permanently racked by pain throughout his body, and for Isabelle, crouching and weeping at his side. Panting, dripping with sweat, sometimes moaning, sometimes delirious, he had reached, one might well say, the limit of human endurance. Each second, each jolt amplified his implacable torture.

At dawn, just before they reached Lyon, he was able at last to fall asleep, but it would take the whole morning and afternoon before they saw the Camargue. It was stiflingly hot in that cell-like *coupé-lit* with its wooden shutters.

When he woke, it was to realize that he could no longer move his limbs. How would he get to the hospital?

It again needed the help of the station staff to lift him, get him down on to the platform, carry him out of the station, and settle him into a cab.

What a sigh of relief Isabelle must have drawn when she saw him lying at last in his narrow hospital bed!

She had him registered under the name of Jean Rimbaud — a pitiful precaution to avoid investigation by the military authorities.

We have no news whatever of the four weeks that followed: Isabelle's first letter to her mother is dated September 22. All the doctors consulted agreed that her brother had no chance of recovering, that he had only a few days or a few weeks to live.

"Stay with him," Dr. Trastour advised her. "It would be cruel to deprive him of your presence."[3]

Of course, when they were in the patient's presence they talked about possible, even probable cure, telling him that he must be patient, so much so that Isabelle seeing him calmer, less congested, his appetite picking up, even began to wonder if it were not she who was being taken in. But the remission was short-lived. He was getting irreversibly weaker, and he knew it. Ah! if only they could find a treatment! Anything (electricity had been mentioned), so that he could use his right arm and walk again with an articulated leg! But scarcely had he expressed this wish than he was aware of its futility; he then began to weep again, and to beg his sister not to abandon him. Isabelle was deeply upset that she had not yet received a letter from her mother: "I beg you, on my knees, to write to me," she implored. "What has happened to you?" It has been suggested that if Mme Rimbaud was behaving so coldly it was because Arthur had pursuaded Isabelle not to marry a rich farmer in Roche.[4] But this smacks too much of romantic fiction. It is more likely that she was displeased because her daughter never mentioned returning home.

But Isabelle was quite incapable of ignoring a poor wretch who was constantly demanding death, and who threatened, if she left him, to strangle himself, or to kill himself in one way or other. "He is in such pain," Isabelle adds, "that I really believe he would do what he says" (October 3). The state of her poor, tortured, fearful brother was profoundly moving: he required constant attention. To justify her presence at his side, Isabelle, in her letter of October 5, appended a "time table" of the day before:

> *Sunday, October 4. I went into Arthur's room at 7 o'clock. He was sleeping with his eyes open, breathing with difficulty, looking so thin and pale with his sunken eyes, and the dark rings around them! He did not wake up straight away. I watched him sleep, saying to myself that he could not possibly live much longer: he looks too sick! After five minutes, he woke up, complaining, as always, that he had not slept all night and had been in great pain; he is still in great pain when he wakes up. He said good morning, as he does every morning, asked me how I was, if I had slept well, etc. I told him that I*

was very well. What is the use of telling him that fever, cough-
ing, and above all anxiety had deprived me of my rest: he has
enough ills of his own!

He then tells me of his night fantasies, the strange things
that happen in the hospital. He accuses the nurses and even
the sisters of abominable things that cannot be, and I tell him
that he has no doubt dreamt it, but he won't be convinced,
and tells me I'm a fool and an idiot.

I then have to remake his bed, without him getting out of
it, which was no easy matter, for he can't bear the slightest
fold under him. His right arm rests on layers of wadding, and
his left arm, which is almost paralysed, is surrounded with
flannel.

Half-past seven. A sister brings black coffee. Then there
are the manual and electrical massages. But none of that had
any effect.

His left leg is still cold and trembling, with a great deal
of pain. His left eye is half shut. He sometimes has palpita-
tions of the heart, which make him gasp for breath. He tells
me that, when he wakes up, he feels his head and heart burn-
ing, and he always has pains in his chest and back, on the left
side.

Isabelle is able to go to the chapel to hear sung mass.

I hurry to get back, because Arthur says that when I'm
not near him he believes that he is already in his coffin.

That day, the long awaited articulated leg arrived. It was the third, but
he could not even try it on.

At eleven o'clock, lunch was brought, but he could not touch anything;
everything seemed repugnant to him. Then came the mail. Isabelle kissed
and moistened with her tears the envelope that contained two letters. She
handed her brother the one addressed to him, but he refused to look at it.

Isabelle goes on:

All day I had to use my ingenuity to stop him doing silly
things. Fortunately, I have some influence over him. His ob-

session is now to leave Marseille for a warmer climate, either
Algiers, or Aden, or Obok. What is holding him here is the
fear that I will not go any further with him, for he can no
longer do without me.
. . . When he wakes up, he looks out of the window at
the sun still shining in a cloudless sky and starts weeping,
saying that he will never see the sun outside again: "I shall go
under the earth," he says, "and you will walk in the sun!"
Thus all day long it is a ceaseless complaint, a nameless de-
spair.

The day ends with the dinner, which the wretched man does not touch, leaving the dessert to his sister and sending back the rest. Then come the visits, with the doctors administering their encouragements; Arthur listens to their good words "with a sort of hope," because he would like to believe them, in spite of everything. "Now the candle has to be lit, for at half-past five it's quite dark in the room. The rest of our day, until 9 o'clock will be spent rubbing the patient, changing linen, arranging the bed, etc. Then he will postpone, minute by minute, the time when I must leave him, then he finally says goodnight, as if I will never see him alive again. And so it is every evening."[5]

Several friends came to visit him: Maurice Riès, who did not realize how seriously ill he was ("When you like," he wrote to him on September 8, "you will be able to get through all the weapons you like, providing you don't tell anyone about it and thus draw the attention of the Italians to it.")[6]

Alfred Bardey also came several times. "He saw Rimbaud again," writes J.-P. Vaillant, "weeping and desperate, showing him his stump. They talked about the old days, then M. Bardey comforted him, assuring him that there were such things as artificial legs, and inviting him to spend his convalescence with him, in the country. Rimbaud was very touched, and wept like a child."[7] Augustin Bernard, a merchant at Aden, also told Mme Méléra of his visits to the Hôpital de la Conception.[8]

A few souvenirs have survived of this painful period: three portraits that Isabelle made of her brother, all reproduced in the *Album Rimbaud.* One shows him with emaciated face, eyes half closed; another, more tragic one, shows him with deep-set eyes, a white skull cap on his head; the third, a mere sketch, shows him stretched out, his right arm swollen by an enormous bandage.

All that remains is to recount the extraordinary day of October 25.

We have only one piece of evidence about it. Isabelle's letter to her mother, dated October 28, which has aroused a great deal of commentary, but whose authenticity is above suspicion. It is a triumphant act of grace: Arthur has faith! Arthur has become converted! Arthur has been touched by divine grace! "He is one of the just, of the elect, a saint, a martyr!"

"I don't believe anyone ever made a more edifying end," the pious sister was to write to Louis Pierquin on December 17, 1892.

This statement has allowed good Catholics, from Claudel to Mauriac, to develop the gospel theme of the return of the prodigal son to his father's house. "Rimbaud is the metaphysical butterfly that God finally pins down in his collection," Mme Briet wrote.[9]

But let us look at things a little more closely.

To begin with, one should not lose sight of the fact that one of the motives for Isabelle's presence—no doubt, with pity, the only one—was her intention, which she actually admitted, of getting her brother to make a "good death." Now, we know that before that day, October 25, no such change had taken place in him: his accusations against the nuns of the hospital show this quite clearly. As Maurice Riès remarked, he swore like a trooper.

On two occasions, the chaplains, Canon A. Chaulier and Father F. Suche,[10] at Isabelle's request, had tried to approach the dying man, but he had received them so badly that they had not dared to speak to him seriously. Rimbaud had remained as he had always been, allergic and hostile to any religious ideas.

And then, on October 25, after the high mass, one of the chaplains went in to see him, talked to him, and heard his confession. As he left the room, he confided to Isabelle: "Your brother has the faith, my child, what did you tell us? He has the faith. I can even say that I have never seen faith of this quality."

Isabelle, her spirits uplifted with joy, dashed into the room, expecting to see her brother radiating happiness—but no, he was "serenely sad."

The following dialogue then took place:

> HE *You're of the same blood as I: do you believe, tell me, do you believe? [A strange question: he knew that she believed, for heaven's sake; she importuned him enough with her invita-*

tions to share her faith; as long as he could remember, she had irritated him with her devotions. What he meant was: behind all this pretence, do you have a sincere, profound conviction?]

SHE   *I believe. Others who are cleverer than I have believed, do believe, and, anyway, I'm sure now. I have proof of it, that is.*

HE   *Yes, they say they believe, they pretend to be converted, but that's so that people will read what they write, it's a form of speculation!*

SHE   *No, they would earn more money by blaspheming.*

HE   *(wanting to embrace her) We may well have the same soul, since we are of the same blood. Well, then, do you believe?*

SHE   *Yes, I believe.* One must believe.

"One must believe." So the game was not won yet; one no longer speaks of the target when it has already been reached. One does not tell a victorious general one must win!

Mischievous commentators have concluded that nothing took place, that Isabelle took her desire for reality, that she elaborated a fantasy of her own on the basis of a few words from the chaplain, whose meaning she did not fully grasp, or quite simply that she lied.

They are wrong. Something really did take place on that Sunday October 25. Arthur was no longer the same person, though he was not the person that Isabelle would have liked him to be either.

Until then God for him had been nothing but the object of hateful sarcasm, and here he was putting his trust in him and begging him to cure him. He turned to Isabelle's God, but it could just as easily have been the God of the Jews or that of the Muslims. In his sister's eyes, he had seen and understood that the faith confers on the believer an unfailing serenity, and this silent example proved to be more effective than any exhortation (which he could not have borne in any case). If faith is a reality, God may be a reality, too, and if he is a reality, he thought, he can cure me. He was using his last strength to cling to this ultimate hope.

"He has not blasphemed since," Isabelle notes. "He calls upon the Crucified Christ, and prays, he prays!"

He also repeated: "Allah kerim!" May God's will be done!

But there was no further change, no further progress. He asked his sister to tidy up his room, because the priest would be back with the sacraments: "You'll see, he'll be here with the candles and lace." But the priest did not come back, and there was no communion, or, it seems, extreme unction.[11] The reasons that Isabelle gives are not very convincing: they did not want to frighten him, he might have spat out the host involuntarily. But this does not accord with what she says of his calm state on that Sunday morning.

Indeed, he asked for nothing: "And he," Isabelle continues, "thinking that he had been forgotten, became sad, but he did not complain."

To conclude, let us say that Rimbaud was not literally converted, and that, if he did not go far in the way of belief, he did go a long way in retreating from unbelief.

However, the disease had progressed in a terrifying way: his stump was so swollen that it formed up to the groin a huge, bony tumor that had become insensitive. The pain had moved into the arms, the leg, and the head. They had to resort to morphine and, from then on, he did not emerge from a comatose state, interrupted only with dreams and delirious episodes. He spoke quietly, but with extraordinary precision, which surprised the doctors. He believed that he was still at Harar; he called his sister Jami; he would suddenly berate her—they had to get to Aden, and first they would have to collect camels, then load the caravan. But why had they let him oversleep? He was expected, he would be late. Then he would begin to cry again. This is Isabelle's last description of the dying man: "He hardly takes anything by way of food, and when he does it is with extreme repugnance, so he is as thin as a skeleton, and has the complexion of a corpse. And all his poor limbs are paralysed, mutilated around him! Oh God, what a pitiful sight!"

On November 9, in a final moment of pseudolucidity, he dictated to his sister a letter to the manager of the Messageries maritimes, preceded by a list of elephant's teeth:

> *Item: one tooth.*
> *Item: two teeth.*
> *Item: three teeth.*
> *Item: four teeth.*
> *Item: two teeth.*

> *Dear Sir,*
> *I am writing to ask whether I have anything left in your account. I wish to change today from that service, whose*

name I can't even remember, but in any case let's call it the
Aphinar service. All those services are there, everywhere, and
I, an unhappy invalid, can find nothing, the first dog in the
street will tell you that.

So send me the prices of the Aphinar services to Suez. I'm
completely paralyzed: so I want to be on board in good time.
Tell me what time I must be carried on board.

But it was not on to a ship of the Messageries maritimes that he was to be carried, but on to the barge of the sinister Charon, the ferryman of the Underworld in Etruscan and Roman mythology. As for the time, he died quietly the following day, Tuesday, November 10, at 10 o'clock in the morning.

Thus was realized Verlaine's wish: in 1889, when the rumor of Rimbaud's death reached Paris, he composed a moving sonnet that ended with the line "Rimbaud! pax tecum sit, Dominus sit tecum!" [May peace be with you, may the Lord be with you!].

He had quietly entered the peace of the beyond.

He was just thirty-seven years old.

On the hospital register was entered the following: "Rimbaud, Jean-Nicolas, merchant, born at Charleville, passing through Marseille, died November 10, 1891, at 10 o'clock in the morning.

Diagnosis: generalized carcinosis."

The death was registered the next day, November 11, on declaration by two employees of the hospital, and signed by Ernest Margnery, deputy mayor of Marseille.

The body was taken to the hospital chapel—an event recorded in its register: "No. 854—In the year one-thousand-eight-hundred-and-ninety-one, on November 11, was brought to this chapel the body of Rimbaud, Jean-Nicolas, deceased at the hospital at the age of thirty-seven years—son of the late Frédéric Jean and Cuif, Marie—bachelor, and was buried with the prayers and ceremonies of the Church" [the last phrase was printed in advance]. [Signed] A. Chaulier."

The same day permission arrived to convey the body to Charleville.

In the deserted chapel a few nuns prayed in front of the simple catafalque placed between candles. Isabelle was grief-stricken, overcome, alone, weighed down by her intolerable pain.

Another patient had taken his place in the death room. In town a clerk filled out the bill for the expenses due to the management of the funeral service by the "heirs of Rimbaud, Jean, thirty-seven years of age, deceased yesterday at the Conception":

—Funeral, sixth class:

—A coffin in oak and lead: 212.60 F.

—A copper plaque, crêpe, various *coupés*, etc.,

Total 458.11 F

The "merchant" Jean Rimbaud left the hospital on November 12, 1891. The poet Arthur Rimbaud returned fifty-seven years later when the following plaque was placed in the main courtyard:

ICI

LE 10 NOVEMBRE 1891

REVENANT D'ADEN

LE POETE

JEAN ARTHUR RIMBAUD

RENCONTRA LA FIN DE

SON AVENTURE TERRESTRE. [12]

All other souvenirs have disappeared. The room in which he died, in the Pavillon des Officiers, has since been demolished, and the site is now occupied by the Rémusat medical laboratory.

On November 13 and 14 Rimbaud made his final return to his native Ardennes. His mother, informed by telegram, immediately made arrangements for his burial, that is to say, room was made in the family vault, between his father and his sister Vitalie. Laborers arrived and built the new compartment. "When the building works were completed," Louis Pierquin recounts, "she herself went down into the ditch to make sure that the dimensions were precisely those on the plan, and that the work was 'well-done.' The laborers who were present at the scene were shocked." [13]

It is certain that it was not Rimbaud's wish to lie in Charleville cemetery, but in that of Harar or Aden. Isabelle mentioned this: "He would have liked to have been buried at Aden, because the cemetery there is on the seashore, not far from his offices. I would certainly have sent his coffin out there if he had insisted on it. He only gave up the idea because of the opposition that I would have encountered." [14]

Mme Rimbaud's tyranny was felt even beyond the grave. However, Isabelle had made certain promises to her brother: "Above all he made me promise not to leave him before he died," she had written to her mother on October 3, 1891, "and to supervise the carrying out of his last wishes, especially concerning his burial."

The *visa d'arrivée* for the body, written up at Charleville police station, bears the date November 14. On that day, about nine o'clock in the morning, Louis Pierquin recounts, Mme Rimbaud and Isabelle went to see the Abbé Gillet, who had become archpriest of Charleville, and ordered a first-class service for ten o'clock. Pierquin continues: "The Abbé Gillet told them that one hour was very short notice, that such a ceremony could not be organized on the spur of the moment, and he added that having been Rimbaud's Religious Instruction teacher (he had the fondest memories of him), he would be happy to arrange for some of his old friends and schoolfellows to attend the funeral. "Don't go on," Mme Rimbaud snapped. "It's no use." So the burial took place at ten o'clock that same day, with all the pomp usually accorded a first-class funeral, but attended by only two persons: Mme Rimbaud and Isabelle."[15]

The bill for the funeral, which is now in the Musée Rimbaud, mentions the presence of five cantors, eight choirboys, twenty orphan girls bearing candles (the whole ceremony costing 528.15 F). One can imagine the panic and rush involved in organizing so many people. Ernest Millot's sister, Mme Létrange, told J.-P. Vaillant that her husband, an organist, played the *Dies irae*. He had been warned at nine o'clock and the ceremony had taken place at half-past ten. "I've got just enough time to get dressed," he remarked, and wondered who could have died in a family known to Mme Rimbaud that made the funeral so urgent.[16]

Similarly, seeing the magnificent hearse ascend the Avenue de Flandre, which leads to the cemetery, people wondered who the obviously important, but unknown individual to be buried could be. No announcement had been made, and no information appeared in the press the following day.

A final blessing from the priest over the gaping ditch, and the two women went back without saying a word. Isabelle was weeping over the brother whom she had loved so much; she was also weeping for herself, now returned to her useless, ponderous existence. Mme Rimbaud, though she shed fewer tears, was also distraught. She had loved her Arthur: she had always loved him and preferred him to the others. He had gone his own way, but in the end he had come to resemble her, strict in duty and honesty, considerate toward others, and determined to conquer through his labors an enviable social position.

Much later, she wrote his funeral oration, and this short piece is reveal-ing: it explains the surprise, the stupefaction, one might say, that overcame her when it was suggested that a monument should be erected to the glory of her son in the Square de la Gare in Charleville. This is what she wrote, part of a letter to Isabelle, dated June 1, 1900: "I have done my duty. My poor Arthur, who never asked me for anything and who, through his work, his intelligence, his good behavior, had amassed a fortune and amassed it very honestly, never deceived anyone: on the contrary, people were responsible for his losing a great deal of money, and a great deal is still owed him and the dear child was charitable, as is well known."

He lies near the entrance to the cemetery under a very simple stone. He was joined by his mother in 1907 ("My coffin," she had asked, "will be laid between my good father and my dear Vitalie on my right, and my poor Arthur on my left"). In 1922, Isabelle completed the family group.

Ever since, on the tomb with its twin stelae, strangers, who have some-times come great distances, pause for a few moments and lay flowers.

Rimbaud had made his sister promise to pay his servant Jami a legacy of 750 thalaris, to be deducted from his account with César Tian. She knew that this Jami was now in the service of M. Felter, manager of the Maison Bienenfeld and Co. of Aden. "He is a young man of twenty-two or twenty-three," she says, "completely illiterate, scarcely understanding a few words of French." Numerous letters had to be written to César Tian, to the French consul at Aden, to Mgr. Taurin-Cahagne, in order to obtain a receipt releas-ing her of all debts. The reply that she received from the Ras Makonnen disappointed her: "Received from Monseigneur Taurin-Cahagne, bishop of the Gallas, the sum of 750 Maria-Theresa thalers from a legacy left by M. Rimbaud to his servant Jami Wadai, and delivered this sum by order of the Ras to the heirs of Jami—Harar, June 7 1893."

In the margin, the Ras had written in his own hand, "Jami's heirs have certainly received 750 thalaris. I confirm this."[17]

To obtain the declaration from Mgr. Taurin-Cahagne, Isabelle had to wait until October 12, 1894.

So the unfortunate Jami had not survived his master, having in all prob-ability fallen a victim to the terrible famine that ravaged Harar in 1891 (an-other victim was Dimitri Righas, who died in November).

"I see from the aforementioned documents," Isabelle wrote to Mgr. Taurin-Cahagne on March 12, 1895, "that Jami did not benefit from his master's generosity, since it is his heirs who have received the gift. I was surprised and sorry to learn of the death of this poor Jami, whom my brother has described as being very attached and very faithful to him. Moreover, he was only about twenty years old I believe. I wonder who his heirs might be. I'm convinced that if my brother had been able to foresee his servant's death, he would have refrained from giving anything to his family. But you must be in a position, Monseigneur, to know whether this family was worthy of such generosity, and I would like to believe that, had it been otherwise, they would not have been allowed to benefit from it."

Mme Rimbaud could not have put it better.

Epilogue

*T*wo weeks after her brother's funeral, Isabelle, opening their daily newspaper, *Le Courrier des Ardennes*, for November 29–30, 1891, was astonished to read an article two-and-a-half columns long, devoted to Arthur Rimbaud, signed L.P.[1]

ARTHUR RIMBAUD

Arthur Rimbaud, one of the best-known members of that constellation that, around 1872, made up the Parnasse contemporain, was buried some days ago in Charleville cemetery.

For about fifteen years, we lost all trace of this comrade, always so difficult to follow; his vagabond temperament and his restless spirit drove him across Europe, of which he knew every language, always tiring of everything and never finding rest.

He was the perfect expression of Baudelaire's "lunatic."

There then follows an account of the author's last meetings with the dead poet.

At Charleville he did not have four friends to confide in, and when, in Paris, in the midst of the coterie in which he shone so brightly, his admirers, Théodore de Banville or Paul Verlaine, begged him to publish the poetry that he trusted to chance, he always refused in the most categorical way. All we know of his work is a slim volume printed in Brussels in 1869, perhaps unknown to himself, and of which we have forgotten the title. Many of his handwritten pieces have been in our temporary possession, but, having neglected to make copies, we can only deplore their irreparable loss today.

More fortunate than us, Paul Verlaine has managed to save from the wreck a few remnants that he has included in his volume Les Poètes maudits. *We would refer the reader to this work, of which a third is devoted to Rimbaud. It is a fairly complete, very truthful study of him.*

Our poet's work, like that of most of the Parnassians, is made up of pieces dazzling in their clarity, perfect in their form, and of others that are incomprehensible, in which the meaning is absolutely sacrificed to the harmony.

Les Effarés is cited as an example of the first kind. The author also mentions Les Assis in reference to the local library.

We shall not try to justify Rimbaud's second, nebulous manner, in which we perceive little more than a beautiful melody.

In poetry, form no doubt holds a high place, but without the idea it is merely a vain appearance, a sterile effort. Tortured by this predisposition to seek always beyond, he gave himself up exclusively to this wave of thought, and was lost in it. All the same he had his worshippers. With Verlaine he founded a school and inspired the sect of the decadents, whose lucrubrations delight certain souls in pain who today pride themselves on their literary taste.

Rimbaud died at the age of thirty-six. His body, brought back from Marseille, rests not far from that of Ernest Millot, a good friend of his, and in our opinion, the best.

L.P.

Poor Isabelle could not believe her eyes. So her beloved Arthur was not just an honest merchant and a skilled explorer, he had also been one of the greatest poets of his day! People remembered him, he had his "worshippers," and, above all, he had been haunted by the need "always to seek the beyond!"

After giving thanks to heaven, she set about trying to discover the identity of this mysterious L.P. (Louis Pierquin).

Casting her mind back, she vaguely remembered that her brother, in her presence, at Roche, had burned several copies of the volume mentioned in *Le Courrier des Ardennes*, but she was only thirteen at the time and that was eighteen years ago!

Of course, she was not unaware that Arthur had been a brilliant pupil at the Collège, and that he had traveled a great deal before settling in Africa. How she would have loved to have known him better! Unfortunately, his sojourns at home were all too short! Hardly had he arrived than he was thinking of leaving again. She had heard long ago, and in none too good terms, of M. Verlaine—but she was not at all sure who he might be: he was probably some writer in Paris.

It all seemed so unhoped for, so wonderful. It had all been worthwhile after all. Arthur was living again: He would never die!

In a flash, she realized that she had a sacred duty: to devote her life and all her strength to the glory of her illustrious brother. To begin with, she must find out exactly what Louis Pierquin knew, over and above what he had said in his article, acquaint herself with the marvelous poems quoted by M. Verlaine in *Les Poètes maudits* (a title that she did not care for at all; her brother's place was in paradise, not among the accursed), and then try to get her hands on the mysterious slim volume, which might not, after all, be irreparably lost.

She had no idea what awaited her.

On December 15, she was shown an article in *Le Petit Ardennais*, a left-wing newspaper that she never read. It was a reproduction of a short article that had recently appeared in *Les Entretiens politiques et littéraires*, written by a certain Monsieur D. (Delahaye): it was a jerkily written account of Arthur's life, containing a great deal of spite and unpleasant revelations.

About the same time, Isabelle was horrified to learn that *Les Illuminations* had been published in 1886 without the author's permission, and, worse, that a scandalous book, *Reliquaire*, consisting of a selection of her brother's poems, with a preface by a certain Rodolphe Darzens, and full of new horrors, had just been published.

But what hurt her most deeply was reading some of Arthur's poems, obviously inspired not by God but by Satan, *Les premières Communions*, for example, or *Le Mal*, or *Accroupissements*, which left no doubt as to his hatred of religion.

So she decided to counterattack, and to impose her own version of the truth. Nobody had known her brother as she had, no one had the right to speak about him. She wrote long letters to the editors of *Le Petit Ardennais* and *Le Courrier des Ardennes* that today cannot fail to raise a smile, in which she declares that her brother had been an exceptional individual from childhood; at school he had been "the most brilliant pupil."

"One of his teachers had taken him to Paris and introduced him to MM. Théodore de Banville and Verlaine, who were struck by the intelligence of this fifteen-year-old child, and set him to write a few poems, several of which are genuine small masterpieces—but it had never occurred to A. Rimbaud to have his verse published, or to derive any gain or fame from them."

Stories about his imprisonment at Mazas and his presence in Paris during the Commune were mere legends. "He continued his education, not in a school, but with various teachers, sometimes in one town, sometimes in another. He'had never been in the service of Holland or deserted in Java. In Africa he had never traded in cotton or skins—the very idea!—but had been a highly respected merchant in coffee, ivory, incense, perfume, and gold ingots. He was highly esteemed by all, by whites and natives alike, for his probity, his kindness, and the purity of his morals. He died like a saint."

Thus was born the "Rimbaud myth" in which nobody has ever believed, but which a distinguished professor at the Sorbonne saw fit to demolish with the sledgehammer of three thousand printed pages.

Isabelle now decided to forbid all publication of her brother's works—his life had been distorted and his thought betrayed. It would be better to sacrifice his reputation altogether, for silence stifles scandal, and she would rather have died than be the cause of scandal.

This did not at all suit Verlaine, who, at the time, was preparing an edition of his old friend's poetic works.

But Isabelle, after four years of obstruction, realized that the current was too strong to resist. She lifted her veto and allowed M. Verlaine to write a preface for her brother's *Poésies complètes* (late 1895).

Since then, the current has grown stronger. Rimbaud is regarded as one of the five or six greatest French poets, and his work is studied throughout the world.

Isabelle's naive hagiography—which she continued, with her husband Paterne Berrichon, until 1914—long ago passed into the anecdotal history of our literature.

Chronology shows that the life of the poet Rimbaud began at the very moment of his death. Should one see it as a sign of destiny that he died in the hospital of the Conception—suggesting the beginning of the formation of a new creature called to life?

He was, as André Gide said, like one of those very distant stars, which, long since extinct, continue to shine in our eyes and will continue to do so for centuries to come.

Since he left this world, his genius has continued to shine, a star of incomparable magnitude in the firmament of French poetry.

NOTES

BIBLIOGRAPHY

INDEX

NOTES

1

1 Preface to Arthur Rimbaud, *Œuvres* (1912).
2 Letter from Mme Rimbaud to Isabelle, May 24–25, 1900.
3 This pleasant square, with its tall trees and its kiosk, was not then called Square de la Gare, for the good reason that the railroad had not yet been built. It did not come into service until October 1858. I am not even sure whether the kiosk existed in 1870.
4 Suzanne Briet, *Rimbaud notre prochain.*
5 Jacques Foucart, "Les ascendances bourguigonnes et franc-comtioses d'Arthur Rimbaud," in *Le Bien public* (Dijon), October 27, 1954.
6 Paterne Berrichon, *Jean Arthur Rimbaud, le poète.*
7 Marcel Coulon, *La Vie de Rimbaud et de son œuvre*, p. 24.
8 Gilles Henry, "Note sur les arrière-grands-parents d'Arthur Rimbaud," in *Etudes rimbaldiennes*, vol. 3 (1972).
9 Colonel Godchot, *Arthur Rimbaud ne varietur*, vol. 1.
10 *Rimbaud vivant*, no. 5 (1974).
11 Jean Bourguignon and Charles Houin, *Revue d'Ardenne et d'Argonne*, November-December 1896.
12 Berrichon, *Rimbaud, le poète.*
13 Suzanne Briet, *Madame Rimbaud.*
14 Cornelia, mother of Tiberius and Caius Gracchus, famous Roman tribunes and orators. Left a widow, with twelve children, she became a byword for the strong-willed woman who devotes all her energies to propagating the ambitions of her children—Translator's note.
15 Berrichon, *Rimbaud, le poète.*
16 Like all the Rimbauds, Mme Briet writes the name of the township as "Roches."
17 Briet, *Madame Rimbaud*

2

1 In his letter to his friend Delahaye of October 14, 1875, Arthur was to call him "Le Némery."

2 Godchot, *Arthur Rimbaud ne varietur,* vol. 1.

3 Berrichon, *Jean Arthur Rimbaud, le poète.*

4 On the subject of Captain Rimbaud's "desertion," see *Revue française de psychanalyse,* (May-June 1975. On his stay at Dijon and his journalistic activities, see the article by H. Lubienski Bodenham in *Rimbaud vivant,* nos. 18–19 (1980).

5 The only manuscript of this poem bears the date May 26, 1871. However, Izambard is right to challenge it, for these verses are obviously later; they have the blackness of the seer's writing of spring 1871. Perhaps Izambard knew the first, less corrosive version of the poem, which Rimbaud revised and darkened later? This would be an explanation.

6 Fowlie, pp. 77–79.

7 It was thought that Rimbaud did not go to school until 1862. M. Stéphane Taute, in the sixth *Cahier du Centre culturel Arthur Rimbaud* (Charleville-Mézières, November 1978), has established that he began school in 1861. As he won prizes at the end of the year 1861–62, one may conclude that he spent the whole year at the Institution Rossat.

8 Information provided by M. René Robinet, former archivist for the Ardennes, at the 98ᵉ Congrès national des Sociétés savantes de Clermont-Ferrand in 1963. Review in *Le Bateau ivre,* no. 20 (September 1966).

9 Extract from *Entre nous,* school magazine of Saint Remi (formerly Institution Rossat), 2d term 1949.

10 Sixth *Cahier du Centre culturel Arthur Rimbaud.*

11 Briet, *Madame Rimbaud.*

12 Paterne Berrichon (*La Vie de Jean Arthur Rimbaud,* p. 32, and idem, *Rimbaud, le poète,* p. 26) dates this notebook from 1862–63. It has been objected that the allusion to the kings of Persia, at a time when ancient history was not yet taught at the Institution Rossat, would suggest that the notebook belonged to a later date: to late 1865, at the earliest. I believe that it represents the first writings and drawings of a very young schoolboy expressing his repulsion for the studies to which he was condemned. See Antoine Adam's note in the Pléiade edition, p. 1027. However, I would agree that the drawing "Navigation," reproduced in *La Grive* of April 1956, is more in keeping with the environment of the Collège, which is situated quite close to the Meuse.

3

1 In France classes are numbered in reverse order, as it were. Thus if one completes one's full time at the *lycée* one will end up in the *classe de première.* The penultimate year is called the *classe de seconde* and so forth. Since no single system of naming the classes is common to the whole English-speaking world, it is preferable to keep the French terms — Translator's note.

2 On Desdouets, see Ernest Delahaye (*Souvenirs familiers*), and Berrichon (his two biographies of Rimbaud), also the *Mercure de France* of January 1, 1955. There is a portrait of him in the *Album Rimbaud.*

3 "Des souvenirs inconnus sur Rimbaud" presented by Pierre Petitfils in the *Mercure de France*, January 1, 1955.

4 Ernest Delahaye, *Rimbaud* (1906), p. 21, and idem, *Rimbaud* (1923), p. 176.

5 Petitfils, *Mercure de France*, January 1, 1955.

6 "Les souvenirs d'un ami de Rimbaud" (Louis Pierquin) introduced by Jean-Marie Carré in the *Mercure de France*, May 1, 1924, and reproduced in the works of the same author (*Lettres de Rimbaud, Les deux Rimbaud*).

7 This Poncelet, who later became a school principal, recounted this fact to Berrichon in a letter dated November 30, 1901 (Collection Matarasso).

8 Almost all these drawings were published by Mme Y.-M. Méléra in the de luxe edition of her *Rimbaud* (1930). The iconography of François Ruchon contains another ("Le marchand de chansons"). Others are still unpublished ("Le Chameau," "L'Eléphant"). The "Dimanche au village" is a modified copy of a cartoon by Albert Humbert ("Croquis agricole") which appeared in *Le Monde comique.*

9 *Mercure de France*, April 1, 1930. The autograph copy of this letter is in the Musée Rimbaud of Charleville-Mézières. The Little Prince's tutor, Auguste Fillon, published a book of memoirs about his illustrious pupil (*Le Prince impérial* [Paris: Hachette, 1912]). There is no mention in it of the correspondence with Rimbaud.

10 On Paul Labarrière, see "Un témoignage tardif sur Rimbaud," by Jules Mouquet, *Mercure de France*, May 15, 1933.

11 The name commonly given to the coup d'état carried out on December 2, 1861, by Louis Napoléon, then president of the Republic—Translator's note.

12 Rimbaud's Latin exercises have been translated and published by Jules Mouquet (A. Rimbaud, *Vers de Collège* [Paris: Mercure de France, 1932]. A Latin discourse, "Apollonius' Speech on Marcus Cicero," is included in the Pléiade edition.

13 Bourguignon and Houin, *Revue d'Ardenne et d'Argonne,*. November-December 1896.

14 Delahaye, *Souvenirs familiers*, p. 43 note.

15 Berrichon (*Rimbaud, le poète*, p. 37) and Mouquet (*Vers de Collège*).

16 Arthur had copied into his ancient history textbook a (perfectly decent) ancient Greek statue. Frédéric took this drawing off him, whereupon it fell into the hands of a certain Rousseau, who hastened to replace the modest figleaf with a respectable male member. He entitled the new work "L'abbé Wuillème in the bath," then, with another pupil, Leroy, slipped the edifying drawing under the seminary door. At an early stage in the investigation, it was thought that Frédéric was the culprit (*Cahier* no. 7 *du Centre culturel Arthur Rimbaud* (Charleville-Mézières, June 1981).

17 Mouquet, *Mercure de France*, May 15, 1933.

18 Marcel Coulon, *Le Problème de Rimbaud, poète maudit*, p. 19.

19 Petitfils, *Mercure de France*, Jan. 1, 1955.

20 This note, which, in *Le Bateau ivre*, no. 14 (November 1955), I describe as unpublished, had in fact already been published in facsimile form in *Les Idées françaises*, 1924, p. 320, by Emile Le Brun. The autograph copy belongs to the Lucien-Graux Collection.

21 Georges Izambard, *Rimbaud tel que je l'ai connu*, articles, souvenirs, and notes collected by H. de Bouillane de Lacoste and Pierre Izambard.

22 Ibid. and *La Grive*, no. 5 (October 1929). It should be said that the version of the *Baiser du Faune* that appeared in *La Jeune France*, July 1886, does not contain Rimbaud's "correction." Fowlie, pp. 47–49.

23 *Creda in unam* was later entitled *Soleil et chair*—Translator's note.

24 Fowlie, pp. 27–35.

25 Ibid., p. 17.

26 Rimbaud was, of course, fifteen on this date—Translator's note.

27 Delahaye, *Rimbaud* (1906).

28 On Bretagne, see the memoirs of Delahaye and of Pierquin and, above all, *Le Bateau ivre*, no. 14 (November 1955).

29 Dehahaye, *Souvenirs familiers*, p. 148.

30 "Le Petit Rimbaud" (unpublished essay by Delahaye), quotation from his book *Les Illuminations and Une saison en enfer de Rimbaud*, p. 27.

31 Petitfils, *Mercure de France*, Jan. 1, 1955.

32 Ibid.

33 Handwritten note by Delahaye in the Bibliothèque littéraire Jacques Doucet, published in *La Bateau ivre*, no. 13 (September 1954).

34 Fowlie, pp. 53–55.

35 The text of this letter will be found in Robert Goffin, *Rimbaud vivant*, pp. 22–23.

4

1 Fowlie, p. 125.

2 Berrichon has provided an excellent commentary on this poem in *Rimbaud, le poète*, p. 68. Marcel Coulon and others believe (wrongly, in my opinion) that these lines refer to Captain Rimbaud's departure around 1860 (when Rimbaud was six years old).

3 Delahaye, *Rimbaud* (1906).

4 Fowlie, p. 93.

5 Izambard, *Rimbaud tel que je l'ai connu*.

6 See *Rimbaud vivant*, no. 16 (1979), review of a work by M. Vandenhoecq on Paul Demeńy in a publication of the Amis de Douai.

7 For the incidents of the nurses and the intercepted convoy see Delahaye, *Souvenirs familiers* (version of *La Revue d'ardenne et d'Argonne*). The incident of the convoy is recounted by Jules Poirier in his work *Mézières en 1870* (Reims, Matot-Braine), p. 48.

8 This date has been challenged by Claude Duchet, "Autour du 'Dormeur du val' de Rimbaud," *Revue d'histoire littéraire de la France*, 1962, p. 371. Rimbaud appears to have left on October 2. I am following Izambard, who says that he came back "about October 8," according to the text of *Vers et Prose* (first term 1911), and "on October 8," according to *Rimbaud tel que je l'ai connu*, p. 71.

9 On Léon Billuart, see the (fairly disappointing) article in *Lettres françaises*, July 5, 1956.

10 Goffin, *Rimbaud vivant.*
11 Ibid.
12 Fowlie, p. 59.
13 Goffin, *Rimbaud vivant.*
14 We know a cartoon, "Prise de Saarbrück," reproduced in Rimbaud, *Œuvres* (1981). This is not the one described by Rimbaud, which was more naive, more popular in style, and which has never been found.
15 Fowlie, p. 63.
16 Izambard, *Rimbaud tel que je l'ai connu.*
17 Fowlie, p. 223.
18 *La Cousine Bette,* novel by Balzac, whose eponymous heroine is a terrifying peasant who becomes a wicked fat society woman—Translator's note.
19 Izambard, *Rimbaud tel que je l'ai connu.* Dame Pernelle, Orgon's mother in Molière's *Tartuffe,* the type of the old scold for whom her daughter-in-law can do nothing right—Translator's note.
20 Petitfils, *Mercure de France,* January 1, 1955.
21 Charles-Marie Desgranges, in his *Morceaux choisis des auteurs français du Moyen Age à nos jours* (Paris: Hatier, 1933), quotes *Le Dormeur du val* with this reference: *"Progrès des Ardennes."* Unfortunately, it is impossible to check this since no copies of *Le Progrès des Ardennes* of this time have been found.
22 Hero of a play by Auguste Vacquerie (1863), the noble benefactor of a young ungrateful thief.
23 See Jules Poirier, *Mézières en 1870.*
24 Fowlie, p. 85.

5

1 Incident recounted by R. Darzens in the preface to *Reliquaire* (1891). It had also been recounted by Félicien Champsaur in his novel *Dinah Samuel* (1883). In the latter work, the facts are presented differently: Max (Gill) appears to have found Cimber (Rimbaud) busy polishing his boots. He would have kept him with him, "but this animal had a penchant for theft and for one of our friends" (Forain?). S. Tanaval (?), a giant of a man, wanted to reprimand him, but Rimbaud-Cimber faced up to him and declared: "I do not fight with horses!" It is anyone's guess how much of this is true.
2 See *Rimbaud vivant* (1974).
3 Delahaye has given the exact location of this cave in a letter to Berrichon, dated June 22, 1897, published in *Le Bateau ivre,* no. 13 (September 1954).
4 Izambard, *Rimbaud tel que je l'ai connu.*
5 Delahaye, *Rimbaud* (1923). Verlaine alluded to this incident in his section on Rimbaud in *Hommes d'aujourd'hui.*
6 This emerges from a police report transmitted from London to Paris on June 26, 1873, published by Auguste Martin as *Verlaine et Rimbaud.* The file of the Belgian secret police ("Forçats libérés") concerning Rimbaud bears the following statement on its cover: "Was a franc-tireur." Delahaye has spoken of "Tirail-

leurs de la Révolution," and Verlaine of the "Vengeurs de Flourens" (*Les Hommes d'aujourd'hui*).

7 Berrichon, *La Vie de Rimbaud*, p. 67.
8 A character in Victor Hugo's *Les Misérables*, *gavroche* being a common Parisian term for "street arab," or "ragamuffin"—Translator's note.
9 Fowlie, p. 81.
10 See *Rimbaud vivant* (1974).
11 Petitfils, *Mercure de France*, January 1, 1955.
12 *La Grive*, no. 61 (April 1949).
13 Fowlie, p. 287.
14 "Les souvenirs d'un ami de Rimbaud" (Louis Pierquin).
15 Berrichon, *Rimbaud, le poète*.
16 See *Rimbaud vivant*, nos. 10 (1976) and 17 (1979).
17 Fowlie, p. 73.
18 Ibid., pp. 91–93. Speaking of absinthe, Verlaine, in his *Confessions* asks: "What fool, then, magnified it into a fairy, into a green Muse?" (part 2, section 3).
19 See *Rimbaud vivant*, nos 10 (1976) and 17 (1979).
20 Fowlie, pp. 303–5.
21 Bourguignon and Houin, *Revue d'Ardenne et d'Argonne*, November-December 1896.
22 Berrichon, *Rimbaud, le poète*.
23 Izambard, *Rimbaud tel que je l'ai connu*.
24 Berrichon, *Rimbaud, le poète*.
25 Mme M.-Y. Méléra, *Résonances autour de Rimbaud*, p. 183.
26 Fowlie, pp. 95–101.
27 Rimbaud was to recount this to Verlaine, and his wife, Mathilde Mauté, was to repeat it in her *Mémoires de ma vie*.
28 Letter from Verlaine to Rimbaud, April 2, 1872, and letter from Rimbaud to Delahaye, June 1872.
29 The head librarian before World War II, M. Manquillet, gave Colonel Godchot (*Arthur Rimbaud ne varietur*, vol. 1, p. 255) a list of the works pertaining to the occult sciences belonging to the Charleville municipal library.
30 Fowlie, p. 65.
31 Delahaye, *Souvenirs familiers*.
32 Delahaye, *Souvenirs familiers*, in *Revue d'Ardenne et d'Argonne*, May-June 1908.
33 The letter to Jean Aicard was published in *La Grive*, July-December 1963, and in *Les Nouvelles littéraires*, September 26, 1963, by M. Pakenham.
34 See Mathilde Mauté, *Mémoires de ma vie*.
35 Indeed, Izambard did not receive his chests of books until four months later at Argentan, his new post (*Rimbaud tel que je l'ai connu*, p. 172).
36 Fowlie, pp. 105–15.
37 Ibid., p. 313.
38 Demény was converted to Rimbaldian *Voyance!* In 1873 Lemerre brought out his collection *Les Visions*, the first poem of which is entitled "Les Voyants" (The Seers). Each of the stanzas of another poem, "Anomalies," begins with "J'ai vu . . ." (I have seen . . .), which is reminiscent of the *Bateau ivre*. There

is one line—"J'ai vu les flots porter des baves amoureuses" (I have seen the waves bearing amorous foam)—which Rimbaud himself would not have been ashamed of. Last, the collection contains a poem entitled "Vision d'Ophélie" and one, "Miniature," dedicated to Verlaine.

39 Fowlie, p. 119.

40 Georges Zayed, *La Formation littéraire de Verlaine*, p. 293.

41 Those who have questioned the attribution of this piece to Rimbaud are, in my opinion, quite wrong. It bristles with expressions that he made peculiarly his own, such as "Vous êtes heureux, vous!" or "Eh bien! Eh bien! j'apprends de belles . . .", or "Tenez, nous sommes aux anges, mon cher," etc.

42 Fowlie, p. 119.

43 Rimbaud read his verse without undue emphasis, but almost convulsively, at feverish speed. "His nervous, still childish voice rendered quite naturally the vibration and power of the words. He spoke at he felt, as it came, in a precipitous outpouring of violent sensations" (Delahaye, *Rimbaud* [1906], p. 86).

44 Delahaye, *Rimbaud* (1906), p. 49 note and *Rimbaud* (1923), p. 41.

45 Fowlie, p. 247.

46 Dehahaye, *Souvenirs familiers*, in *Revue d'Ardenne et d'Argonne*, November-December 1908.

6

1 Later, in dozens of comic poems, which he called "coppées," Verlaine tried to imitate this tone, but what he produced is a curious mixture of Ardennais, Artesian, and rural speech in the manner of d'Onésime Boquillon, a naive, but cunning country poet, who was very fashionable around 1875–80.

2 P. Verlaine, "Nouvelles notes sur Rimbaud," *La Plume*, November 15–30, 1895.

3 On Verlaine and Petrus Borel, see Zayed *La Formation littéraire de Verlaine*, p. 294.

4 This letter, in the Bibliothèque de Bordeaux, was published for the first time by Jean de Maupassant in 1923, in the *Revue philomathique de Bordeaux et du Sud-Ouest*.

5 P. Verlaine, *Les Beaux-Arts*, December 1, 1895. In the section devoted to Albert Mérat in his *Hommes d'aujourd'hui*, Verlaine mentions his lack of enthusiasm when Rimbaud arrived in Paris.

6 See my study of Rimbaud's manuscripts in *Etudes rimbaldiennes*, vol. 2 (1970).

7 Information supplied by Charles Beaumont, *Mercure de France*, October 1, 1915.

8 Letter from Delahaye to Godchot, in *Arthur Rimbaud ne varietur*, vol. 2, p. 141.

9 The Glatigny hypothesis turns up for the first time in a letter from Léon Vanier to Louis Pierquin, dated January 26, 1893. The legend arose around the time of Rimbaud's death: an anonymous notice in the *Echo de Paris* of November 12, 1891, claimed that Hugo spoke his historic words while stroking Rimbaud's head, and that Rimbaud, suddenly moving away, murmured: "Il m'emmerde,

ce vieux birbe." According to Lepelletier, Rimbaud regarded Hugo as an un-
inspired, conventional poetaster (*Echo de Paris*, July 25, 1901).

10 Delahaye, *Rimbaud* (1923), p. 43 note.

11 Drawing reproduced in a catalogue for a book sale at the Hôtel Drouot, May
29, 1968.

12 On Henri Mercier, see Michael Pakenham's study in the *Revue des Sciences
humaines*, July-September 1963.

13 This opéra bouffe in three acts, with music by Henri Litolff, was produced on
October 18, 1871. It was, according to one critic, "a succession of farts in the
Offenbach manner."

14 See H. Matarasso and P. Petitfils, "Rimbaud, Verlaine, Germain Nouveau, and
l'Album zutique," *Mercure de France*, May 1961.

15 The autograph copy, which belonged to Paul Gachet, the son of the famous
Dr. Gachet of Auvers-sur-Oise, is reproduced in Briet's *Rimbaud notre prochain*.

16 Like this one, for instance, recounted by Delahaye, and published by Henri
Guillemin in *Mercure de France*, October 1, 1954 (Rimbaud is speaking): "It's
silly, I know, but I used to get a lot of fun out of passing myself off as a filthy
pig. People would believe everything I said. One day, for instance, I told some-
body how I had gone into Cabaner's room while he was away, found a cup of
milk waiting for him, beat off over it, and came in it. People laughed, then
repeated it as true."

17 The building, demolished in the early 1930s, housed a cabaret, the annex of
the *Caméléon*, which was in the Boulevard du Montparnasse, where the poets
of the late 1920s gave public readings.

18 *Le Miroir du monde*, 1936.

19 In 1893, at the time when Wilde and Lord Alfred Douglas met Verlaine. "I had
previously met Verlaine one day when I was with Oscar Wilde," Douglas writes.
"We spent some hours together in a café drinking absinthe, an apertif that I
found sickening. It was a year before the catastrophe" (*Oscar Wilde et quelques-
uns.*)

20 Lepelletier's mother died on September 29, 1871.

21 Deverrière wrote to Izambard on January 2, 1872: "Rimbaud has been in Paris
for two or three months, with Verlaine, the poet and friend of Père Bretagne"
(Izambard, *Rimbaud tel que je l'ai connu.*) Thus Verlaine was suggesting that
Rimbaud was still living in his house: Mme Rimbaud had to be reassured.

22 See *Le Figaro littéraire*, April 28, 1951. Jules Lefranc (*Revue Palladienne*, no.
17, 1952) has remarked that there was once a gate into the Montparnasse cemetery opposite the Rue Campagne-Première, giving access to the 21st and 22nd
divisions. This gate has since been removed. See *La Bateau ivre*, no. 9 (March
1952).

23 Berrichon, *Rimbaud, le poète*.

24 The *Sonnet du combat* was published in *La Renaissance littéraire et artistique*,
April 12, 1873.

25 This version by R. Darzens (Preface to the *Reliquaire*) is, in my opinion, preferable to Verlaine's (Preface to Rimbaud's Poésies complètes, [1895]), in which
the blow from the sword-stick was delivered at Carjat in the dining room, across

the table. In 1895 Verlaine was trying not to blacken Rimbaud too much in his sister's eyes.

26 See Godchot, *Arthur Rimbaud ne varietur*, vol. 2, p. 159.

27 Germain Nouveau made a subtle allusion to the incident in his letter to Jean Richepin of April 17, 1875, when referring to his projected collection, which would be in serried Alexandrines like the soldiers of Philibert de Lorme, the man with the string. "But you know more than Carjat about nothingness—and you can see from this what sort of a thing it may be."

28 *Le Sagittaire*, October 1901.

7

1 Delahaye, *Rimbaud* (1923), p. 162.

2 Fowlie, p. 151.

3 A. Adam, ed., *Œuvres complètes de Rimbaud*, Pléiade edition (1972), p. 943.

4 Fowlie, p. 217.

5 The arietta referred to comes from Act 2, Scene 7:

> "*Dans nos prairies*
> *Toujours fleuries*
> *On voit sourire*
> *Un doux zéphyr, etc.*"

A collection of eighteenth-century players, including *Ninette à la cour*, figures in the list of objects left by Verlaine in the Rue Nicolet in July 1872. To these "Ariettes oubliées" Verlaine devoted in all nine poems of the *Romances sans paroles*, including the fifth that begins with the line "Le piano que baise une main frêle," and evokes "Un air bien vieux, bien faible et bien charmant."

6 Edouard Chanal, successor to Henri Perrin, himself successor to Georges Izambard at the Collège de Charleville. Laure, Edmond Lepelletier's sister. Anatole Guérin, manager of the newspaper *La Ligne droite*, which was published at Charleville, at this time.

7 This "someone very important in Madrid" (that is, at the Café de Madrid) was Antoine de Tounens, a native of Périgueux, M. Mauté's home town, who called himself "roi de Patagonie et d'Araucanie." He recruited subjects by selling decorations (the "steel crown") and noble titles. Verlaine met him at the house of Dr. Antoine Cros, who was to succeed him on the throne. See Jean Raspail, *Moi, Antoine de Tounens, roi de Patagonie* (Paris: Albin Michel, 1981).

8 Henri Regnault, a painter whose talent equaled his patriotic fervor, killed at Buzenval, January 24, 1871.

9 See Jules Rais, "Les dernières lettres inédites de Paul Verlaine," *Revue des vivants*, 1923.

10 See Léandre Vaillat, *En écoutant Forain* (Paris: Flammarion, 1931).

11 Mme Verlaine, *Mémoires de ma vie*.

12 In his work *The Design of Rimbaud's Poetry*, Mr. John Porter Houston points out that Rimbaud's "chansons" bear an astonishing resemblance to the religious poetry of the celebrated Madame Guyon, the friend of Fénelon, not only in style and rhythm, but also in vocabulary. See *Le Bateau ivre*, no. 18 (July 1964).

13 Fowlie, p. 137.

14 Ibid.

15 Ibid., p. 133.

16 Cazals and Le Rouge, in *Les Derniers jours de Paul Verlaine*, quote this song to the tune of "Saute, saute, Bourguignonne":

> *"Dans la vill' de Paris,*
> *Merde, merde pour Versailles.*
> *Dans la vill' de Paris,*
> *Y a deux académies.*
> *L'une ousq'ils sont quarante,*
> *Qui vivent de leurs rentes,*
> *L'autre au Quartier latin*
> *Qui s'tient chez le chand'vin."*

The "Academie d'absinthe" was replaced by a butcher's shop before 1910.

17 Fowlie, p. 143. This poem and the "chansons" of the Hôtel de Cluny were rediscovered in 1906. They were in Forain's possession. It is thought that when he came to see Rimbaud, he retrieved them in his room after his departure in July 1872.

8

1 "Les souvenirs d'un ami de Rimbaud" (Louis Pierquin).

2 François Porché (*Verlaine tel qu'il fut*, p. 198 note) was the first to point out that, according to Delahaye, Rimbaud was on the train.

3 Fowlie, p. 151.

4 Ibid., p. 201.

5 Ibid., p. 151.

6 Ibid., pp. 145–47.

7 See D.-A. de Graaf, "Autour du dossier de Bruxelles," *Mercure de France* August 1, 1956.

8 Fowlie, p. 235.

9 See my article on "L'Architecture rimbaldienne," *Nouvelles littéraires*, August 24, 1967.

10 In his works on Verlaine and Rimbaud in England, Mr. V. P. Underwood provides innumerable details concerning the entertainment offered by London toward the end of the year 1872: plays, exhibitions, shows of various kinds.

11 Fowlie, p. 239.

12 Ibid., p. 233

9

1 Delahaye, *Rimbaud* (1906), p. 115.
2 "Nouveaux documents sur Rimbaud: le journal de sa soeur Vitalie presenté par H. de Bouillane de Lacoste et H. Matarasso," *Mercure de France*, May 15, 1938. Text in the Pléiade edition.
3 *La Table ronde*, November 1954.
4 "Liège, que j'avais vue aussi—tenez, le jour même de la chute de Thiers en 1873. Cela ne me rajeunit guère" (P. Verlaine, *Onze jours en Belgique*). Thiers fell on May 24, 1873. The news did not reach Liège until Monday May 26.
5 Fowlie, pp. 251–53.
6 *Revue d'Ardenne et d'Argonne*, September 1901, p. 191.
7 Underwood, *Rimbaud et l'Angleterre*.
8 Delahaye, *Rimbaud* (1923), p. 52.
9 Underwood, *Rimbaud et l'Angleterre*.
10 Delahaye, *Verlaine* (1919), p. 170.
11 Fowlie, p. 189.

10

1 Underwood, *Rimbaud et l'Angleterre*.
2 In his declaration of July 12, 1873, to the Brussels examining magistrate, Rimbaud is wrong in saying that he arrived in Brussels on Tuesday morning. In the morning of Tuesday July 8 he was still in London.
3 Delahaye, *Rimbaud* (1906), p. 125.
4 The discovery of this curious and moving picture was announced by Maurice Monda in *Le Figaro littéraire*, April 5, 1947. It belongs to M. Matarasso. About Jef Rosman and the dubious widow Pincemaille, see H. Matarasso, *Mercure de France*, November 1, 1947. On the most likely Madame Pincemaille-Porson, see D.-A. de Graaf, *Mercure de France*, August 1, 1956.

11

1 Fowlie, pp. 187–89.
2 Ibid., p. 173.
3 Ibid., p. 193.
4 Berrichon, *Rimbaud, le poète*.
5 Fowlie, pp. 208–9.
6 Facsimile in the thesis of H. de Bouillane de Lacoste, *Rimbaud et le problème des Illuminations*.
7 See D.-A. de Graaf, "Autour du dossier de Bruxelles," *Mercure de France*, August 1, 1956.
8 Godchot, *Arthur Rimbaud ne varietur*, vol. 2, p. 274.

9 Jean Richepin, *Revue de France*, January 1, 1927.
10 Berrichon, *Rimbaud, le poète.*
11 "Les souvenirs d'un ami de Rimbaud" (Louis Pierquin).
12 Underwood, *Rimbaud et l'Angleterre.*
13 Ibid.
14 See H. de Bouillane de Lacoste, *Rimbaud et le problème des Illuminations,* and André Guyaux, "L'écrivain et son scribe: Germain Noveau copiant deux textes des Illuminations," *Rimbaud vivant,* no. 10 (1976).
15 Jean Richepin, *Revue de France*, January 1, 1927.
16 Here is an example: the poem *Le Refus* (*Valentines*) opens with this declaration:

> "*Je suis pédéraste dans l'âme,*
> *Je le dis tout haut et debout.*
> *Assis, je changerais de gamme,*
> *Et couché sur un lit, Madame,*
> *Je ne le dirais plus du tout.*"

and ends with this denial:

> "*Or, je ne suis pas pédéraste;*
> *Que serait-ce si je l'étais!*"

17 Underwood, *Rimbaud et l'Angleterre.*
18 Vitalie's diary was published (not in its entirety) by H. de Bouillane de Lacoste and H. Matarasso in *Mercure de France,* May 15, 1938. Text in the Pléiade edition.
19 These three letters, and two, less interesting ones, from Isabelle (July 9 and 17, 1874) are included in the Pléiade edition. The manuscripts are in the Musée Rimbaud, Charleville-Mézières.
20 Underwood, *Rimbaud et l'Angleterre.*
21 Bourguignon and Houin, *Revue d'Ardenne et d'Argonne,* September-October 1897.
22 "Sur les traces de Rimbaud," *Mercure de France,* May 1, 1947.
23 Underwood, *Rimbaud et l'Angleterre.*
24 Fowlie, p. 245.

12

1 Bourguignon and Houin, *Revue d'Ardenne et d'Argonne,* September-October 1897.
2 See D.-A. de Graaf, *Revue de Philologie et d'Histoire,* vol. 34 (1956); see also *Rimbaud vivant,* no. 11–12 (1977).
3 Berrichon, *La Vie de Rimbaud.*
4 At the end of the "Lettre du baron de Petdechèvre" (Geneva: Edition Pierre

Cailler, 1949) is the reproduction of a drawing by Rimbaud representing the old town of Stuttgart, and part of the drawing that appears on his letter of March 5, 1875, to Delahaye.

5 Information provided by D.-A. de Graaf. See *Rimbaud vivant*, nos. 11–12 (1977), with an engraving representing Dr. Luebke's house.

6 Henry Guillemin, "Connaissance de Rimbaud," *Mercure de France*, October 1, 1954, p. 241.

7 Underwood, *Verlaine et l'Angleterre*, p. 270.

8 *Cahier Doucet*, plate 17.

9 Drawing reproduced in Verlaine's *Nos Ardennes* (Geneva: P. Cailler, 1948).

10 Delahaye, *Rimbaud* (1923).

11 Ibid., p. 61. On Henri Mercier, see Michael Pakenham, *Revue des Sciences humaines*, July-September 1963.

12 First publication in *Le Bateau ivre*, May 11, 1949.

13 *Cahier Doucet*, on the back of plate 71.

14 *Les Entretiens politiques et littéraires*, December 1891.

15 Delahaye, *Rimbaud* (1923).

16 Article reproduced from *Barbarie et Poésie* (1928).

17 Delahaye, *Verlaine* (1919), p. 233.

18 *Cahier Doucet*, plate 24.

19 Ibid., on the back of plate 17.

20 Rimbaud's *Ebauches* (Paris: Mercure de France), p. 208.

21 *Cahier Doucet*, on the back of plate 67.

22 The lists of English, German, and Spanish words copied out by Rimbaud are reproduced in H. de Bouillane de Lacoste's *Rimbaud et le problème des Illuminations*.

23 *Cahier Doucet*, on the back of plate 10.

24 Ibid., on the back of plate 17.

25 Delahaye wrote to Verlaine (on the back of plate 31 of the *Cahier Doucet*) that according to a former pupil at "Barbadaux," Germain Nouveau, imitating the "too glorious model" (Rimbaud), prepared one evening a punch in a chamberpot according to the practice of the pupils who had slipped out of the Collège (supported by a drawing). Sometimes, it has been said, Nouveau accompanied his pupils in their nocturnal outings.

26 Extract from the sales catalogue of autograph manuscripts, March 12, 1936 (Blaizot, expert). See Verlaine's *Œuvres poétiques* (1951), p. 1197.

27 Delahaye, *Rimbaud* (1906), p. 173 note.

28 *Cahier Doucet*, on the back of plate 68.

29 Ibid., on the back of plate 89.

30 Bourguignon and Houin, *Revue d'Ardenne et d'Argonne*, September-October 1897.

31 Louis Pierquin, "Sur Arthur Rimbaud," *Le Courrier des Ardennes*, December 31, 1893.

32 Bourguignon and Houin, *Revue d'Ardenne et d'Argonne*, September-October 1897.

33 Delahaye, *Rimbaud* (1923).

34 *Cahier Doucet*, plate 2.

13

1 *Cahier Doucet*, on the back of plate 105.
2 Delahaye, *Rimbaud* (1923), p. 63 note.
3 "Les souvenirs d'un ami de Rimbaud" (Louis Pierquin).
4 See the memoirs of Ernest Letrange (Louis's son) in *La Grive*, no. 83 (October 1954).
5 *Cahier Doucet*, on the back of plate 64 (the drawing concerns the elections of February 20, 1876).
6 Drawing reproduced for the first time in *La Revue blanche*, April 15, 1897.
7 Bourguignon and Houin, *Revue d'Ardenne et d'Argonne*, September-October 1897.
8 *Cahier Doucet*, plate 12.
9 Ibid., plate 10.
10 An extract from the register of the War Department was published by Dr. Marmelstein in the *Bulletin des Amis de Rimbaud* (supplement to *La Grive*, no. 37 [July 1937]). An (illegible) photographic reproduction of the Bandung Register is to be found in D.-A. de Graaf, *Rimbaud et la durée de son activité littéraire*, p. 136. This register was destroyed during World War II.
11 Fowlie, p. 223. It has been said that this text was suggested to Rimbaud by propaganda leaflets urging young men to volunteer for military operations in Algeria.
12 See the *Utrescsch Dagdlad*, June-July 1976.
13 M. Van Dam, "Le légionnaire Rimbaud—Episodes d'une vie aventureuse" (Jakarta: *de Fakkel*, February 1941). See also Serge Guy Luc, *France-Asie*, June 1946, and Mohammed Sjah, *Indonesia*, no. 10, October 1954; Louis-Charles Demais, "Arthur Rimbaud à Java," *Bulletin de la Société d'études indochinoises*, vol. 42, no. 4 (1967): 337–49.
14 See Dr. Marmelstein, *Mercure de France*, July 15, 1922.
15 *Cahier Doucet*, on the back of plate 41.
16 Letter published by D.-A. de Graaf, *Revue des Sciences humaines*, October-December, 1951.
17 "Sur les traces de Rimbaud," *Mercure de France*, May 1, 1947.
18 Bourguignon and Houin, *Revue d'Ardenne et d'Argonne*, September-October 1897.
19 V. P. Underwood, "Rimbaud le marin," *Mercure de France*, December 1960, *Rimbaud et l'Angleterre*, pp. 201–15.
20 Ernest Delahaye, *Les Illuminations et Une saison en enfer de Rimbaud*, p. 16 note.
21 Underwood, *Rimbaud et l'Angleterre*, p. 217.
22 This letter was published for the first time, at my instigation, in *Le Figaro littéraire*, May 20, 1961. Facsimile in *Album Rimbaud*.
23 See Henri Thétard, "Arthur Rimbaud et le cirque," *Revue des deux mondes*, December 1, 1948.
24 *Cahier Doucet*, on the back of plate 18 representing Delahaye gathering plants with a friend—or pupil.
25 Letter published by de Graaf, *Revue des Sciences humaines*, October-December 1951.

26 Bourguignon and Houin, *Revue d'Ardenne et d'Argonne*, September-October 1897.

27 On the back of a drawing, in the *Cahier Doucet*, showing Rimbaud put out at not being able to meet Chanel, professeur de rhétorique at the Collège (Bibliothèque littéraire Jacques Doucet).

28 "Les souvenirs d'un ami de Rimbaud" (Louis Pierquin).

29 Letter in the Bibliothèque littéraire Jacques Doucet.

30 See de Graaf, *Revue des Sciences humaines*, April-June 1955. If Rimbaud had visited the Exposition of 1878, he might have met Verlaine there (see my *Verlaine*, p. 244).

31 *Cahier Doucet*, on the back of plate 78.

32 Pierquin, "Sur Arthur Rimbaud," *Le Courrier des Ardennes*, December 31, 1893.

33 "Les souvenirs d'un ami de Rimbaud" (Louis Pierquin).

34 Rimbaud's only allusion to his father's death is this passage from his letter of April 24, 1879, to his mother: "Only today have I been able to get this power of attorney from the chancery." On Rimbaud's family life we have only very partial documents: those letters that were considered too private or concerned his family have not been published—or were altered, or censored by Isabelle and Berrichon.

35 This was suggested by J.-M. Carré, *Lettres de la vie littéraire d'Arthur Rimbaud*, and refuted by H. Guillemin, *Mercure de France*, June 1, 1953.

36 Underwood, *Rimbaud et l'Angleterre*, p. 223, quotation from an article by R. Milliex, "Le premier séjour d'Arthur Rimbaud à Chypre," which appeared in *Kupriakai Spoudai* (Nicosia) in 1965. A photograph of the places appeared in *Le Figaro*, September 18, 1954.

37 Delahaye, *Rimbaud* (1906), p. 185.

38 Ibid., p. 186.

39 Drawing reproduced for the first time by Charles Donos in *Verlaine intime* (1898).

40 Lidia Herling Croce, "Rimbaud à Chypre, à Aden et au Harar, documents inédits," *Etudes rimbaldiennes*, vol. 3 (1972).

14

1 *Barr Adjam*, Memoirs of Alfred Bardey, preface by Joseph Tubiana (Centre national de la Recherche scientifique, 1981). I have reproduced those passages concerning Rimbaud in *Etudes rimbaldiennes*, vol 1 (1968).

2 Goffin, *Verlaine et Rimbaud vivants*.

3 L. Robecchi-Brichetti, "Rimbaud—Ricordo di uno soggiorno nell' Harar," *Bollettino della Società geografica italiana*, ser. 3, vol. 4 (1891): 23–24.

4 See A. Provost, "Sur les traces africaines de Rimbaud, Aden, Ethiopie," *Revue de France*, November 1, 1928. The authentic photograph of the Bardey Agency was reproduced in *Illustration*, September 21, 1940, and reproduced in the *Al-*

bum Rimbaud, p. 243. At Harar visitors are shown a "Rimbaud house," with an upper story with raised gallery accessible by a broad external staircase; it was in fact built in 1900, after Rimbaud's death.

5 *Barr Adjam.*

6 Letter from Alfred Bardey to P. Berrichon, March 21, 1901, *Revue d'Ardenne et d'Argonne*, July 1901.

7 *Mercure de France*, May 15, 1939.

8 *Barr Adjam.*

15

1 See Godchot, *Arthur Rimbaud ne varietur*, vol. 1.

2 Letter from Delahaye to Verlaine, Dec. 31, 1881, *Cahier Doucet*, on the back of plate 36.

3 Letter from Rimbaud to the French consul at Aden, January 28, 1883 (Pléiade edition), and letter from Alfred Bardey to P. Berrichon, January 20, 1898 (*Mercure de France*, May 15, 1939).

4 The photograph on the terrace was published by F. Ruchon (*Rimbaud, documents iconographiques*) in 1946; the one "in a coffee grove" appears in the Banderole edition of *Une saison en enfer* (1922) and in two forms in the aforementioned book by F. Ruchon; the photograph in the banana grove is reproduced in *Etudes rimbaldiennes*, vol. 3 (1972).

5 Preface to Arthur Rimbaud, *Œuvres* (Paris: Mercure de France, 1912).

6 Méléra, *Résonances autour de Rimbaud.*

7 *Mercure de France*, May 15, 1939.

8 Alfred Bardey had withheld the announcement of his death and funeral service, which was celebrated on August 31, at the Catholic Mission at Harar (see J.-P. Vaillant, *Rimbaud tel qu'il fut*, and *Bar Adjam*).

9 *Mercure de France*, May 15, 1939.

10 Briet, *Rimbaud notre prochain.*

11 Thus we have the "evidence, fifty-eight years after Rimbaud's death, of a Capuchin friar to a member of the American legation at Addis-Ababa" (H. Gillemin, *La Table ronde*, September 1953).

12 *Mercure de France*, May 15, 1939.

13 Petitfils, *Mercure de France*, January 1, 1955.

14 Photograph reproduced in *Etudes rimbaldiennes*, vol 3 (1972).

15 Berrichon, *La Vie de Rimbaud.*

16 *Mercure de France*, May 15, 1939.

17 Petitfils, *Mercure de France*, January 1, 1955.

16

1 Ugo Ferrandi, Letter to Ottone Schanzer, published by Benjamin Crémieux in *Les Nouvelles littéraires*, October 20, 1923.

2 Petitfils, *Mercure de France*, January 1, 1955.
3 Briet, *Rimbaud notre prochain*.
4 Lemay, quoted ibid.
5 Jules Borelli, *L'Ethiopie méridionale: Journal de mon voyage aux pays Amhara, Oromo et Sidama* (September 1885 to November 1888) (Paris: Maison Quantin, 1890).
6 H. Dehérain, *Figures coloniales françaises et étrangeres*, (Paris: Société d'éditions géographiques, maritimes et coloniales, 1931), letter not published in the Pléiade edition.
7 Starkie, *Arthur Rimbaud in Abyssinia*, pp. 90–91.
8 Borelli, *L'Ethiopie méridionale*.
9 This receipt is to be found in the Musée Rimbaud, Charleville-Mézières. It was reproduced in *Le Goéland*, no. 96 (June-July 1949).
10 Offprint of the *Bulletin de géographie historique et descriptive*, no. 1 (Paris: Imprimerie nationale, 1897).
11 Ruchon, *Rimbaud, documents iconographiques*, plate 74.

17

1 Berrichon, *La Vie de Rimbaud*.
2 Text in Mario Matucci, *Le dernier visage de Rimbaud en Afrique*.
3 Ibid.
4 Extract from Ugo Ferrandi's diary appeared in *La Table ronde*, January 1950. A complete copy of this diary is to be found in Novara Library.
5 The photograph, which first appeared in Ottorino Rosa's *L'Impero del Leone di Giuda*, is reproduced in *Etudes rimbaldiennes*, vol 3, (1972), with the legend "Une rue du quartier central." This house was demolished by Menelik's grandson, Lij Yasu, governor of Harar.
6 See *Correspondance* de Rimbaud et d'Ilg, Introduction by Jean Woellmy (Paris: Gallimard, 1965).
7 Jean and Jérome Tharaud, *Le passant d'Ethiopie*.
8 *Revue hebdomadaire*, August 27, 1932.
9 Berrichon, *La Vie de Rimbaud*.
10 *Corriere della Sera*, May 28, 1965.
11 Text in Matucci, *Le dernier visage de Rimbaud en Afrique*.
12 *Mercure de France*, May 15, 1939.
13 *Les Nouvelles littéraires*, January 16, 1947.
14 Letter from Jules Borelli to P. Berrichon in *La Vie de Rimbaud*, p. 184. Information provided by A. Bardey, quoted by Delahaye in *Les Illuminations et Une saison en enfer de Rimbaud*, p. 70 note.
15 Letter published by Carlo Zaghi in *Nuova Antologia*, August 16, 1940, p. 405.
16 *Mercure de France*, May 15, 1939.
17 See Pierre Ripert, *Marseille*, no. 52 (July-September 1952).
18 *Mercure de France*, May 15, 1939.
19 Photograph in André Dhotel, *La Vie de Rimbaud*. The building is said to have

been Rimbaud's house. This is obviously a mistake, for it would be very curious if Rimbaud's house was surmounted by a cross!

20   On Mgr. Jarosseau see Gaëtan Bernonville, *Mgr Jarosseau*, and Omer Denis, *Mgr Marie-Elie Jarosseau* (Toulouse: Edition du Clocher, 1951).

21   H. Célarié, "A propos de Rimbaud, souvenirs d'Ethiopie," *Le Temps*, June 10, 1933, article reproduced in *Ethiopie XXe siècle*, by the same author.

22   Ugo Ferrandi, Letter to Ottone Schanzer, in *Les Nouvelles littéraires*, October 20, 1923.

23   *Revue hebdomadaire*, August 27, 1932.

24   Ugo Ferrandi, Letter to Ottone Schanzer, in *Les Nouvelles littéraires*, 20 Octobre 1923.

25   Petitfils, *Mercure de France*, January 1, 1955.

26   *Le Figaro littéraire*, articles by Jean-Paul Vaillant (October 16, 1954) and R. Etiemble (October 23, 1954).

27   Jules Mouquet, "Un temoignage tardif sur Rimbaud", *Mercure de France*, May 15, 1933.

28   *Les Nouvelles littéraires*, January 16, 1947.

29   Berrichon, *La Vie de Rimbaud*.

30   Unpublished document from the Bibliothèque littéraire Jacques Doucet.

31   Jean-Paul Vaillant, *Rimbaud tel qu'il fut*.

32   Ibid.

33   Letter from Alfred Bardey on February 15, 1923, published in *Carrefour*, November 2, 1949.

34   See André Billy, *Le Figaro littéraire*, December 24, 1940. On André Tian, see *Mercure de France*, October 1, 1954.

35   The young decadents had turned Rimbaud into a myth, and attributed certain incoherent sonnets to him.

18

1   See Méléra, *Rimbaud*, and Henriette Célarié, *Le Temps*, June 10, 1933 and *Ethiopie XXe siècle* (Paris: Hachette, 1954).

2   Ward usually reserved for officers of the merchant navy.

3   An obvious lapse of memory: this should be the right leg.

4   Pierre Ripert, *Marseille*, no. 52 (July-September 1952).

5   Berrichon, *La Vie de Rimbaud*.

6   Isabelle Rimbaud, in *Ebauches d'Arthur Rimbaud* collected by M.-Y. Méléra., p. 177.

7   See *La Grive*, no. 61 (April 1949).

8   Robert Goffin, *Rimbaud vivant*.

9   The term *terrier des loups* (wolves' lair) is Rimbaud's own; it occurs in a letter from Maurice Riès to Emile Deschamps, dated March 15, 1929 (Pléiade edition p. 815). Isabelle spoke of "terre des loups."

10   The memoirs of Dr. Henri Beaudier were published in the *Bulletin des Amis de Rimbaud* (*La Grive*, January 1933). See Goffin, *Rimbaud vivant*, p. 56.

19

1 Isabelle Rimbaud, "Le dernier voyage de Rimbaud," *La Revue blanche*, October 15, 1897, reprinted in Arthur Rimbaud, *Reliques* (1922).
2 Ibid.
3 Ripert, *Marseille*, no. 52 (July-September 1952).
4 Méléra, *Résonances autour de Rimbaud*.
5 Isabelle Rimbaud, "Rimbaud mourant," *Mercure de France*, April 15, 1920, republished in *Reliques*.
6 Unpublished letter in Bibliothèque littéraire Jacques Doucet.
7 Vaillant, *Rimbaud tel qu'il fut*.
8 Méléra, *Résonances autour de Rimbaud*.
9 Briet, *Rimbaud notre prochain*.
10 These names have been provided by Ripert in the review *Marseille* (July-September 1952). Canon Chaulier, who signed the register of the hospital chapel when Rimbaud's body was taken to it, appears to have died in 1904, according to Pierre Arnoult (*Rimbaud*, 1955, p. 496). In 1891 he was over sixty. His portrait appears in the *Album Rimbaud*. The Abbé Suche was younger—nothing is known about him.
11 Isabelle wrote to P. Berrichon, on December 30, 1896, to say that her brother had asked for a second confession and had received extreme unction (?).
12 Plaque erected by the Marseille literary group "Les Amis d'Arion," on October 10, 1946, on the initiative of the poet Toursky, in the presence of the prefect of the Bouches-du-Rhône and a number of important personalities.
13 See the memoirs of Louis Pierquin, *Mercure de France*, May 1, 1924, and reproduced in the books by the same author (*Lettres de Rimbaud, Les deux Rimbaud*). Mme Rimbaud even tried out the grave for her own size (according to her letter to Isabelle, June 1, 1900).
14 *Ebauches de Rimbaud*, p. 180.
15 See the memoirs of Louis Pierquin, *Mercure de France*, May 1, 1924.
16 Vaillant, *Rimbaud tel qu'il fut*.
17 Document of the Musée Rimbaud, Charleville-Mézières.

Epilogue

1 On February 8, 1890, *La Petit Ardennais* had published an article on the poet Arthur Rimbaud, signed "Pierre l'Ardennais" (Marcel Coulon?) (*Le Bateau ivre*, no. 20 [1966]). But Isabelle did not know this, because she never read that newspaper.

BIBLIOGRAPHY

A complete bibliography of Rimbaud would fill a volume of several hundred pages. I have had to confine myself to a fairly strict selection. As far as the poet's own works are concerned, I mention only the original editions, the critical editions, and editions in print today, excluding innumerable intermediary editions, which have often been superseded, de luxe editions, or illustrated works.

Studies of Rimbaud have been included, though the list does not claim to be exhaustive. (All the works on Verlaine refer also to Rimbaud. I would refer the reader to the bibliography in my *Verlaine* [Paris: Julliard, 1981].)

Of the enormous mass of articles in reviews and newspapers I have referred only to those that contribute something new.

When articles have been collected in volume form, I indicate only the volume.

Lastly, I have regretfully been unable to find appropriate room for works by non-French authors.

Works by Rimbaud

Original Editions

Une Saison en enfer, Bruxelles, Alliance typographique J. Poot & Cie, 1873.
Les Illuminations, notice par Paul Verlaine, Paris, publications de *la Vogue*, 1886 (texte paru dans *la Vogue*, n°s 5, 6, 7, 8, 9, du 13 mai au 21 juin 1886).
Reliquaire, poésies, préface de Rodolphe Darzens, Paris, Genonceaux, 1891.
Les Illuminations et une Saison en enfer, Paris, Léon Vanier, 1892. *Une Saison en enfer* avait été publié dans *la Vogue* du 6 au 27 septembre 1886.
Poésies complètes, préface de Paul Verlaine, Paris, Léon Vanier, 1895.
Lettres (Egypte, Arabie, Ethiopie) réunies par Paterne Berrichon, Paris, Mercure de France, 1899.
Œuvres (vers et proses), préface de Paul Claudel, Paris, Mercure de France, 1912.
Poésies (fac-similé des autographes ou copies de Verlaine), Paris, A. Messein, 1919 (Les manuscrits des maîtres).

Les Mains de Jeanne-Marie, notice de P. Berrichon, Paris, au Sans pareil, 1919.
Les Stupra, sonnets, Paris, imprimerie particulière, 1923.
Un Cœur sous une soutane, intimités d'un séminariste, Paris, Ronald Davis, 1924.
Ce qu'on dit au poête a propos de fleurs, Paris, Le Livre, 1925.
Voyage en Abyssinie et au Harar, Paris, La Centaine, 1928.
Correspondance inédite (1870–1875), introduction de Roger-Gilbert Lecomte, Paris, Les Cahiers libres, 1929.
Lettres de la vie littéraire d'Arthur Rimbaud, édition en partie originale due à Jean-Marie Carré. Nouvelle Revue française, 1931.
Vers de Collège, introduction et notes de Jules Mouquet, Paris, Mercure de France, 1932.
Poèmes de l'Album Zutique. Introduction de Pascal Pia, Lyon éditions de l'Arbalète, 1943.
Album Zutique, introduction et notes de Pascal Pia, Paris, Cercle du Livre précieux, 1962. Deux volumes dont l'un donne le fac-similé de l'Album.
Correspondance (avec Alfred Ilg), 1888–1891. Introduction et notes de Jean Voellmy, Paris, Gallimard, 1965.

Collected or Separate Editions. Critical Editions

Poésies, édition critique de H. de Bouillane de Lacoste, Paris, Mercure de France, 1939.
Une Saison en enfer, édition critique de H. de Bouillane de Lacoste, Paris, Mercure de France, 1941.
Les Illuminations, édition critique de H. de Bouillane de Lacoste, Paris, Mercure de France, 1949.
Lettre du Voyant (15 mai 1871 à Paul Demény), Fac-similé de l'autographe ayant appartenu à Henri Saffrey. Paris, Edition Messein, 1954 (publication due à Henri Matarasso).
Pages choisies par H. de Bouillane de Lacoste, Paris, Hachette, 1955 (Classiques Vaubourdolle).
Pages choisies par R. Etiemble, Paris, Larousse, 1956. Réédition 1972.
Œuvres, Introduction d'Antoine Adam, notice de Paul Hartmann. Paris, Club du meilleur livre, 1957.
Poèmes, Introduction de Pierre Moreau, notes de Michel Decaudin. Paris, Hachette, 1958.
Œuvres, Edition établie par Suzanne Bernard. Paris, Garnier frères, 1960. Nouvelle édition mise à jour et complétée par André Guyaux, 1981.
Œuvres poétiques, Préface de Michel Decaudin. Paris, Garnier-Flammarion, 1964.
Illuminations, Introduction d'Albert Py. Genève-Paris, Droz-Minard, 1967. Réédition 1969.
Poésies, Derniers vers, Une Saison en enfer, Illuminations, Edition de Daniel Lewers. Paris, Le Livre de poche, 1972.
Œuvres complètes, édition établie par Antoine Adam, Paris, Gallimard, Bibliothèque de la Pléiade, 1972.
Poésies, Une Saison en enfer, Illuminations, Préface de René Char, commentaries de Louis Forestier. Paris, Gallimard, 1973 (collection « Poésie »).
Lettres du Voyant (13 et 15 mai 1871), Commentaires de Gérald Schaeffer, introduc-

tion de Marc Eigeldinger (« La voyance avant Rimbaud »). Genève-Paris, Droz-Minard, 1975

Œuvres poétiques (extraits) par Daniel Dubois, Paris, Bordas, 1975 (« Univers des Lettres »).

Pages choisies par Jean-Pierre Giusto, Paris, Hachette, 1976.

Poésies, édition critique établie par Marcel A. Ruff, Paris, Nizet, 1978.

Une Saison en enfer, Les Illuminations, Reproduction des éditions originales, présentation de Roger Pierrot. Genève, Slatkine Reprints, 1979 (collection « Ressources »).

Œuvres poétiques complètes présentées par Alain Blottière, préface de Maurice Juin, Paris, Laffont, 1980 (collection « Bouquins »).

Ce qu'on a dit au poète a propos de fleurs, florilège de Agnès Rosentiehl. Fac-similé du manuscrit, illustrations et commentaires, Paris, Gallimard, 1981.

Poésies et table de concordances rythmiques et syntaxiques, deux volumes. Edition du Centre d'études Arthur Rimbaud de l'Université de Neuchâtel sous la direction de Marc Eigeldinger, Neuchâtel, A la Baconnière, 1981 (collection « Langages »).

Studies (Books and Articles)

Acremont (Henri d'), « En Abyssinie sur les traces de Rimbaud », in *Revue hebdomadaire*, 27 août 1932.

Adam (Antoine), « L'énigme des Illuminations », in *Revue des Sciences humaines*, décembre 1950.

Ammer (K.-L), *Arthur Rimbaud, Leben und Dichtung*, préface de Stefan Sweig, Leipzig, Insel-Verlag, 1907.

Arnoult (Pierre), *Rimbaud*, Paris, Albin Michel, 1943. Réédition 1955.

Auvinet (Louis-Francis), *Aspects psychologiques d'Arthur Rimbaud*, Bordeaux, Delmas, 1941.

Bardey (Alfred), *Barr Adjam, souvenirs d'Afrique orientale (1880–1887)*, préface de Joseph Tubiana, Centre National de la Recherche Scientifique, 1981.

Barokas (Bernard), *Rimbaud*, Paris, Duculot, 1981 (collection « Travelling »).

Barrère (Jean-Bertrand), « Les *Voyelles* telles quelles? », in *Revue d'Histoire littéraire de la France*, 1974, n° 2.

Baudry (Jean-Louis), « Le texte de Rimbaud », *Tel Quel*, n°s 35 et 36 (1968–1969).

Bauer (Gérard), « Arthur Rimbaud », *Historia*, janvier 1967.

Bernard (Jean-Marc), «L'idée d'anarchie dans la vie et l'œuvre d'Arthur Rimbaud », *Revue critique des idées et des livres*, 10 juin 1911.

Bernard (Suzanne), « Etat présent des études sur Rimbaud », *l'Information littéraire*, 1962, pp. 55–59 et 93–102.

Berrichon (Paterne), *La vie de Jean Arthur Rimbaud*, Paris, Mercure de France, 1897.

————*Jean Arthur Rimbaud, le poète (1854–1873)*, Paris, Mercure de France, 1912.

Bertozzi (Gabriele Aldo), *Rimbaud attraverso i movimenti d'avanguardia*, Roma, Luciano-Lucarini, 1976.

Billy (André), « La maladie et la mort du poète », *le Figaro*, 8 novembre 1941.

Bonnamy (Georges), *Rimbaud, l'homme aux semelles de vent* (Théâtre), Paris, Debresse, 1941.

Bonnefoy (Yves), *Rimbaud par lui-même*, Paris, LeSeuil, 1961 (« Ecrivains de toujours»).

Bouillane de Lacoste (Henri de), En collaboration avec Pierre Izambard, « Les sources du *Bateau ivre* », *Mercure de France*, 15 août 1935.

———En collaboration avec Edouard de Rougemont et Pierre Izambard: « L'évolution psychologique d'Arthur Rimbaud d'après son écriture », *Mercure de France*, 1ᵉʳ novembre 1936.

———En collaboration avec Edouard de Rougemont: « Verlaine, éditeur de Rimbaud », *Mercure de France*, 15 juin 1937.

———En collaboration avec Henri Matarasso: « Nouveaux documents sur Rimbaud (Lettres d'Alfred Bardey à Paterne Berrichon) », *Mercure de France*, 15 mai 1939.

———*Rimbaud et le problème des Illuminations* (Thèse de doctorat), Paris, Mercure de France, 1949.

Bourguignon (Jean) et Houin (Charles), « Poètes ardennais: Arthur Rimbaud », *Revue d'Ardenne et d'Argonne*, sept articles de novembre 1896 à juillet 1901.

Breton (André), *Flagrant délit*, Paris, Thésée, 1949 (réédition Pauvert, 1964).

Briet (Suzanne), « Isabelle "habillée" par Emilie Rimbaud », *le Bateau ivre*, nᵒˢ 7–8, mars 1951.

———*Rimbaud notre prochain*, Paris, Nouvelles éditions latines, 1956.

——— « Le Cahier des dix ans », *la Grive*, avril 1956.

———*Madame Rimbaud, essai de biographie*, lettres de Mme Rimbaud, Paris, Minard, 1968 (« Les Lettres modernes »).

Brunel (Pierre), *Rimbaud, anthologie thématique*, Paris, Hatier, 1973 (collection « Thema-Anthologia »).

Caddau (Pierre), *Dans le sillage du capitaine Cook ou Arthur Rimbaud le Tahitien*, Paris, Nizet, 1968.

Carré (Jean-Marie), *Les Ardennes et leurs écrivains: Michelet et Taine, Verlaine et Rimbaud*, Charleville, Rubens, 1923.

——— «Les Souvenirs d'un ami de Rimbaud » (Louis Pierquin), *Mercure de France*, 1ᵉʳ mai 1924, recueillis dans les *Lettres* et *les Deux Rimbaud*.

———*La Vie aventureuse de Jean-Arthur Rimbaud*, Paris, Plon, 1926. Rééditions 1943 et 1949.

——— « Rimbaud a-t-il détruit sa *Saison en enfer?* », *les Nouvelles littéraires*, 18 septembre 1926.

———*Les Deux Rimbaud*, Paris, les *Cahiers libres*, 1928.

———*Lettres de la vie littéraire d'Arthur Rimbaud*, Paris, Gallimard, 1931.

——— « Arthur Rimbaud en Ethiopie », *Revue de France*, 1ᵉʳ juin 1935.

———*Autour de Verlaine et de Rimbaud*, présentation de dessins de Ernest Delahaye, Verlaine et Germain Nouveau, Université de Paris, 1949. Réédition Gallimard.

Cartier (Marius), *Rimbaud, sa vie, son œuvre*, Bienne (Suisse), 1956.

Castelnau (Jacques), *Rimbaud*, Paris, Tallandier, 1944.

Celarié (Henriette), « A propos de Rimbaud, souvenirs d'Ethiopie », *le Temps*, 10 juin 1933. Recueilli dans *Ethiopie XXᵉ siècle*, Hachette, 1934.

Chadwick (Charles), *Etudes sur Rimbaud*, Paris, Nizet, 1960.

——— « La correspondance de Rimbaud », *Revue d'Histoire littéraire de la France*, 1965, pp. 693–694.

———*Rimbaud*, London, The Athlone Press, 1979 (collection « Athlone French Poets »).

Charvet (Louis), *Rimbaud, notre frère*, Paris, Editions Rougerie, 1972.

Chauvel (Jean), *L'Aventure de Jean-Arthur Rimbaud*, Paris, Seghers, 1971 (collection « L'Archipel »).

Chisholm (Alan Rowland), *The Art of Arthur Rimbaud*, Melbourne University Press, 1930.

Clauzel (Raymond), *Une Saison en enfer et Arthur Rimbaud*, Paris, Société d'éditions littéraires et techniques E. Malfère, 1931.

Cohn (Robert Greer), *The Poetry of Rimbaud*, Princeton University Press, 1973.

Colban (Jean-Claude) et Blottière (Alain), « Rimbaud en Ethiopie », *Réalités*, juillet 1977.

McCombi (John), *The Prince and the Genie*, The University of Massachusetts, 1972.

Coulon (Marcel), *Le problème de Rimbaud, poète maudit*, Nîmes, Gomez et Paris, Crès, 1923.

———*Au cœur de Verlaine et de Rimbaud*, Paris, Le Livre, 1925.

———*La Vie de Rimbaud et de son œuvre*, Paris, Mercure de France, 1929.

——— « Les *vraies* lettres de Rimbaud arabo-éthiopien », *Mercure de France*, 15 mars 1929.

——— « Les gains de Rimbaud en Abyssinie », *L'Archer*, avril 1931.

Daniel-Rops, *Rimbaud, le drame spirituel*, Paris, Plon, 1936.

Davies (Margaret), *Une Saison en enfer d'Arthur Rimbaud*, analyse du texte, Paris, Minard, 1975 (Archives des Lettres modernes).

Debray (Pierre), *Rimbaud, le magicien désabusé*, Paris, Julliard, 1949 (collection « Témoins de l'Esprit »).

Decaudin (Michel), « Travaux italiens sur Rimbaud », *Revue de Littérature comparée*, septembre 1963.

Dehérain (Henri), « La carrière africaine d'Arthur Rimbaud », *Revue de l'Histoire des colonies françaises*, 1916, 4e trimestre. Etude reprise et complétée dans *Figures coloniales françaises et étrangères*, Paris, Société d'éditions géographiques, maritimes et coloniales, 1931.

Delattre (Jean-Luc), *Le déséquilibre mental d'Arthur Rimbaud*, Paris, Le François 1928.

Delahaye (Ernest) (sous les initiales M. D.), « Sur Rimbaud », *Entretiens politiques et littéraires*, décembre 1891.

———*Rimbaud*, Paris-Reims, Editions de la Revue de Paris et de Champagne, 1906.

——— « A propos de Rimbaud, souvenirs familiers », onze articles de la *Revue d'Ardenne et d'Argonne* de mars 1907 à mai 1909. Texte repris, en partie seulement, dans *Souvenirs familiers à propos de Rimbaud, Verlaine et Germain Nouveau*, Paris, Messein, 1925.

———*Rimbaud, l'artiste et l'être moral*, Paris, Messein, 1923. Réimpression sous le titre *Rimbaud*.

———*Les Illuminations et Une Saison en enfer d'Arthur Rimbaud*, Paris, Messein, 1927.

———*La part de Verlaine et de Rimbaud dans le sentiment religieux contemporain*, Paris, Messein, 1935.

Demais (Louis-Charles), « Arthur Rimbaud à Java », *Bulletin de la Société d'études indochinoises*, 1967, tome XLII, n° 4.

Denis (Yves), « Deux glosses de Rimbaud: *Après le déluge et H.* », *les Temps modernes*, 1968, pp. 1261 et 1878.

Dhotel (André), *L'Œuvre logique de Rimbaud*, Mézières, Editions de la Société des écrivains ardennais, 1933.

————*Rimbaud et la révolte moderne*, Paris, Gallimard, 1952 (collection « Essais »).

————*La Vie de Rimbaud*, Paris, Editions du Sud (Albin Michel), 1965 (collection « Vies et Visages »).

Duchet (Claude), « Autour du "Dormeur du val" de Rimbaud », *Revue d'Histoire littéraire de la France*, 1962, pp. 371–380.

Dullaert (Maurice), « L'Affaire Verlaine-Rimbaud », *Nord* (Bruxelles, 4ᵉ cahier, 1930. Autre édition, Paris, Messein, 1930.

Eaubonne (Françoise d'), *La vie passionnée d'Arthur Rimbaud*, Paris, Seghers, 1956.

————*Verlaine et Rimbaud ou la fausse évasion*, Paris, Albin Michel, 1960.

Eigeldinger (Frédéric S.) (en collaboration avec André Gendre), *Delahaye, témoin de Rimbaud*, Neuchâtel, A la Baconnière, 1974.

Eigeldinger (Marc), *Rimbaud et le mythe solaire*, Neuchâtel, A la Baconnière, 1964.

d'Ermatingen Ribi, Essai d'une rythmique des Illuminations d'Arthur Rimbaud, Zurich, Uto, 1948.

Etiemble (René), *Le Mythe de Rimbaud*, Paris, Gallimard. Tome I: *Genèse du Mythe* (1869–1949), Bibliographie, 1954, réédition 1968. Tome II: *Structure du Mythe*, 1952, rééditions 1961 et 1970.

————*L'Année du centenaire*, 1961.

————*Le Sonnet des Voyelles*, 1968 (collection « Essais »).

————*Nouveaux aspects du Mythe de Rimbaud dans le monde slave et communiste*, Paris, Centre de documentation universitaire, 1964.

Etiemble (René) et Gauclère (Yassu), *Rimbaud*, Paris, Gallimard, 1936 (collection « Essais »). Rééditions 1950 et 1966.

Faurisson (Robert), « A-t-on lu Rimbaud? », *Bizarre*, 4ᵉ trimestre 1961. Editions Pauvert, 1971.

Felsch (Angelika), *Poetische Struktur und Kontext*, Bonn, Bouvier, Verlag, Hebert Grundmann, 1977.

Fénéon (Félix), « Les "Illuminations" d'Arthur Rimbaud », *le Symboliste*, 7–14 octobre 1886. Recueilli dans ses *Œuvres complètes*, Genève, Droz, 1970 (tome II).

Fondane (Benjamin), *Rimbaud le Voyou*, Paris, Denoël & Steele, 1933.

Fongaro (Antoine), « Les échos verlainiens chez Rimbaud et le problème des *Illuminations* «, *Revue des Sciences humaines*, avril-juin 1962.

Fontainas (André), *Verlaine, Rimbaud—Ce qu'on sait de leurs relations, ce qu'on en présume*, Paris, Librairie de France, 1931.

Fontaine (André), *Génie de Rimbaud*, Paris, Delagrave, 1934.

Forbes Duncan, *Rimbaud in Ethiopia*, Hythe, Volturna Press, 1979.

Foucart (Jacques), « Les ascendances bourguignonnes et franc-comtoises d'Arthur Rimbaud », *le Bien public* (Dijon), 27 octobre 1954.

Fouchet (Max-Pol), « Avec Rimbaud à Harar », *les Nouvelles littéraires*, 14 mai 1970.

Fowlie (Wallace), *Rimbaud. The myth of Childhood*, London, Dennis Dobson, 1946.

————*Rimbaud*, New York, New Directions Books, 1946.

————*Rimbaud*, University of Chicago Press, 1967.

Frankel (Margherita), *Le Code dantesque dans l'œuvre de Rimbaud*, Paris, Nizet, 1975.

Frohock (Wiebur Merill), *Rimbaud's Poetic Practice, Image and Theme in the major poems*, Harvard et Oxford, University Press, 1963.

Fumet (Stanislas), *Rimbaud, mystique contrarié*, Paris, Plon, 1966 (« La Recherche de l'absolu »).

Fusero (Clemente), *Vita et poesia di Rimbaud*, Milano, « Corbacchio » Dall'Oglio, 1951.

Gascar (Pierre), *Rimbaud et la Commune*, Paris, Gallimard, 1971 (collection « Idées »).

Gengoux (Jacques), *La Symbolique de Rimbaud*, Paris, Editions du Vieux Colombier, 1947.

————*La pensée poétique de Rimbaud*, Paris, Nizet, 1950.

Gilbert-Lecomte (Roger), *Arthur Rimbaud*, Montpellier, Bruno Roy, 1972.

Giusto (Jean-Pierre), *Rimbaud créateur*, Paris, Presses Universitaires de France, 1980 (collection « Publications de la Sorbonne, série Littérature », n° 13).

Godchot (colonel), *Arthur Rimbaud ne varietur*, Nice, chez l'auteur, Tome I (1854–1871), 1936; Tome II (1871–1873), 1937.

Goffin (Robert), *Sur les traces d'Arthur Rimbaud*, Paris, Editions du Sagittaire, 1934.

————*Rimbaud vivant*, avant-propos de Jean Cassou, Paris, Corrêa, 1937.

————*Rimbaud et Verlaine vivants*, Paris, Bruxelles, L'Ecran du monde, sans date.

Graaf (Daniel Adriaan de), *Rimbaud et la durée de son activité littéraire*, Assen (Hollande), Van Gorcum & Cie, 1948. Ouvrage paru chez le même éditeur, la même année, sous le titre: *Arthur Rimbaud, homme de Lettres*,—« Autour du dossier de Bruxelles », *Mercure de France*, 1ᵉʳ août 1956.

————*Arthur Rimbaud, sa vie, son œuvre*, Assen, Van Gorcum, 1960.

Grall (Xavier), « Rimbaud somalien », *le Monde*, 15 février 1976.

————*Arthur Rimbaud, la marche au soleil*, Paris, éditions Mazarine, 1980.

Guerdon (David), *Rimbaud, la clef alchimique*, Paris, Robert Laffont, 1980 (« Aux portes de l'étrange »).

Guillemin (Henri), « Rimbaud est-il mort chrétiennement? », *le Figaro littéraire*, 9 mai 1953.

———— « Approche de Rimbaud », *La Table ronde*, septembre 1953.

———— « Rimbaud fut-il communard? », *le Figaro littéraire*, 10 octobre 1953.

———— « Connaissance de Rimbaud (nouveaux documents inédits) », *Mercure de France*, 1ᵉʳ octobre 1954.

Guiraud (Pierre), « L'évolution statistique du style de Rimbaud et le problème des *Illuminations* », *Mercure de France*, octobre 1954.

————*Index des mots des Illuminations d'Arthur Rimbaud*, Paris, Klincksieck, 1954.

Guyaux (André), « A propos des *Illuminations* », *Revue d'Histoire littéraire de la France*, septembre-octobre 1977.

Hackett (Cecil A.), *Le lyrisme de Rimbaud*, Paris, Nizet et Bastard, 1938.

————*Rimbaud l'enfant*, préface de Gaston Bachelard, Paris, J. Corti, 1948.

————*Rimbaud*, Cambridge, Bowes and Bowes, 1957.

————*Autour de Rimbaud*, Paris, Klincksieck, 1967.

————*Rimbaud, a critical introduction*, Cambridge, University Press, 1981.

Héraut (Henri), « Du nouveau sur Rimbaud: la solution de l'énigme des *Voyelles* », *Nouvelle Revue française*, 1ᵉʳ octobre 1934.

Houin (Charles) (voir Jean *Bourguignon*).

────── « Iconographie d'Arthur Rimbaud », *Revue d'Ardenne et d'Argonne*, septembre 1901.

Houston (John Porter), *The design of Rimbaud's Poetry*, Yale (U.S.A.), University Press, 1963.

Izambard (Georges), *Rimbaud tel que je l'ai connu*, Recueil des écrits de G. Izambard établi par H. de Bouillane de Lacoste et Pierre Izambard, Paris, Mercure de France, 1946.

Jacquemin-Parlier (E.), *Un diagnostic médico-littéraire: le poète ardennais Jean-Nicolas-Arthur Rimbaud*, Strasbourg, Editions universitaires, 1929.

Jasmin (Claude), *Rimbaud mon beau salaud*, Montréal (Canada), Edition de jour, 1969.

Kittang (Atle), *Discours et Jeu*, essai d'analyse des textes d'Arthur Rimbaud, Grenoble, Presses universitaires, 1975.

Kunel (Maurice), *Verlaine et Rimbaud en Belgique*, Liège, Solédi, 1945.

Lacambre (J. H.), *L'instabilité mentale à travers la vie et l'œuvre littéraire de Jean Arthur Rimbaud*, essai de psychologie pathologique, Lyon, La Source, 1923.

Lefranc (Jules), « Roche. La maison Rimbaud », *Revue Palladienne*, avril-mai 1949.

Le Hardouin (Maria), « Arthur Rimbaud et sa mère », *Revue des deux mondes*, 15 août 1961.

──────*Rimbaud le transfuge*, Lyon, E. Vitte, 1962.

Locker (Malka), *Rimbaud, le poète qui s'enfuit*, Paris, Presses du temps présent, 1965.

Lovinescu (Horia), *Rimbaud*, Bucarest, Editions Univers, 1981.

Lubienski Bodenham (H.), « Le capitaine Rimbaud à Dijon (1864–1878) », *Rimbaud vivant*, nᵒˢ 18–19 *(1980)*.

Macé (Gabriel), « Rimbaud "recently deserted" », *Nouvelle Revue française*, avril-mai 1978.

Magny (Claude Edmonde), *Arthur Rimbaud*, Paris, Pierre Seghers, 1949 (Poètes d'aujourd'hui, nᵒ 12). Réédition en 1966.

Mallarmé (Stéphane), « Arthur Rimbaud », *The Chap Book* (Chicago), 15 mai 1896. Texte repris dans *Divagations*, Paris, Fasquelle, 1897.

Marmelstein (J.-M.), « Rimbaud aux Indes néerlandaises et à Stuttgart », *Mercure de France*, 15 juillet 1922.

────── « Rimbaud soldat », *Bulletin des Amis de Rimbaud*, nᵒ 6 (*La Grive*, juillet 1937).

Martin (Auguste), *Verlaine et Rimbaud. Documents inédits tirés des archives de la Préfecture de Police*, tirage à part en 1944 d'un article paru dans *la Nouvelle Revue française* le 1ᵉʳ février 1943.

Matarasso (Henri) et Petitfils (Pierre), « Rimbaud, Verlaine, Germain Nouveau et l'Album Zutique », *Mercure de France*, mai 1961.

──────*Vie d'Arthur Rimbaud*, préface de Jean Cocteau, Paris, Hachette, 1962.

──────*Album Rimbaud*, Paris, Gallimard, 1967, Bibliothèque de la Pléiade.

Mathieu (Bertrand), *Orphisme: Rimbaud et Henry Miller*, Paris, La Haye, Mouton, 1970.

Matucci (Mario), *Le dernier visage de Rimbaud en Afrique*, Paris, Marcel Didier, 1969.

Mauté (Mathilde) (ex-Mme Verlaine), *Mémoires de ma vie*, Paris, Flammarion, 1935.

Méléra (Marguerite Yerta), *Rimbaud*, Paris, Firmin-Didot, 1930 (édition courante et édition de luxe avec dessins de Rimbaud).

———— « Arthur Rimbaud », *Ebauches*, Paris, Mercure de France, 1937.

————*Résonances autour de Rimbaud*, Paris, Editions du Myrte, 1946.

Mijolla (Alain de), « La "désertion" du capitaine Rimbaud », *Revue française de psychanalyse*, mai-juin 1975.

Miller (Henry), *Rimbaud*, Lausanne, Mermod, 1952 (collection « La Grenade »). Ouvrage récrit par l'auteur et publié sous le titre *le Temps des assassins, essai sur Rimbaud*, traduit de l'américain par P. S. Temple, Paris, J. Oswald, 1970.

Mondor (Henri), *Rimbaud ou le génie impatient*, Paris, Gallimard, 1955.

———— « Paul Valéry et *le Bateau ivre* », *Revue de Paris*, février 1957.

Montal (Robert), *L'Adolescent Rimbaud*, Lyon, Armand Henneuse, 1954.

————*Rimbaud*, Paris, Editions universitaires, 1968.

Morizot (Jean-Claude), *Claudel et Rimbaud*, Paris, Minard, 1976, Bibliothèque des Lettres modernes.

Morrissette (Bruce), *La Bataille Rimbaud—l'Affaire de la « Chasse spirituelle »*, Paris, Nizet, 1959. Traduction de *The Great Rimbaud forgery*, Saint Louis, Washington University Studies, 1956.

Mouquet (Jules), « Un témoignage tardif sur Rimbaud » (Paul Labarrière), *Mercure de France*, 15 mai 1933.

————*Rimbaud raconté par Verlaine*, Paris, Mercure de France, 1934.

———— « Une version nouvelle d'un poème de Rimbaud » « Trois baisers »), *Mercure de France*, 1er avril 1934.

———— « Rimbaud et le Parnasse contemporain », *Bulletin du Bibliophile*, mars 1946.

Musso (Frédéric), *Arthur Rimbaud*, Paris, Pierre Charron, 1972 (collection « Les Géants »).

Nicoletti (Gianni), *L'Inferno di Rimbaud attraverso l'analisi della « Saison en enfer »*, Venezia, Gruppo Editoriale Veneziano, 1948.

————*Arthur Rimbaud dans Poeti maledetti dell'Ottocento francese*, Torino, Unione tipografico-Editrice Torinese, 1954.

————*Rimbaud, una poesia del "canto chiuso"*, Torino, Edizione dell'Albero, 1965, 2e édition, Bari 1968, 3e édition, Napoli, 1972.

————*Rimbaud "Una stagione in Inferno", "Illuminazioni"*, Milano, Mondadori, 1979.

Noulet (Emilie), *Le Premier visage de Rimbaud*, Bruxelles, Edition du Palais des Académies, 1953. Réédition en 1973.

Paillou (P.-H.), *Arthur Rimbaud, père de l'existentialisme*, Paris, Libraire académique Perrin, 1947.

Payen (Pierre), *Rimbaud-Voyelles, cent ans après le secret est dévoilé*, Monte Carlo, Editions Hals, 1974.

Perrier (Madeleine), *Rimbaud, chemins de la création*, Paris, Gallimard, 1973 (Essais).

Petitfils (Pierre) (voir Matarasso Henri),« Arthur Rimbaud à Douai, ou les chercheuses de poux retrouvées », *Bulletin du Bibliophile*, 1945, n°s 5 à 10, pp.
227 à 234.

———*L'Œuvre et le visage d'Arthur Rimbaud*, essai de bibliographie et d'iconographie, Paris, Nizet, 1949.

——— «Des souvenirs inconnus sur Rimbaud », *Mercure de France*, 1er janvier
1955.

———(en collaboration avec Joseph Deschuytter) « Paul-Auguste Bretagne (1837–
1881), souvenirs inédits », *le Bateau ivre*, n° 14 (novembre 1955).

——— « L'Architecture rimbaldienne », *les Nouvelles littéraires*, 24 août 1967.

——— « Les manuscrits de Rimbaud », *Etudes rimbaldiennes*, tome II (1970).

——— *Verlaine*, Paris, Julliard, 1981.

Petralia (Franco), *Bibliographie de Rimbaud en Italie*, Firenze, .Editions Sansoni,
1960.

Peyre (Henri), *Rimbaud vu par Verlaine*, Paris, Nizet, 1975.

Piérard (Louis), « L'édition orginale d'*Une Saison en enfer* », *Poésie 42* (P. Seghers),
janvier 1942.

Pierquin (Louis), (Voir Jean-Marie Carré).

——— « Arthur Rimbaud », *le Courrier des Ardennes*, 29–30 décembre 1891.

——— « Sur Arthur Rimbaud », *le Courrier des Ardennes*, 31 décembre 1893.

Plessen (Jacques), *Promenades et Poésie. L'Expérience de la marche et du mouvement
dans l'œuvre de Rimbaud*, La Haye et Paris, Klincksieck, 1967.

Poulet (Georges), *La poésie éclatée, Baudelaire, Rimbaud*, Paris, Presses Universitaires de France, 1980.

Ray (Lionel), *Rimbaud*, Paris, Pierre Seghers 1976 (« Poètes d'aujourd'hui »).

Reboul (Yves), « Les problèmes rimbaldiens traditionnels et le témoignage d'Isabelle
Rimbaud », *Revue des Lettres modernes*, 1972 et 1976.

Rhodes-Peschel (Enid), *Flux and reflux: ambivalence in the poems of Arthur Rimbaud*, préface d'Etiemble, Genève, Droz, 1977.

Richepin (Jean), « Germain Nouveau et Rimbaud, souvenirs inédits », *Revue de
France*, 1er janvier 1927.

Richer (Jean), « Le délire raisonné de Rimbaud », *les Nouvelles littéraires*, 17 septembre 1971.

———*L'Alchimie du verbe de Rimbaud ou les jeux de Jean-Arthur*, Paris, Didier,
1972.

Rickword (Edgell), *Rimbaud, the boy and the poet*, London, Heineman, et New York,
A. Knopf, 1924.

Rimbaud (Isabelle), *Mon frère Arthur*, Paris, Camille Bloch, 1920.

———*Reliques*, Paris, Mercure de France, 1922.

Rimbaud (Vitalie), *Journal* présenté par H. de Bouillane de Lacoste et H. Matarasso,
Mercure de France, 15 mai 1938. Tirage à part, 36 pages.

Ripert (Pierre), « En marge du Symbolisme, Rimbaud, Verlaine, Germain Nouveau
et Marseille », *Marseille*, n° 18, juillet-septembre 1952.

Rivière (Jacques), *Rimbaud*, Paris, Kra, 1930. Réédition Emile Paul, 1938, et Gallimard, 1977, avec un dossier 1905–1925 préparé par Roger Lefèvre.

Roach (Robert Clive), *Index du vocabulaire du Symbolisme et Index des mots d'Une
Saison en enfer*, Paris, Klincksieck, 1962.

Robinson (Judith), *Rimbaud, Valéry et l'incohérence harmonique*, Paris, Minard, 1979 (« Archives des Lettres modernes »).

Rolland de Reneville (André), *Rimbaud le Voyant*, Paris, Aus Sans pareil, 1929. Rééditions 1938, Denoël & Steele, et 1947, La Colombe.

―――― « Verlaine témoin de Rimbaud », *les Cahiers de la Pléiade*, printemps 1950.

Ruchon (François), *Jean-Arthur Rimbaud, sa vie, son œuvre, son influence*, Paris, ancienne Librairie Honoré Champion, 1929.

――――*Rimbaud, documents iconographiques*, Genève, Pierre Cailler, 1946.

Ruff (Marcel A.), *Rimbaud, l'homme et l'œuvre*, Paris, Hatier, 1968 (« Connaissance des Lettres »).

Segalen (Victor), *Le double Rimbaud*, préface de Gérard Macé, Montpellier, Fata Morgana, 1980.

Silvain (René), *Rimbaud le précurseur*, Paris, Boivin, 1945.

Solmi (Sergio), *Saggio su Rimbaud*, Milano, Einaudi, 1974.

Solomon (Petre), *Rimbaud, o calatorie spre centrul cuvintului* (Rimbaud, un voyage au centre de la Parole), Bucarest, Editions Albatros, 1980.

Soupault (Philippe), « Sur les traces de Rimbaud », *Europe*, mai-juin 1973.

Starkie (Enid), *Rimbaud in Abyssinia*, Oxford, Clarendon Press, 1937. Edition Française: *Rimbaud en Abyssinie*, Paris, Payot, 1938.

――――*Arthur Rimbaud*, London, Faber and Faber, 1938. Réédition complétée, London, Hamish Hamilton, 1947 et 1961.

―――― « Sur les traces de Rimbaud », *Mercure de France*, 1er mai 1947.

Strentz (Henri), *Arthur Rimbaud, son œuvre*, Paris, Éditions de la Nouvelle Revue critique, 1927.

Tharaud (Jean et Jérôme), « Rimbaud à Harrar », *Candide*, 19 novembre 1941.

Thisse (André), *Rimbaud devant Dieu*, Paris, José Corti, 1975.

Tian (André), Polémique avec miss Enid Starkie, dans *le Feu* (Aix-en-Provence), juin-juillet 1941.

―――― « Fin du mystère Rimbaud », *Confluences*, mai 1942.

―――― « A propos de Rimbaud », *Mercure de France*, 1er octobre 1954.

Underwood (Vernon Philip), *Verlaine et l'Angleterre*, Paris, Nizet, 1956.

―――― « Rimbaud le marin », *Mercure de France*, décembre 1960.

――――*Rimbaud et l'Angleterre*, Paris, Nizet, 1976.

Vaillant (Jean-Paul), *Rimbaud tel qu'il fut*, Paris, le Rouge et le Noir, 1930.

―――― « Abdoh Rinb, Rimbaud serviteur de Dieu », *le Figaro littéraire*, 16 octobre 1954.

Verlaine (Paul), Voir Jules Mouquet et Henri Peyre.

Verstraete (Daniel), *La chasse spirituelle d'Arthur Rimbaud, les Illuminations*, Paris, Editions du Cerf, 1981 (« Le Bonheur de lire »).

Whitaker (Marie-Joséphine), *La structure du monde imaginaire de Rimbaud*, Paris, Nizet, 1972.

Wing (Nathanaël), *Present appearances, aspects of poetic structure in Rimbaud's Illuminations*, University of Mississippi Press, 1974.

Wolfenstein (Alfred), *Rimbaud, Leben Werk Briefe*, Berlin, Internationale Bibliotek, 1930.

Zech (Paul), *J.-A. Rimbaud, Ein Querchnitt durch sein Leben und Werk*, Ebda, 1927, réédition 1947.

Collected Studies

Hommage de l'Ardenne à Rimbaud et à Verlaine, Charleville, Société des Ecrivains ardennais, 1925.
Rimbaud, Paris, Hachette, 1968 (« Génies et Réalités »).
Essai de sémiologie poétique, Paris, Larousse, 1971.
Aujourd'hui Rimbaud. Enquête de Roger Munier, Paris, Minard, 1976 (« Archives des Lettres modernes »).
(Cinq) *Etudes sur les « Poésies »* de Rimbaud, sous la direction de Frédéric Eigeldinger, Neuchâtel. A la Baconnière, 1979 (« Languages »), et Paris, Payot, même année.
Le Mythe d'Etiemble, Paris, Didier, 1979 (Etudes de littérature étrangère et comparée).

Periodicals

Special numbers devoted to Rimbaud

Le Grand Jeu, printemps 1929.
Espoir, novembre 1936.
Poésies 41 et 42 (p. Seghers).
Biblio, mai-juin 1949.
La Grive (Mézières), octobre 1954.
Cahier du Collège de Pataphysique, n° 17–18, 1954.
Europe, novembre 1954 et mai-juin 1973.
Le Magazine littéraire, n° 73, février 1973.
Littérature, n° 11, octobre 1973.
La Voix des Poètes (« Les Pharaons »), printemps 1975.
Bérénice (Rome), en français, 1981.

Rimbaud Periodicals

Publications de la Société des Amis de Rimbaud.

Bulletin des Amis de Rimbaud, Supplément de la revue ardennaise
La Grive, (7 numéros), de janvier 1931 à avril 1939.
Le Bateau ivre (20 numéros), de janvier 1949 à septembre 1966.
Etudes rimbaldiennes (Minard, éditeur à Paris), 3 tomes: 1968, 1970, 1972.
Rimbaud vivant (21 numéros), de 1973 à 1982.

Publications de Charleville-Mézières

Arthur Rimbaud dans les collections municipales de la Bibiothèque et du Musée: Catalogue général (1966) et supplément (1969).

Cahiers du Centre culturel Arthur Rimbaud, présidé par André Lebon (7 cahiers), de mars 1969 à juin 1981.

Autre publication sous la direction de Louis Forestier:

Cahiers A. Rimbaud (Minard, éditeur à Paris), 4 volumes: 1972, 1973, 1976, 1981.

INDEX